The Voice in the Machine

Building Computers That Understand Speech

Roberto Pieraccini

D1340133

The MIT Press
Cambridge, Massachusetts
London, England

This book was set in Sabon by Toppan Best-set Premedia Limited. Printed and bound in the United States of America.

Library of Congress Cataloging-in-Publication Data

Pieraccini, Roberto, 1955–
The voice in the machine : building computers that understand speech / Roberto Pieraccini.
    p.   cm.
Includes bibliographical references and index.
ISBN 978-0-262-01685-8 (hardcover : alk. paper), 978-0-262-53329-4 (paperback : alk. paper)
1. Machine learning. 2. Speech processing systems. I. Title.
Q325.5.P54   2012
006.4'54—dc23
2011030566

To my parents,
who gave me the wings.
To my children,
so they can fly.

Contents

Foreword

The holy grail of speech technology has been the creation of machines that can recognize and understand fluently spoken human speech and respond in an appropriate manner. Unfortunately, despite millions of hours of research, the technology behind talking machines is still in its infancy, and the promise of machines with the intelligence and capability of HAL (in the movie *2001: A Space Odyssey*) or R2D2 and C-3PO (in the *Star Wars* movies) remains beyond our current (and foreseeable) capabilities.

The key question that needs to be answered for speech research to make real and steady progress toward building intelligent talking machines is whether there is something fundamental in human language and speech that we do not yet understand well enough to replicate in a machine. To answer this question, we must examine the paths we have taken to build intelligent machines and the progress we have made in speech recognition, speech understanding, speech synthesis, and dialog systems over the past seventy years.

Is it absolutely essential that there be a single solution to building intelligent machines that recognize and understand speech and respond appropriately to virtually any query? Clearly, human-machine interactions will generate enormous paybacks that justify the effort that has gone into building such machines. These paybacks will enable us to do our jobs faster, smarter, better (depending on the task being tackled), and, in some cases, with less frustration at waiting for human attendants to help answer our questions or solve our problems. Perhaps we should just continue along our current path and design specialized voice interactive systems for different applications such as customer care, help desks, services, banking, and investing. The ongoing success of these systems certainly justifies efforts to design others for still other applications.

That said, there is today a huge disconnect between our expectations for intelligent machines and what such machines can actually do. It is not easy to bridge the gap between working systems in the business world and a generalized speech understanding system that can handle any scenario of interest. What is the cause of such a gap? What can be done to significantly reduce it? Do we understand the problems sufficiently? Do we have any novel thinking about potential solutions or methods for bridging the gap over the next few years or decades? And, most important, will acquiring better knowledge of how humans handle language actually help us build more intelligent talking machines? These are all questions raised and duly considered in this book.

The Voice in the Machine is thus about the complexity of language and the difficulty of building machines that can recognize speech and understand spoken language

- with an accuracy of recognition and understanding approaching that of humans
- for any speaker, with any accent
- in any environment, and
- for any application.

Pieraccini explains in nonspecialist terms (and without the support of signal processing or statistical mathematics) the various processes that occur in *human speech recognition* (HSR) and compares them to those which have evolved over the past seventy years in *automatic speech recognition* (ASR) and *natural language understanding* (NLU). He shows how natural language understanding and dialog systems have enabled speech researchers and developers both to build viable working systems for a range of applications from dictation to customer care and to introduce those systems into industry, where they are successfully used by millions of customers per day. By comparing and contrasting human language acquisition with statistical training methods for machine learning, he also shows that, even though machine learning has made a great leap forward from statistical methods of learning speech signal properties, how humans acquire one or more mother tongues in the early years of life is still a far more robust process that cannot be easily replicated with machine learning methods.

Most of his chapters deal with speech recognition and understanding and trace their evolution from waveform methods, to artificial intelligence approaches, to template-matching statistical methods, and ultimately to statistical methods based on the *hidden Markov model* (HMM) characterization of speech statics and dynamics. Pieraccini tells how simple isolated-digit recognition machines have evolved into highly sophisticated approaches to dictation and ultimately to natural language understanding and how a talking machine with almost natural voice quality has formed the basis for an entire class of "dialog systems" in which the machine interacts with the customer by understanding the meaning of each utterance, considering prior history and other factors, and then responding intelligently according to a dialog model and a set of rules for dialog management.

With more than thirty years of experience in the speech recognition area, and a recognized expert in virtually every aspect of speech processing, Roberto Pieraccini is uniquely qualified to write about the complexities of speech recognition and natural language understanding. In *The Voice in the Machine,* he has done a superb job of explaining those complexities in nonspecialist terms.

Lawrence Rabiner
January 2011

Acknowledgments

Dear Mom and Dad, this book is dedicated to you. Most certainly I would not have had an exciting career in science and technology, and I would not have written this book if you had not always fostered and cherished, since I was a little child, my inner desires to build stuff, my curiosity to always know how things work, and without the unconditional confidence you always instilled in me. Mom, you have always been great. Your kindness and open-mindedness, your love for life, for people and for their stories, your always wise and fearless take on the little and big problems of existence defined me and what I am. Dad, I still remember the strophe from the Ulysses canto of Dante's Inferno you always recited to me: "*Fatti non foste a viver come bruti, Ma per seguir virtute e conoscenza*" ("Ye were not made to live like unto brutes, But for pursuit of virtue and of knowledge"). That strophe became the leitmotif of my life. Too bad you are not here anymore. You would have loved to see this book finished and published.

Dear colleagues of my many work adventures; all of you who mentored me, taught me, told me stories, sat down with me for long coffee breaks or lunches to talk about science, technology, life; all of you who shared with me the enthusiasm of new ideas, the excitement of good results, the frustration of bad ones, the foreshadowing of solutions to the most difficult problems; you all contributed to the writing of this book. Even though I mention only some of you here, the list of those who have been influential in my career, and thanks to whom I understood most of the things explained here, is definitely too long. But you know who you are. In particular, I want to thank you, dear Giulio (Modena), Roberto (Billi) and Enrico (Vivalda)—sadly no longer among us—for having given me a unique chance to work with you at CSELT, one of the most prestigious research centers in telecommunication in Europe at the time, and for having infused in me the first sparks of that love for human language and speech which has stayed with me for all of my work life. Thanks, Carlo (Scagliola). Although we've never worked at the same place and at the same time, I have always felt you have been, besides a great friend, one of my mentors. Your point of view on speech recognition gave me a jump start on many aspects of it and helped me shape the philosophy of my research. Many thanks to you for having described to me, for the first time, how the "grammar-driven connected word recognition" algorithm works in such simple and intuitive terms that I still use your way to describe it and to think about it, even in this book. And also many thanks to you, Carlo, for having encouraged me to spend some time at Bell Laboratories—which became more than ten years—and for having introduced me to the Bell Labs people who then invited me there.

Dear Aaron (Rosenberg), Larry (Rabiner), and Bishnu (Atal). You have been my mentors, a source of inspiration, and my role models at that special and magical place that was called Bell Laboratories. This book wouldn't be this book if I hadn't met you, and if I hadn't spent precious time with you all. Thanks, Larry, for having read one of the first drafts of *The Voice* and for your insightful and useful, as always, suggestions and comments. Also, thank you for encouraging me to get into this endeavor and in many other endeavors in my career.

Dear Esther (Levin), we worked together for almost a decade. We solved existing problems, discovered new ones to solve, invented new stuff, fought on our different views (and yes … you were right most of the time). We strived for greatness, novelty, surprise, and new and unconventional solutions. Your clear and crisp insight into the complexity of things, and your strong aversion to nonsense, helped me understand things I wouldn't have understood in any other way, and learn how to discern what works from what doesn't.

Dear Mazin (Gilbert). I have always enjoyed talking to you, and cherished our friendship. You were the first to strongly encourage me to write this book, from a vague idea to a real project. You and I worked together during the first phases of it, you greatly helped me catalyze my thoughts about its structure, its style, its content.

Dear David (Nahamoo), Phillip (Hunter), Jay (Wilpon), Jim (Flanagan), John (Makhoul), Michael (Picheny), Mike (Phillips), Pascale (Fung), Steve (Young), Sasha (Caskey), Jeff (Sorensen), Juan (Huerta), Renato (De Mori), and everyone else who, at some point in time, worked with me in some way or another, and with their wisdom and deep understanding of the technology of speech was influential to me, spent time answering my questions, opened my eyes to new ideas, told me their technological stories, and gifted me with their insights on "computers that understand speech." My most sincere thanks to you. Many of your thoughts and points of view are expressed in this book.

Thanks, Zor (Gorelov), for the many discussions we had on the business of speech, and for your insight about it. Thanks, Ruth (Brown), Victor (Goltsman), Alan (Pan), and all other colleagues at SpeechCycle, for the long conversations, the hours spent together, and the shared excitement of the constant challenge of trying to understand speech and its business.

Thank you, dear Bernd (Moebius), Bob (Carpenter), Caroline (Drouin), David (Suendermann), DC (Cymbalista), Eric (Woudenberg), Keelan (Evanini), Krishna (Dayanidhi), Julia (Hirschberg), Gianfranco (Bilardi), Leide (Porcu), and everyone else who read all or some of the parts of the early versions of the manuscript, and always gave me precious feedback. And a huge thank you to you, my dear friend Jonathan Bloom, for reading one of the final versions of the whole manuscript, all of it, and for having given me the most insightful remarks, both as a professional in the field as well as an accomplished writer. I totally enjoyed our lunch breaks where we discussed at length each one of the chapters, concept by concept, paragraph by paragraph, interlacing that with our always interesting discussions about art, literature, cinema, and life.

Dear Ada (Brunstein), Katherine (Almeida), Marc (Lowenthal), James (DeWolf), and the whole MIT Press staff. Thanks for believing in this book and proposing it for publication, and for the constant help you have given me. Thank you, Jeffrey (Lockridge), for your critical reading and deep understanding of *The Voice*, and for helping me sound like a native English speaker.

Thanks, dear and sweet Francesca (Gherardi). As you know, I owe you the conception of the idea of writing this book, which originated when you invited me to give a 3-hour talk about speech technology at the University of Florence, in front of an audience of biologists, psychologists, and anthropologists. It turned out to be one of the most fun talks in my life, and gave me the confidence that I could talk about computers that understand speech to nontechnical people.

My thanks also to all of you who contributed to the technology of computer speech with passion, brilliance, and perseverance, and whose name I've mistakenly left out. Any inaccuracies and omissions are my own.

Dear Daniele and Alessandra, my children, this book is dedicated to you. Talking to you, getting your fresh perspective on life, science, literature, theater, the internet, music, and cinema has always been a refreshing source of inspiration for me. And, even though you might not have realized it, some of the ideas we discussed made it into this book. Thanks, Dan, for having read an early draft of the manuscript, and for helping me streamline my English and my thoughts. Thanks, Alex, for just being there and listening to me and to my stories, with your beautiful, young, calm, and explosive energy. I love you both.

Introduction: The Dream of Machines That Understand Speech

Queen Mary, University of London. September 2009. Scientists from four continents gather for their annual meeting: the workshop of the Special Interest Group on Discourse and Dialogue. Over the course of two days, a truly heterogeneous group of researchers—those who study humans, those who study machines, and those who try to make machines behave like humans—comes to the podium to talk about . . . talking. And, among other things, about talking to machines. And all of these people, with their different interests, backgrounds, and scientific goals, seem to get along very well.

Dan Bohus, a young scientist at Microsoft Research, presents something that impresses even some of the old, disenchanted technologists who have seen hundreds of demonstrations and listened to thousands of talks. Dan talks about what he characterizes as "situated interactions," those where machines are embedded "deeply into the natural flow of everyday tasks, activities and collaborations."[1] These machines may be robots, regular computers, entertainment systems, automobiles, or avatars impersonating a virtual living being on a monitor screen. In fact, the avatar that comes to life in the video shown by Dan during his talk did so in a monitor installed as an experiment in a cafeteria at Microsoft (figure I.1).

The avatar on the monitor isn't a real person but tries to behave like one. Although we see only her face, she's fairly convincing. She talks with a synthetic computer voice while moving her mouth in synch with what she says. She looks straight ahead, but her eyes move almost imperceptibly as if she were alive. And if you get closer to her, she actually seems to see you, stare at you, and engage you in a conversation. Someone who was accidentally looking at her found it quite unnerving when she asked a question. She can play trivia games, give ground transportation information, and make reservations. She can track more than one person at a time, follow their eyes, react when they're looking at her, talk to them, listen, and understand what they say. But what does "understand" mean? How can a machine understand speech? How can a machine respond? That's what this book is about.

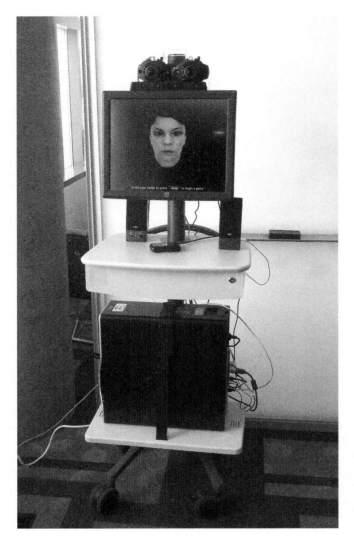

Figure I.1
View of Microsoft avatar face and computer rack for the 2009 situated interaction experiment. ©2010 Microsoft. All rights reserved.

My First Conversational Machine

Let's go back a little in time. My friend Roberto Billi and I built our first talking machine in Italy in 1982. To be precise, it wasn't just a machine that talked; it was a machine that could understand what we would say—in a very limited sense—and respond. It was a conversational machine. The place was one of the most prestigious industrial laboratories in Italy, the Center for Telecommunication Studies and Laboratories (CSELT), the research center of the Italian telephone company.[2] Computers at that time were big, expensive, and slow, with hard disks the size of washing machines and a capacity less than a hundredth of the flash memory sticks you buy today for a few dollars. Speech, collected by a microphone, reached the computer through another custom-built bulky machine, an analog-to-digital converter. The voice of the computer was generated by a completely separate machine, a tall rack full of printed circuits, which had made the news a few years earlier as the first "talking computer" built in Italy. It was called "MUSA" (*MU*ltichannel *S*peaking *A*utomaton) and spoke like a tipsy Italian with a pronunciation problem (figure I.2). But it was intelligible and very futuristic.

Figure I.2
CSELT research scientist working on an Italian spoken dialog system of the early 1980s and MUSA, the first Italian stand-alone machine for text-to-speech synthesis. From the historical archive of CSELT, courtesy of Telecom Italia.

Because general computers in the mid-1980s were so slow, building a program that could recognize even simple single-word utterances with a delay of a second or so required the help of an expensive number-crunching machine specifically programmed to perform special tasks. This came in the form of a shiny new FP100 floating point array processor, which continuously exchanged data with the main computer, a DEC PDP 11/60, via complex data uploading, downloading, and synchronizing procedures. So there we were, with a general-purpose minicomputer, a refrigerator-sized speaking automaton, a number-crunching box, and another box to transform speech collected by the microphone into a digital representation.[3] And after programming for months with other team members in three different computer languages, taking turns at the few teletypes and the even fewer primitive terminals, we gave life to our first, quite lame conversational machine.[4] It could do only two things: make single-digit calculations

User: Compute <pause> three <pause> times <pause> six
Machine: Three times six is eighteen . . . What else?

and provide the telephone extensions of all sixteen people in our department

User: Telephone <pause> Roberto <pause> Billi
Machine: The number of Roberto Billi is six three nine . . . What else?

Of course, the conversational machine couldn't actually dial the extensions. That would have required another box, which we didn't have. But the demonstration was quite impressive anyway. So impressive in fact that Piero Angela, the host of a famous science show on Italian public television, *Quark*, wanted to include our conversational machine in a story on advances in computer technology. After spending about a week with the show's producer, camera crew, directors, and photographers, and waiting another three months to find out which Wednesday evening our story would be aired, we saw our conversational machine finally get its 45 seconds of fame.

Thank You for an Enjoyable Game

Let's take another little jump back in time. The dream of building a talking computer is much older than the 1980s. Surely, the talking computer most imprinted in the collective imagination is HAL. In Arthur C. Clarke's and Stanley Kubrick's science fiction masterpiece *2001: A Space Odyssey*, the HAL 9000 (HAL being an acronym for *H*euristically Programmed *AL*gorithmic Computer) was built on January 31, 1997, at the HAL Plant in Urbana, Illinois.[5] It was deployed on the *Discovery One* spaceship in 2001, when the saga begins. HAL becomes the story's villain when it decides the mission is being endangered by the human crew and "terminates" all of them except Dave Bowman, who eventually deactivates it. HAL isn't a visibly anthropomorphic computer: it has no legs, arms, or hands. It's represented by a single camera eye. Its body is essentially the entire ship, and everything there is under its complete control, including the lives of the astronauts kept in suspended animation. Its humanlike intelligence is conveyed by its ability both to talk in a soothing voice and to make autonomous decisions. A conversation HAL has with Frank, one of the astronauts, shows that it even has manners:

Frank: Um . . . anyway, Queen takes Pawn.

HAL: Bishop takes Knight's Pawn.

Frank: Lovely move. Er . . . Rook to King One.

HAL: I'm sorry, Frank. I think you missed it. Queen to Bishop Three. Bishop takes Queen. Knight takes Bishop. Mate.

Frank: Ah . . . yeah, looks like you're right. I resign.

HAL: Thank you for an enjoyable game.

Frank: Yeah. Thank you.

Did HAL truly enjoy the game in the way humans enjoy things they are passionate about? Or was its comment simply one of a number of different voice recordings, like "You are a better player than you used to be" or "You should work on your openings," programmed by the Urbana engineers to come up randomly at the end of each game it won?

Science fiction lets us compare technological predictions with actual realities if we're lucky enough to live during the time when the story is set. Produced in 1968, *2001: A Space Odyssey* shows technology developed only three decades later. Did technology in 2001 even remotely resemble what the movie portrayed? David G. Stork, a researcher in computerized lip reading at the Tokyo-based Ricoh Company, conducted a thorough analysis of the gaps existing between the science fiction predictions of Kubrick's movie and actual technological advances around 2001.[6] Indeed, if you watch the movie now, most of its technology seems outdated. There are no cell phones, no Palm Pilots, no fancy computer graphics or windows, no mouses— and people actually take notes with pencil and paper! But, then, who could have predicted the Internet and the Web, Google search, *Wikipedia,* and the Internet Movie Database back in 1968? Certainly, Kubrick spent a lot of time at IBM, AT&T's Bell Laboratories, and several other ivory towers of computer technology before shooting the movie. When Bowman sets about deactivating HAL, it sings "Daisy Bell" for him, its voice becoming slower, deeper, and graver as it "dies."[7] Kubrick was most likely inspired by a meeting with pioneer of computer music Max Mathews of Bell Labs, who played him a version of "Daisy Bell" sung by a synthetic computer voice. Yet there is a huge gap between most of the technology of *2001,* the movie, and 2001, the reality. Most of the movie's technology actually looks quite dated from the perspective of someone living in 2001, except for one thing: we didn't have then, nor do we now, computers like HAL that talk and understand speech. Our computers are better than most humans at playing chess, memorizing enormous numbers of facts, and making split-second decisions that can control complex machines like jet planes and nuclear plants. But they aren't better than, nor even as good as, we are in two of our most common and natural activities— talking and understanding speech. Is that just a failure of our technology? Is it because human language is good only for humans, but not for computers? Or is it, rather, because there is something fundamental in human language and speech that we don't yet understand well enough to replicate in a machine?

Let me be clear. We humans communicate in a wide range of different ways that aren't speech. Written language, smoke signals, gestures, and sign language are all manifestations of the power and variety of human communication. Speech, which is based on sound signals emitted by our vocal apparatus and captured by our hearing, is only one of the ways we communicate but, without doubt, the way most often used by the whole of humanity. Computers that interact with humans using speech appear in nearly all science fiction stories and movies. Thus, in Robert Wise's 1951 sci-fi movie *The Day the Earth Stood Still*, Gort, a traditional anthropomorphic robot that looks to be made of tin cans, understands speech even though it can't talk: Gort doesn't say a single word throughout the whole movie. Indeed, just by watching the robot, we've no idea whether it actually understands speech or just a simple set of commands issued by its alien master, Klaatu. And in Isaac Asimov's 1950 novel *I Robot,*, Chief Robopsychologist Susan Calvin explains that the first generation of robots could easily understand speech, but they couldn't *produce* it. If, however, we go further back, to Fritz Lang's 1927 silent movie *Metropolis,* we can find a beautiful robot woman, Futura, that can both understand speech and speak.[8]

It's widely believed that the two acts of spoken language communication, understanding and producing speech, aren't equally complex. Small children learn to understand what we say to them months, even years before they learn to speak. Perhaps this commonly observed occurrence is at the origin of the popular belief that producing speech is more difficult than understanding it. We simply aren't as impressed by computers that understand spoken commands as we are by computers that talk in a more or less natural and human-sounding voice. And we're generally more attracted by people who speak well than by people who understand well. There's no obvious way to add flourishes to understanding, to make it charismatic, as some of us can make speech. Indeed, we often take speaking as a reflection of intelligence. If someone doesn't speak, or at least do something equivalent to it like writing or using sign language, there's no proof that person actually understands what we've said. As it happens, however, understanding speech and speaking are both enormously sophisticated and complex activities. We can't speak well if we don't understand what we're saying. And we can't build a machine that speaks if it doesn't also understand at least some of what it's saying. How can you know, for instance, how to pronounce "read" in "I read the book a year ago" and in "I will read the book tomorrow" if you don't understand that the first happened in the past and the second will happen in the future? Both activities, which are so natural and come so easily to virtually all of us, are indeed so complex that we haven't been able to build machines that speak and understand speech with anywhere near the flexibility of humans. At least not yet. But, even if you recognize that the talking ability of machines is light-years away from the talking ability of humans, you can still appreciate the enormous effort that scientists and technologists have put into trying to endow machines with even minimal capabilities of speaking and understanding speech. Using only such capabilities, however, we can build machines that can greatly benefit our society. Talking machines aren't just a gimmick to impress the general public; they're a useful extension of our interactive capabilities that can make us faster, smarter, and better at some tasks.

Press or Say 1

We forget the good things that technology has brought us when we run up against its limitations. We curse computers; we call them "dumb" because they seldom do what we want them to without also annoying or frustrating us with their complexity and the need for us to be computer geeks to deal with them. We often forget that, without computers, our planes, trains, and automobiles wouldn't be as safe as they are; without them, we wouldn't be able to do most of the things we're used to doing. Computers let us communicate with people around the world at any time and from any place, buy tickets or goods online, take pictures and see them right away . . . and the list could go on forever. Computers are the heaven and hell of today's world. They are heaven when you browse through thousands of pictures of your loved ones or listen to the songs you've stored at almost no cost on a minuscule hard disk. They are hell when you struggle to retrieve what you've stored inside them, when they behave in incomprehensible, utterly complex, and nonsensical ways, or when the agent at the desk can't check you in on the next flight because . . . the computer is slow or down that day. But, like any other technological device around us, computers are products of human minds. They can't be perfect. Humans aren't. Our bodies are the product of millions of years of evolution, and still we get sick, we malfunction, we get old and die. Computers have been here for slightly over fifty years, a mere instant in evolutionary terms. How could we even compare them to humans?

You may curse computers, but you're forced to use them, so you often find yourself disliking them, especially when they try talking to you. You dial an 800 number and, instead of a human, you get a computer saying, "Thanks for calling.

This call is important to us. Please press or say 1 for sales, press or say 2 for billing inquiries, and press or say 3 for anything else." Damn, you grumble. Why don't I have someone, a human being, talking to me? Is my call really all that important to them? I want to talk to an agent! I want to talk to a *real person*!

But the plain truth is we *can't* talk to a real person anytime we want and for every possible request. AT&T, the telecommunications giant that was created by Alexander Graham Bell in 1885, used to be a monopoly with nearly a million employees serving millions of customers. There was a time, many years ago, when making a telephone call meant talking to an operator, a human being who would connect your home telephone with the person you wanted to call by plugging wires into a switchboard. Endless rows of operators sat at their switchboards, with roving managers making sure that everything went smoothly twenty-four hours a day, seven days a week. "I'd like to call John Smith in Chicago," you might say. "There are many John Smiths in Chicago," the operator might reply. "Do you know where he lives?" "Uh . . . yes, he lives on Clark Street." "Thank you. Please hold while I connect you."

But human operator assistance for all callers all the time was simply not sustainable. The exponential growth in telephone customers inevitably led to an exponential growth in the need for operators. Technology historians observed that "in a few years AT&T would have had to hire everyone in the U.S. to be able to continue its operations."[9] Fortunately, AT&T invented the automatic telephone switch, and callers could dial the parties they wanted without any operator assistance by looking up their numbers in a telephone book. But that advance came with trade-offs. What about the hundreds of thousands of telephone operators who lost their jobs? And was looking up a number in a big bulky book and having to dial it on a rotary telephone more convenient than asking a human operator to complete the call for you? Probably not. But would you really rather talk to Mabel at her switchboard every time you wanted to call someone? Technology is often a mixed blessing. We get one thing at the expense of something else. We get cheap telephone calls to anywhere and at any time at the expense of some convenience.

Technology moves ahead, no matter what we do, no matter what we think of it. Technological progress is most often driven by business and economies of scale, not just by the real needs of people. But that's not always a bad thing. Economies of scale necessitate automation, and automation, once we get used to it, makes our lives easier. Machines that talk and understand speech are an example of that, and a reality today. And, as the technology evolves, they'll become even more pervasive in the future for a variety of applications. They'll make our lives easier, until they become invisible; they'll just be part of our everyday lives, something we take for granted, like a computer keyboard or mouse, or the Web. That's the fate of any good technology.

I remember when I saw my first computer mouse. I was stunned. Today I don't think about it. The mouse is there; when I move it on my desk, my cursor, the image of a little arrow, moves on my monitor screen among icons of documents, folders, and such. Sophisticated computer programs, graphics, and electronics are required to move that little arrow on the screen in sync with my movements of the mouse. But, most of the time, I'm completely unaware of that and actually think I'm *directly* moving the arrow, not just sending signals to the electronics and programs behind it.

Now consider the difference between clicking and double-clicking. Yes, you have to think about it if you really want to explain what the difference is. But you don't have to think when you actually click and double-click the icons and the links on your virtual desktop, just as you don't have to think how to move and balance your body when you walk. It's second nature for most of us, including small children, who today learn the difference even before they learn how to read. You use a mouse without perceiving there is complex technology behind it that coordinates your actions with the corresponding actions on a computer screen. We say that such technological advances are "invisible" because they work flawlessly and unobtrusively most of the time.

Have talking machines become invisible? Has interacting with them become second nature to us? Not yet. Clicking and double-clicking are very simple communicative acts, and the technology behind them is both simple and quite mature. On the other hand, the technology behind talking machines is still in its infancy, and there is a huge distance between what we expect talking machines to do and what they actually can do today. That's why talking machines aren't invisible. Not yet. But there's no doubt that great progress has been made.

The Future as We Know It

Talking to a "Press or say 1" 800 number can be a frustrating experience if you expect it to be like talking to a trained human agent. But this is a relic of the past, the vestige of a technology evolving with each passing day through the efforts of thousands of scientists and technologists around the world. Today's talking machines have the potential to do so much more. They can understand the voices of millions of people, make sense of thousands of different words and concepts, follow simple commands, provide information, and solve problems as well as—and sometimes better than—humans. You must keep in mind, however, that language, and speech in particular, is probably the most sophisticated invention of our species. It has evolved inseparably from and in the most powerful alliance with our minds. Indeed, we humans wouldn't have evolved in the ways we have without a language as complex and as sophisticated as human language. *The Voice in the Machine* is about the complexity of language and how difficult it is to build machines that can understand it. You'll see that computer speech technology has taken much longer to reach maturity than other technologies. Yet we're still trying to build better and better talking machines, driven, on the one hand, by the dream of re-creating intelligence, language, and speech in a computer and, on the other, by the needs of business and automation.

If you could visit any of the hundreds of academic and industrial labs involved in computer speech research around the world or attend any of the dozens of international conferences on the topic held every year, you'd get a vivid glimpse at the future of talking machines, at avatars like the one at the beginning of this introduction that talk and show a full range of emotions. You'd see how you can speak and control your entertainment system from anywhere in your living room without having to carry a remote, how you can speak to a machine in English and hear your voice come out in Chinese. These are just a few of the technological marvels available today in the research labs. However, these and many others won't be widely available outside the labs until they become cost effective. More than fifty years of research has made these achievements possible despite the enormous complexity of human speech.

The first chapter of *The Voice in the Machine* considers how we speak, how we understand speech, what makes human language so complex, and why it's so difficult to build talking machines. The product of hundreds of thousands of years of evolution, human language is a major advantage that has helped our species survive and thrive—and do so without armor plates to protect us from the assaults of stronger and bigger predators, without powerful jaws or fangs or claws to catch and kill our prey, and without fur to protect us from the elements. Our unprotected bodies are built for language. We have an extremely sophisticated vocal apparatus, much more sophisticated than that of almost any other living creature, which allows us to produce and combine sounds to form words, the building blocks of speech and, indeed, to express any concept our minds are capable of conceiving. We've developed complex mechanisms to string words together into sentences to convey meanings that reflect ideas and mental representations of the world. And we've developed correspondingly complex mechanisms to translate word-sounds into actual words and sentences and these words and sentences back into ideas and conceptual representations. Yet speaking and understanding speech seem as easy to us as walking, seeing, and breathing. They are "invisible"—we speak and understand speech without having to think about either. How can we replicate all that in a machine?

Chapter 2 tells how pioneers in the field of computer speech have reengineered human speech capabilities into machines. Although a Hungarian scientist at the court of Empress Maria Theresa of Austria invented a machine that could reproduce human speech in the late 1700s, serious scientific attempts to reproduce and understand human speech weren't made until the late 1930s and the 1950s, respectively. At that time, lacking computers, scientists had to build dedicated circuit boards to give life to their talking inventions. When digital computers and devices that could digitize sounds and transform them into numbers became available, more and more research fueled the dream of building talking machines. The first most effective systems that could understand simple words and phrases weren't electronic models of the human auditory system, but those which relied on the brute-force approach of matching speech to recorded patterns.

Chapter 3 talks about the tension between placing speech and language capabilities into computers and finding brute-force solutions to highly simplified versions of the "speech understanding" problem. Artificial intelligence (AI) has given rise to talking machines with reasoning capabilities that can logically come to conclusions based on the knowledge compiled by experts. The brute-force approach has proved superior, not because it is more informed, but because of the difficulties the artificial intelligence approach has encountered in compiling the vast and ever increasing amounts of knowledge required to recognize simple utterances, like ten-digit phone numbers or the names of the people you want to call. When the AI and the brute-force or engineering approach came into conflict, we realized that putting all of the knowledge necessary to understand speech manually into a computer would be an endless process that would never show practical results. We understood the importance of endowing machines with the capability of acquiring the knowledge they required automatically and autonomously. That capability came in the form of statistical learning.

Chapter 4 explains statistical learning and the modeling of human speech. By casting speech recognition and understanding as communication problems and solving them with an elegant mathematical formulation, we obtained one of the most effective models for building machines that understand speech with minimal manual input, the hidden Markov model (HMM), which serves as the basis of modern speech recognition.

Once we developed an effective model to teach a talking machine how to understand speech, the next step was to raise its performance to levels acceptable for practical purposes. Chapter 5 recounts the long journey from primitive working machines to sophisticated ones that could understand naturally spoken utterances with vocabularies of thousands of words. Collecting ever larger quantities of data and evaluating progress in an accurate and scientific manner acted as the forces behind a continuous and unrelenting improvement of the technology. Chapter 6 considers the challenge of moving computer speech technology to the next level. A machine that recognizes spoken words is useless if it can't ask questions, respond to them, and make intelligent use of what it knows. That ability is called "dialog."

Although most of *The Voice in the Machine* is devoted to teaching machines how to understand spoken language and react to it, chapter 7 addresses producing speech, which, we should remember, is as complex as understanding it.

Chapter 8 describes the beginning of the long and difficult process of building commercially viable talking machines, machines that both fulfill a variety of business purposes and are cost effective. Chapter 9 tells how the business of talking machines that understand speech and speak has evolved and how companies have been formed and infrastructures, standards, and practices created to bring speech technology to nearly everyone. And, concluding that the future is not what we dreamed it would be and is evolving in ways we couldn't have predicted, chapter 10 asks where we go from here. Will we end up with a C-3PO as our best friend—or with a computer that just understands speech?

1

Humanspeak

Speaking is like walking. We do it without thinking about *how* we do it. When you speak your mother tongue, you don't think about how the concepts, ideas, images, intents, and voices in your mind become first words and then sounds produced by specific and precise movements of your tongue, lips, and jaw. And you don't think about how your ears transform those sounds into electrical impulses that travel to your brain and become words, and then concepts, ideas, images, intents, and voices again. Speaking and understanding speech are as natural as walking, recognizing the faces of your friends, or finding your way home from work.[1] But there was a time very early in your life when you didn't know how to speak, walk, or make sense of the world around you. Do you remember when you learned to do all those things? And if you had to teach them to a nonhuman intelligence, an alien life-form from outer space, or a machine, how would you do that? Where would you start?

There are times, of course, when we do perceive the complexity hidden within speaking. For instance, some of us have to relearn how to speak and perform other natural activities when our brains or some other parts of our bodies are injured in an accident or damaged by disease. But, less dramatically, many of us perceive the complexity of language when we try to learn a second language as adults. All of a sudden, speaking and understanding are no longer natural. You have to focus consciously on the rules of grammar and syntax, strain to recall words you've memorized, and articulate them using sounds that are alien to your ears. Indeed, even when you've lived in a foreign country for decades, and even when your command of the grammar, syntax, vocabulary, and idioms of its language is excellent, native speakers still perceive your accent as foreign. You still make little, almost imperceptible mistakes in pronunciation or intonation that are the telltale signs of your original, first language. There's something in the language we learn when we are very young that leaves its mark on us for the rest of our lives.

This chapter provides a glimpse into the hidden complexity of spoken language. Only by understanding that complexity can the nonspecialist appreciate the difficulties inherent in building a machine that understands and produces speech. As you'll see in reading this book, you don't have to fully understand how spoken language works—not that we do fully understand it today—to build a machine that understands speech at least to some degree. But even though building such a machine is a technology—rather than a science—and one developed by engineers to achieve measurable goals, it's important to have at least a simplified scientific idea of the inherent complexity of language to appreciate the successes, failures, and struggles that many researchers and technologists experienced to make machines do even a slight semblance of what we do so naturally and effortlessly.

My primary purpose in this chapter is not to teach language theory, which is definitely beyond my knowledge and background as a computer scientist and technologist, but to make my general readers aware of certain characteristics of language that will open a window on its enormous complexity and our efforts to unravel and harness that complexity within a talking machine. To that end, I've simplified certain notions and usages of linguistics and related fields to the point that specialists may find them not entirely accurate or conventional according to accepted thinking and practices in their fields.

Learning a Language

You start learning your first language almost right after you're born, but your first language skills show up only around your first birthday. You may have grown up in a multilingual environment and learned more than one language, but, no matter how many languages you learned at that early age, those will be your mother tongues for the rest of your life. Although today we know quite a lot about language learning from the experimental point of view, how we actually acquire our mother tongues as children is still largely a mystery. Whatever your ethnicity or culture, you learn your first language in much the same way, with much the same milestones at much the same ages.[2] During your first year of life, you start babbling and exercising your ability to produce a large variety of sounds. Around your first birthday, you start pronouncing and understanding simple words, naming the objects, toys, food, and people or pets around you. At around two, your vocabulary begins to catch up with the vocabulary of the adults in your lives, and you start combining words to express more complicated concepts and ideas. This is the beginning of learning that will progress into your adolescence: from two-word phrases to whole sentences with a vocabulary that will grow richer and richer every day. It's estimated that a college graduate knows, on average, about 20,000 words.[3]

Producing and understanding speech aren't independent activities. When, as a healthy child of about one, you start experimenting with the speech sounds of your mother tongue, the continuous feedback you receive through listening to yourself is essential for the development of your vocal system.[4] Children born deaf never develop the ability to articulate speech that people with normal hearing have. This isn't because their vocal systems are incapable of normal speech, but because, lacking the necessary feedback from hearing, they can't fine-tune the articulation of speech sounds.

One of the peculiarities of human language is that we speak it fluently only if we learn it before adolescence. Any language you learn after puberty will retain the signs of your mother tongue. And children denied the opportunity to learn any language before puberty are unlikely to learn a language at all thereafter. So-called feral children, children who were kept isolated, didn't learn a language at an early age, and couldn't learn a language thereafter, are used as anecdotal proofs of the impossibility of learning a first language later in life.[5] But, in one of the many paradoxes of human language, even though people with no physical or mental disabilities can never learn a language if they haven't learned one early enough in their lives, severely disabled people with highly limited communication channels to the outside world can eventually excel in the use of language. Take the phenomenal example of Helen Keller, who, blind and deaf from the age of one and a half, used her only available communication channel—touch—to learn how to finger-spell and read with Braille at seven, went on to get a college degree, and eventually wrote many books and articles.

However surprising these facts may be, what's even more surprising is that healthy children can learn a language at all in such a short period of time after their birth and with such seemingly limited exposure to linguistic data.[6] We all learned a language as children, but we don't remember how. Can you even remember a time when you didn't understand what people around you were saying, when you couldn't speak to them, and when sounds like "me" and "you" barely made any sense to you? Nevertheless, you learned your mother tongue extremely well and with a great mastery of language skills in just a few years, years during which your comprehension and intellectual capability weren't as strong and as refined as they are now, at least you believe they weren't. If you could do that so easily and so perfectly when you were so little and so otherwise incapable, why can't chimpanzees and dogs? And why can't machines?

Unlike chimps and dogs, we humans evolved to be physiologically specialized for speech. The sophistication of our vocal and auditory systems surpasses that of most, if not all, other animals. Unlike them, we can speak because we're hardwired for speech. Moreover, again unlike other animals, we humans can use a sophisticated language even if we can't speak. If we're deaf, we can communicate using sign language, which has as much expressivity and sophistication as any spoken language. Why can't other intelligent and social animals like chimpanzees learn a sign language anywhere near as sophisticated as our own?[7] We must certainly possess some innate capability to learn and master language—what Noam Chomsky has called a "language organ"—unavailable to any other living species on earth.

The Language Organ

A professor of linguistics at the Massachusetts Institute of Technology (MIT) since 1955, Noam Chomsky is probably one of the most controversial and influential language theorists of our times. Modern neurolinguistics and psycholinguistics provide radically different points of view on the process of human language acquisition, and experimental studies evidence that tends to disprove Chomsky's hypothesis. I want to briefly discuss it here, however, to provide readers with another convincing element of the complexity of human language and our inability to completely explain it.

According to Chomsky, we humans are born with a *language organ,* part of our brains that is genetically hardwired to learn language.[8] Active for only a few years after our birth, this organ atrophies and becomes useless when we reach puberty. The case of feral children, our difficulty in learning and mastering a second language as adults, and phenomena like the creole languages tend to support Chomsky's hypothesis.[9]

On the other hand, there is much that does not. Children learn their first language in circumstances uniquely different from those of adults learning a second language.[10] To start with, children don't have any other language to influence and distract them before they learn how to speak. Nor do they have any other way to communicate or make their needs known in a clear and effective manner. Thus their motivation to learn a first language is clearly much stronger than any motivation adults might have for learning a second one. Small children also receive the attention of the people around them in ways they'll never experience later in their lives. Parents exercise extreme patience during child development, repeating sounds and words over and over, correcting mistakes, encouraging acquired skills, and teaching new ones. As a child, you're allowed to learn your first language at your own pace and without any external obligation or exam, and you can even have fun doing it. And, what's more, you're exposed to your mother tongue, often the only language you hear, for most of the time you're awake. How many hours of speech do children listen to and process during their first few years of life? Thousands! Even when fully immersed in a second language, can an adult receive anything like the same patience, attention, and constructive criticism from native speakers that a child does when learning its first language at home?

We All Speak the Same

Let's assume we *are* born with a language organ, then how much of the language we first learn to speak do we inherit with that organ? Does a child born to French parents inherit some grasp of French, however limited? Would a French-born infant adopted by Japanese parents speak Japanese with a *French* accent?

Although we humans speak thousands of different languages, all of them different in sound, structure, and grammar, as children born and raised in any one of the thousand different linguistic environments we learn our mother tongue in much the same way, over the same length of time, and with the same final result, in terms of capabilities and expressivity. Thus, if you're a child born to French parents and raised in a Japanese-speaking environment, you'll learn Japanese as well as a child born to and raised by Japanese parents, and with no trace of a French accent. So the language organ, if we do have one, is presumably hardwired for learning language in general, rather than any specific language. But is there what Chomsky calls a "universal grammar," an innate structure that is the skeleton of all human languages?

We're often amazed at how different the thousands of human languages seem to be, but what's all the more amazing is how intrinsically similar they are. If we observe them from an outsider's perspective, for instance, from the point of view of an extraterrestrial alien, all human languages sound like different dialects of the same language: *humanspeak*. To start with, all human spoken languages are based on a relatively small collection of basic speech sounds called "phonemes."[11] Languages use phonemes singly or, far more often, in combination to form basic units of meaning called "words." Some words, such as the nouns *chair, Bob, dog,* and *happiness,* refer to objects, living things, or concepts. Other words, such as the verbs *sit, create,* and *belong,* describe actions and the relations between things. Still other words, such as the adjectives *red, smart,* and *this,* modify or describe the nouns they accompany. We know that all human languages have nouns and verbs, most have adjectives, and some have other functional words, such as prepositions and articles, that help make language more precise.[12] Finally, most human languages change words by adding prefixes and suffixes to give them slightly different meanings—adding *-s* to *house,* for example, changes it from the singular to the plural *house_s_.* Viewed from a distance, all human languages use more or less the same mechanisms. And that's not restricted to words. All languages have more or less strict sets of rules that prescribe how words should be put together to construct sentences, although the particular rules may differ from language to language. For instance, some languages require adjectives to come before nouns, whereas others allow adjectives to follow nouns. The set of all the rules that govern the creation of correct sentences is called "syntax," and the systems of rules that describe syntax are called "grammars." As you soon realize when you set about learning foreign languages, each language has its own grammatical rules—with plenty of exceptions.

Although different languages may have different grammatical rules, Chomsky's hypothesis holds that there's an underlying, unique, and universal grammar that has the power and flexibility to account for all of them—and for all their rule variations. At least in principle, and again according to Chomsky's hypothesis, by setting the appropriate parameters of this universal grammar, each child on earth learns its mother tongue no matter what that is. For instance, a child reared in a language environment where adjectives typically come before nouns, as they do in English, would set the parameters of its universal grammar to account for that pattern, just as a child reared in a language environment where adjectives follow nouns, as they do in Italian and French, would set the parameters of its universal grammar to account for that different pattern. According to the hypothesis, the general code of the universal grammar is part of your genetic makeup, and you configure its parameters while learning your mother tongue during your first years of life. You learn which rules of the universal grammar are in use in your mother tongue, and which aren't, as you learn to speak its words.

The spoken form of words—and, indeed, their written form as well—is mostly arbitrary and derived from cultural convention.[13] There are no deep reasons, beyond those of a historical nature, why today in English a house is called a "house" and a dog is called a "dog." You could make up completely new words and call a house a "wampum" and a dog a "barkyu" without in any way affecting the underlying power of language. The true essence of human language, Chomsky tells us, is not in the spoken, written, or gestured form of the words but in the underlying universal structure that's part of our collective human culture and genetic patrimony, which differentiates us from all other animal species.

To summarize, viewed from afar, all human languages are quite similar. They all build all possible words starting from a small number of fundamental sounds, and they all put together words to form meaningful sentences and phrase according to a set of rules. And if there's an innate universal grammar, it includes all the possible rules of all the possible languages. We abide by those which match the language we hear during the first years of our lives and ignore those which don't. But how does spoken language work? How do we produce and understand speech?

The Speech Chain

Figure 1.1 shows the ideal path, called the "speech chain," that spoken language follows from the brain of the speaker to the brain of the listener.

Speech begins as a concept or idea in the speaker's brain. This concept or idea generates an electrochemical signal that, when sent through the motor nerves, activates the vocal muscles of the mouth and produces speech sounds. These sounds then travel through the air as sound waves to the listener's ears, where they're transformed into electrochemical signals that, when sent through the sensory nerves to the listener's brain, reconstruct the original concept or idea. At the same time, in a feedback link partly through the air but mainly through the bones of the skull, speech also goes back to the speaker's ears. This feedback link allows us, as speak-

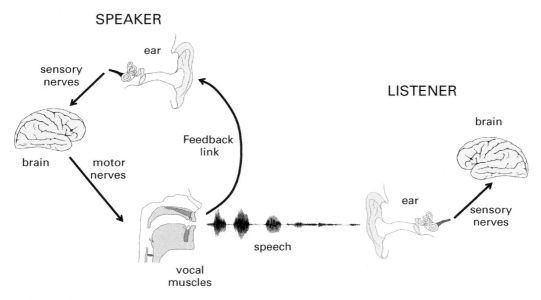

Figure 1.1
Human speech chain. Adapted from P. Denes and E. Pinson, *The Speech Chain* (Bell Telephone Laboratories, 1963).

ers, to finely and continuously adjust the delicate movements of our vocal organs to produce intelligible speech. You need feedback to perform any complex activity. You couldn't draw if you didn't see your drawing, you couldn't walk, run, or ride a bike if you didn't perceive every change in acceleration and pressure in your body, and you couldn't speak properly if you didn't hear your speech.

When humans speak, a lot happens in the brains of both speaker and listener that we don't know much about. But the structure of language itself can give us a rough idea of what *might* happen there. Linguists break language down into layers corresponding to different *linguistic levels* of abstraction. Each layer represents the knowledge needed to map the layer above with the one below. With these linguistic levels, we can draw a more complex speech chain (figure 1.2).

We must certainly have in our brains a model of the world around us. We know that people live in houses and rent hotel rooms, a giraffe is an animal with a long neck and four legs, tables have four legs but don't move, and humans have two legs but generally move around a lot. These and countless other ideas and facts occupy the highest level of abstraction, and the level *before* language: *world knowledge*. The level below world knowledge, and the first level of language, *semantics*, is defined as the ability to represent knowledge generally in structured meaningful elements, where each element has a precise role and function. For instance, an

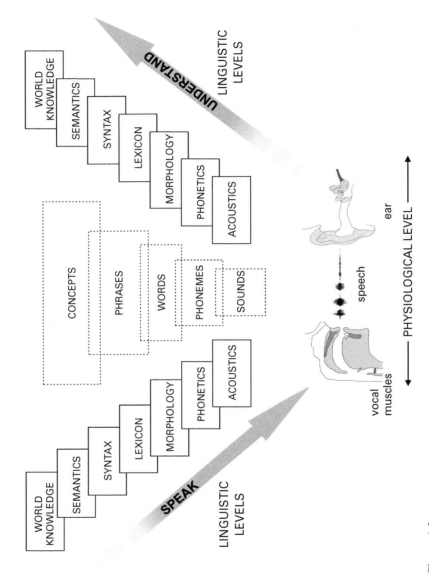

Figure 1.2
Linguistic layers of abstraction involved in the speech chain.

invitation to a party expressed as WHEN: 07/12/2008 @ 7PM; WHERE: 135 W 11TH STREET; OCCASION: STEVE'S BIRTHDAY is a formal semantic representation whose elements WHEN, WHERE, and OCCASION have well-defined meanings for all of us. The second level of language, *syntax*, expresses all the rules that govern putting words together to represent the meaning expressed by semantics. The third level of language, *lexicon*, is the knowledge of the words and their meaning, while the fourth level, *morphology*, is the knowledge of how words change their spoken or written form to perform slightly different roles. For instance, in English, if you see more than one horse, you say "horse<u>s</u>," and if you say "walk<u>ed</u>" rather than "walk," you're referring to something that happened in the past. The fifth level of language, *phonetics*, is the knowledge of phonemes and how words are built as sequences of them.[14] And finally, the sixth level of language, *acoustics*, is the knowledge of what phonemes sound like and how to produce them by moving your vocal organs. Your acoustic knowledge is then translated into motor nerve signals that actually make your vocal organs produce the sounds of the words, which are combined in phrases and sentences to speak the concept or idea you have in mind. This is the part of the speech chain that goes from concept or idea to speech. When you listen to someone speak, you follow the part of the speech chain that goes in the opposite direction, from speech to concepts or ideas. Your acoustics knowledge detects which phonemes were spoken, your phonetics knowledge tells you how these phonemes can be formed into words, your morphology knowledge actually forms the phonemes into words and phrases, your syntax knowledge structures these words and phrases into sentences, your lexicon knowledge tells you what the words of these sentences can mean, and your semantics knowledge tells you what they actually do mean to reconstruct the original concept or idea the speaker had in mind and map that to your knowledge of the world.

The Thoughts behind the Words

Let's follow the speech chain with a simple example. Imagine that I'm sitting out on the deck of my house glancing over at my neighbor, who's grilling a sausage in his backyard. The neighbor's telephone rings, and when he runs inside to pick it up, my dog runs into his backyard and, in one swift gulp, eats the sausage. That's the story, the idea, the concept, the sequence of images in my mind. The image of my dog eating the neighbor's sausage is the climax of my little story, but it's not the only thing that lingers in my mind. There are live perceptions of smells and sounds: the smells of the juicy grilling sausage and freshly cut grass; the sounds of the neighbor's telephone ringing, birds chirping, insects buzzing, a car driving by. There are also all sorts of body sensations: the feeling of my body pressing down on the chair, the sun shining on my skin, the little itch on my right eyelid. And there are other things in my mind: my feeling hungry and wanting very much to eat a sausage, my funny feeling at seeing my neighbor's puzzled and comical reaction when he comes back to find his delicious sausage gone. There are, in fact, too many ideas, images, perceptions, and feelings to communicate all of them at the same time. So my saying something has to start with selecting a small number of relevant things from among the large number that are in my mind at that precise instant.[15]

Meaning

I know what I want to say. I get up from my chair and walk the few steps to my neighbor's backyard to tell him what happened. While I'm going there, my mind has probably already arrived at a semantic description of the idea I've selected from among the many different things in my mind: "Something did something to something else." And, yes, the first something is my dog—whose name is Ares—the second something is the action of eating, and the third something is the sausage. The speech act begins to take shape; my brain has selected just one little idea from the thicket of connected and unconnected perceptions and feelings in my mind and put it in a structured form. It's not a collection of sensations, but a much simpler and crisper idea than the images, sounds, and feelings that were floating in my mind a minute ago. It's ready to travel from my brain to the brain of my neighbor in a concise package through the speech chain. We can even represent that structured semantic expression—"Something did something to something else"—as a simple formula, like

$$S \xrightarrow{A} O$$

where S is the something that performs the action A on the something else, O.[16] Here S is the dog, the subject of the action; A is the action of eating; O is the sausage, the object of the action; and the arrow represents the direction of the action: from S to O, and not the other way around. O, A, and S are general symbolic variables, placeholders that represent objects or actions or their meanings, whether in the real world or in the world of ideas. But now we need to put the real characters of my story into the formula, which might then look like this (figure 1.3).

Since pictures are difficult to draw, we can use more specific symbols—symbols, not words—to refer to the objects or actions of the real story:

$$DOG \xrightarrow{EATING} SAUSAGE$$

At this point, DOG, SAUSAGE, and EATING are still symbols and not yet words. They're unspoken placeholders, pointers to internal images of my dog, Ares, my neighbor's sausage, and the act of eating.

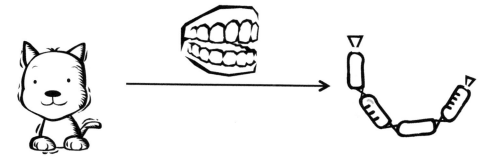

Figure 1.3
Symbolic nonverbal representation of the "dog eating sausage" concept.

What happened to the other ideas that were discarded during the initial selection process? Are all the smells, images, sounds, and feelings lost? Yes, most of them are lost just as I begin to speak and will never reach my listener's mind. Consciously or unconsciously, I decided to leave them out of my speech act because I thought they weren't relevant. Some of them—like my funny feeling—may be inferred by my listener, who knows the context, has probably had a similar experience before, and can relate to what I'm saying and add other unspoken details. This is one of the many complications with language: it's not precise. It doesn't describe accurately our ideas, images, feelings, and all that's associated with the huge amount of information that continuously reaches our senses. It can't; there's too much to convey through a channel as narrow and time limited as speech. Spoken language is just a rough approximation and simplification of what's in our minds. It suggests but doesn't describe ideas precisely and completely; it assumes that listeners, with their general knowledge of the world and their experience, will be able to interpret its approximate description of our concepts and ideas and reconstruct at least part of the vast amount of information lost in the process of speaking. But this reconstruction is occasionally mistaken, leading to misinterpretation of a speaker by a listener. On the other hand, when a lot of common contextual information exists between speaker and listener, very little spoken language is needed to precisely convey concepts and ideas. Take the famous story about Victor Hugo, who in 1862, after publication of *Les Miserables,* wired his publisher to learn how sales were going. Hugo telegraphed the single character "?" and his publisher responded with a "!"

But we could, if we wanted, include more elements to express our ideas and the properties and relationships among them. So in my simple example, I could add the fact that the dog belongs to me and the sausage belongs to my neighbor, and I

Figure 1.4
Semantic network representation with more elements of the "dog eating sausage" concept.

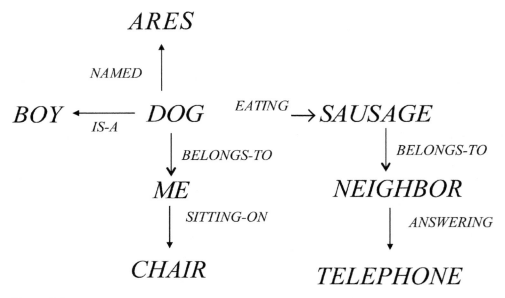

Figure 1.5
More complex semantic network with still more elements of the "dog eating sausage" concept.

could represent that by putting more arcs and symbols in our semantic formula (figure 1.4).

I could also add that my dog's name is Ares, he's a male, and I was sitting on a chair and my neighbor was answering the phone at the time the mischief took place (figure 1.5).

By adding more and more information to describe the reality of what happened in greater and greater detail, we arrive at what linguists call a "semantic representation," a symbolic formula that tries to capture the complexity of the meaning. We don't know whether our minds actually use this type of representation, or even whether our brains process this, or a similar, kind of formula to generate and understand phrases and sentences. This is just one of the many formalisms developed by semanticists to represent concepts, ideas, and their relationships.

The Whole World in a Computer

Technologists have been thinking for years of using a formalism like the one shown in figure 1.5 or any of the many others developed by linguists, semanticists, and computer scientists to represent all the world facts and knowledge in a structure that can be stored and used by computers. We can use powerful formalisms not only to represent things, but also to derive other facts. For instance, from our semantic formula, you could infer that my neighbor owns a telephone and that his telephone is out of reach from where he generally grills his sausages. We can build computer programs that know how to handle the algebra of semantic formulas and thus can derive many additional facts. The ability to derive facts from facts is called "inference," and it's one of the manifestations of what's commonly regarded as intelligent behavior.

Indeed, a vast and ambitious project called "Cyc" (pronounced like the "cyc" in "encyclopedia") was undertaken in 1984 at the Microelectronics and Computer Technology Corporation in Texas under the supervision of Stanford professor Douglas Lenat.[17] The project eventually gave rise to a company called "Cycorp" in 1994. The goal of the Cyc project, and then of Cycorp, is to create a complete repository of all *human commonsense knowledge*—the general knowledge we humans have that, among other things, allows us to speak to one another and to make reasonable assumptions about what's not said and what doesn't need to be said, in a conversation. For instance, that birds fly but dogs don't, that small birds don't eat sausages, that all animals die and stay dead, that a house is larger than a box of chocolates, that if you jump from the roof of a house you may get badly hurt or killed, that Snow White and the Seven Dwarfs are fictional characters, and so are Superman and Santa Claus, and that a fictional character may sometimes jump from the roof of a house without getting hurt are all examples of human commonsense knowledge. Commonsense knowledge plays an integral part in the interpretation of language and, in principle, could be used as an integral part of an intelligent machine. However, as of this writing, no one has found a way to completely automate the gathering of commonsense knowledge. The Cyc project, though it's gathered 2.5 million facts and rules concerning more than 150,000 concepts over the course of its twenty years, is still far behind the knowledge possessed by even the simplest human being,[18] and there's a lot of skepticism about its eventual success.[19]

On the other hand, almost unexpectedly, a digital repository of all world knowledge sprang up in the mid-1990s and, after a little more than fifteen years, has reached proportions never seen before: the Web. Containing far more information than the Cyc database, compiled by a few dozen researchers, the Web is growing at mind-blowing speed, with millions of contributors all around the world. Unfortunately, the Web isn't structured: it's a vast assemblage of mostly free-form documents in English and many other languages, audio recordings, images, and videos. The knowledge is there all right, but there's no simple way for computers to understand and formalize the vast amount of it on the Web and to make rational and logical inferences following its links. For instance, there's no easy, standardized way for a computer to infer from the biography of Mozart on *Wikipedia* that because he was born in 1756, exactly six years after the death of Johann Sebastian Bach, he and Bach couldn't possibly have ever met. In order to infer that, computers would need to fully understand written language, which is only marginally less complex than understanding spoken language. And, of course, computers can't do that today, or can't do that as well as humans do.

Another project of vast proportions, called the "Semantic Web," which started about the same time as the Web, is attempting to make it easier for computers to understand the world knowledge stored on the Web *without* having to fully understand written language.[20] It does this by marking documents, more or less by hand, with semantic tags. For instance, on the *Wikipedia* page about Mozart, it might put an annotation stating, in a formal semantic language easily interpretable by a computer program and similar to the semantic language we saw before, that

[January 27, 1756] is-the [birth-date] of [Wolfgang Amadeus Mozart].

If we would do that for all or most of the pages of the Web, and with a standardized set of agreed-upon markers, computers could, in principle, perform logical inferences about the vast and ever growing amount of knowledge contained on the Web. And they could, again in principle, answer questions like

Did Wolfgang Amadeus Mozart and Johann Sebastian Bach ever meet?

Unfortunately, there's a problem with the Semantic Web project, similar to the problem with the Cyc project: these markers have to be inserted by hand. The difference is that, for the Semantic Web project, we have millions and millions of contributors, so that eventually it may work, at least to the extent that projects like *Wikipedia* work today. But in the opinion of many, the ultimate tool that would provide the Web with meaning will be based on automated programs that can understand written language. So even though there's a lot of interest in the Semantic Web around the world, there's an equal amount of interest in the language research community about building machines that can understand facts in written English and thus can also insert semantic markers automatically.

Syntax and Words

Syntax, the next linguistic level below semantics, governs the combination of words, the elements used to construct meaning, into phrases and sentences. Semantics and its formulations deal with symbolic representations that include *objects*, like DOG and SAUSAGE, *properties*, like BELONG-TO, and *actions*, like EATING. The symbols of semantics are not words but need to be translated into words of a specific language. Thus the symbol DOG—or the little image of a dog in figure 1.3—becomes the word *dog* in English, but also *chien* in French, *cane* in Italian, and *perro* in Spanish. Language uses words in specific syntactic roles like nouns, adjectives, and verbs to refer to objects, properties, actions, and other constituents of meaning. The set of words of a language is often referred to as its "lexicon" or "vocabulary."

Words by themselves, even without the help of syntax, are extremely powerful when the speaker and the listener share the same speech context. I could probably just say, "Dog eat sausage," and my neighbor, still puzzled by the mysterious disappearance of his sausage, and even more puzzled by my Tarzan-like way of speaking, would probably understand what I meant, even though it is not a proper, syntactically correct sentence. With the help of a shared speech context, listeners can fill in the missing information, even if what they hear is broken English. So that if I removed an important syntactic element like the verb and shouted, "Dog sausage!" my neighbor would probably still get what I meant to say, just because my neighbor and I share a common context. Understanding would be impossible without that. Although context helps our listeners decode the meaning of even badly mangled sentences, we generally don't speak in pidgin-like sentences like "Dog eat sausage" unless we have a serious communication problem, as we might when learning a foreign language.[21] Rather, we use syntax to shape our sentences. Syntax eases the process of understanding by clearly indicating the functional role of each word in a phrase or sentence. On the other hand, even a sentence like "Dog eat sausage" has a syntactic structure, unlike "Eat sausage dog" or "Sausage dog eat"—although, given the strong hints provided by the context and by proper intonation, my neighbor would probably understand either of those variants as well. Indeed, Yoda English in *Star Wars* is perfectly understandable to almost all English speakers despite its uncommon word order.[22] Often an essential syntactic cue necessary for conveying a clear message, word order in a language like English, determines which words refer to the subject and which refer to the object upon which an action is performed. Although it seems natural for English speakers to derive a cause-effect or subject-object relationship from word order, this isn't true for all languages. Latin, the language of the ancient Romans, is one of the most striking examples of how word order can have little or no effect on the meaning.

Latin writers and orators used word order to convey style more than syntactic information. Like many other languages, Latin relies heavily on word variations called "inflections" rather than on word order or prepositions to assign functional roles to the elements of sentences. Thus, at least in principle, listeners could infer the correct meaning of a Latin sentence from the inflections of its words no matter what order they were in. Latin uses word inflections to assign different functional roles, like subject, object, destination, possession, or instrument of an action. Thus, in the Latin sentence "Ioannes amat Mariam" (John loves Mary), the inflection *-es* indicates that "Ioannes" is the subject and the inflection *-am* that Mary is the object, so that, in principle, even if we shuffle the words, as in "Amat Mariam Ioannes" or "Mariam Ioannes amat," the sentence's meaning remains the same. It's John who loves Mary, no matter who comes first in the sentence. If, however, we want to say that it's Mary who loves John, we need to change some word inflections, "Mariam" to "Maria" and "Ioannes" to Ioann*em*," as in "Maria Ioannem amat" or "Amat Ioannem Maria."

Inflections, the small variations of words that indicate their functional roles in a phrase or sentence, are the subject of morphology. English has a somewhat simpler morphology than other languages. Think, for instance, of how many variations a common verb like *walk* has: *walks, walked,* and *walking.* Just three. Now look at all the variations of the corresponding verb in Italian, *camminare*:

cammino, cammini, cammina, camminiamo, camminate, camminano, camminavo, camminavi, camminava, camminavamo, camminavate, camminavano, camminai, camminasti, cammino', camminammo, camminaste, camminarono, camminero', camminerai, camminera', cammineremo, camminerete, cammineranno, camminerei, camminerestin, camminerebbe, cammineremmo, camminereste, camminerebbero, camminassi, camminasse, camminassimo, camminaste, camminassero, camminato, camminando, camminante.

Thirty-eight variations in all—and that goes for *all* Italian verbs! How can we possibly learn all the variations for all the verbs in a language like Italian? Fortunately, human language has evolved in a smart way: regularity is the basis of morphology. Although there are many exceptions, most variations are regular variations. Words in English have a stem, for instance *walk*, which generally doesn't change, or changes very little, and a set of standard suffixes. Typical suffixes for English verbs are *-s, -ed,* and *-ing*. On the other hand, common words are often irregular, like the verbs *have, be, do,* and *go.* In that case, both the stem and the suffix change, as in "go" and "went." But that's not really a problem. English speakers hear and use these words so often they have plenty of opportunities to learn all the variations by heart.[23]

Whereas English has a quite simple morphology, languages like Arabic have a more sophisticated way of changing words: they routinely apply one or more prefixes and suffixes to word stems to change their meaning. For example, in Arabic, *bait* (house) can become *baitena* (our house), *baitekum* (your house), *baiteha* (her house), *baiteho* (his house), *baituh* (its house), or *baitum* (their house). The Arabic determinative article *Al* is also attached to words as a prefix—that's why most English words of Arabic origin start with "al," like *alcohol, algebra,* and *alembic.* But not every "Al" at the beginning of an Arabic word is an article. Take the words *Al-yawm,* meaning "the day," and *Alyawm,* meaning "today." Only in *Al-yawm* is the prefix *Al-* an article, whereas in *Alyawm* it's an integral part of the word. Different languages use inflections in different ways. Some languages insert what are called "infixes" in the middle of words to change their meaning. For instance, in Tagalog, spoken in the Philippines, the infix *-um-* transforms the word *bili,* meaning "buy," into *bumili,* meaning "bought."

To further complicate things, in many languages, like French, Spanish, Portuguese, and German, nouns have a gender. A word's gender in these languages is generally signified by its article, whereas articles in English—*the, a,* and *an*—are gender neutral. For instance, in Italian, the articles *il, la, lo,* and *le* are gender specific and have to agree with the gender of the nouns they accompany. It's obvious that the gender of a word for "man" should be masculine and the gender of a word for "woman" should be feminine. But what about the gender of a word for "table," which has no natural biological gender? Why is the word for "table" masculine in Italian (*il tavolo*) but feminine in French (*la table*)? The bad news is that grammatical gender is, by and large, arbitrary. That said, I should point out that adjectives in languages with gender-specific articles also have to match the gender of the nouns they modify. And there's more! Certain languages, such as Italian, modify nouns by adding suffixes to indicate "big," "small," "small and pretty," "bad," and "small" in a disparaging way. So a *casa* (house) can become a *casona* (big house), a *casina* (small house), a *casetta* or *casuccia* (small and pretty house), a *casaccia* (bad house), or a *casupola* (small house in a disparaging way).

Morphology is tightly entwined with syntax and participates in the construction of well-formed sentences. Although a sentence like "Eat dog sausage" may be interpreted correctly in certain specific contexts, it's certainly not a well-formed sentence. "Dog eats sausage," though better formed from the syntactic point of view, is still missing some elements that would make it easier for the listener to interpret it. Just as semanticists have found ways to formalize meaning, so linguists have devised ways to formalize syntax with rules. A *grammar* is a set of rules that describes the syntax of a language. Grammars describe—or prescribe, depending on your linguistic school and point of view—how you can put together words to form correct phrases and sentences. At the listener's end of the speech chain, grammars are the ground upon which you're able to analyze and semantically interpret sentences. We'll discuss grammars in greater detail in the next section.

Colorless Green Ideas

An apparently simple, though completely impractical, way to fully represent the syntax of a language would be to compile a table of all possible syntactically correct or well-formed sentences. If you had that table, you could use it to find the well-formed sentences you need for any possible occasion and to verify whether any given sentence was syntactically correct or not. As an additional benefit, you could also store there all the possible semantic interpretations of each sentence, using a formulation like the one in figure 1.5. A grammar represented as a table of all possible sentences would look pretty much like a very large phrase book for tourists in a foreign country.

Could you compile a table that included *all* possible well-formed sentences of a language? Of course not. Every known human language comprises an infinite number of well-formed phrases and sentences, and thus that table would have to contain an infinite number of entries. And though we don't know for sure how many words are in a language, especially if we include all the possible proper names, brand names, acronyms, and abbreviations, we might well consider their number to be unbound and potentially infinite as well. We can always invent new words, and we do that all the time. Think of all the new words that didn't exist a few decades ago and have become popular only recently. The word *Internet*, in common use today, didn't exist in 1980. And the same is true for words like *anime*, *netizen*, *WiFi*, and *iPod*.

So with a potentially infinite number of words and infinite possible combinations of them, you can create an infinite number of sentences. But even if you could create a table with an infinite number of entries, it would take an infinite amount of time to search through it. Can our brains store an infinite list of sentences and search through it to find a specific well-formed one in a finite amount of time every time we speak? No, they can't, and neither can a machine, no matter how powerful it is. There must be a better solution than storing a grammar as a table.

The first step to reduce the complexity of the list of possible sentences in a language is to replace each word with a symbol representing its lexical category, or part of speech. Thus your list would include all the possible correct sequences of *parts of speech*, rather than all possible sequences of words. If you took only every possible part of speech of each individual word, you could use the simplified table as a grammar. This is a big simplification since the infinite number of sequences of different words that share the same representation in terms of parts of speech would all become just one entry in our table. For instance: "The dog eats the sausage," "The cat likes the mouse," "The boy reads the book," and infinitely many other such sentences could be represented by a single entry in our grammar phrase book:

Determiner Noun Verb Determiner Noun[24]

And to indicate that the above sequence is indeed a sentence, you could use the standard formulation

Sentence → Determiner Noun Verb Determiner Noun

Linguists use the arrow (→) symbol to specify grammar rules and to indicate that a functional role, for instance, that of a "sentence," can be broken down into a sequence of other functional roles, like "determiner" and "noun." Also, for the sake of simplicity, linguists use short symbols to express functional roles, such as

$S → DET$ N V DET N

To see how this compact formula can represent an infinite number of sentences, let's expand the various symbols for functional roles, which linguists call "nonterminal symbols," into real words, which linguists call "terminal symbols" because they can't be broken down any further. This expansion of nonterminal symbols into real words can be represented by adding other rules to our compact phrase book, such as

$DET → the, a$

$N → dog, cat, boy, sausage, mouse, book, bike, car, bank, . . .$

$V → eats, likes, reads, breaks, builds, banks, . . .$

The items listed on the right-hand side of the rules separated by commas, which linguists and computer scientists call "disjunctions," represent alternative ways of breaking down the symbol on the left-hand side. So the word *the* is a *DET*, or determiner, but so is the word *a*. Similarly, *dog* is an *N*, or noun, like *cat*, *boy*, or *sausage*. Now you can build as many sentences as you want by using the right words in our vocabulary to replace the symbol in the *S* rule, for instance:

The dog eats the sausage

The cat likes the mouse

The boy reads a book,

and many others by trying all the possible allowed combinations. All of these are well-formed sentences of English obtained by following a simple syntactic rule and a set of vocabulary rules. Because we established earlier that a language has an infinite number of words, you can therefore build an infinite number of well-formed sentences using just this one *S* rule.

On the other hand, among these well-formed sentences, you'll find an infinite number that make little or no sense at all, like "The book eats a boy," "A bike builds the dog," and "A dog likes the book." What's wrong with your rule? Nothing.

Syntactic rules prescribe how to build grammatically correct sentences that sound like good English. But they say nothing about whether those sentences make any sense. A sentence can be perfectly grammatical, yet meaningless. "Colorless green ideas sleep furiously" is a perfectly grammatical English sentence that makes no sense.[25] Meaning is the domain of semantics, whereas syntax only tells you how to build grammatically correct sentences. But just as grammatical correct sentences aren't always meaningful, so meaningful sentences aren't always grammatically correct, like the sentence "Dog eat sausage" from my mischievous dog story.

Although the *S* rule accounts for an infinite number of sentences, all of them must have the same structure: *determiner-noun-verb-determiner-noun*. It can't account for sentences with even a slightly different structure like "The fat dog eats the grilled sausage," and there are infinitely more such sentences. If you want to account for them as well, you need to add new rules to your grammar. For instance, you need a rule that allows for one adjective in front of each noun, like

$S \rightarrow DET\ ADJ\ N\ V\ DET\ ADJ\ N$

But, as you may have already guessed, if you start adding rules to describe all possible sentence structures, you'll end up with an infinite number of rules. It seems like there's no way to escape infinites in language. The harsh truth is that there are infinitely many possible sentence structures that are grammatically correct. For instance, you would need to add a rule for one adjective in front of each noun, but also one for two adjectives in front of one of the nouns, as in "The big fat dog eats the grilled sausage," another for two adjectives in front of the second noun, three adjectives, four, and so on. There's actually no limit to the number of adjectives you can put in front of a noun in English and in many other languages. If you take a grammatically correct English sentence with as many adjectives as you like and add another one, it's still a grammatically correct English sentence. On top of that, English, like many other languages, allows you to insert *relative clauses* into sentences, as in "The big fat dog **that ate the sausage** likes the cat." And, again, there's no limit to the number of relative clauses you can insert into a sentence. Any grammatically correct sentence remains grammatically correct, no matter how many relative clauses you insert into it, so long as these, too, are grammatically correct:

This is the farmer sowing his corn that kept the cock that crowed in the morn that waked the priest all shaven and shorn that married the man all tattered and torn that kissed the maiden all forlorn that milked the cow with the crumpled horn that tossed the dog that worried the cat that killed the rat that ate the malt that lay in the house that Jack built!

So you're back to square one. Although you've eliminated one infinite set of rules by using parts of speech rather than words, you end up with another infinite set of rules governing all possible sentence structures with all possible adjectives, relative clauses, and many other variations we've not even considered. And since there's no prescribed maximum number of words in a grammatically correct English sentence, you have yet another infinite set of rules to contend with. Is there any way around all these infinite sets of rules? Yes, there is, and fortunately linguists have found it. Their way around relies on what mathematicians and computer scientists call "recursion," which allows you to represent an infinite number of grammatically correct sentence structures with a finite number of rules. It does so by defining intermediate elements as placeholders to represent more complex elements. For instance, you can define an intermediate element called "noun phrase," or *NP*, to represent a noun, as in

$NP \rightarrow N$

or a noun with another word that complements it, such as the sequence of an adjective and a noun:

$NP \rightarrow ADJ \ N$

At this point, you can use the trick of recursion and state that, by adding an adjective in front of a noun phrase, what you get is *still* a noun phrase, or

$NP \rightarrow ADJ \ NP$.[26]

This last rule is powerful indeed since it allows you to represent a noun with *any number* of adjectives in front of it, thus an infinite number of possible phrase structures. For instance, you can start with a noun:

$NP \rightarrow dog$

and then continue to apply the recursive *NP* rule by putting an adjective in front of each noun phrase we form, thus forming a new noun phrase, which in turn can have an adjective in front of it, and so on. "Fat dog" is a noun phrase, and so are "fat ugly dog," "big fat ugly dog," "ferocious big fat ugly dog," and so on to infinity. All of these infinitely many noun phrases are represented by just one simple expression:

$NP \rightarrow ADJ \ NP,$

which is called a "recursion" because the symbol on the left-hand side appears also on the right-hand side. You can rewrite the *S* rule as

$S \rightarrow DET \ NP \ V \ DET \ NP,$[27]

which now represents any possible sentence having nouns preceded by any number of adjectives. And you can use the same recursion trick for inserting any number of relative clauses and to represent sentences as long and elaborate as the nursery rhyme about the farmer and the house built by Jack.

So, at least in principle, using parts of speech to represent all possible words, and using recursion to represent all possible sentence structures, you can arrive at a relatively small set of rules—a grammar—to describe all possible sentences in a language. Linguists write grammars, among other things, to help students learn languages, and computer scientists write grammars to help computers interpret written or spoken human language. The bad news is that linguists, grammarians, and computer scientists haven't yet been able to completely describe the syntax of any human language with such grammars. Even though they can make a good approximation for languages like English, Italian, and Chinese, the peculiarities and exceptions present in almost every human language make full and complete formalization nearly impossible. And even though written language displays a certain regularity, writing a full grammar for spoken language is out of the question. Why? Because the truth is, we don't speak grammatically. Spontaneous speech simply isn't grammatical. Just listen to normal conversations. Consider the following sample, said to a travel agent:

From um sss from the Philadelphia airport um at ooh the airline is United Airlines and it is flight number one ninety-four once that one lands I need ground transportation to uh Broad Street in Phileld Philadelphia what can you arrange for that?[28]

What grammar written by a grammarian can ever describe and predict such a sentence? There are repetitions, false starts, phrases connected without conjunctions, unexpected changes of subject, and many other ungrammatical artifacts. But anyone with enough knowledge of spoken English would be able to understand. And how about expressions used over and over in conversation, like "As if . . ." "So?," "Totally," "A couple few people," and so on? Are they grammatical?

A grammar is supposed to *describe*, not *prescribe,* our language. So saying that we don't speak grammatically is a contradiction in terms. We speak the way we speak, and linguists try to approximate language patterns in our speech using grammar formalisms. We shouldn't expect any formal grammar to represent and explain all possible forms and expressions of language in the real world any more than we should expect the laws of physics to describe all physical processes and events in the real world. Laws of physics are approximations—however accurate—based on a simplified model of the world. You can use Newton's and Bernoulli's laws to compute the trajectory of a paper airplane, taking into account drag and the shape of the plane. But you can't predict how the irregularities in the plane's shape, the temperature and thus density of the air, and the presence of dust and other objects, like a big insect, the plane might encounter during its flight will cause its actual trajectory to vary from its computed one. Nevertheless, you also can't say the paper plane *doesn't follow* the laws of physics. The laws of physics aren't there to be *followed.* They're useful mathematical tools that allow physicists and engineers to make close, often very close, predictions. Similarly, grammars are useful linguistic tools that can help us understand a language, learn a new one, and eventually build programs to help us deal with language, like the program trying to correct my grammar on the word processor I'm using to write this book.

What Is Speech?

Let's descend from the more abstract levels of language to the more concrete levels of speech. In my story, I finally tell my neighbor: "My dog ate your sausage." How did I speak that? How did I go from the sequence of words in my mind to the uttered sounds? What *is* speech?

Speech is produced by your vocal apparatus, which includes your vocal cords, mouth and nasal cavities, *velum* or soft palate, lips, and tongue (figure 1.6).

Indeed, there are similarities between the human vocal apparatus and a wood-wind instrument, a clarinet, for example. The clarinet is a cylindrical pipe, open at the bell end and closed at the mouthpiece, with holes along its length. Its mouthpiece

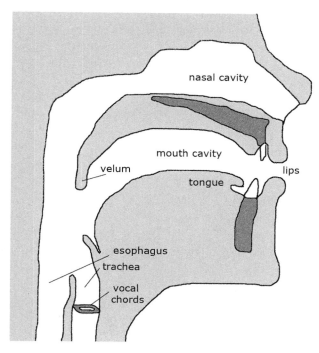

Figure 1.6
Cross-section of human vocal tract.

has a slit blocked by a flexible reed. When a player blows air through the mouthpiece, the reed vibrates, causing the slit on the mouthpiece to open and close rhythmically. This, in turn, causes the cylindrical air column within the instrument to resonate, producing the sound of a clarinet. The length of the resonating air column determines the *fundamental frequency* of the sound, hence the musical note that's played. By opening and closing the holes on the body of the clarinet, the player changes the length of the resonating air column and thus produces different notes.

So, in very simple terms, the beautiful sound of a clarinet is produced by a not so beautiful sound—a vibrating reed. The narrow, cylindrical shape of the resonating air column within the instrument determines the color of the sound, which we perceive as that of a clarinet, rather than of a saxophone (with a more conical air column) or a bassoon (with a wider and longer air column). Human speech is produced in a similar way. Your vocal cords, muscular folds at the beginning of your windpipe or *trachea*, vibrate like the reed of a clarinet. You can feel that vibration by lightly touching your throat while you speak. And just as the vibration of a clarinet's reed causes its air column to resonate, so the vibration of your vocal cords causes the air column in your vocal tract to resonate as well. But the shape of the space within your vocal tract is a good deal more elaborate and complex than the cylindrical space within a clarinet. As a result, the sound produced—speech—is even more interesting than the sound of a clarinet. Evolution has provided us with a more sophisticated mechanism to change the geometry of our resonating air column than opening or closing the holes of a clarinet: a tongue, jaw, and lips, which open or close access to our mouth cavity, and a soft palate (velum), which opens or closes access to our nasal cavity.

There is one fundamental difference, though, between how a clarinet player and a human speaker produce sounds. A clarinet player produces different notes by changing the length of the resonating air column within the instrument, but the shape of that column (measured by its radius) remains always the same. On the other hand, when you speak, by changing the position of your jaw, lips, tongue, and velum, you change the *shape* as well as the length of space within your vocal tract and thus its resonating properties. The different shapes of that space determine the different sounds of human speech.

There is no musical instrument that can change the shape of its resonating cavity in the many ways that the human vocal tract can, but we can imagine building such an instrument. Its body would be a flexible pipe, not a rigid one like a clarinet or a trumpet, with something like lips that could open and close in a round or elongated shape at one end. It would have some internal movable part, a tonguelike blade, which could be maneuvered to change the actual shape of the internal cavity. And, finally, it would have another, nose-like pipe, connected with the main cavity, which

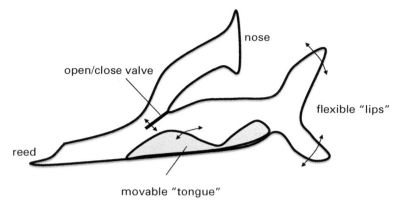

Figure 1.7
Fictional musical instrument for reproducing human speech sounds.

could be opened or closed by a valve, and, in cross-section, might look like the diagram in figure 1.7.

Such an instrument could play notes with a variety of colors and make different sounds much like those produced in human speech. The notes would sound "a-ish" at times, "o-ish," at others, and "e-ish," at still others, and, yes, when the valve would open the instrument's nose, they would definitely sound nasal, like a "n" sound.

Wolfgang von Kempelen, a Hungarian scientist who spent most of his life at the court of Empress Maria Theresa in Vienna, built an instrument like the one just described during the last decades of the eighteenth century in the attempt to generate a human voice artificially.[29] A bellows provided the flow of air across a reed used to simulate the vocal cords. The mouth and the nose pipes were made of rubber. A trained operator needed to use both hands to make Kempelen's machine speak. While one hand was operating the bellows, the other hand could open or close the nose cavity and change the resonating properties of the machine's mouth cavity by partially covering its opening.

An Infinity of Sounds

What shape does your vocal tract assume when you pronounce different sounds? We know that, for making an "oo" sound, you have to round your lips in a closed shape, and you have to widen them for an "ee" sound. But what happens inside your mouth when you do this? During the early years of phonetic research, many scientists asked that question. X-rays provided the answer.[30] If we took an X-ray image of your mouth while pronouncing the vowel sound /a/, as in "sofa," we'd notice that your tongue was forming a small hump toward the center of your palate.

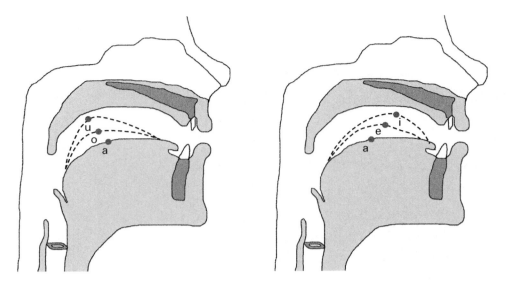

Figure 1.8
Different tongue positions for the production of different vowels.

The hump of your tongue is closer to the front of your mouth when you say the vowel sounds /e/, as in "bet," and /i/, as in "bit," and toward the back for the vowel sounds /o/, as in "bode," and /u/, as in "boot." This is clearly shown by the diagrams of tongue positions for different vowel sounds in figure 1.8.

Your lips are also involved in producing vowel sounds. For instance, when you make the vowel sound /u/, as in "boot," your lips are rounded, whereas they're flat when you make the vowel sound /e/, as in "bet."

You produce different vowel sounds by changing the position and elevation of your tongue with respect to the roof of your mouth, as well as the shape of your lips. The place where your vocal tract shows the most constriction when you pronounce a speech sound is called the "place of articulation." Phoneticians started characterizing all the individual speech sounds by their place of articulation, whether in the front, center, or back of the mouth, and by the height of the tongue, whether high, middle, or low. The chart in figure 1.9 characterizes English vowel sounds by place of articulation, on the horizontal axis, and by height of tongue on the vertical one.

For instance, to make the high-front vowel sound /i/ in "beet," your tongue hump constricts your mouth cavity and leaves a small opening in the front. If you push your tongue both down—creating a wider opening—and toward the back of your mouth, you make the low-front vowel sound /e/ in "bet."

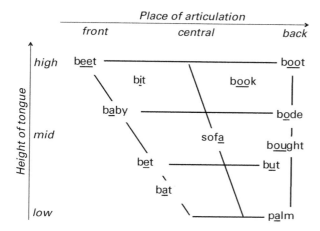

Figure 1.9
Vowel articulation chart representing place of articulation and height of tongue for the U.S. English vowels.

Vowel sounds—and some consonant sounds like /s/ or /z/—are called "stationary sounds," meaning that their characteristics don't change when you produce them. Once your vocal tract assumes the right configuration, it remains like that for the whole duration of each such sound. Thus you can make an /a/ sound last for as long as you want without changing the position of your tongue and lips. But you can't do that with some of the consonant sounds because they're dynamic. Try, for instance, to make a /t/ sound last for a few seconds. It's impossible. And that's because some consonant sounds, like /t/, are the product of rapidly moving parts of our vocal apparatus and not steady sounds.

Consonant sounds like /t/, /p/, and /b/ are called "stops" or "plosives." You produce them by constricting your vocal tract and temporarily stopping the flow of air with the tip of your tongue (as in /t/ and /d/), your lips (as in /p/ and /b/), or your glottis in the back in your mouth (as in /k/ and /g/). You then release the air in a short burst, like a little explosion (which is why they're also called "plosives"). Moreover, your vocal cords briefly vibrate when you make the sounds /b/, /d/, and /g/, whereas they're still when you make the sounds /p/, /t/, and /k/. Which leads us to another distinction among the different speech sounds of English. Those produced when your vocal cords vibrate—all the vowel sounds and some of the consonant sounds like /b/, /d/, and /g/—are called "voiced," whereas those produced when your vocal cords are still are called "unvoiced." But, if that's so, how do you produce unvoiced speech without the sound produced by the vocal cords? There is indeed an alternative source of sound besides your vocal cords for some of the speech sounds, and that's the hiss of the air you release to make sounds such as /s/ and /f/, which are called "unvoiced fricatives." But there are also sounds called "voiced fricatives," which you produce by releasing air in a hiss while also vibrating your vocal cords, as in the sounds /v/ or /z/.

You've many other ways of producing the different speech sounds. You make sounds called "nasals," like /m/ and /n/, by lowering your velum and thus coupling your mouth and nasal cavities. You make peculiar vowel-like sounds called "liquids," like /l/ and /r/, by positioning and moving your tongue in very specific ways. You make dynamic vowel sounds called "glides," like /j/ and /w/, and dynamic consonant sounds called "affricates," like /ts/ and /ch/, by combining plosive and fricative sounds. Although all these speech sounds belong to English, all languages have their own sounds, which differ in both their articulation and their acoustic characteristics. The human vocal apparatus can assume an endless number of configurations to produce an endless number of stationary and dynamic sounds. Although different languages generally evolve with different sounds, you can find, if not exact, then at least near correspondences between the sounds of two different languages, like English and Italian. For instance, the /r/ sound pronounced between two vowel sounds in Italian, as in the word "terra" (earth), doesn't exist in English. But it's very close to the "flapped-t" sound that U.S. English speakers make when they say the /t/ in words like "little." An Italian using an Italian /r/ to pronounce the word "little" as /lirol/ would sound almost like someone from Brooklyn, but not quite.

As you may have noticed, indicating the sounds of speech with the letters of the alphabet creates a problem, one often overcome by giving well-known example words: the /u/ sound, as in "boot," or the /e/ sound, as in "bet." That's because, for many languages like English, the relationship between the written form of a word and its pronunciation is quite complex and often arbitrary. But even for languages like Italian, where that relationship is simpler and more consistent, there's still a problem identifying sounds in unique and unambiguous ways. For instance, does the /e/ sound of the Italian word "sera" (evening) sound exactly like the /e/ sound of the English word "bet"? Not really. So how do you clearly distinguish the Italian /e/ from the U.S. English /e/? Phoneticians, who study the sounds of human speech, have developed a standard alphabet of symbols for representing all the sounds of all the known languages. It's called the "International Phonetic Alphabet" (IPA), and it's periodically updated as new languages and new speech sounds are discovered, studied, and classified. Founded in 1886, the organization that maintains the IPA is called the "International Phonetic Association," also known as the "IPA."[31] The latest (2005) revision of the International Phonetic Alphabet includes more than 100 symbols, which, alone or combined, can describe all the sounds of the languages known today, including even the tones of Chinese and the clicks of Zulu.[32]

The Other End of the Chain

Let's get back to my dog and his sausage. Now that I, as a speaker, have explained to my neighbor about the missing sausage, it's time to see what happens to my neighbor as a listener. Whereas the speaker's end of the speech chain goes from meaning to speech, the listener's end goes the opposite way: from speech to meaning. However sophisticated your vocal apparatus may be in producing the different sounds of speech, your auditory apparatus is just as sophisticated in collecting those sounds and sending them to your brain, which then transforms them back into meaning.

The human ear is particularly sensitive to sounds in the range of frequencies between 200 and 5,500 cycles per second (hertz, abbreviated as "Hz"). It's certainly no happy accident that this range coincides exactly with the frequency range of human speech. Our voices and ears evolved together to provide us humans with the marvelous and powerful mechanism of spoken language. The human ear is an assembly of three functional parts, the outer ear, the middle ear, and the inner ear, as shown cross-section in figure 1.10.

The outer ear is the external part, the one in direct contact with the air. The visible part of the outer ear, the *pinna*, is a skin and cartilage cup whose function is to capture enough acoustic energy to convey even the faintest sounds to the *eardrum* at the end of the auditory canal. The eardrum, besides protecting the delicate mechanisms in the middle and inner ears from the outside environment, has the primary function of transferring the sound vibrations to the *ossicles*, three tiny bones known as the "hammer," "anvil," and "stirrup." These connect to form a lever that transfers an amplified version of the vibrations of the eardrum to the *oval window*, the part of the inner ear in direct contact with the stirrup.

In the inner ear, a snail-shaped, coiled, and tapered tube filled with liquid, the *cochlea* (Latin for "snail") transforms the sound vibrations into an electrical signal, which it sends to the brain through the auditory nerve. An electroacoustic microphone, a much simpler device than the human ear, also transforms sounds into an electrical signal, an electronic replica of the sound waves as they move through the air. If you plot the electrical signal generated by a microphone and the instantaneous pressure of the air in proximity to those sound waves through time, the plots look very similar, practically identical. So, from now on, I'll call the time plot of both the electrical signal and its corresponding sounds a "waveform." Figure 1.11 shows the waveform of "My dog ate your sausage."

The horizontal axis represents the passing of time, from 0 to 1.9 seconds, and the vertical axis represents the instantaneous value of the electrical signal generated by the microphone; we aren't interested in the actual values, but only in their variation through time. If you look at the waveform, you can identify areas of higher

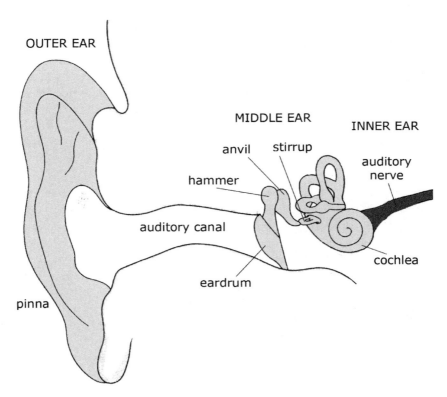

Figure 1.10
Diagram of the human ear.

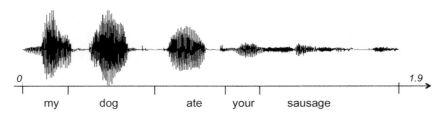

Figure 1.11
Speech waveform.

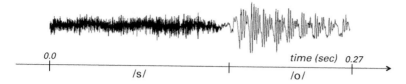

Figure 1.12
Enlarged portion of the speech waveform in figure 1.11 for the sounds /s/ and /o/ at the start of the word "sausage."

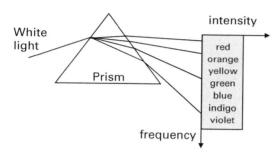

Figure 1.13
Spectrum of white light.

loudness—that is, higher values of the signal—especially corresponding to the mid portion of the words "my," "dog," and "ate," whereas the words "your" and "sausage" are spoken at considerably lower loudness. A zoom-in can show you that there are portions of the waveform that are highly periodic, corresponding to voiced sounds, and others that are more noise-like, corresponding to the unvoiced sounds, like the sound /s/ at the beginning of the word "sausage," as shown in figure 1.12.

For its part, the cochlea of the inner ear generates a more interesting and sophisticated representation of sound than the waveform electrical signal of a microphone, one that is related to the frequency content of sounds. What the cochlea does to the colored sound of speech is, in a way, equivalent to what a prism does to light. A prism breaks light into the spectrum of its color components. When you look at the spectrum of white light, you'll see that its individual color components have more or less the same intensity (figure 1.13).

But when you shine a ray of colored light on the same prism, you'll see that the intensity of the spectrum is not distributed equally among the different color components as it is for the white light.

For instance, in figure 1.14, reddish light has a higher intensity toward the red end of the spectrum, whereas bluish light has a higher intensity at the other or blue

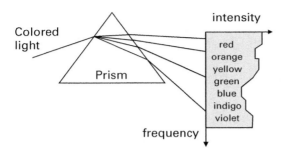

Figure 1.14
Spectrum of colored light.

end of the spectrum. Similarly, the colored sound of human speech can be broken down into a set of individual pure tones, each having a different frequency and intensity. And just as colored light comprises different individual colors with different frequencies and intensities, so colored sound comprises different individual pure tones with different frequencies and intensities. If you look at the colored sound of speech in the same way you do the spectrum of light, you get an idea of the type of information the cochlea sends to the brain.

Reading Speech

A *spectrogram* is a visual representation of a signal that shows the evolution of its spectral content through time. Spectrograms are widely used in speech science because they are more effective than waveforms for the visualization of the information contained in speech. Whereas waveforms show the variation through time of the overall intensity of a signal like that of speech sounds, spectrograms represent the variation through time of individual frequency components. By looking at a waveform, you can identify both areas of higher and lower loudness and areas where speech is highly periodic, indicating the presence of voiced sounds. But there's very little you can infer about what was actually said simply by looking at a waveform. Spectrograms are a much richer representation of speech sounds; with some training, you could learn to identify which spectrogram corresponds to which sounds and words. Look at the spectrogram of "My dog ate your sausage" in figure 1.15, for instance, where the corresponding waveform is included for reference.

The horizontal axis in the spectrogram represents time, as it does for the waveform, whereas the vertical axis represents frequency, which goes from 0 to 8 kHz. The darker bands of the spectrogram represent higher intensities of particular frequency components at particular times. These darker bands, which seem to move through time toward higher or lower frequencies, are typical of speech spectrograms

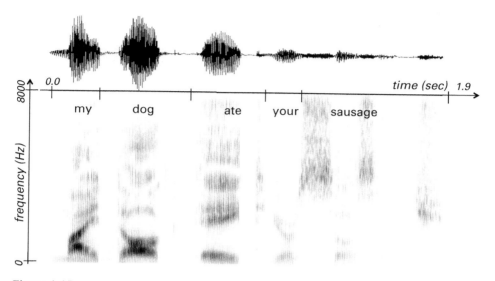

Figure 1.15
Waveform and spectrogram of "my dog ate your sausage."

and are called "formants." They correspond to the frequencies where the sound energy is more concentrated due to the resonating properties of the vocal tract at those particular times. The lines in figure 1.16 highlight the first three formants— called "F1," "F2," and "F3"—for "my dog."

Formants correspond to the more intense portions or stronger colors of the light spectrum. As the shape of the vocal tract changes dynamically, so do the frequencies at which it resonates, and formants are a manifestation of that. Most voiced sounds, such as vowel sounds, are characterized by recognizably typical patterns, especially for the first three formants. In fact, there's a one-to-one relationship between place of articulation and height of the tongue, on the one hand, and the frequency values of F1 and F2, on the other, as shown in figure 1.17.

Thus, as the place of articulation—the position of the tongue's hump—moves from the back to the front of the mouth, correspondingly, the second formant moves from lower to higher frequencies. And as the height of the tongue's hump decreases, the frequency of the first formant increases.

Produced by the hissing sound of air released through the lips, unvoiced sounds such as the phonemes /s/ and /f/ don't have a formant structure but instead exhibit a noise-like frequency distribution. For instance, you can see how the unvoiced /s/ sound at the beginning of the word "sausage" in the spectrogram of our sample utterance looks pretty much like a random, unstructured pattern concentrated at the higher frequencies.

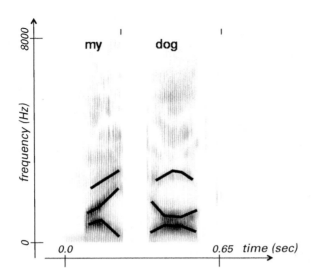

Figure 1.16
Tracing of the first three formants (F1, F2, F3) on a spectrogram of "my dog."

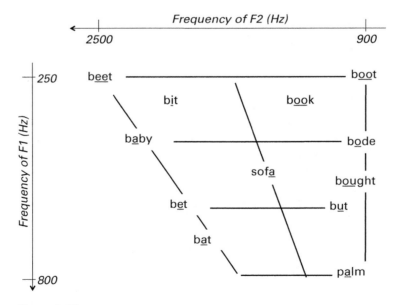

Figure 1.17
Vowel articulation chart for the U.S. English vowels based on the values of F1 and F2.

If you study many spectrograms in many different speech contexts, you can actually learn to read what was actually said from its spectrogram. Indeed, a number of speech scientists have successfully learned how to read spectrograms as a way to learn more about the acoustic properties of speech. In particular, Victor Zue, now codirector of the Computer Science and Artificial Intelligence Laboratory at MIT, reached an unheard-of level of accuracy in spectrogram reading. He developed this skill during his research work in the 1980s and subsequently made a science out of it, formulating a well-defined process that enabled other people to reach the same level of skill. He went on to establish a spectrogram-reading course that's still taught at MIT and other institutions where speech science is part of the curriculum.

Scientists have developed sufficient understanding of spectrogram representation to shed light on what the cochlea does to a speech signal. Although many details of the mechanisms associated with hearing and speech understanding are still a mystery, we know that the cochlea sends information to the brain in a form somewhat similar to that of a spectrogram. Transmitted by the ossicles of the middle ear, sound vibrations create waves in the liquid within the cochlea. The spatial characteristics of these waves depend on the frequencies of the sound. The cochlea has groups of hair cells of different lengths that move with the waves, pretty much like kelp beneath the sea. Each group of hair cells is receptive to a different group of frequencies and sends a different signal to the auditory nerve depending on its position within the cochlea. The auditory nerve combines all the signals received from the different groups of hair cells into a single, complex signal, which it then relays to the brain. Similar, in principle, to a spectrogram, this complex signal reflects the evolution of the frequency content of the sound through time.

Because brain functions are far more difficult to investigate than the anatomy and physiology of organs, no one knows exactly what happens next. The only thing we know for sure is that the human brain must indeed be highly specialized and sophisticated to be able to interpret and understand the content of speech.

The Variability of Speech

How does your brain go from individual sounds to words? You've seen that spoken words are sequences of distinct sounds, phonemes, which are characteristic of each language. But you've only to look at a spectrogram or a waveform to realize that there's not always a clear boundary between one phoneme and the next in speech. For instance, looking at the waveform and spectrogram of "away" in figure 1.18, can you tell where each phoneme starts and ends?

You can't move the articulatory mechanism of your vocal tract instantaneously from one configuration—one particular phoneme—to the next. Your normal

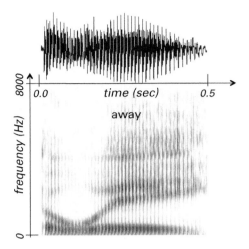

Figure 1.18
Waveform and spectrogram of "away."

speaking rate is somewhere between five and ten phonemes per second; your articu-latory muscles simply can't move much faster than that. For instance, between the first phoneme of the word "away," /ə/, and the next one, /w/, you have to move your vocal tract from a central-mid to a back-high configuration, while rounding your lips. You move your articulatory muscles relatively fast, though gradually and not instantaneously, when you speak these phonemes at a normal rate. As you do, the first two formants, F1 and F2, gradually, however quickly, move from higher to lower frequency. As you can see in the spectrogram, there's no specific point where the /ə/ sound clearly ends and the /w/ sound clearly begins.[33]

What you need to keep in mind is that, unless spoken in isolation and for dem-onstration purposes, speech sounds are never stationary. They're always in motion, from one sound to the next. Because of the dynamic nature of speech, each indi-vidual phoneme serves as transition from the one before it to the one after in the utterance. In reality, even though some speech sounds, such as vowel sounds, show relatively long stationary portions, there's nothing really stationary in normal speech. Thus speaking is like walking not only because you do both without thinking about how you do them, but also because you never reach a pure stationary state in either: you're always in a precarious balance moving your muscles from one configuration to the next.

The continuous transition between consecutive phonemes is known as "coarticu-lation." Even though speech sounds are continuously morphing from one to the other, we hear them as individual and consistent sounds. For instance, we perceive a /w/ sound always as a /w/ even though its acoustic characteristics differ and continuously change depending on the phonemes before and after it. Unfortunately, it's quite difficult to replicate in a machine this invariance of sound perception independently of the phonemic context. You could start, for instance, by calculating all the possible phonemic contexts for the 46 different phonemes in spoken English. Each phoneme can appear in 2,116 (46 × 46 = 2,116) possible combinations of a preceding and following phoneme. And if you consider each speech sound in context as a different sound, there are at least 97,336 (2,116 × 46 = 97,336) acoustically different speech sounds, each one of them with its characteristic acoustic pattern. Of course, you could make the simplifying assumption that the phonemes beyond those immediately before and after a given phoneme have no significant effect on it. Unfortunately, that's not always the case. And granted that some of the nearly 100,000 combinations of speech sounds are unpronounceable, like the sequence /tdt/, and thus would never appear in spoken English, even a number less than half as large gives you an idea of the magnitude of acoustic variability in speech and the multitude of different patterns we need to consider if we want to build a machine that understands speech.

Coarticulation is only one of the sources of variability of speech sounds. There are others that are only minimally related to the acoustic properties of the individual sounds. You've seen that your vocal cords generate a periodic signal that is then modulated by your vocal tract to create all the vowel sounds and all the voiced consonant sounds, like /m/ and /v/. What's known as the "fundamental frequency" or "pitch" of your vibrating vocal chords can vary between 60 and 350 Hz in normal speech.[34] For comparison, the middle C on a piano keyboard corresponds to a pitch of 261 Hz. However, pitch doesn't distinguish one phoneme from another. You can speak the same voiced speech sound at different pitches and still perceive it as the same sound. Indeed, when you sing a song, you use a different pitch, corresponding to each note of the melody, for each of the voiced sounds of the lyrics, without affecting your or your listeners' comprehension of those sounds. An /a/ sound, as in "baby," is perceived as an /a/ sound whether it's sung as a C or a G-sharp. Indeed, there are some languages, like Chinese, where rapid variations of pitch are used to characterize different words composed of the same phonemes. These variations, which are characteristic of *tonal* languages like Chinese and some African languages, concern small speech segments of short duration, like a syllable. With the exception of tonal languages, the variation of pitch is used in normal speech to add color or additional meaning to the spoken message. For instance, in English as well as other languages, a rising pitch at the end of an utterance makes it sound like a question, if that's not already clear from its syntactical structure. To demonstrate that, speak the single word "raining" with a raising pitch on the last syllable:

raining

By doing that, you put an acoustic question mark at the end of the word that makes it sound like "Is it raining?" And you can answer that question with a declarative utterance by simply repeating "raining," this time using a falling pitch as an acoustic exclamation mark:

raining

You can also use pitch in conjunction with loudness and the duration of words or syllables as a way to emphasize a particular word or phrase, for instance, "Julia" in the following sentence to indicate that it's Julia, and not Mary, who went to the market:

Julia went to the market

Similarly, you can do so to emphasize the word "market" instead, to mean that Julia went to the *market,* and not, for instance, to school:

Julia went to the market

Pitch, loudness, and the variable duration of speech segments are called "supra-segmental features" of speech because they're not confined to each individual acoustic segment, but extend "above" the whole structure of words, phrases, or entire utterances. When you speak, you commonly use these features to stress a particular syllable in each word—to determine which syllable has the lexical stress[35]—and thus to distinguish, for instance, the noun "<u>pre</u>sent" from the verb "pre<u>sent</u>." Generally, it's not the absolute value but the change pattern of the supra-segmental features that adds meaning, a pattern linguists call "intonation" or, more formally, "prosody."

Suprasegmental features can be extremely important in helping us deliver the right message in conversational speech, even in very short utterances. Think of how many different meanings you can give the word "okay," depending on your intonation. You can go from a neutral acknowledgment, meaning "I agree with what you say," to a doubtful question, meaning "Do you understand that?"—all by just changing your intonation of a single word. Your intonation not only conveys different meanings, but also reflects—often unconsciously—much of your mental state and feelings. How you feel, whether tense, happy, upset, or shy, often comes out in the way you speak, through the pitch, volume, and duration of your speech sounds, your intonation.

All Voices Are Unique

Men, women, adults, children, old people, people with a speech impediment, people from different regions, people with an accent because they grew up in a different country all have different voices. You recognize categories of speakers—for instance, men versus women—and familiar voices simply because they sound different to you. The size and shape of each individual vocal tract, the different characteristics of the skull, the shape of the lips, the size of the cheeks and the tongue, all contribute to the infinite variety of human voices. No two of us sound alike, and even if our voices may have similar acoustic characteristics, each of us is slightly different in the way we articulate the same sounds, pronounce the same words, and form the same phrases and sentences, in other words, each of us has a different speaking style. When it comes to acoustic differences, we need to include the effects of the environment. Voices sound different in an open field, a theater, and a carpeted office. The different reverberation properties of these places affect the spectral character-istics of speech sounds before they reach your ears, as does background noise made by cars, airplanes, dogs barking, computers humming, telephones ringing, and other people talking. Moreover, in the presence of extremely loud noises, you change the way you speak: you tend to raise your voice and exaggerate your articulation. But your perception of speech sounds ignores all that. You always perceive a /m/ sound as a /m/ sound, for instance, whether it's spoken by a young woman, a child, an adult man, or someone with a Spanish accent, whether it's part of an angry retort or a declaration of love, and whether you hear it during a play in a big theater, someone whispers it into your ear on the beach, or shouts it during a crowded and noisy cocktail party. To your brain, a /m/ sound is a /m/ sound is a /m/ sound, no matter what, even though all of these /m/ sounds have different acoustic characteristics. Your brain does something marvelously sophisticated: it perceives the basic sounds, the phonemes, as invariant elements even though each physical realization of them is different. But, at the same time, it clearly perceives all the other sources of acoustic variability that accompany those phonemes. Even though you also perceive the acoustic differences of the voices of those who speak to you and of your speech environment, you're able to isolate the speech of each individual in the clamor of a cocktail party. And even though all of these sources of acoustic variability are mixed in the sounds that reach your ears, your brain can isolate each one of them. Indeed, no machine that's yet been built or even designed can today match our human ability to perceive speech in extreme acoustic situations and sort out all the different sources of sound.

Time Flies like an Arrow

The variability of the acoustic patterns discussed above certainly gives you an idea of the complexity underlying the recognition of speech sounds. As we move to higher levels of abstraction on the listener's end of the speech chain, however, things don't get any easier. Keep in mind that language is intrinsically both ambiguous and parsimonious: relying on the shared bulk of knowledge between speaker and listener, it evolved to assign many different meanings to the same common words and to let listeners sort them out from speech contexts. Take a common word like "bank," a noun with many different meanings or senses: the bank where you put your money, the bank of a river, a bank of clouds, and so on. But "bank" is also a verb with a variety of senses: airplanes bank, clouds bank, you can bank a pile of dirt, skiers can bank around a turn, or you can just "bank on it." So, when you hear a word like "bank," you can't immediately know which sense is meant or which specific part of speech it is, although you might first think of the most common "bank," a noun and where you put your money. Syntax can help you remove ambiguity and assign the correct role and sense to each word in a sentence based on all the other words. But not always. Unfortunately, there are cases where syntax is itself ambiguous, and the same phrase or sentence can be interpreted differently according to different grammatical rules. Consider the famous example

Time flies like an arrow.[36]

If you take "time" to be a noun, "flies" a verb, "like" a preposition, and "arrow" a noun, you're led immediately to the sentence's most obvious meaning: "Time goes by as fast as an arrow." But the problem is, the word "time" can also be a verb, as in "time with a stopwatch," and the word "flies" can also be a plural noun, as in "swarm of flies." So this sentence can also mean "Time the flies as you would time an arrow" or "Time the flies as fast as an arrow" or even "Time the flies flying in an arrow formation." Thus, if "time" acts as a verb, "flies" has to be a noun, but, depending on whether the preposition "like" refers to the action of timing or to the flies themselves, there are still two possible interpretations of "like an arrow."

Alas, we're not done yet. The word "time" can also be an *adjective,* as in "time bombs," "time sales," and "time spans." So why not "time *flies*" as well? And, of course, "like" can also be a *verb.* So, if we can like summer afternoons or ice cream, what's to prevent "time flies" from liking an arrow? All of which is to say, when syntax doesn't help you determine which interpretation of a sentence makes most sense, you need to resort to higher knowledge, like semantics, or, better still, to the actual, real-world context you're experiencing. When you meet an old friend you haven't seen for more than twenty years, then "Time flies like an arrow" assumes a very precise and unambiguous meaning.

So language, apart from all its other complications, is highly ambiguous by its very nature. Chances are that any sentence you form has more than one meaning, and, we're lucky we can still understand one another. In reality, however, being very parsimonious, language simply can't afford to have a different word for every different meaning. Yes, anything you say can be interpreted in different ways, and the correct interpretation requires a common context. But we have that common context. It's the knowledge substrate of our humanity, the culture that defines our unique species.

Eagles and Airplanes

So now you know. Language is complex, and we know very little about how we humans manage this complexity. Although we understand the physiology of the organs that produce and perceive speech, as we move toward the brain activities that handle language, our understanding becomes vaguer and vaguer. We have theories, but we don't know exactly what mechanisms our brains use to represent concepts and ideas and transform them into syntactic structures and sequences of words, and how these structures and sequences are ultimately transformed into motor nerve stimuli that activate our articulator muscles when we speak. We know that the cochlea in the inner ear generates a complex signal that represents the spectral information of the speech sounds we hear, but we don't know exactly how the brain uses that signal to extract the individual phonemes, arrange them into words, perform a syntactic analysis, and then come to a semantic representation of the concepts and ideas that makes sense in the immediate context we find ourselves in at a particular moment in time. We don't even know whether the brain disentangles the complex signal on the different linguistic levels—semantic, syntactic, lexical, morphological, phonetic, and acoustic—or skips that by making direct associations between sequences of sounds and concepts or ideas. We can make educated guesses based on the experimental evidence from perceptual tests and studies of anomalous behavior caused by disease or accident, but we don't know for sure. We humans are the masters of a language of incomparable complexity among all living species, but we don't understand, at least not yet, exactly how it works. And, nevertheless, we want to build machines that speak and understand speech.

Will having a better understanding of how we humans handle language help us build more-intelligent talking machines? And should machines that imitate human behavior be based on the same mechanisms we know or presume humans use? Kempelen's speaking machine was indeed an attempt to imitate the physiology of human vocal organs. Say you wanted to build, today, a modern computerized version of Kempelen's machine. You could indeed create a computerized machine to simulate the vocal tract; define a reasonable mathematical mechanical model of the tongue, lips, jaw, and velum; and compute the acoustic characteristics of the resulting sounds by solving the equations that govern the mechanics and motion of the air in a resonating cavity of a given shape and size. You could then link each individual speech sound to the corresponding articulation sequences and build a computer program that, for any utterance, would compute the actual movements of the simulated vocal tract, solve the equations, and generate synthetic speech. And in fact many researchers have been taking just this approach for decades.[37] But attempts at exactly simulating the highly complex mechanics of speech production haven't yet been able to produce natural-sounding synthetic speech, at least not as well as other approaches have. The problem is that our lack of knowledge about the fine articulatory details of speech production and the inherent complexity of creating an accurate mechanical model of the vocal tract inevitably give rise to a computationally expensive and still crude approximation of human speech. And even if you had a more accurate mechanical model of speech articulation, the computation needed for solving all the motion and fluid equations in real time—while the computer was speaking—would be beyond the capacity of today's commercial computers.

Consider instead a simpler and more brute-force approach, one that would abstract essential elements of speech rather than precisely imitate vocal tract physiology. For instance, you could create an inventory of audio clips of speech segments, like phonemes, syllables, or words, recorded by a human speaker. With a complete inventory of these sound clips, you could then synthesize any utterance by splicing them in the correct order. Thus, rather than building a machine that functions as humans do, you could build a fast, sophisticated, but intrinsically simpler machine that worked by assembling sounds from a catalog of recorded sounds: a smart reproducer of recorded speech samples. If you used the right technology for splicing sounds in a seamless way, with a large inventory of elemental speech units and a lot of engineering, the effect could be compelling: a machine that spoke without simulating any moving parts, a machine that used a fundamentally different concept than the one used by humans, yet sounded very much like a human. Of course, the brute-force approach has many limitations when compared to a powerful mathematical mechanical model of the vocal tract. But we can't yet build a talking machine based on a mathematical mechanical model, whereas, despite all the limitations of the brute-force approach, we have built talking machines using it, machines that have worked for many years now with compelling results.

However enticing it may seem to build a machine that uses humanlike mechanisms for accomplishing what humans do, such an approach has proven to be impractical not only in understanding and generating speech, but in many other areas of machine intelligence. It's a known and widely accepted fact today that machines don't have to replicate the same mechanisms used by humans, or whatever we believe these mechanisms to be, to exhibit intelligent behavior. Machines that produce and perceive speech, recognize images and handwriting, play chess, and translate languages without imitating humans stand as proof of this fact.

To appreciate why replicating human mechanisms is not always the best way of having machines exhibit human intelligence, you need to understand that the computational characteristics of the human brain are fundamentally different from those of modern computers. Whereas digital computers derive their power from a relatively small number of fast computational elements—processors—that are sparsely connected and share data through a limited number of channels, the human brain is an abundantly interconnected assemblage of an immense number of computational elements—neurons—that are both far slower and far less powerful than a computer chip. By way of comparison, a commercial top-of-the-line 2010 Intel personal computer chip—microprocessor—is capable of performing more than 100 billion operations per second, whereas the response of a human neuron is a mere 1,000 impulses per second. But the brain is composed of some 100 billion neurons, whereas a commercial PC has typically only one or a couple of computer chips. A back-of-the-envelope estimate of the computational power of the human brain based on those numbers is around 100 trillion operations per second, roughly 1,000 times more powerful than a commercial computer chip today.[38] After all, 1,000 is not that big a number. At the current rate of increase in a computer speed, we may see, in a decade or two, chips that match or exceed the computational power of the human brain.

But computational speed or power is not the only fundamental difference between a digital computer and the human brain. Data access and the type of processing achieved are also key differentiators. A computer chip generally includes a single processing unit, the *central processing unit* (CPU), which performs operations in a sequential way—one operation at a time. Even when you run simultaneous tasks on a home computer, for instance, printing a document while browsing the Web and receiving an e-mail, or chatting with several remote users at the same time, the CPU is still running in a sequential fashion. In fact, each fraction of a second, the CPU dedicates a small amount of time to each one of the tasks, giving you the illusion that you're doing things in parallel on the same computer. Since the birth of the electronic computer, we've developed effective ways of programming single CPUs that mostly rely on procedural mechanisms: first do A, then do B, then do C, and so on. Moving from a single CPU to a massive assemblage of computational elements—parallel computing—is indeed a hot topic in computer science today. Blue Gene, the high-performance computer built by IBM in 2004 for solving genetic analysis problems, could assemble as many as 65,000 individual processors to reach computational powers in the hundreds of trillions of operations per second. Its successor, IBM Roadrunner, built in 2008, has roughly twice as much power. A computer like that—not your typical home computer—is very close to matching and even exceeding the raw computational power of a human brain. If that's true, why can't we use a machine like Blue Gene or Roadrunner to replicate the human mechanism of speech production, hearing, understanding, and intelligent behavior in general?

The problem, beyond the cost of such a supercomputer, is that parallel supercomputers still have severe limitations in data access when compared with the human brain. The 100 billion neurons of a human brain are linked together by incoming and outgoing information channels that are connected by specialized junctions called "synapses." The neurons, with all their specialized connections, form a huge network that acts as both the program and the data of our brains. New connections are created and others are destroyed every time we learn or memorize something. It's estimated that a human brain includes some 100 trillion connections—synapses—which provide storage for an estimated 100 terabytes (100 million megabytes) of data and programs. The brain apparently knows how to access all this data in a rapid and efficient way through its immense network of neuron connections for performing activities that seem natural to us, like speaking, walking, or seeing. Today's parallel supercomputers are nowhere close to that. Moreover, a massive supercomputer like IBM's is programmed in much the same way as a single-chip home computer is, using step-by-step procedures. The brain, with its huge parallel computational architecture, is most likely *not* programmed with step-by-step procedures. The phenomenal performance of the brain in activities such as speaking and playing chess must come from different programming paradigms, which, as of today, we simply don't understand. And, of course, even if we did know how to program a brain-like machine, we wouldn't know what program to write.

We know so little about how our brains transform concepts and ideas into speech, and speech into concepts and ideas, that we wouldn't be able to replicate it in a brain-like machine.

But if I had to name just one of the features that differentiate the human brain from any machine we might build, it would probably be its ability to continuously learn. We're each born with a brain that initially knows little more than what other animals do. It knows how to control your internal functions, how your heart beats, how you breathe, and how, as an infant, you suck milk for your survival. As a newborn, your ability to control and coordinate your limbs through your senses of touch and sight, what we call "hand-eye coordination," is rather limited, and you certainly don't know how to speak or understand speech. But evidently, your brain is endowed with the power to let you learn. Indeed, before too many years, you learn how to use your hands, to walk, to speak, and to eat with a knife and fork. And you go on to learn math, history, science, and music. Your ability to continuously learn is exactly what digital computers currently lack, though they're starting to acquire it to a very limited degree thanks to scientific disciplines such as machine learning. But, still, most of what computers do today has been painfully programmed, step by step, by humans. If we want to build machines that replicate sophisticated human activities, like speaking and seeing, we need to give them, first and foremost, the ability to learn.

Thus, there is a deep divide between how the human brain functions and how a modern computer does, and this divide can't be bridged by today's technology. Asking whether we can teach machines to behave like humans by replicating human mechanisms in them is an ill-posed question, especially given that, by and large, we don't know how those mechanisms work. If you want to build a talking machine, you need to exploit the computational power of today's computers using today's programming models. Airplanes don't flap their wings, yet they can fly faster and farther than eagles. And though few airplanes can land on the top of a mountain, and none can dive down to catch its prey, reproduce, and care for its babies, all airplanes can carry humans and things from one place to the other in the fastest and safest way, which is what they're built to do, and which is definitely not what eagles do. Airplanes and eagles thus have different purposes or goals, so it makes little sense to compare what each can and can't do. Today's talking machines may not have mouths, tongues, and ears, but they can reasonably produce and understand speech, and they'll do it better and better with each passing year. But you shouldn't expect them to do what humans do in all, or even most, situations. Just as it makes little sense to compare eagles and airplanes, it makes even less sense to compare talking machines and humans. Like laptop computers, TVs, cars, and airplanes, talking machines are devices created to expand the capabilities of human beings, not to imitate them.

2

The Speech Pioneers

Wolfgang von Kempelen perfected his speaking machine over the course of more than thirty years, completing and exhibiting it in 1804, shortly before his death. But he was famous for having built another machine, in 1770, one that could play chess and win most of the time, even against chess masters. Or so it seemed. Shaped like a human dressed in Turkish clothes sitting at a chess table, the machine was known as "the Turk."[1] For decades, Kempelen took his Turk on tour around Europe and the United States. His highly popular automaton attracted the attention of the press and of notables such as Napoleon Bonaparte and Benjamin Franklin, both of whom played against it, and lost.

Automatons were all the rage at that time. Jacques Vaucanson, a contemporary of Kempelen, built one that could play a flute, as well as a duck automaton that could flap its wings, drink water, eat food, and even "digest" it.[2] But playing chess was, without any doubt, a far more difficult behavior to imitate than flute playing or wing flapping. Indeed, to play chess and win, a machine had to analyze the positions of all the pieces on the chessboard and react to each of its opponent's moves with a legal and intelligent move of its own. The number of possible positions and moves in any game of chess is so large, however, that it would have been simply impossible to build a machine that could react intelligently to all of them with the technology available in 1770. And, in fact, Kempelen's Turk was nothing more than a well-engineered hoax: a human chess master, concealed inside a box beneath the chess table, operated the chess-playing automaton through a system of levers and magnets.

It's said that, at the end of each chess exhibition, Kempelen would pull out an alphabet board and invite the audience to ask his automaton questions. The Turk would spell out its answer to each question by pointing a stick to the appropriate letters on the board. But the spectators, though ready to accept the possibility that Kempelen's machine could play chess, weren't ready to believe that it could also understand speech and answer questions. Faced with growing skepticism and fearing exposure, Kempelen soon removed the question-answering routine from the Turk's repertoire.

Building machines that could speak, understand speech, and display intelligent behavior was part of the collective dream well before the 1700s, as it is today. And people perceived back then, just as they do today, that it would be far more difficult for an automaton to understand speech than, for instance, to play chess. But the dream of building a machine that could understand speech persisted through the centuries until we developed more technologically advanced tools and came to know far more about the complex phenomena behind speech and language.

The Voder

Although *The Voice in the Machine* is mainly about understanding speech, producing and understanding speech are two faces of the same coin: we can't intelligently discuss one without discussing the other. After Kempelen's success in mechanically reproducing the sounds of human speech with bellows and rubber mouths, many scientists tried to replicate his results using more elaborate mechanical and electronic devices.

Let's jump ahead a century and a half to the New York World's Fair of 1939, whose main theme was technological innovation, at a time when the United States was just coming out of the Great Depression. In Manhattan, a few miles from the fair, Bell Laboratories, the research arm of the American Telephone and Telegraph giant, was revolutionizing world technology with its advanced innovations.[3] Among them was the Voder (an acronym for *Voice operation demonstrator*),[4] the first electronic speech synthesizer, created by Bell Labs scientist Homer Dudley, and one the main attractions of the AT&T exhibit at the World's Fair (figure 2.1).[5]

Vannevar Bush, one of the pioneers of analog computing, wrote in a 1945 article: "At the 1939 World's Fair a machine called a Voder was shown. A girl stroked its keys and it emitted recognizable speech. No human vocal cords entered into the procedure at any point; the keys simply combined some electronically produced vibrations and passed these on to a loud-speaker."[6] Actually, building a speaking machine came as a by-product of Dudley's research on compressing speech for more efficient transmission on telephone channels. What do speech compression and speech production have to do with each other? And what *is* speech compression, after all?

Before the first satellite communication systems were developed in the 1960s, and long before high-capacity fiber optics were in commercial use in the 1970s, telephone signals traveled mostly on copper wires. A technique called "carrier multiplexing," invented in 1910 by Major George O. Squier, enabled several individual telephone signals to be mixed into a single "multiplexed" electrical signal that could be transmitted on the same wire.[7] At the receiving end, the multiplexed signal could then be separated into the individual telephone signals with minimal degradation.

SCIENCE NEWS LETTER, *for January 14, 1939*

ENGINEERING

Now a Machine That Talks With the Voice of Man

Voder Combines Electrical Currents to Produce Synthetic Speech; Converses at Signal From Keys

See Front Cover

NATURE took hundreds of thousands of years to teach man how to speak.

In two years, scientists have taught a machine how to talk, translating into real words and sentences signals punched into its controlling keyboard.

Controlled by a skilled operator who has learned how to mix the sounds the device's two electric discharge tubes produce, it combines varying electric currents that an amplifier turns into real speech. No phonograph records of any kind are ever used. It is the first device that actually creates human speech.

The name of this new robot is the Voder.

"Practice makes perfect," it told its first enthusiastic hearers at its debut before the Franklin Institute. It isn't perfect yet. But the Voder was good enough to convince its audience that the Fourth of July orators and, perhaps, even opera singers may some day have to look to their laurels.

This new synthetic orator will "lecture" with his "electrical accent" at the New York and San Francisco world fairs.

It is a compact machine resting on a small table, plus as many loudspeakers as are necessary to reach the audience. It has a pair of keyboard units, more than a dozen other controls and an electrical circuit featuring a vacuum tube and a gas-filled discharge tube.

It builds up speech from 22 fundamental sounds from which speech organs also create spoken words. The operator, in using the device, analyzes phonetically the words the machine is to speak, then duplicates the sounds, and therefore the words, by pressing the proper keys and controls.

The Voder proved itself to be quite an able talker at the hands of Mrs. Helen Harper of New York, first of 24 telephone operators to be trained in its use, and S. S. A. Watkins, Bell Telephone Laboratories scientist who taught it to speak. When members of the audience suggested even such difficult foreign phrases as "Hasenpfeffer" and "Com-ment allez-vous?" it repeated "Hasenpfeffer" and "Comment allez-vous?" with perfect aplomb.

The machine resulted from efforts of Bell scientists H. W. Dudley and R. R. Riesz in fundamental telephone research. They developed an electrical speech analyzer and a speech synthesizer, both of which were demonstrated at the Harvard Tercentenary. The former machine fed an electrical control pattern into the synthesizer. With the exception of the organ-like keyboard, all its parts are in regular telephone use.

When the subject of the Bell exhibit at the New York and San Francisco fairs came up, it was suggested that the machine that talked, when the analyzer fed it the proper pattern, would be a fit display—particularly if it could be made to speak when an operator punched a keyboard instead of merely seeing that the analyzer continued feeding it the proper signals.

Two fundamental types of sound are involved in human speech—the relatively musical note of the vocal cords, and a sibilant hiss which can be recognized most easily in a whisper. These sounds the machine imitates. The vocal sound comes from a vacuum tube, while the sibilant is produced in a gas-filled tube. The tubes themselves do not actually produce the sounds; what they do is produce an electric wave whose pattern corresponds to the sounds in question and which is converted into sound in an amplifier, just as occurs in a radio receiver.

These two fundamental sounds are given proper pitch by punching the right one or ones of 10 keys which control electric filters. Changes in intonation, as in asking a question, are made by raising or lowering a foot pedal. Three special tabs provide the "stop" consonants, "t", "p", etc.

The Voder is actually the superior of any human being alive in one respect, for it can speak in tones ranging from lowest bass to highest soprano, as determined by the flick of a knob. Ordinarily, however, it speaks in a firmly masculine baritone.

THE VODER
The young lady striking keys is creating a man-like voice. This and the cover picture are from the Bell Telephone Laboratories.

Mr. Riesz is also known for his work in connection with the development of the artificial larynx. He and his associates are accustomed to calling the Voder "Pedro" after the Brazilian emperor, Dom Pedro. Dom Pedro, when he listened to a demonstration telephone, then newly invented, at the Centennial Exposition in 1876, exclaimed, "My God! It talks!"

Heart of the device is a "relaxation oscillator," which produces a saw-toothed wave from the discharge tubes, instead of the rounded wave of a pure musical note. The machine has considerable difficulty with the so-called transitional consonants, such as "l" and "r", but otherwise its speech is clear.

Science News Letter, January 14, 1939

GEOLOGY—PHYSICS

Research By-Product Saved $500,000 During Depression

THERE is nothing much more fundamental than the constitution of the earth itself and the rocks that lie beneath our collective feet. In Washington there is a modest building full of laboratories where a handful of scientists are struggling with this problem.

During the World War the scientists at the Carnegie Institution's Geophysical Laboratory interrupted their program long enough to help create an American optical glass industry without which our

Figure 2.1

Article on the Voder published in the January 14, 1939, issue of *Science News Letter*. From the Science Service Historical Images Collection, National Museum of American History, courtesy of Bell Telephone Laboratories.

However, there's a physical limit to the number of signals that can travel on a wire without degrading their reception. That limit is expressed in terms of total *bandwidth,* the range of frequencies contained in the final transmission signal, measured in hertz.

Thus, if we limit the frequency range of an individual telephone signal from a minimum of 0 Hz to a maximum of 4,000 Hz—4 kilohertz (kHz)—to accommodate the core frequency range of normal human speech, that signal would have a bandwidth of 4 kHz.[8] A single multiplexed signal comprising ten individual telephone signals, each with a 4 kHz bandwidth, would have a total bandwidth of $10 \times 4 = 40$ kHz. The bandwidth, or capacity, of a transmission channel, whether a wire, cable, or microwave communication channel, is the range of frequencies that can pass over it without being significantly affected by distortion. It depends on the physical characteristics of the channel, such as its length, geometry, and, in the case of a cable transmission channel, the type of insulation between the wires. Since the typical bandwidth for telephone speech is 4 kHz, to transmit ten telephone signals with minimal distortion, you'd need a channel, using a cable for instance, that could accommodate a bandwidth of at least 40 kHz. If you tried to transmit more than ten 4 kHz signals on such a channel, each individual telephone signal would be irreversibly distorted at the receiving end. Like a water pipe, a communication channel simply can't carry more than its physical capacity permits.

The *broadband coaxial cable,* invented at AT&T in 1929 and experimentally first installed between New York and Chicago in 1936, pushed the capacity of a single telephone "wire" to hundreds of individual telephone signals. But even that wasn't enough. With an increasing number of customers, and with more and more cities, towns, and villages being connected throughout the country, AT&T was constantly looking for ways to increase the capacity of its network without increasing its expenses by adding more and more cables across the whole country. If there was a way to reduce the bandwidth of each individual telephone signal, the same network would be able to transmit more signals without the need for additional cables.

The problem is, you can't reduce the bandwidth of a speech signal simply by removing high-frequency components. Indeed, human speech includes frequency components that extend above 10 kHz, although the sensitivity of the human ear is quite modest for frequencies that high. If, however, you reduce the bandwidth of telephone speech from 10 kHz to 8, 6, or 4 kHz, for instance, that speech will start to sound more muffled and less crisp, more "telephone-like." At bandwidths narrower than 4 kHz you'd have a hard time understanding what was said. *Intelligibility,* the degree to which spoken words can be understood, is a way to characterize the quality of speech as we manipulate its spectral content. We can measure intelligibility as the proportion of correct guesses made by experimental subjects when asked to listen to various degrees of processed speech and to report what they hear.

Irvin Crandall and Harvey Fletcher started working on speech intelligibility at Bell Labs during the second decade of 1900. In 1917, Crandall noted: "It is possible to identify most words in a given context without taking note of the vowels. . . . The consonants are the determining factors in . . . articulation."[9] You can readily see that consonants carry most of the information in speech by looking at two versions of the same sentence, the first with the vowels removed:

Sp__ch _s th_ m_st _ff_ct_v_ m__ns _f c_mm_n_c_t__n.

It's not hard to guess the original words—"Speech is the most effective means of communication"—but the situation is altogether different if the consonants are removed, leaving only the vowels:

__ee__ i_ __e _o__ e__e__i_e _ea__ o_ _o__u_i_a_io_.

Unfortunately, because most consonant sounds are characterized by high-frequency components, reducing the bandwidth of a telephone signal impairs the listener's ability to discriminate among them. As Crandall went on to explain:

"Take him to the map" has a very different meaning from "take him to the mat," and a handyman may waste a lot of time fixing a "faucet" when the faulty component was actually the "soffet." Pole, bole, coal, dole, foal, goal, told, hole, molt, mold, noel, bold, yo, roll, colt, sole, dolt, sold, toll, bolt, vole, gold, shoal, and troll all share the same vowel sound, only differing in the consonants with which it is coupled, but the difference can drastically change the meaning of a sentence. Consonant sounds have this critical role in most languages, including French, German, Italian, Polish, Russian and Japanese. And of course, consonants occur frequently in speech. "P" and "t," one of the most commonly confused pairs, account for over 10 percent of the phonemes in simple speech. "F" and "s" are 6.8 percent, "m" and "n" another 10.3 percent, and so on. Overall, more than half of all phonemes are consonants.[10]

To better understand the importance of high frequency in consonant sounds, look at the spectrograms of two words, differing only in their initial consonant sound when frequencies above 3.4 kHz have been blanked out (figure 2.2).[11]

Apart from the usual variability of speech, the reduced spectrograms of the two words look almost exactly the same. But with the frequencies above 3.4 kHz restored, you can immediately see that the two words are actually different (figure 2.3). The initial speech sound of the first word has a much stronger component at higher frequencies than that of the second word. And, in fact, the first word is "sold," whereas the second is "fold."

Removing the higher frequencies made the spectrograms of the two words look, and the words themselves sound, almost the same.

Limiting speech to a bandwidth of 4 kHz was a compromise between intelligibility and cost made in the early years of the telephone network, but that same bandwidth is still used today. Speech limited to 4 kHz has the typical muffled quality of telephone speech. For consonant sounds that are mainly characterized by

Figure 2.2
Spectrogram of two different words, with frequencies above 3,400 Hz blanked out.

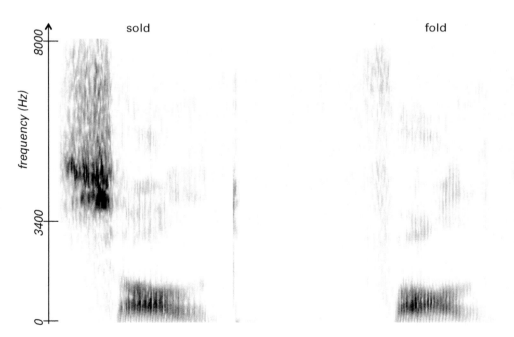

Figure 2.3
Full spectrogram of two words in figure 2.2, with their identities revealed.

high-frequency differences, such as /p/, /t/, /f/, and /s/, it's sometimes hard to tell one sound from another over the telephone, and we often need to spell out our words by example: "'p' as in 'Peter,'" "'t' as in 'Tom,'" "'s' as in 'Sam,'" "'f' as in 'Frank,'" and so on. That said, a bandwidth of 4 kHz is wide enough for us to carry on normal telephone conversations, as people have been doing for more than 100 years. But if that bandwidth were narrowed further, intelligibility would become so poor that communication would be nearly impossible.

Even though 4 kHz has proven to be the minimum bandwidth for acceptable intelligibility over the telephone, the information contained in speech could, in principle, be compressed into a signal with a bandwidth much narrower than that. In 1937, Homer Dudley invented a device that could do just that; in his patent filing, he noted that

> the number of movable or variable elements of the vocal system that are controlled as parameters to give the desired speech production and that are movable or variable substantially independently of one another by the muscles of the vocal system is small . . . of the order of ten. Moreover, for each of the physical elements the minimum time in which it can go through a complex cycle of change in position is not less than one-tenth of a second. Consequently, each independent variable has a fundamental frequency of not over ten cycles per second while engaged in speech production.[12]

In other words, there are no more than ten physical elements in our vocal tract that produce the different speech sounds, and those elements can't change their shape and position faster than ten times a second because our muscles can't move faster than that. Thus, at least in principle, we could identify the shape and position of these ten elements in a speaker's vocal tract and transmit their values ten times a second in such a way that, at the receiving end, we could reconstruct the content of the original speech. Think of a system that transmits, ten times a second, the exact position of a speaker's tongue, lips, velum, and so on, and another system that moves the tongue, lips, velum, and so on of a mechanical model of the vocal tract according to the received positions and shapes. If you could do that, you'd only need a bandwidth of a few hundred hertz, an order of magnitude narrower than the current 4 kHz bandwidth of the telephone signal. For a telephone company, that would translate into an order of magnitude more signals that could be transmitted on the same network, significantly increasing the number of potential customers for virtually no additional investment in cable infrastructure.

Unfortunately, detecting in real time the position and shape of the ten elements of the vocal tract that produce speech just from the speech signal collected by a microphone is no easy task. This information is indecipherably encoded within a signal having a bandwidth of thousands of hertz and a lot of redundancy, redundancy that's hard to remove to get to the essential information. That was, in essence, the problem that Homer Dudley tried to solve by building a machine that would

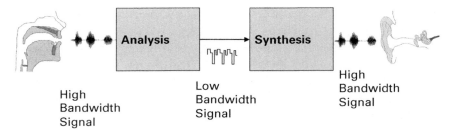

Figure 2.4
High-level diagram of a speech compression system based on the Vocoder concept.

compress speech to its essential content at one end and reconstruct it in an intelligible manner at the other. He called his machine the "Vocoder" (a contraction of "Voice Coder"); it consisted of two parts or modules, called "Analysis" and "Synthesis" (figure 2.4).

The analysis module would compress speech before the transmission, from a wide-bandwidth to a narrow-bandwidth signal, so that many more compressed speech signals could be accommodated on a communication transmission channel with a limited overall bandwidth. The synthesis module, at the receiving end, would reconstruct an intelligible version of the original speech. Dudley solved the problem of compression, not by finding the shape and position of the vocal tract elements, but by analyzing speech into a series of contiguous frequency bands and retaining only high-level summary information about them. He also detected whether a segment of speech was voiced (produced by the vibrations of the vocal cords) or unvoiced (produced by the flow of air through the mouth). That information alone, if coded into a signal that could be transmitted on a cable, would require a bandwidth of only 300 Hz. In reality, however, the signal reconstructed at the receiving end of Dudley's Vocoder sounded quite degraded with respect to the original speech, although it was still *almost* intelligible, indeed, enormously more intelligible than an equivalent 300 Hz bandwidth speech obtained by simply filtering out high-frequency components.

Dudley realized that, by having the Vocoder's synthesis module store typical frequency information for each speech sound, as in a catalog, he could make it produce speech independently of the analysis module. By creating a signal corresponding to the stored frequency band information, he could then re-create, or synthesize, each speech sound, associating the keys of a keyboard with the individual speech sounds and using them to combine the sounds in sequences to synthesize spoken words and sentences. Dudley did in fact build just such a machine in 1939, the Voder, using a special keyboard complemented by a wrist bar to control whether each generated sound was voiced or unvoiced, buzz-like or noise-like, and a pedal to control the pitch and to allow for intonation changes. It's reported that it took more than one year to train operators to synthesize utterances of reasonable quality, but, once trained, they could play the Voder like a concert piano. Jim Flanagan, one of the pioneers of computer speech, recalls:

When Homer retired from Bell Labs, I found one of the original ladies trained to operate the Voder for the World's Fair. She had retired earlier. We found one of the Voders in the basement of Bell Labs and cleaned it up. We got some very antique vacuum tubes at one of the distributors on Route 22, from their attic or someplace. We got it working, and she agreed to come to Homer Dudley's retirement. We asked, "Do you think you can make this thing talk?" She said, "Oh sure. What do you want it to say?" "Say, 'hello, how are you?'" She sat down and gave a virtuoso performance on the Voder.[13]

Although the Voder's synthesized speech was barely intelligible, sounding hollow and mechanical, robot-like, it was a big achievement for its time and marked the beginning of electronic speech processing technology. Unfortunately, both the Vocoder and the Voder were too expensive to put into commercial use, more expensive than any potential gains from using them on the telephone network.

Apart from the one being mechanical and the other electronic, Kempelen's speaking machine and Dudley's Voder differed in a fundamental way. To produce speech-like sounds, Kempelen's machine imitated the human vocal tract, whereas Dudley's Voder synthesized a sound signal *without* imitating the vocal tract. Dudley took a purely engineering approach, viewing speech as a sound signal with particular spectral characteristics—regardless of the way humans produced it.

AUDREY

We had to wait thirteen years after Dudley built his Voder, a machine that attempted to produce speech, before someone built a machine that attempted to *recognize* speech, at the receiving end of the speech chain. In 1952, three Bell Labs scientists, K. H. Davis, Rulon Biddulph, and Stephen Balashek, published a detailed description of the AUDREY (*AU*tomatic *D*igit *RE*cognition) machine, which could recognize spoken digits.[14] For each digit spoken into its microphone, AUDREY would light a corresponding bulb on its front panel. The three scientists wrote:

We are faced with the problem of actually determining what was in the mind of the speaker, knowing that his ability to express his thought as a sound may differ from that of another speaker or even from his own previous utterance of the same sound. Therefore we are not looking for something that matches any standard sound exactly, but rather something that resembles one standard more closely than any other.[15]

It was clear to the speech recognition pioneers that the main problem they faced was that each utterance of the same word differs at least slightly, whether spoken by a different or by the same person. This is true for nearly every activity we perform as humans. Take handwriting. You can sign your name as many times as you like, yet each time your signature will look different, however slightly. You can learn how to exercise fine control over your hand when you write, but no two strokes will ever come out the same, even for the same letter in the same word. Or take speaking. You can repeat the same word as many times as you like, and each time it will come out differently: your intonation, timing, and the quality and duration of each sound you produce will differ slightly. If that's so for any two repetitions of the very same word by the very same person, how could we possibly build a machine that can recognize speech at all? The answer is that, to recognize speech, a machine doesn't have to rely on exact matches: it can instead recognize features of sounds and the words that vary minimally across repetitions and, to be more specific, that vary less across different repetitions of the same sounds and words than across different repetitions of different sounds and words. AUDREY was one of the first machines to recognize speech using this approach.

Formants, you may recall, correspond to the frequencies at which our vocal tract resonates when we speak, in other words, to the frequencies with the highest value of sound energy for the speech sounds we produce as speakers. When our vocal tract changes shape from sound to sound, the frequency value of the formants changes as well. Just by looking at the first two formants, F1 and F2, you can recognize most of the speech sounds even when you don't actually hear them. So, if the set of words to recognize is small enough, for instance, the digits from zero ("oh") through nine, just by looking at the changing values of F1 and F2 for any spoken word from that set, you can get a good idea of which word it is. K. H. Davis and his colleagues plotted sample F1 and F2 values for each of the spoken digits. Figure 2.5 shows plots for the digits "one," "five," "seven," and "nine," where each dot represents particular values of the first and second formants at a particular time.

By looking at the plots, the Bell Labs scientists realized that each spoken digit had its own characteristic pattern on the F1/F2 plane, although, of course, that pattern varied slightly from one utterance of the digit to another. Thus they couldn't make a precise one-to-one comparison of the plot of each incoming utterance of a particular digit with a stored electronic version of its plot. They needed a less exact way to compare incoming with stored formant patterns, one that would be forgiving of small differences. So they divided the F1/F2 plane into nine squares, as shown in figure 2.5. For each spoken digit, they measured how long the formant patterns stayed, on average and relatively, in each of the nine squares. For instance, for the digit "one," the patterns stayed about half the time in square 8 and about half the time in square 9; for the digit "five," the patterns stayed about half the time in square 9, a little more than a quarter of the time in square 8, and a little less than a quarter of the time in square 7—as you can see in the plots of "one" and "five"

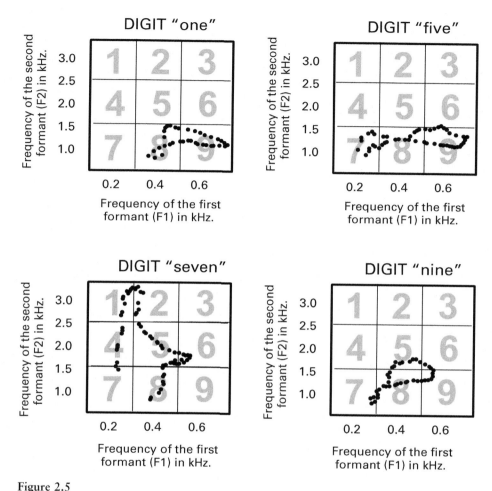

Figure 2.5
Plots used by AUDREY to define the characteristic patterns for each vowel sound.

in figure 2.5. Taking the average amounts of time spent by formant patterns in each square of the F1/F2 plane, the scientists characterized each spoken digit by nine numbers corresponding to the nine squares. From each unknown spoken digit, AUDREY extracted the values of F1 and F2 at regular intervals of time, measured how often these values appeared in each square, and compared these numbers with those stored for each digit. It recognized the unknown spoken digit as the one whose set of numbers was closest to that of a particular stored digit and lit the corresponding bulb on its front panel. AUDREY did all this with analog electronic circuits, and its accuracy wasn't bad at all: between 97 and 99 percent for a male subject speaking clearly and slowly. Like the Vocoder, AUDREY was an impressive achievement for its time. But, again like the Vocoder, it was and remained just an experiment. As Jim Flanagan and colleagues explained in 1980:

AUDREY occupied a six-foot-high relay rack, was expensive, consumed substantial power and exhibited the myriad maintenance problems associated with complex vacuum-tube circuitry. More important, its reliable operation was limited to accurate recognition of digits spoken by designated talkers. It could therefore be used for voice dialing by, say, toll operators, or especially affluent telephone customers, but this accomplishment was poorly competitive with manual dialing of numbers. In most cases, digit recognition is faster and cheaper by push-button dialing, rather than by speaking the successive digits.[16]

Recognizing Speech Is Difficult

An automatic speech recognizer (ASR) is a machine that takes speech sounds as input and identifies the words that were spoken, displaying them on a computer monitor (figure 2.6) or in any number of other possible ways.

AUDREY was the first automatic speech recognizer reported in a scientific journal, and its limitations highlight most of the speech recognition challenges. First of all, AUDREY couldn't work properly unless the speaker paused between words. Unlike written text, however, there are no spaces between words in normal speech, and speaking . . . with . . . pauses . . . between . . . words . . . is . . . quite . . . unnatural. In normal speech, nothing marks the end of one word and the beginning of the next. Coarticulation—the tendency of a speech sound to morph gradually into the following one—makes things even more difficult since successive sounds sometimes merge into a single sound, like the digits "one" /wən/ and "nine" /nīn/, which, when pronounced in sequence without a pause, as in normal speech, become/wənīn/, with just one single /n/ sound and no clear separation between them, as shown by the spectrogram in figure 2.7.

Though capable of what was called "isolated-word" or "isolated-speech recognition," AUDREY couldn't separate words as spoken in normal speech and thus worked only when a speaker paused between consecutive words. The machine

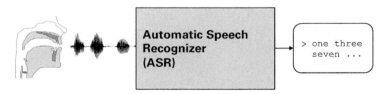

Figure 2.6
Automatic speech recognition as a system transforming input speech into text.

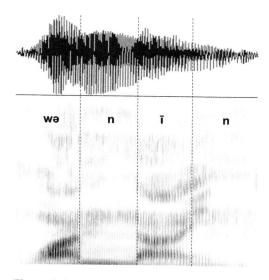

wə   n   ī   n

Figure 2.7
Waveform and spectrogram of "one nine" spoken without a pause between words.

capability of recognizing naturally produced speech without pauses between words—
what was called "connected-speech recognition"—wouldn't be possible until decades
after AUDREY.

The need for pauses between words wasn't AUDREY's only limitation; it had to
be tuned and tweaked for each individual speaker:

After preliminary analysis of the speech of any individual, the circuit can be adjusted to
function satisfactorily for the speech of that individual. The recognizer is not, however, in its
present form, capable of such accuracy on speech of a series of talkers without adjustment
for each talker. If no adjustment is made, accuracy may fall to as low as 50 or 60 percent in
a random digit series.[17]

As we all know, different speakers have different voices with different acoustic
properties. The formant frequencies, and thus also the patterns on the F1/F2 plane,
vary slightly from speaker to speaker, so that AUDREY needed to be slightly
adjusted with each different speaker to maintain a reasonable level of accuracy. This
need, called "speaker dependence," is another problem that affected earlier efforts
at speech recognition. A *speaker-dependent* speech recognizer needs to be tuned for
each different speaker, as opposed to a *speaker-independent* system, which works
for everyone—or almost everyone—right out of the box.[18]

AUDREY could recognize digits and digits only. And only in U.S. English. Such
a speech recognizer could be used to dial telephone numbers or to collect numeric

information like social security or account numbers, dates, and times, all by voice. But it would be useful to extend its recognition capabilities to words other than digits, such as the names of people or places or the words of simple commands. Unfortunately, AUDREY was hardwired to recognize digits, and recognizing other words would have required major modifications to its circuitry. And even that might not have worked. AUDREY's discriminating factor among words, patterns of the F1 and F2 formants, which mostly characterize vowel sounds, wouldn't have worked for discriminating between words with the *same* vowel sounds, like "dog" and "log" or "Tokyo" and "Kyoto," which would have sounded all alike to AUDREY's ears.

After AUDREY, the three main challenges of speech recognition technology would remain the same for decades: speaking style, speaker independence, and vocabulary size, graphically represented by the speech recognition evolution space in figure 2.8.

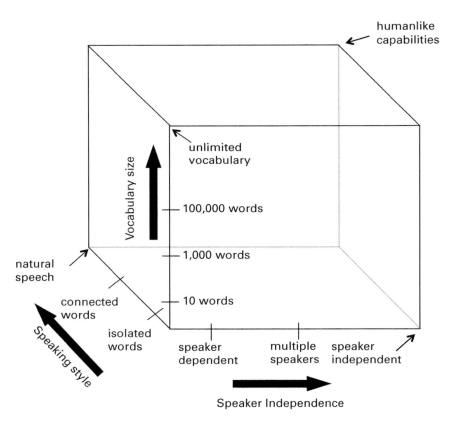

Figure 2.8
Speech recognition complexity space.

Moving along the speaker independence dimension, speech recognition evolves from speaker-dependent systems, which require training for each user, to multiple-speaker ones, which work reasonably well for a predefined set of users, to speaker-independent systems. The speaking style dimension characterizes the evolution of the speech recognizer's ability to interpret speech from the early isolated-word recognizers, which force the speaker to pause between words, to connected-word recognizers, which force the speaker to carefully articulate words, to recognizers that interpret natural, unconstrained speech. Finally, the vocabulary size dimension tracks the evolution of systems to handle larger and larger vocabularies. The upper right corner of the cube represents humanlike capabilities.

The Illusion of Phonetic Segmentation

AUDREY opened the way for speech recognition research. It showed that building a machine that could understand speech wasn't an impossible dream after all. Based on its success, Stephen Balashek and other scientists at Bell Labs, such as Dennis Fry, Peter Denes, and Homer Dudley himself, continued to pursue speech recognition. They realized that, to get beyond the limitations of the simple pattern-matching approach, they needed a fundamentally different speech recognition strategy. That strategy, called the "phonetic segmentation approach." would start by identifying the individual phonetic elements in the utterance. Segmenting utterances into individual speech sounds and reliably detecting their phonetic identity would give you a solid basis for a general speech recognition solution. If you knew which sounds, or phonemes, were spoken, you could group them into words, the words into phrases, and the phrases into sentences and reconstruct, level by level, the human speech chain. That was a reasonable approach. But Balashek, Denes, Dudley, and many other researchers in the years to come succumbed to the illusion that phonetic segmentation was the Holy Grail of speech recognition.

Despite all the effort, knowledge, and attention to detail scientists put into building phonetic segmentation machines, these machines performed poorly at the phonetic level, introducing errors that inevitably entailed other errors at the lexical level, resulting in speech recognition of mediocre accuracy. A key reason for their poor performance was the assumption that phonemes were discrete and easily identifiable, whereas, in fact, they are continuous and ever changing. And though our brains certainly have a deep knowledge of the different speech sounds, we don't know how they start to understand and interpret those sounds, whether they segments utterances into individual phonemes or proceeds in a different way. AUDREY, with its pattern recognition approach, set quite a high bar for performance. Other analog speech recognizers built in the years immediately after it brought only marginal improvements. Speech recognition needed a more powerful machine, one that was right around the corner: the computer.

The Computer's Mouth and Ears

Although the first digital computer, ENIAC (*Electronic Numerical Integrator And Computer*), had been built during World War II, digital computers didn't appear on the scene of speech research until the early 1960s. AUDREY and other recognition systems of the 1950s were based instead on specifically designed analog electronic circuits. As it happens, using a digital computer to process speech sounds isn't a straightforward process. Digital computers are designed to handle a whole range of numbers, such as

14, 17,894, 78.34, 1.005, −35.78, . . . ,

whereas speech sounds and the electrical currents they generate in microphones aren't numbers but continuously varying phenomena called "signals," such as the one shown in figure 2.9.

Signals and numbers would seem to have nothing in common. But Bell Labs scientists Harry Nyquist and Ralph Hartley thought otherwise. They showed that we could indeed represent a signal by a sequence of discrete numbers in 1928, long before the first digital computer was built.

While working to improve the efficiency of telegraph transmissions, Nyquist discovered that a continuous signal could be exactly characterized by samples taken at regular intervals at a rate higher than or equal to twice its highest frequency.[19]. So that if you had a signal whose frequencies weren't higher than 4,000 Hz (4 kHz), for instance, and you took at least 8,000 samples per second, you could exactly describe that signal with the samples alone. Mathematically, you could reconstruct the original signal exactly from the samples without any loss; Nyquist and Hartley prescribed a precise procedure for that reconstruction.

Twenty years later, in 1948, another Bell Labs scientist, Claude Shannon, universally recognized as the father of modern information theory, mathematically formalized what would come to be known as the "sampling theorem."[20] Let's take a closer look at the sampling process. Signal samples are values of a signal taken at regular

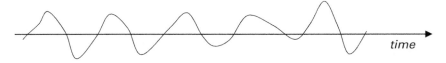

time

Figure 2.9
Signal.

Figure 2.10
Sampled signal.

intervals. For instance, the bold dots in the figure 2.10 are samples of the signal shown by the dotted line.

According to Nyquist, Hartley, and Shannon, if you take enough samples, you can use them alone to represent the whole signal without any loss. The line that connects the plotted dots of consecutive samples provides no additional information, and you can ignore it without losing anything from the original signal, which you can completely and exactly reconstruct from the samples at any time. In other words, the samples and the signal are practically the same thing: the sequence of discrete numbers representing the amplitude of successive samples is an exact numerical version of a continuous signal—an exact *digital* representation of an analog signal.[21] As such, it can be handled by a digital computer, to which the signal would look like nothing more than a long string of numbers:

375 782 3 −825 −26 710 578 −322 −456 2 689 680 −14 −56 4 890 780 457 −4 5 . . .

Once you've converted a signal into numbers, you can use a computer to perform a whole series of interesting operations on it. Whereas classical signal processing prescribes how to limit the bandwidth of a continuous signal with a specifically built electronic filter, digital signal processing can do the same thing with a *digital* filter, by applying series of mathematical operations called "algorithms" on the numerical representation of the signal.

Working with digital representations of signals and computer programs is easier and provides greater flexibility than building electronic circuits with resistors, capacitors, wires, and soldering irons. Once you created and tested a computer program, you could make any number of copies of it at virtually no cost, whereas you would need to separately build, and test, each copy of an electronic circuit. And any copy of your computer program would perform exactly the same on the same data at any time, whereas imperfections in the components or assembly of any copy of an electronic circuit you might build would produce at least slight variations in its performance. And, most important, computers would enable you to perform highly sophisticated operations, again at virtually no cost, operations that would require exceedingly complex and expensive analog circuitry.

Thus digital computers raised the level of what we could do with signals to what no one would have ever dared with analog circuitry because of the extreme complexity and cost. They make it easy for us to plan and perform experiments to test different conditions, and they allow us to fine-tune methods and processes. They allow us to collect, store, manipulate, and visualize data in ways that weren't even conceivable before. In other words, with Nyquist, Hartley, and Shannon's discoveries, and as the main instrument for testing theories and building signal manipulation and transformation devices, computers opened a whole new dimension of research on signals, and in particular on speech.

When the advantages of using computers for signal processing became clear, research laboratories started to look for economic and effective ways to convert analog signals into their corresponding digital representations and the other way around. Commercial devices that would do that, called "A/D" and "D/A converters," first became available in the early 1960s. Back then, they were so expensive and bulky that few labs could afford them or had the space to accommodate them. Today they're ubiquitous, so cheap and small that virtually every device we interact with, whether personal computer, MP3 player, cell phone, digital TV, CD or DVD player, includes an A/D or a D/A converter, or both.

With the advent and the availability of A/D and D/A converters, speech research made slow, but unrelenting and irreversible progress, moving from the realm of electronic ad hoc circuitry to that of general-purpose computers. Instead of designing and building complex electronic circuits, speech scientists wrote computer programs. Yet because early computers were too slow to run complex speech analysis programs in real time, scientists had to perform most of their experiments offline and definitely not in real time on batches of recoded speech samples. A pioneer and visionary who understood, early on, the value of using computers for speech research, Jim Flanagan remembers how, in the early times at Bell Telephone Laboratories when A/D converters weren't yet available, he digitized a dozen or so utterances by displaying their waveforms on the oscilloscope and taking down sample amplitudes by hand—thousands for every second of speech![22]

But even when the analog-to-digital converters became available, the digitizing process was still long and labor intensive. Typically, you recorded speech samples on analog magnetic tapes and hand-carried them to your lab's A/D converter, most likely the only one available, which you had to reserve in advance. Then, after a few hours or days, depending on how many utterances needed to be digitized, the technician operating the A/D converter would hand you back digital magnetic tapes containing the numeric versions of the analog utterances you'd recorded. You jealously guarded these tapes, using them over and over in as many studies and experiments as you could because of the prohibitive cost of acquiring new ones.

Although speech researchers successfully performed many computer simulations offline, the challenge for the 1960s was real-time speech recognition with computers. Spectral analysis, in particular, requires a large amount of computation, which earlier computers couldn't perform in real time. The speech recognition prototypes of the 1960s and early 1970s were hybrid systems, which used special devices for the most intensive computations and general-purpose computers for the rest.

Templates and Time Warps

With the advent of digital computers, many laboratories around the world started research programs in speech recognition, where knowledge of speech, its production, and the acoustic characteristics of the individual phonemes assumed central importance. Seeking a general solution to the problem of speech recognition, most of the researchers pursued the phonetic segmentation approach. A few researchers took a completely different approach, however, looking at speech recognition primarily as an engineering problem.

To see why a divide formed between the linguistic and engineering approaches, consider how linguists and engineers differ in what they do. Linguists, as scientists, try to answer fundamental questions, such as "How do humans understand speech?" They build hypotheses, or models, of what the answers might be, and some try to make the models of those answers work in machines—to get machines, for instance, to understand speech like humans. Engineers, on the other hand, try to solve specific problems, such as "How can we build a machine that can be controlled by speech?" Being pragmatic, they use models created by scientists if they think these might help them solve the problem at hand. If not, they redefine the problem so that they can solve it with the means and tools available to them.

The 1952 AUDREY machine was a solution to the speech recognition problem reduced to engineering terms that could be solved with the technology available at the time. The speech recognition engineers of the 1960s took a similar tack. They didn't try to solve the general problem of speech recognition, but a much narrower, more specific problem that could be expressed as follows: "How can we build a machine that, under certain agreed-upon conditions, will recognize all the words a user speaks to it?" Let's first agree, they might have said, that the machine will have a limited set of words—a restricted vocabulary—and that the user of the machine will speak to it using only words from that vocabulary and not any others. And let's also agree on two more conditions: that the user will (1) pause long enough before and after speaking each word for the machine to easily identify when a spoken word starts and when it ends and (2) go through a training phase, during which the machine will be attuned to the user's particular way of speaking. Given these agreed-upon conditions, the engineers' most successful solution to that narrower problem, and one of the first engineering approaches to speech recognition after AUDREY, was what came to be known as the "template-matching approach."

The idea behind word templates is at once simple and intuitive. Imagine having stored an exemplar or *template* of every word in the restricted vocabulary for your machine to recognize. You first ask the user of your machine to record all the words you want the machine to recognize. This operation is called "training" or "enrollment." Then, when the user speaks any one of those words again, your speech recognition machine compares that just-spoken word with all the stored word templates and recognizes it by selecting the template that's the most similar.

But even though the idea of word templates is simple in principle, there are a few details that need to be worked out. What does "the most similar" mean? How do you compute how similar a just-spoken word is to a stored word template? Do you store each word template as a digitized waveform and try comparing it sample by sample with the digitized waveform of the just-spoken word? That turns out to be a bad idea. Waveforms are highly variable, even when they're of the same word spoken by the same person at different times. The individual samples of waveforms of different utterances of the same word would therefore look extremely different. To get an idea of how pointless it would be to compare waveforms sample by sample, first look at the waveform segment in figure 2.11, which represents some 40 milliseconds of the initial portion of the word "one."

Now look at the two waveform segments in figure 2.12.

One of them is the initial portion of a different utterance of "one" and the other is the initial portion of an utterance of "man"—all three utterances made by the same person at different times. Can you tell which waveform segment is "one" and which is "man" just by comparing them, point by point, with the sample in figure 2.11? Most likely not—in fact, the second segment of figure 2.12 is "one." The problem is that waveforms contain too many irrelevant details. It's like trying to recognize the species of a plant by comparing it in every single detail—the precise

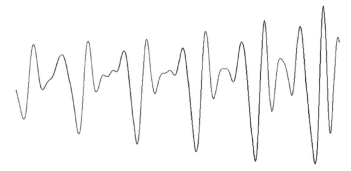

Figure 2.11
Segment of waveform of the initial portion of an utterance of the word "one."

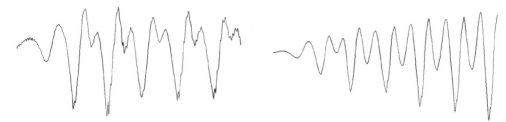

Figure 2.12
Mystery waveforms 2 and 3.

number, position, and shape of all its leaves and all its branches—with the plants pictured in a gardening book. It's hard to find similarities when you look at things with too much detail. But if you look at the waveforms of spoken words with too *little* detail—from too great a distance, so to speak—there isn't much to help a machine identify the words they represent.

Another way for a machine to discriminate among different spoken words would be to compare their spectrograms. As we've seen, spectrograms contain a lot of information on what was said, and they have patterns that are characteristic of each individual sound. Moreover, as we know, the human ear itself creates a tridimensional (frequency-intensity-time) spectrogram-like representation of speech sounds for further processing in the brain. Yet raw spectrograms also have too many irrelevant details, so that comparing them point by point would be both cumbersome and of little help.

The template-matching approach needed a version of spectrograms that could make different repetitions of the same word look similar, despite variations in insignificant details, that would blur the irrelevant differences but keep the high-level characteristics. Such a version would indeed help a machine discriminate among different spoken words. One way to get it is to look at spectrograms at a lower resolution, both in time and frequency. To illustrate how that might work, let's take the spectrogram of a spoken word in figure 2.13.

When we consider broader intervals of time and frequency, we obtain what's called a "quantized" representation of a spectrogram, one that may be less sensitive to the little differences between the various utterances of the same word. Figure 2.14 shows how it might look.

In choosing a time interval or *frame* of the right size, you need to consider how fast we move our articulatory muscles when we speak. Looked at for a 10-millisecond interval, for instance, our vocal tract would appear quite still. Thus a 10-millisecond frame is typically considered to be a good choice for the minimum temporal resolution of human speech. Higher resolutions won't bring us any

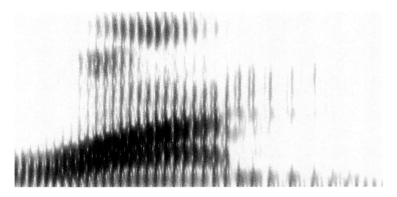

Figure 2.13
Raw spectrogram of a word.

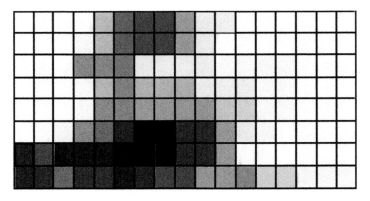

Figure 2.14
Spectrogram of word in figure 2.13 quantized into frequency/time intervals and intensity levels.

additional information; lower resolutions may actually miss important information for the discrimination of speech sounds. Likewise, choosing a frequency interval of the right size is typically based on how accurately the human ear hears frequencies.[23]

Figure 2.14 represents the intensities of the quantized spectrogram with squares in different shades of gray, but in the internal representation of a computer, each square would be a number corresponding to the average intensity of the spectrogram in that particular interval of time and frequency. (the figure is for illustration purposes; the time and frequency intervals are not in scale with the actual intervals used in practice). Thus, inside a computer, the quantized spectrogram of an utterance would take the form of a tabular array of numbers called a "matrix," like the one shown in figure 2.15.

2.5	2.4	2.5	2.4	4.8	7.9	7.7	7.6	5.8	4.3	1.2	1.1	0.9	0.5	0.2	0.1	0.2
2.4	2.3	2.4	2.7	3.9	7.4	7.1	7.2	6.1	4.1	1.3	1.2	0.7	0.3	0.1	0.1	0.1
2.5	2.2	2.5	7.5	6.9	7.2	3.2	2.8	3.3	3.2	2.6	3.1	0.8	0.4	0.3	0.2	0.1
2.2	2.1	2.0	2.2	5.3	6.5	5.8	5.3	5.4	3.5	3.7	3.5	1.1	0.3	0.1	0.2	0.1
2.1	2.2	2.3	2.3	6.1	7.1	6.5	6.7	6.1	5.9	5.5	52	1.2	0.6	0.4	0.4	0.3
2.3	2.2	2.5	6.8	6.2	7.8	9.9	9.9	8.7	7.9	6.1	2.1	1.5	0.2	0.4	0.2	0.4
9.8	8.7	9.1	9.3	9.1	9.7	9.9	9.9	8.6	8.2	6.3	2.8	1.1	0.3	0.3	0.3	0.3
9.3	8.9	8.2	8.9	8.7	9.5	8.7	8.5	8.5	7.8	8.1	8.3	7.1	6.6	4.2	3.9	2.8

Figure 2.15
Matrix of feature vectors obtained from the quantized spectrogram in figure 2.14.

Each column of the matrix representing an utterance is called a "feature vector" and corresponds to a 10-millisecond slice of time: a frame of speech. Each number in the feature vector measures the spectral intensity in the corresponding interval of frequencies at a particular time within that frame of speech. A typical feature vector might have from ten to thirty numbers, depending on the sophistication of the speech recognition system. Once you've represented every frame of speech by numbers, you can measure how similar two different frames of speech are by measuring the distance between the corresponding feature vectors.[24]

You now have two important concepts to help your machine recognize spoken words by comparing them to stored word templates: first, the feature vector, a list of numbers to represent broad spectral characteristics of speech sounds for each 10-millisecond frame of speech, and, second, the distance between corresponding feature vectors to compare different speech frames and measure how similar they are. Your next step is to compare all the frames of speech for one utterance with all the frames of speech for another, for instance, all those for an unknown spoken word with all those for a stored word template, and to measure how similar they are. There's an added problem, however: different utterances have, in general, different durations, and thus different numbers of frames of speech. How can you compare, frame by frame, two utterances with different numbers of frames?

Although it's obvious that utterances of words of different lengths most often have different durations, even two utterances of the same word may have different durations. One can be faster or slower than the other. But that's not the only

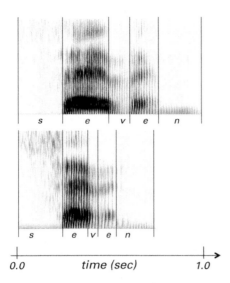

Figure 2.16
Spectrograms of two different utterances of "seven."

problem; their speech sounds may be faster or slower in different ways. For instance, look at the spectrograms of two utterances of "seven" in figure 2.16.

The first utterance is spoken more slowly than the second, and thus its spectrogram looks considerably longer. But you might also notice that the initial /s/ sound is pretty much the same length in both utterances, whereas the other sounds are shorter in the second utterance. The /s/ in the first utterance is about as long as the /e/ that follows, whereas the /s/ in the second utterance is about twice as long as the corresponding /e/. Time doesn't move in a straight line across different pronunciations of the same word; it "warps" at different rates for different sounds. When you make a frame-by-frame comparison between two utterances, you need to make sure that you align corresponding frames of speech, frames that belong to the same speech sounds. Only by doing that can you be sure to get a good match and find the maximum possible overall similarity. If, on the other hand, you don't take into account the different time warps inside words, as in the examples above, you may end up comparing frames of speech for an /e/ with frames for a /v/ and a /n/. So that the similarity you find between two utterances of the same word may be smaller than the similarity between utterances of different words. And the whole template matching strategy will fail.

You're that much closer to a successful template-matching approach. You understand that time warps differently inside slower or faster utterances of the same word and that when you compare frames of speech, you need to make sure you compare frames for the same speech sounds. Intuitively, think of making each word template of a rubber sheet, and of stretching or compressing it differently along the horizontal dimension to try to make it fit the quantized spectrogram of the unknown utterance. If you do that for each word template in your machine's inventory, you may find the one that matches the unknown utterance better than all the others. That template is most likely the one that corresponds to the word that was spoken. What you just did is called "dynamic time warping" (DTW), and to understand how to do it in an optimal or best possible way, you first have to understand how to find the best path in an intricate network of intersections.

Best Decisions and Your Daily Commute

The solution to the dynamic time-warping problem came as an application of the groundwork done in the 1950s by Richard Bellman, a math professor at Stanford University with a passion for number theory. In the early 1950s, Bellman spent some time as a consultant for the RAND Corporation working on problems related to planning and decision processes.[25] At that time, Bellman invented a procedure he called "dynamic programming," which would become a pillar of modern decision theory and operational research.[26] Known as "Bellman's optimality principle," it would also become one of the basic mathematical tools for modern speech recognition. In Bellman's own words, dynamic programming is a method aimed at "finding the best sequence of decisions related to an optimization problem." But it can be described in simpler terms, as you'll see in the following practical example.

Many of us drive from home to work every morning. Every morning, we choose one of a number of different routes: some longer, some shorter, some flat, some hilly, some with tolls and little traffic, and others with no tolls but constant traffic. As a daily commuter, you want to find the best route, but you first have to decide what "best" means. A necessary first step to find the best of anything is to agree on a criterion for judging when something is better than something else, when a particular route is better than another in our example. For instance, valid criteria for judging your best route—for "optimizing" your route—might be how long it takes you, how much gas you have to use, or how much money you have to spend overall. Let's say you want to minimize the total expense of your daily commute, calculated as the sum of the costs of gasoline, tolls, and car wear and tear (estimated as a certain number of cents per mile). Consider a network of intersecting road segments where all your possible routes from home to work are plotted (figure 2.17).

The numbers in the network are your average costs for driving each segment: the sum of what gasoline, tolls, and car wear and tear will cost you for that particular stretch of road, from intersection to intersection. For instance, it would cost you

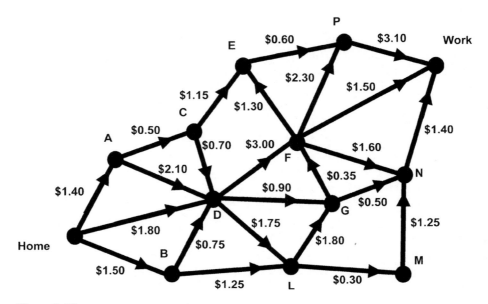

Figure 2.17
Network of all possible routes from home to work, with associated costs of each segment between consecutive intersections.

$1.50 to go from home to intersection B and then $0.75 to go from intersection B to intersection D, and so on. Thus the total cost of your commute is the sum of all the individual road segment costs. For instance, following the Home–B–D–G–N–Work route would cost you $1.50 + $0.75 + $0.90 + $0.50 + $1.40 = $5.05, whereas the route Home–A–C–D–G–F–Work would cost you $1.40 + $0.50 + $0.70 + $0.90 + $0.35 +.$1.50 = $5.35. You now have all the elements for finding your cheapest route, but how do you do that in the most efficient way? You may be tempted to take the cheapest alternative at each intersection, but this strategy—called a "greedy strategy"—won't work. In fact, what can seem a good immediate choice because it's cheaper may lead to a more costly and longer path later, with more traffic, or more tolls. The Home–A–C–D–G–F–Work route, chosen by following a greedy strategy, turns out to be more expensive than the Home–B–D–G–N–Work route. In fact, if you follow a greedy strategy, you don't minimize your overall expense, you simply take the next cheapest segment, which may force you into something more costly later. In effect, you blindly follow a short-term plan. On the other hand, a more costly segment taken at a certain point may put you on a route that becomes much cheaper later on and allows you to save on your overall expense. That said, how do you make the best decision—determine the best route to take—at each intersection?

You could try to find the best route—to solve what's known as the "best-path problem"—by simply listing all the possible routes with their total costs and choose the best one, that is, by finding what engineers and mathematicians would call an "exhaustive solution" to your problem. Although, in our example, there are only 55 different routes, most of the time, the number of possible routes is very high, too high to easily enumerate and choose the best one from all of them. And the bad news is that the number of possible routes grows exponentially with the number of intersections. So that, if you've an average of 3 possible choices at each intersection—left, right, or straight—and you've 11 intersections in the network of road segments from home to work, your overall number of possible routes is 3 to the power of 11 (3^{11}), or 177,147. With 15 intersections, your overall number of possible routes jumps to more than 14 million, and, with 20, to almost 3.5 billion! Mathematicians and computer scientists don't like things that grow exponentially because they soon become unmanageable. Even with a relatively small number of decision points—the intersections in our example—11, for instance, it becomes close to impossible to enumerate and choose from among all the possible routes. So, in most cases, the trivial solution simply isn't practical. Enter Bellman's dynamic programming procedure.

Bellman's procedure is based on the observation that if you select the best path that leads from your starting point to any intermediate intersection, that path is part of the best path among all paths through that particular intersection. Assuming you're going through that particular intersection, you can disregard all other paths that lead to it. To see how this method works, take intersection D and select the best path that leads to it from home. There are four possible ways you can get to intersection D: directly from home, from intersection A, from intersection B, and from intersection C, with costs of $1.80, $3.50 ($1.40 + $2.10), $2.25 ($1.50 + $0.75), and $2.60 ($1.40 + $0.50 + $0.70), respectively. Evidently, if you had to go through intersection D, the best path to it, the one with the smallest cost, is the direct path from home. That's also part of your overall best path, again assuming you have to go through D. Of course, you don't know yet if your best route would go through intersection D, but you'll remember that, just in case it would. So you can remove from your consideration all the other possible ways to reach D because you know they'll never be part of your best path. You'll also remember the cost of the best partial path going through any of the other intersections for which you've made a best decision, in parentheses in figure 2.18. The best decision for intersections A, B, and C is "trivial" because only one segment leads to each one of them.

Now do the same for intersection L. You can get to L from intersection B, with a cost of ($1.50) + $1.25 = $2.75 or from intersection D with a cost of ($1.80) +$1.75 = $3.55. So your best path to intersection L definitely goes through intersection B. If you continue to analyze all the intersections in an orderly way and

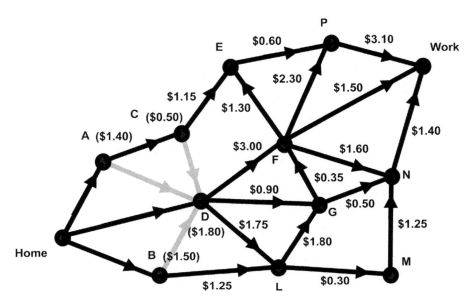

Figure 2.18
Application of Bellman's dynamic programming procedure to select the least costly segment leading to intersection D from home and intersection A, B, or C.

determine, for each one of them, the best path among those coming from all the previous intersections and remove all the others, you'll end up with one, and only one, overall best path to work, namely, Home–D–G–F–Work, as shown in figure 2.19.

Your best overall path from home to work will cost you $4.55. It may be a little more expensive than what you thought, but the good news is that what you did to reach that result—use Bellman's dynamic programming procedure—was far easier than calculating the cost of all the possible paths. In fact, you only had to calculate the cost of all possible paths to reach each of the eleven intersections from home to determine the best path to it, taking advantage of the calculations you'd already made to determine the best path to reach all the previous intersections leading to it. And since the total number of possible paths is exponentially larger than the number of intersections, you saved yourself an exponentially larger number of calculations.

Finding Your Way in Time Warp Land

You now know how to find the best path—the path with the smallest cost—even in a network with a large number of intersections and without having to perform

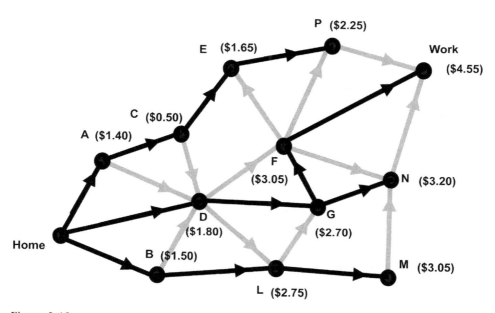

Figure 2.19
Application of Bellman's dynamic programming procedure to the whole network leads to the elimination of all nonoptimal segments for each intersection.

an exponentially larger number of calculations. But what does solving the best-problem have to do with the problem of aligning utterances and templates? Well, as I hinted before, dynamic programming will also help you solve the time-warping problem. You can clearly see the similarity between the two problems—driving from home to work and dynamic time warping—in figure 2.20, where the second problem is represented on what engineers call an "alignment grid."

On the vertical axis, you've the frames of speech for a word template stored in your speech recognizer, let's say the template for "seven." On the horizontal axis, you've the frames of speech for the unknown word—which also happens to be "seven" in our example, but your machine doesn't yet know what it is. Every point of the grid corresponds to a particular frame of the template and a particular frame of the unknown word, each frame corresponding to a feature vector. Each of the many paths through the intersection points or *nodes* of the grid—one path is shown in figure 2.20—corresponds to one of the many possible frame-by-frame alignments between the stored word template and the unknown word. Or, to put it another way, each path on the alignment grid is a specific time warp of the stored word template trying to match the unknown word. The task for your speech recognizer is to find the best time warp, the one with the smallest "cost" of alignment. The

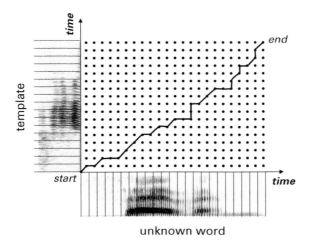

Figure 2.20
Grid used to represent all possible alignments between a stored word template and the sequence of feature vectors of an unknown word. One of the possible alignments is shown as a line connecting the grid nodes and going from the initial to the final frames of both representations.

word template corresponding to the best of all time warps is the one most similar to the unknown word: its word and the unknown word are a match.

Every path segment connecting pairs of nodes on the alignment grid represents the cost of aligning the corresponding frames of the stored template and the unknown utterance: the larger the dissimilarity between the frames, the larger the cost of alignment. You can compute the cost by calculating a measure of dissimilarity, a distance, between the corresponding feature vectors. Thus the total cost of aligning these vectors is the sum of all the individual distances between them. Since time moves from left to right and from bottom to top on the alignment grid, so do all the possible paths. The path segments connecting the nodes on the grid follow a regular network, and you calculate their alignment costs as the distances between corresponding feature vectors, as represented in figure 2.21, which shows an enlarged portion of the alignment grid with all the possible paths between nodes.

A horizontal path segment between two nodes of the alignment grid corresponds to stretching the word template in time—to matching more vectors of the unknown word to the same vector of the template. Similarly, a vertical path segment corresponds to compressing the template in time—to matching more of the template's frames to the same frame of the unknown word. A diagonal path segment between nodes on the grid corresponds to matching both feature vectors and frames of the template to those of the unknown word linearly, without stretching or compressing them in time. It should be clear now that the problem of finding the best alignment

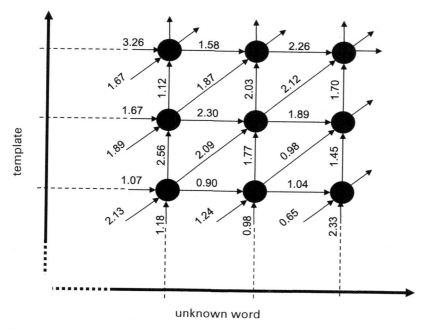

Figure 2.21
Enlarged portion of the alignment grid showing the allowed paths among nodes and the associated alignment costs.

between a template and the unknown word is similar to that of finding the best path; in both cases, you're looking for the solution with the smallest overall cost. And you now know that you can solve the problems using Bellman's dynamic programming procedure in a computationally efficient way.

The first paper reporting a dynamic programming solution of the template-matching problem for speech recognition was published by the Soviet scientist T. K., Vintsyuk in 1968.[27] Hiroaki Sakoe and Seibi Chiba presented a similar solution at a 1970 conference in Japan.[28] But it wasn't until 1973, when the Japanese scientist Fumitada Itakura came to Bell Telephone Laboratories to work in the acoustic research department headed by Jim Flanagan, that Bellman's dynamic time-warping technique—dynamic programming—was used in speech recognition research by U.S., and later European, laboratories.[29]

Even with Bellman's dynamic programming, however, DTW–based speech recognition still required a great deal of number crunching. At a rate of a feature vector every 10 milliseconds of speech and assuming an average word duration of 500 milliseconds, each word representation had an average number of 50 feature vectors. Thus each alignment grid had $50 \times 50 = 2,500$ nodes, and dynamic time warping required computing the vector distance for each node as well as the best move to the next node on the alignment grid. For a vocabulary of ten words, the digits "zero" ("oh") through "nine," for instance, a machine had to perform a DTW alignment for each one of the ten templates, with a total number of calculations of the order of 2,500 × 10 = 25,000. DTW speech recognition was thus a "computational hog" that challenged even the fastest general-purpose computers of the 1970s. Real-time machines required special hardware; it took hours, sometimes days, to compare different configurations and tune the needed algorithms offline. And even after all that, Sakoe and Chiba reported in 1978, "a NEAC-3100 computer . . . required about 3 seconds for each digit word recognition and about 30 seconds for [each] geographical name recognition [from a list of fifty]."[30] Thus, even if dynamic time warping provided a reasonably accurate solution to the problem of isolated-word recognition with a small vocabulary for a single speaker, real-time speech recognition on general-purpose computers was out of the question unless technologists could build and optimize special and far more powerful digital hardware for the dynamic time-warping computations.

Machines Are Made of Parts

Although whole-word template matching has a limited use today,[31] the search for the best path on a grid using dynamic programming is still the foundation of all modern speech recognizers. But keep in mind that a template-matching speech recognizer is a complex machine and that DTW template matching is only one part of it, albeit the most important one. Poor performance by *any* component would make even a powerful technique like dynamic programming useless. Besides DTW template matching, the template-matching speech recognizer has at least two other key components: the end-point detector and feature extraction, which transforms speech into a sequence of feature vectors, as shown in figure 2.22.

The function of the end-point detector is a very delicate one indeed. It's responsible for detecting when each word actually starts and ends—for distinguishing the word from the silence that precedes and follows it. If the detector makes a mistake, if it cuts off the first or last part of the word it then sends along to the other two key components of the speech recognizer, no matter how good and accurate its feature extraction and DTW template matching are, the speech recognizer, as a whole, is bound to fail.

In principle, the task of an end-point detector is simple: to distinguish between silence and speech. And, looking at a waveform of a speech sound, such as the one in figure 2.23, you might conclude that silence is simply the absence of any signal, a flat line with zero energy.

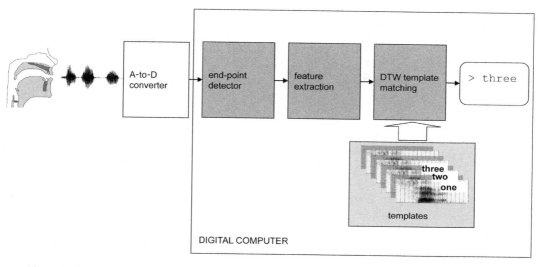

Figure 2.22
Schematic diagram of a template-matching, isolated-word speech recognition system.

Figure 2.23
End-point detection.

So, you might further conclude, it shouldn't be difficult to build a component that separates the parts of a speech signal with sound energy from those with none or, more simply, that separates speech sounds from silence. Unfortunately, it's not that easy. First of all, silence is almost never completely silent. Noise permeates all but the most scientifically controlled acoustic environments. The murmur of a distant air conditioner, the whooshing of traffic outside, the hum of a refrigerator, the blaring of police sirens, the crying of a baby next door, the barking of a dog down in the garden, or, even worse, the chattering of people at a neighbor's cocktail party or in a restaurant across the street—any or all of these sounds can be in the background of a speaker's voice. How to build an end-point detector that ignores this background noise, as the human ear does, is no easy problem to solve. Indeed, even the smartest end-point detector can mistake background noise for speech or the other way around. Thus the end-point detector can mistake some consonant sounds, like /f/ or /s/, which are quite faint and noise-like, for background noise and wrongly cut off the first of last part of a word. Another problem arises when the uttered word includes within it a stop or plosive, like /t/, /p/, or /b/, which is essentially silence followed by a short burst of energy. A not-so-smart end-point detector can mistake the silence preceding the burst of energy in a stop consonant sound for the silence at the end of a word and cut off rest of the word. Because cutting off the first or last part of a word can lead to irreversible mistakes by a speech recognizer, the design of an accurate end-point detector has played a pivotal role in the development of functional speech recognition systems.

The next key component of a template-matching speech recognizer, as you saw in figure 2.22, is feature extraction, the module that transforms the speech signal into a sequence of feature vectors. No matter how well designed and realized the core DTW speech recognition algorithm is, if the feature extraction fails, the whole machine fails. Researchers did all they could to find the best features for optimal speech recognition, especially during the early years of the template-matching approach.

The Ignorance Approach

The success of dynamic time warping in the 1970s drew the attention of several laboratories around the world to template-matching techniques. After all, building a DTW isolated-word speech recognizer was relatively easy. All you had to do was pure engineering: collect templates for each word of the restricted vocabulary and store them on a computer, then implement end-point detection, feature extraction, and the DTW algorithm on that same computer. You didn't have to be a linguist, understand phonetics, or be able to read spectrograms to build a speech recognizer. Which helped explain the widespread popularity of the template-matching approach in research centers around the world. Scientists concentrated on the problem of computational complexity by trying to make the DTW search more and more efficient. To enhance the speech recognizer's ability to discriminate among spoken words, they developed ways to extract more-representative features and templates that could work better across different speakers, thus avoiding the need to train the speech recognition machine for each specific user.[32]

On the other hand, one of the main criticisms leveled at the dynamic time-warping approach by the more scientifically and linguistically oriented speech recognition researchers of the 1970s was that it had no knowledge of, nor basis in, fundamental linguistic phenomena. Yes, with DTW, you could engineer a speech recognizer that would work for a few words spoken in isolation, but you couldn't scale the technology up to solve the general speech recognition problem. Dynamic time warping was a brute-force approach designed to solve only an oversimplified and constrained version of the speech recognition problem. It was based on an "ignorance model"—as the more linguistic-oriented scientists used to say—and not on an approach that would benefit from the vast amount of knowledge regarding human language accumulated through the years. There was no apparent way to relax the limitations of the template-matching approach and move toward larger and larger vocabularies, true speaker independence, and recognition of natural speech without pauses between consecutive words. Even the recognition of just one word required huge amounts of unintelligent computation that had no real linguistic basis. And if a template-matching speech recognizer made a mistake, if dynamic time warping produced a higher distance score for the correct word and lower one for a wrong word—and that would happen sometimes—there was no easy way to understand why that happened and give a rational explanation for it. And thus there was also no easy way to revise and improve the performance of the machine based on knowledge about a particular phonetic or acoustic phenomenon, as systems based on phonetic segmentation would allow. The only thing you could do was collect better templates, extract more-representative features, and invent better template distance measures based on experimental evidence that certain configurations performed better than others. And every time you had to add a new word to the restricted vocabulary, or change the vocabulary altogether, or train the system for a different user, you had to collect new word templates. In other words, the template-matching approach was regarded by many speech recognition researchers as little more than *kludge,* a derogatory engineering term for an ad hoc, inelegant solution to a problem.[33] Foremost among researchers sharing this point of view were linguists who, for years, had pursued the knowledge-based approach, following the attractive principles and philosophy that first defined the term *artificial intelligence.*

3

Artificial Intelligence versus Brute Force

The dream of building intelligent computers with humanlike reasoning capabilities has fascinated scientists and laypeople alike since the early 1950s. The idea that computers weren't just giant calculators but could also manipulate nonnumeric information and draw intelligent conclusions—whatever we might mean by the word "intelligent"—has been engrained in the collective imagination. It's been taken up by the press, featured in movies and science fiction literature, and supported by popular (however unfortunate) terms like "electronic brain." In a 1950 *Scientific American* article, the father of information theory, Claude Shannon, described how computers could be made not only to play chess but also "to work on symbolic elements that represent words, propositions, and other conceptual entities."[1] In 1956, Allen Newell, Herbert Simon, and J. C. Shaw invented a computer program, called the "Logic Theorist," that could prove theorems from the *Principia Mathematica* of Alfred North Whitehead and Bertrand Russell. That same year, interest in the new discipline bloomed during the Dartmouth Summer Research Project on Artificial Intelligence, a two-month conference organized at Dartmouth College in Hanover, New Hampshire, by the young mathematician John McCarthy. The conference attracted famous scientists, including Shannon, from Bell Telephone Laboratories, Newell, from the RAND Corporation in Santa Monica, California, Simon, from the Carnegie Institute of Technology in Pittsburgh, and Arthur Samuel, from IBM. The name "artificial intelligence" stuck—indeed, "AI" is now part of our common vocabulary—and referred to efforts to develop computer programs that showed reasoning behaviors characteristic of human intelligence, such as inference. Most of the participants at the Dartmouth conference would go on to become key contributors to the field of AI.

In 1962, MIT received a $2.2 million grant from the U.S. Department of Defense to study "machine-aided cognition," another term used for artificial intelligence. By the mid-1960s, AI had become the focus of hundreds of research projects all around the world, to include, of course, building machines that could understand language.

At the end of the 1960s, Terry Winograd, from MIT, created a program called "SHRDLU" that could carry on a simple dialog with a user typing on a teletype.[2] The conversation was restricted to an artificial world of objects—called a "blocks world"—displayed on a computer screen with the simple graphics of the time.[3] You could type a sentence like "FIND A BLOCK WHICH IS TALLER THAN THE ONE YOU ARE HOLDING AND PUT IT INTO THE BOX," and SHRDLU would respond: "BY 'IT,' I ASSUME YOU MEAN THE BLOCK WHICH IS TALLER THAN THE ONE I AM HOLDING," a pretty sophisticated response for a computer.[4]

By the 1970s, it was generally agreed that artificial intelligence could realize the dream of building intelligent machines in just a few years. Many scientists, advisors, and decision makers strongly believed in the strategic importance of AI; the U.S. government, educational institutions such as MIT, Carnegie Mellon University, and Stanford University, and corporations such as IBM invested considerable amounts of money into artificial intelligence research.

Expert Systems

The term *expert systems* refers to AI programs that, by storing and being able to navigate a large amount of knowledge, can act like human experts to solve common problems in a specific field, such as medicine, resource planning, or engineering. To build an expert system, you need to solve at least three problems: how to acquire knowledge specific to a certain class of problems—for instance, diseases or nuclear plant accidents; how to represent this knowledge in a form computers can read; and how to develop a mechanism that can use it to solve given problems. The main assumption behind expert systems was that you could acquire the knowledge you needed by interviewing experts and represent it in a digital form as I F-THEN-ELSE rules. You could then use the whole set of rules in a program that, starting from evidence of certain facts, would *infer* a number of truthful conclusions.

MYCIN, developed at Stanford University in 1970, was one of the earliest expert systems.[5] Its goal was to diagnose blood infections based on patient symptoms and to recommend treatments based on clinical results.[6] Hundreds of rules were manually created from interviews with doctors and represented in MYCIN's memory as IF-THEN-ELSE statements like

---

IF

the infection is primary-bacteremia

AND

the site of the culture is one of the sterile sites

AND

the suspected portal of entry is the gastrointestinal tract

THEN

There is suggestive evidence of 0.7 that infection is bacteroid.

Given a number of facts, such as a patient's blood test results, MYCIN would attempt a diagnosis by triggering the rules that mentioned those facts in their IF part. These rules would generate some conclusions, which would be used as facts for other rules, and so on in a chain of inference from the initial facts to the final diagnosis. This process was carried out by the expert system's inference engine, which typically could work using rules of any number and type, provided they were expressed with the right formalism.

Expert systems were applied in a wide range of specialized fields from medicine and biology, to engineering, law, and finance, to linguistics. Although understanding spoken language requires large amounts of semantic, syntactic, lexical, morphological, phonetic, and acoustic knowledge, as long as the knowledge was represented in a suitable form, any general inference engine would be able to draw conclusions from observed facts, much as it would in any other field using expert systems. But whereas experts in medicine, biology, engineering, law, and finance can often articulate many of the rules they use in their everyday decisions, expert speakers of a language are generally unaware of most of the rules they use to understand common speech.[7] Indeed, unless they're trained linguists, few speakers know, for instance, why a /t/ sound is perceived as a /t/, what the difference between a /t/ and a /d/ sound is, and what the rules are that govern the interpretation of different syntactic constructs. And no matter how well we understand speech, like walking, skiing, or biking, it's one of those things nearly all of us find hard to explain in specific rules.

The idea of building machines that understood speech as expert systems was quite attractive. Indeed, most of the laboratories engaged in artificial intelligence research had at least one project targeted at developing expert systems that understood language and speech. An expert system's rules for recognizing plosive speech sounds or the /b/ sound, in particular, might have looked like this:

IF

a pause is followed by a voiced low-energy segment

AND

the time between the beginning of the pause and the beginning of the voiced segment is more than 20 milliseconds

THEN

The segment is a **voiced plosive**

ELSE IF

the time between the beginning of the pause and the beginning of the voiced segment is 20 milliseconds or less

THEN

The segment is an **unvoiced plosive**.

---

or

IF

the segment is a **voiced plosive**

AND

it is followed by a **vowel**

AND

both the second and the third formants rise to their stationary value

AND

the burst of energy after the stop is weak

THEN

The segment is **/b/**

If you could compile enough of these rules, from lower-level acoustic, phonetic, and morphological knowledge to higher-level lexical, syntactic, and semantic knowledge, your expert system's inference engine would be able to start with fundamental acoustic facts, like pauses or high-energy voiced segments of speech, and to proceed, level by level, up the inference chain to higher-level conclusions about words, phrases, sentences, and finally meanings, the ultimate goal of a speech understanding system. If during its ascent from lower-level acoustic facts to higher-level inferences, one or more crucial facts were missing, the expert system engine could descend back down the chain of inference until the truth about the missing facts was either affirmed or negated. Artificial intelligence scientists found this schema of upward and downward inference both elegant and highly attractive. It seemed to replicate the process of human cognition, or at least our understanding of it. In a word, it seemed "intelligent" since, at any point, the AI scientists could trace back the chain of inference, from the final conclusions to the initial facts, and analyze why the expert system had made a particular decision based on its rules and the available knowledge. And if the decision was deemed to be wrong, leading to false conclusions or erroneous results, the scientists could always correct the rules, include exceptions, or add more knowledge where they felt the system was weak.

But, unfortunately, life wasn't going to be that easy for them. First, the number of rules they needed to describe all observable speech phenomena, especially at the acoustic and phonetic levels, was astoundingly large. Indeed, it was virtually impossible to cover all the possibilities. But even if they somehow managed, in order to implement each rule, they needed computer programs that could identify and characterize facts like "pause," "low-energy segment," "significantly larger than," "second and third formant rise," and so on. And most of those facts couldn't be identified accurately enough to provide the level of truth the inference system needed to work properly.

Take pauses, for example, one of the basic elements of speech. Detecting pauses in speech is important because, among other things, pauses characterize plosives, like /t/ and /d/. The duration of a pause can also determine the type of plosive.[8] But even a simple fact like "a pause longer than 20 milliseconds" is hard to verify with 100 percent accuracy. First, your expert system has to detect a pause. But, as you learned when we discussed end-point detection, detecting pauses in the presence of background noise is hard to do. Then, having detected the pause, your system has to determine whether it's longer than 20 milliseconds. Does its rule still apply if the pause is just 19.99 milliseconds? No, your expert system won't trigger the rule in that case because the rule clearly states that the pause has to be "*longer* than 20 milliseconds." And your system's rules are inflexible: either they apply or they don't. By contrast, physical phenomena are *not* inflexible, black or white, either or. They're characterized, not by hard and fast thresholds, but by fuzziness. Yes, it may well be true that, generally, the pause associated with a certain plosive is longer than 20 milliseconds, but your system will almost certainly encounter utterances of the same plosive where the pause before it is *shorter* than 20 milliseconds, and utterances of a *different* plosive where the pause before it is slightly longer. And thus making a hard decision based on a hard and fast threshold is bound to fail sometimes. And this failure, when it happens, even if it happens very seldom, will trigger the wrong rule, which, in turn, will trigger other wrong rules, and inevitably lead to the wrong conclusion, when your system's inferential house of cards will collapse—often enough, however seldom, to make your expert system based on that wrong decision unusable for practical purposes.

The main problem with earlier systems of speech recognition based on artificial intelligence was that, in assuming knowledge could be used to infer conclusions based on a number of physical facts, they didn't take into account that verifying those facts often required hard decisions—and that the physical phenomena of speech were better characterized by probabilities than by certainties. When AI scientists became aware of that, they designed speech recognition systems that delayed hard decisions, maintaining a number of unconfirmed facts, or hypotheses, until the inference process could generate sufficient evidence to prove all but the most likely hypotheses wrong. Such a system, to stay with our example, could avoid deciding whether a pause was actually longer than 20 milliseconds by characterizing it with a *likelihood* of being longer than 20 milliseconds.[9] In other words, after scoring each rule based on the estimated likelihood of the facts that supported it, the system would trigger many rules at once according to their scores. The success of this strategy depended on whether the scores reflected the actual likelihood of the hypotheses and on whether the system combined these hypotheses in a meaningful way. With many rules triggered at the same time, however, the chains of rules generated an exponentially growing number of combined hypotheses that challenged the computational power of any available computer at that time. Eventually, the system had to come to a decision, based, for instance, on the combined hypothesis scores. The correctness of the decision ultimately depended on the scoring mechanisms, and there was no way to optimize the accuracy of the results in a principled way. Tuning and optimizing the systems were lengthy and expensive experimental procedures that required an enormous amount of both data and computational power, neither of which was readily available in those days.

Thus, despite the popularity and the aura of scientific interest surrounding expert system speech recognizers, they weren't very successful from the performance point of view. Building prototypes with even limited capabilities was difficult and required the collaboration of several experts in disparate fields such as computer science, phonetics, linguistics, and engineering. That said, the inherent limitations of the AI approach weren't evident at the time. Because extensive experimental evaluations of speech recognition systems were both difficult to carry out and alien to the artificial intelligence way of thinking of the time, none of the AI–based speech recognition systems was ever significantly compared with other systems. Nor was the performance of earlier versions of the AI systems, except in rare instances, tracked against successive versions. Indeed, for the most part, anecdotal evidence of their functionality was the only proof that they worked at all. How well they worked remained unclear. Most of the AI researchers were more interested in the novelty, elegance, and scientific attractiveness of their approach, and in how closely their models resembled plausible models of human cognition, than in the actual performance of their systems.

Whither Speech Recognition?

John R. Pierce, executive director of the Communication Sciences Research Division at Bell Telephone Laboratories, had spent most of his brilliant career in vacuum tube research and satellite communication and had helped develop Telstar 1, the first commercial communication satellite. He was a hard-core engineer and first-class scientist, famous for his witty remarks. "Artificial intelligence is real stupidity," he once said, "I thought of it the first time I saw it," and "After growing wildly for years, the field of computing appears to be reaching its infancy." Having seen a few less-than-encouraging results and the lack of a scientific approach to evaluation, Pierce became skeptical about the possibilities and the seriousness of the field of artificial intelligence in general and AI–based speech recognition in particular. In June 1969, he published a letter entitled "Whither Speech Recognition?" in the *Journal of the Acoustical Society of America* (*JASA*), home of several important and seminal articles on speech recognition:

Speech recognition has glamour. Funds have been available. Results have been less glamorous. When we listen to a person speaking—much of what we think we hear is supplied from our memory. . . . General-purpose speech recognition seems far away. Social-purpose speech recognition is severely limited. It would seem appropriate for people to ask themselves why they are working in the field and what they can expect to accomplish. It would be too simple to say that work in speech recognition is carried out simply because one can get money for it. That is a necessary but not sufficient condition. We are safe in asserting that speech recognition is attractive to money. The attraction is perhaps similar to the attraction of schemes for turning water into gasoline, extracting gold from the sea, curing cancer, or going to the moon. One doesn't attract thoughtlessly given dollars by means of schemes for cutting the cost of soap by 10 percent. To sell suckers, one uses deceit and offers glamour. . . . Most recognizers [speech recognition researchers] behave, not like scientists, but like mad inventors or untrustworthy engineers. The typical recognizer gets it into his head that he can solve "the problem." The basis for this is either individual inspiration (the "mad inventor" source of knowledge) or acceptance of untested rules, schemes, or information (the untrustworthy engineer approach).[10]

Simply put, Pierce didn't believe there was any commercial reason for using speech to communicate with machines. Keyboards, cards, and magnetic tapes were already performing that task and performing it well. But, most of all, he didn't believe you could build machines that would understand spoken language "phoneme by phoneme or word by word." People, he pointed out, recognize language "not because they hear the phonetic features or the words distinctly but because they have a general sense of what a conversation is about." And thus his opinion was that a "general phonetic typewriter is simply impossible unless the typewriter has intelligence and a knowledge of language comparable to those of a native speaker of English."

Pierce was, in principle, right. To build machines that would understand spoken language, you had to capture and encode a lot of the linguistic rules we humans follow naturally and unconsciously when we speak, an extremely difficult task in itself. Pierce was also right in thinking that the technology available at his time didn't measure up to that task. Rule-based AI systems required the laborious effort of many scientists and experts to gather sufficient knowledge and encode it in a form computers could read. And even with all the rules AI scientists could gather and years of work performed by top-notch experts in linguistics, phonetics, and computer science, most of the systems built by AI scientists had produced only dubious results. Worse than that, their progress could not be assessed in any measurable form. On the other hand, the brute-force engineering approach of template matching and dynamic time warping had produced at least some results that were both measurable and interesting, albeit in very limited tasks: the recognition of a handful of words uttered by a specific speaker. Nevertheless, the general sentiment was that template-matching approaches were not advancing science and couldn't be scaled up to achieve humanlike recognition of speech. Having said his piece on all that, as an executive director of AT&T, Pierce banned any further investment in speech recognition by his corporation and, as a government advisor, he recommended that the United States stop funding academic research in the field.

For his part, Jim Flanagan, then a department head in the speech research laboratory, later told me:

At that time, there were various opinions in Bell Labs about speech recognition. . . . John [Pierce] was my executive director: my boss's boss. He essentially said we were not going to do any work on speech recognition, even if we were asked to, because it was not that promising. My feeling was that there were problems, but also opportunities. My response to John was: John, we are also interested in talker identification. He said, okay, we support that. I did not go into the fact that most of the digital processing and the algorithms for talker verification were very similar to speech recognition. That was about 1971. I went to the international acoustic conference in Japan and got to know a lot of Japanese scientists. There I met [Fumitada] Itakura, from NTT [Nippon Telegraph and Telephone], who had done a lot of good work on speech coding. I asked him to come and visit us as a scientist. . . . He came in 1972 and stayed for two years. . . . I told him we were not permitted to work on speech recognition, but since he was a visiting scientist supported by his company, he could work on whatever he wanted. So, in a few months, he could demonstrate a speech recognition system for flight information based on DTW. . . . For two years, Bell Labs did not do the research, but we were blessed by Itakura working on speech recognition.[11]

The ARPA Speech Understanding Project

Despite Pierce's letter and against his advice, in the early 1970s, the U.S. government funded the first large-scale speech understanding project, which would generate some of the fundamental ideas still used in modern commercial speech recognizers. In 1958, the Department of Defense had established the Advanced Research Project Agency (ARPA) "for the direction or performance of such advanced projects in the field of research and development as the Secretary of Defense shall, from time to time, designate by individual project or by category."[12] ARPA, later called "DARPA" (Defense Advanced Research Project Agency), was the U.S. response to the Soviet Union's conquest of space (with the launching of the artificial satellite Sputnik on

October 4, 1957), and the agency's original mission was that of assuring that the United States, and its military in particular, achieved and maintained a technological lead over other countries.[13] In 1962, ARPA created the Information Processing Technology Office (IPTO) with the intent of directing artificial intelligence research toward large-scale domains. As Allen Newell explained:

The DARPA support of AI and computer science is a remarkable story of the nurturing of a new scientific field. Not only with MIT, Stanford and CMU [Carnegie Mellon], which are now seen as the main DARPA–supported university computer-science research environments, but with other universities as well . . . DARPA began to build excellence in information processing in whatever fashion we thought best. . . . The DARPA effort, or anything similar, had not been in our wildest imaginings.[14]

One of the first directors of IPTO, J. C. R. Licklider, was firm in his belief that artificial intelligence, central to the development of technology for intelligent command and control military operations, was also central to ARPA's mission. Carnegie Mellon University, MIT, Stanford University, and the Stanford Research Institute received large amounts of financial support for AI research from ARPA. Smaller amounts were granted to other educational institutions, such as Columbia, Brown, and Rutgers Universities and the University of Pennsylvania.[15]

The target domains of AI research ranged widely, from problem solving and theorem proving, to graphic visualization, to pattern recognition and included natural language and speech processing as well. IPTO's director Lawrence Roberts created the Speech Understanding Research (SUR) program in 1971 with the intention of pushing the evolution of artificial intelligence toward solution of the general speech understanding problem. It's important to note here that IPTO's target was speech *understanding,* not just recognition—ideas and concepts, not just sequences of words. Not surprisingly, the proposal for the ARPA Speech Understanding Research program was sharply criticized and strongly opposed by a committee of the National Academy of Science chaired by John R. Pierce.

Initially, IPTO set quite stringent requirements for the SUR systems: recognition of any utterance drawing on a vocabulary of 10,000 words spoken by any user in any acoustic environment. As members of IPTO's advisory committee, Newell and Licklider helped set more reasonable requirements: recognition of utterances in a specific domain of conversation drawing on a vocabulary of only 1,000 words spoken by any of a select group of cooperative users in a quiet room. Moreover, the participating labs would be allowed to train their systems for each of the users. Under the revised requirements, the goal was to build machines that, by the end of the program, would understand more than 90 percent of the utterances in a "few times real time" on a 100 MIPS (million instructions per second) computer, a fairly powerful machine in 1970.

IPTO allocated $15 million to the Speech Understanding Research program for a five-year period, with the intention of pursuing a five-year follow-up project should the program succeed. Carnegie Mellon University, the Stanford Research Institute, MIT's Lincoln Laboratory, Systems Development Corporation (SDC), and Bolt, Beranek and Newman (BBN), a Boston consulting company with a long history in acoustic research, used part of the funds to establish their own speech understanding research lab. The SUR program ended in 1976 with four working systems. Systems Development Corporation built a system that answered questions on facts about ships, such as "How fast is the *Theodore Roosevelt*?" Bolt, Beranek and Newman built a system, called "HWIM" (*Hear What I* Mean), that answered travel questions, such as "What is the plane fare to Ottawa?" Carnegie Mellon created two systems, the first of which was called "Hearsay II," that inventoried and retrieved documents, answering questions such as "Which computer science abstracts refer to the theory of computation?" Built using the AI–based expert system approach, the SDC system, HWIM, and Hearsay II made heavy use of rules at all levels of knowledge. A sketch of the architecture of an early version of HWIM, shown in figure 3.1, will give you an idea of how complex these systems were.

The second Carnegie Mellon system, called "Harpy," took the brute-force template-matching dynamic time-warping approach to speech recognition. Despite being a technological outlier, Harpy was the only SUR system that got close to the goals initially set by IPCO; with 95 percent accuracy in speech understanding, it was far ahead of all the other systems. The only problem was that Harpy, like most DTW template-matching systems, was a computational hog; using a then state-of-the-art PDP-KA10 computer, Harpy took 4 minutes to process a sentence that took only 3 seconds to speak—*eighty* times real time instead of the "few times" required by the SUR program.[16] The runner-up was Carnegie Mellon's Hearsay II, with 74 percent accuracy. Bolt, Beranek and Newman's HWIM took third place, with 44 percent, trailed by Systems Development Corporation's system, with only 24 percent accuracy.[17]

Because the SUR program failed to define a formal and fair evaluation process at its outset; because the four different vocabularies in four different speech domains made determining which SUR system worked best difficult, if not impossible; and because of its generally missed goals, despite the partial success of Harpy, ARPA decided to terminate the program without a follow-up. The general feeling was that speech understanding research wasn't sufficiently developed to merit government funding.[18] But even though the speech understanding project seemed to prove Pierce right, it was not entirely a waste of money. In hindsight, we can say that Harpy provided a deeper understanding of the technology needed to develop modern speech recognition and understanding systems, most of which use algorithms developed during the SUR project. And the other unsuccessful SUR systems, the AI–based ones, provided helpful insights into speech and computer science that are still referred to today.

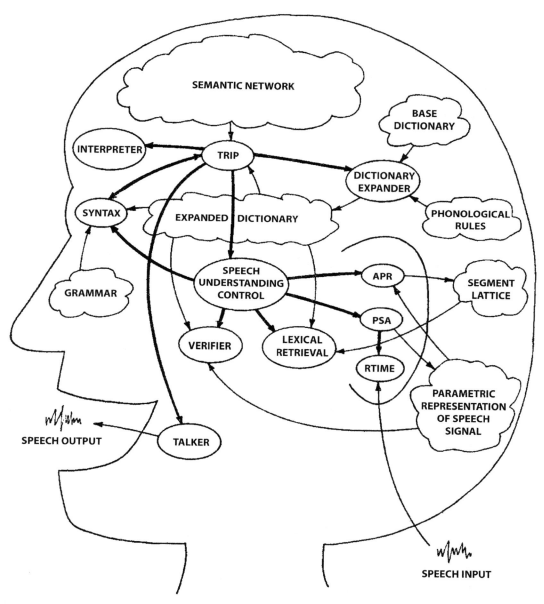

Figure 3.1
Architecture of an early version of the HWIM system. APR, acoustic-phonetic recognizer; PSA, signal processing component; RTIME, real-time signal acquisition. From Bertram Bruce, "HWIM: A Computer Model of Language Comprehension and Production," BBN report no. 4800, Bolt, Beranek and Newman, Inc., Cambridge, Mass., March 1982. Graphic courtesy of Raytheon BBN Technology Corporation and of the University of Illinois at Urbana-Champaign. Drawing by Bertram C. Bruce, 1982. Special thanks to Marie Meteer and John Makhoul for finding and providing a scan of this drawing.

The complex, rule-based HWIM, Hearsay II, and SDC systems shared the same overall philosophy, differing mostly in how they composed and triggered rules for forming hypotheses at higher and higher linguistic levels. For instance, HWIM relied on what its designers called an "island-driven parser": the system first triggered acoustic rules to detect "islands" of reliable acoustic facts anywhere in the utterance; it used these islands to form hypotheses about the acoustic portions of the utterance; it then triggered phonetic rules, which would take these acoustic hypotheses, and having detected reliable islands of phonetic facts, build other hypotheses spanning larger (phonetic) portions of the utterance, and so on from one linguistic level to the next higher one. Finally, the system would merge the highest-scoring hypotheses to create sentence hypotheses at the syntactic level.

Hearsay II used a different, "blackboard" scheduling process. Different processors at the acoustic, phonetic, lexical, and syntactic levels each triggered rules to constantly read and write hypotheses from and to specific portions of a common storage area called the "blackboard." For instance, the lexical processor constantly read hypotheses from the area of the blackboard written by the phonetic processor and wrote specific word hypotheses in its own area of the blackboard; these were constantly read by the syntactic processor, which wrote first phrase hypotheses and then, from these, sentence hypotheses in its own area of the blackboard. However, neither HWIM nor Hearsay II had a good strategy to estimate which hypotheses were most likely to lead to the correct result in the fastest way. Both systems often waded—computer scientists would say "thrashed"—through tens of thousands of hypotheses drawn at the different linguistic levels in order to find the most likely ones. Both based the scoring of hypotheses on empirical considerations, which, though reasonable, weren't optimized and thus couldn't guarantee a high level of success. In other words, relying only on empirical evidence, the systems could provide no theoretical guarantee that the highest-scoring hypothesis was also the correct one. That was the fundamental problem with most AI–based speech recognition systems.

Raj Reddy's lab at Carnegie Mellon built Hearsay II in the most evident rule-based AI tradition, but Reddy hedged his bets with Harpy, a non-rule-based system he built together with Bruce Lowerre, taking the more pragmatic engineering approach. The main idea behind Harpy was to define a network of templates that would represent all permissible utterances, and then use dynamic programming to find the path in the network that most closely resembled the unknown input utterance. As an extension of the template-matching approach from isolated to connected words, Harpy proved to work much better than the more sophisticated artificial intelligence knowledge-based systems. To understand how and why it did, we need to go back to dynamic time warping.

From Isolated to Connected Words

Although dynamic time warping (DTW), which matched whole-word templates with feature vector representations of unknown utterances, was a workable solution to the problem of isolated-word recognition, the problem of recognizing naturally spoken "connected" speech, where nothing clearly marks the end of one word and the beginning of another, seemed to require something more. But however difficult and unsolvable this second problem might appear to be, its solution proved to be a straightforward extension of the DTW concept, a solution that, as in most cases, became evident after expressing the problem in the right terms.

It turned out that trying to directly segment connected speech into individual words was the wrong approach. As you now know, segmentation is always difficult, requiring a hard decision, and making hard decisions in an uncertain world leads to irreversible hard mistakes. Hence the unintuitive and unconventional idea of giving up on segmenting input utterances into words as a first step of the process and of delaying any hard decisions for as long as possible. That meant considering any frame of speech in the unknown utterance to be a potential boundary between consecutive words, making word hypotheses of all possible segmentations, and finding the most likely one among them, according to an overall optimality criterion. You might think that finding the most likely word hypothesis when you don't even know how many words were spoken, let alone which words were spoken, is an impossible task. But it's not. Let's revisit the alignment plane we used for dynamic time-warping recognition of isolated words.

The difference between isolated- and connected-word recognition happens at the word boundaries. In the isolated-word case, because we know the utterance to be recognized contains one and only one word, all possible DTW alignments have to match each frame of the unknown utterance with the corresponding frame of the template being aligned, from the first frame of speech to the last.[19] Moreover, to reduce the computational requirements of the alignment algorithm, only a certain amount of distortion is allowed, which means considering only paths that would deviate only a certain amount from the diagonal of the alignment plane. In other words, for each template, the DTW considers only alignment paths such as those in the highlighted area of figure 3.2.

If the unknown utterance contains more than one word, because any of its frames of speech can be the start or end of a word, you have to consider a different, more complex type of alignment, represented by a more complex alignment plane where, once an alignment path between a template and a portion of the unknown utterance reaches the end frame of the template, it continues to any possible initial frame of all the templates that can potentially follow. This process is schematized in figure 3.3.

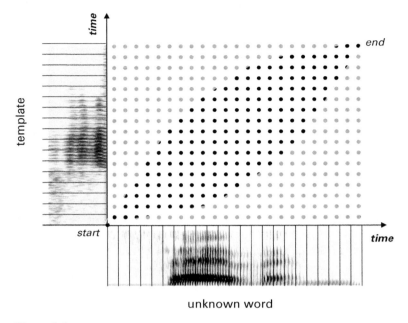

Figure 3.2
Alignment grid for performing dynamic time warping for isolated words showing the area where the search for the best path is performed in order to reduce the computational load.

Although the network of all possible paths representing all possible alignments of all sequences of templates with the unknown utterance—thus all possible sequences of words—is quite intricate, using Bellman's dynamic programming, you can find the best path with a reasonable number of computations, a number that doesn't grow exponentially with the number of templates and words in the vocabulary and the number of frames of speech for the input utterance. But, as a listener, you can do better than that. When you recognize connected words—as opposed to isolated words—you can take advantage of what you already know: that not all sequences of words are permissible. That knowledge, which can greatly reduce a speech recognizer's computational burden and help it to avoid making unreasonable mistakes, is nothing more or less than a grammar.

Using Grammars

Even with the great simplification derived from using Bellman's dynamic programming procedure, the recognition of connected words with DTW alignment still requires a lot of computation. For every initial template frame, the speech recognizer

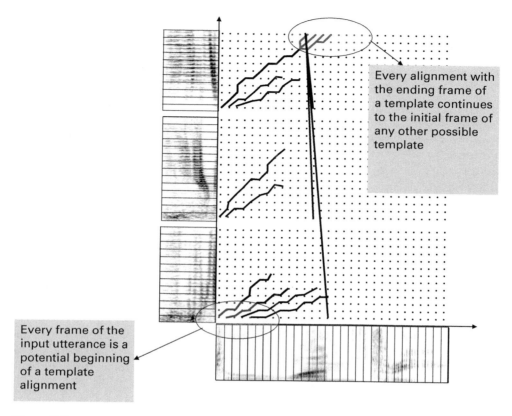

Every alignment with the ending frame of a template continues to the initial frame of any other possible template

Every frame of the input utterance is a potential beginning of a template alignment

Figure 3.3
Alignment grid for template-matching connected-speech recognition. Each one of the templates can potentially align with any portion of the unknown utterance. When a path reaches the end of a template, all the possible template beginnings are tried next.

has to decide which is the best path among all those coming from all possible previous word templates, and it has to do so for each frame of speech in the unknown input utterance. In other words, it has to consider the possibility that a new word can start at each frame of speech in the unknown utterance. That said, for almost all vocabularies and applications, not all sequences of words are permissible.[20] There are two clear advantages for a speech recognizer to consider only permissible sequences of words: doing so will (1) require less computation, sometimes significantly less, and (2) prevent the recognizer from mistaking a grammatically impossible sentence for a permissible spoken one.

Consider a simplified blocks world in which all you can say are things like

Put the red pyramid on top of the yellow cube

Push the yellow sphere to the right of the green sphere

Remove the yellow pyramid.

By combining actions, like "put," "move," and "remove," objects, like "sphere," "cube," and "pyramid," properties like "red," "green," and "yellow," and location qualifiers like "on top of," "to the right of, " and "to the left of," you can come up with quite a large number of different statements. Yet the set of permissible sentences is quite restricted and structured as compared to all possible sequences of words. For instance, it's quite easy to predict which words will follow any given word and which won't, as long as the sentence is within the grammatical constraints of the blocks world. Every grammatically correct sentence will start with an action, such as "put." The next word will refer to a specific qualified object, such as "the green cube" or "the yellow pyramid." Then there may be a location qualifier, like "on top of" or "besides the," and finally there may be another object, like "the red sphere" or "the green cube." You can capture all these regularities in grammar rules, as you've seen earlier, and you can use these rules to constrain the speech recognizer to search only among the permissible sequences of words. For instance, if an alignment path reaches the final frame of the template for "the," it will continue to the initial frame of the templates of for "green," "red," or "yellow," the three permissible words that can follow. Grammar rules substantially reduce the amount of computation required by dynamic time warping and prevent the speech recognizer from mistaking senseless sentences like "The move put cube here" for permissible sentences like "Remove the red sphere" simply because they sound alike.

Computer scientists have a penchant for anything that can be expressed as a network of nodes and interconnections. Networks, which can be easily and conveniently represented as programming structures, lend themselves to solutions, such as dynamic programming and the search for the best path, that computer scientists know how to do quite well. An attractive property of certain grammars is that they can be expressed as networks of the type known as "finite state machines," where "machines" refers, not to a real machines made with wires, wheels, or electronic circuits, but to computer mechanisms programmed to follow well-defined procedures.[21] If you can describe what it does, step by step, and represent that in a computer form, you've a "machine" in this sense.

You can characterize anything we know in the world, to include real and computer machines and even living organisms, as being in any one of a number of possible states at any point in time. In general, the number of these possible states can be very large, even infinite. But, for practical purposes, we often consider only a small—finite—number of them, and computer scientists use finite state machines to help them do just that. An example of a very simple finite state machine is the power switching mechanism in an appliance like a television, which is generally in one of three possible basic states: "off," "on," and "standby." Now, there are actions you can take that change the state of a thing, that cause what computer scientists call a "state transition." For instance, if you plug a TV in, you cause a state transition from "off" to "standby." Then, if you push the power button on its remote, you cause another state transition, from "standby" to "on." The effect of an action you take may differ from state to state. If you push the power button on the remote when the TV is in its "off" state—because it's unplugged—nothing will happen; the TV will stay in its "off" state, but if you do so when the TV is "on," it will go into "standby"

In diagramming finite state machines, computer scientists typically use circles to represent states and arrows to represent state transitions. Both states and state transitions have labels. The state labels identify each state with a number or name, so you know which state you're talking about. The state transition labels identify the actions or events that trigger the state change. Consider our example of the TV power switching mechanism, diagrammed as a simple finite state machine in figure 3.4.

Besides representing state transitions of TVs and other devices, you can use finite state machines to represent and describe in a compact form all the permissible sentences in a defined language. If you follow state transitions labeled with words from

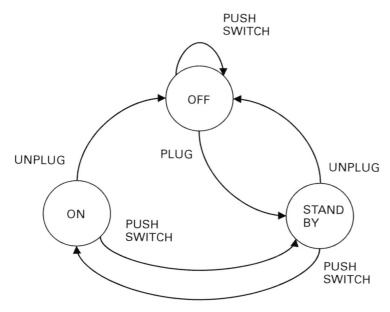

Figure 3.4
Simple finite state machine.

an initial or start state and take note of each word at each transition, when you reach the end state, you'll have one such permissible sentence in that language. By exploring all the possible transitions, you can get to all its permissible sentences. The finite state machine shown in figure 3.5, for instance, represents our simple blocks world language.[22]

Following the arrows, try to find all the permissible things you can say with the restricted vocabulary and within the syntactic structure of the simplified blocks language. After the start state, you've only four permissible words you can use to begin a sentence: "put," "move," "remove," and "take." If you choose the "put" transition, you go to state 1, where you have only one permissible next word: "the." You then go to state 3, where you have three permissible next words: "red," "green," and "yellow." If you choose "yellow," you go to state 4, and if you then choose "sphere," you go to state 5. And so on, until you reach the end state. Proceeding in this way, no matter what particular path you take, you end up with a permissible—legal—sentence in the blocks language.

A finite language state machine can compactly represent a large number of sentences. The machine of our example is quite simple, yet it represents a total of 504 permissible sentences. A slightly larger machine, one with 10 nodes and 5 transitions per node, could represent as many as $5^{10} = 9,765,625$ permissible sentences while excluding an infinite number of impermissible or illegal ones. A paradoxical aspect of finite state machines is that quite simple machines can represent large, indeed infinite, numbers of sentences. Take, for instance, the "looped" finite state machine shown in figure 3.6.

Although it uses some of the words of the previous machine (figure 3.5), it's much simpler in structure, with only three states and ten state transitions—by comparison, the previous machine has sixteen states and twenty-eight state transitions. Note that there's a state transition with *no* symbol, represented by an unlabeled arrow that arcs back from state 1 to the start state.[23] That unlabeled arrow represents a recursion. By following the state transitions of this machine, including the unlabeled recursion one, you can generate an infinite number of sentences; all the combinations of the eight words in sequences of any possible length, from one to infinity: PUT, PUT MOVE RIGHT LEFT CUBE, SPHERE SPHERE CUBE CUBE PYRAMID PUT MOVE THE CUBE SPHERE . . . Every time you reach state 1, you have the choice of ending the string of words or going back to the start state and adding more words. This simple machine represents an infinite number of permissible strings with any number of words from among those defined there. If, however, you want to limit the number of permissible strings of words to a finite number of well-structured sentences, you need to create a more intricate machine, like the one in figure 3.5. The power of a finite state language machine is that of being able to reduce the infinity of possibilities to a reasonable size, represent them in a compact

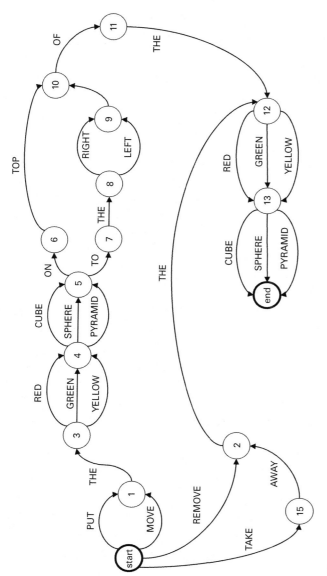

Figure 3.5
Simplified blocks language represented as a finite state machine.

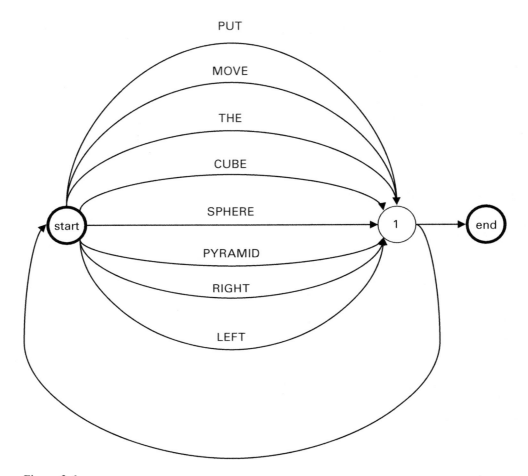

Figure 3.6
"Looped" finite state machine representing an infinite number of sentences with all word combinations of length from one to infinity.

manner, and still fully represent the complexity of the underlying language. That's exactly what you need for your speech recognizer.

Putting It All Together

Let's return to our template-matching approach, and see how a finite state machine can help your speech recognizer recognize spoken sentences that belong to a set represented by the machine. Think of a template as itself a finite state machine,

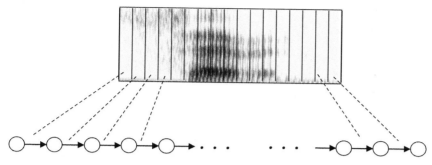

Figure 3.7
Finite state machine representation of a sequence of feature vectors representing a speech template.

where each state transition corresponds to a frame of speech and its corresponding feature vector.

The concept of a finite state machine can be easily extended, and its state transitions can represent not just symbols or words, but also physical phenomena of any type, such as time slices or frames of speech or, better still, feature vectors. So the machine shown in figure 3.7 is a finite state representation of the sequence of feature vectors that constitute a template. Any state transition, shown by an arrow from one state to the next, corresponds to a feature vector. If you follow the machine from its first state to its last, you encounter exactly the sequence of feature vectors that make the whole template.

Going back to finite state machine in figure 3.6, if you substitute for each word transition the appropriate word template machine, you create an extremely large machine where each transition represents a particular feature vector corresponding to a particular frame of a specific template. Figure 3.8 shows a portion of this now fully *composed* machine.[24]

Any path through the machine is a potential sequence of template frames and their corresponding feature vectors. The machine represents all possible sequences of them. Given an input utterance represented as a sequence of feature vectors, you want your machine to find the sequence within it that most closely resembles that utterance. And it will—if you allow it to do a certain amount of dynamic time warping. What you've done is reduce the problem of recognizing grammatically correct speech made up of connected words to the problem of finding the best path in a network. And again, Bellman's dynamic programming procedure is the answer to that. No matter how large your network is, Bellman's procedure guarantees that you'll find the best path sooner or later, depending on how fast your computer is. It may take a long time, but not a time that increases exponentially with the size of

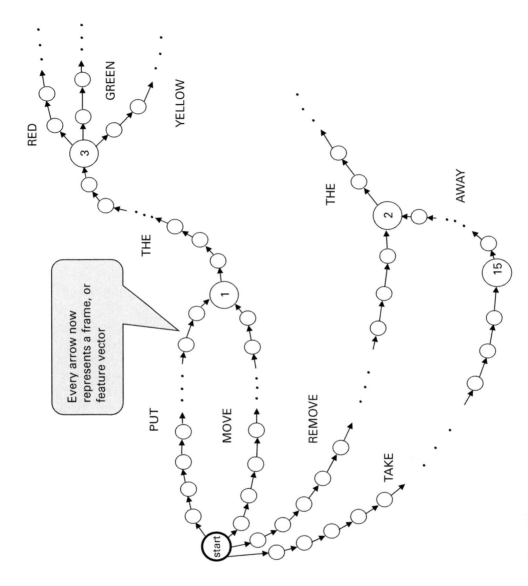

Every arrow now represents a frame, or feature vector

Figure 3.8
Fully composed finite state machine, representing all permissible sequences of template feature vectors allowed by the language definition.

your network and the length of the input utterance. What you have is an alignment problem, no different from the alignment problem you encountered in moving toward isolated-word recognition, where you had to align each of the individual templates and the unknown utterance. You now have a huge alignment grid, with all possible state transitions of your network—corresponding to all feature vectors—representing all permissible sentences on the vertical axis and with all frames of speech in the unknown utterance on the horizontal one. The paths on this huge alignment grid, though not regular, as in the case of isolated words, are governed by the state transitions on the language finite state machine. Each intersection on the alignment grid corresponds to matching a specific feature vector on the language finite state machine with a specific feature vector of the unknown utterance. The cost of that intersection corresponds to the distance between the corresponding feature vectors. The solution to the connected- speech recognition problem consists in solving the best-path problem in this huge grid of intersections. And the computationally effective solution to that problem is the DTW alignment algorithm.

The recognition of connected speech from the engineering point of view was thus nothing more than a search for the best path in a large network: a jackhammer, brute-force approach. Harpy worked exactly like the finite state machine search just described. Bruce Lowerre and Raj Reddy, who built Harpy at Carnegie Mellon in 1971 for the ARPA Speech Understanding Research project, created a finite state machine that represented all permissible sentences that could be spoken using its restricted vocabulary of 1,000 words—all the sentences that were proper English queries in the document retrieval speech domain, that is. Rather than creating a template for each word, which would have been quite unmanageable, they represented each word either as linked smaller templates of phonetic units or, if it had phonetic variants, as a finite state machine with alternative pronunciations. For example, a word like "tomato," which could be pronounced either as /tomahto/ or /tomeito/, would be represented by a finite state machine like the one in figure 3.9, where each state transition corresponds to a specific phonetic unit.

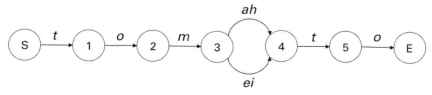

Figure 3.9
Finite state machine representing phonetic variations of the word "tomato."

Harpy's final composed network consisted of some 15,000 interconnected phonetic templates.[25] To make it easier for its speaker-dependent system to adapt to new speakers, Reddy and Lowerre automated the collection of templates for a set of training utterances from each speaker who participated in the experiments.[26]

The search space for connected-speech recognition—the grid that represents all permissible alignments of an input unknown utterance with the network of all permissible utterances—may be very large. Thus, for a 2-second input utterance with 200 frames of speech, given that Harpy had 15,000 stored templates with an average size of 10 frames, the number of points in the alignment grid would be $15,000 \times 200 \times 10 = 30,000,000$. Thirty million decision points that needed to be searched by the dynamic programming algorithm was definitely too much computation for a 1970 computer. Even with a modern computer, it would take many seconds, if not minutes, for the recognition of a single utterance. Back then, it would have taken several hours. To show that Harpy could actually work, if not in a few times real time, then at least in a few minutes, Lowerre and Reddy had to improve on the best implementation of the dynamic programming algorithm. They introduced simplifications and approximations to the algorithm to speed up the search and find the *approximately* best path—a "good enough" solution. And they succeeded admirably.[27] With an understanding accuracy of 95 percent, Harpy was a great computer science and engineering achievement for its time.

In the years to come, variations of the search mechanism implemented by Harpy would be used by most connected-speech recognizers developed all around the world. ARPA's Speech Understanding Research project clearly showed that brute force could produce better results than artificial intelligence. But there were still issues that needed to be resolved, chief among them, how to build a sentence network that could generalize to new sentences *outside* the initial set.

One of the main problems with the template-matching approach was how to select appropriate phonetic templates that would work for different vocabularies and different speakers. The solutions adopted in Harpy and in other brute-force systems tried to extract the templates more or less automatically from recordings of many different speakers and to merge those templates to achieve the greatest degree of speaker independence. Doing this required a lot experimental trial-and-error tuning, however, and resulted in only modest performance. Although it was clear that acquiring larger and larger amounts of data was the key to improving that performance, template-matching systems couldn't easily be scaled up for a number of reasons. Deriving phonetic templates, even if automated, wasn't very accurate, and acquiring more data inevitably meant acquiring more templates, which slowed down the search.

At about the same time as the SUR project, an IBM speech recognition group led by Fred Jelinek, who had gotten his Ph.D. in electrical engineering at MIT, started work on an approach based on formal mathematical and statistical theories. Meanwhile, at Carnegie Mellon, graduate students Jim and Janet Baker, who would go on to play an important role in the history of the business of speech technology, pursued a purely statistical approach to speech recognition in their doctoral work. In 1974, the Bakers joined Fred Jelinek's group at IBM's T. J. Watson Research Center in Yorktown Heights, New York. The collaboration of these three researchers with other mathematicians and computer scientists in Jelinek's group would give rise to the modern theory of speech recognition.

4

The Power of Statistics

"Whenever I fire a linguist, our system performance improves," quipped Fred Jelinek during a natural language processing workshop in 1988.[1] Sixteen years later, in 2004, on receiving the prestigious Antonio Zampolli Prize in Lisbon, Jelinek told his fellow researchers why he'd parted company with linguists and how he'd turned to statistics to improve his speech recognizer.[2] This chapter retells his story.

An electrical engineer from what's now the Czech Republic, in the mid-1970s, Fred Jelinek headed up one of the most innovative, and at the time most controversial, speech recognition research teams at IBM's T. J. Watson Research Center in Yorktown Heights, New York. Whereas most other speech researchers were investing their hopes and efforts in the knowledge-rich AI approach, Jelinek and his team believed they could solve the speech recognition problem by using mathematics, statistics, and communication theory.

IBM had invested in AI research from the outset. IBM's Arthur Samuel, an AI pioneer and participant at the famous 1956 Dartmouth conference, had created one of the first and most successful checker-playing machines. IBM considered speech recognition to be a strategic technology for its business: typewriters were an important sector of its market, and a voice-activated one would be a "killer application" for the corporation.

Thus, in the mid-1970s, Jelinek's group found itself working on the recognition of sentences drawn from an artificially constrained language called "Raleigh" and represented by a large finite state network, similar to the one used in Harpy. An IBM manager with a background in linguistics insisted that the team adopt an AI expert system approach, complete with phonetic rules based on linguistic knowledge. And in fact the team actually built a phonetic-linguistic AI–based speech recognizer, whose word recognition accuracy came in at around 35 percent. After a while, the manager linguist departed the scene—it's not clear whether he was actually fired, left IBM on his own, or simply lost interest in speech recognition—and Jelinek's team approached the recognition problem in a new and completely different way. By using statistical models of phonemes derived automatically from data, and without introducing any linguistic expertise, the team managed to more than double the word recognition accuracy of its system, to 75 percent. And even when it then tried to cripple the system by representing words as sequences of characters, rather than phonemes—an extremely rough approximation for a language like English—the system's accuracy was still superior to the one built along pure linguistic lines. Embellishments aside, Jelinek's story is testimony to the power of statistical models as compared to pure linguistic knowledge when it comes to automatic speech recognition.

The statistical approach pursued by the IBM researchers represented speech recognition as a theoretical communication problem, also known as the "noisy channel model." Speech starts from a sequence of symbolic representations of words in the mind of a speaker. These symbolic representations then activate the vocal apparatus of the speaker to form the speech sounds ultimately conveyed as an acoustic signal to the ears of the listener or the microphone of a computer. Since we know so little about what happens during this transformation of the symbolic representations of words into an acoustic signal—speech—you might as well consider all that as noise added to the original message. From the point of view of your speech recognizer, all you're interested in are the words; everything else is simply noise. That's the assumption behind the noisy channel model, a hidden mechanism that takes a clean symbolic representation of words—the one in the mind of the speaker—and transforms it into an unclean, messy, speech-like acoustic signal, with all the problems you've already learned about. But what if you could communicate the words directly to the listener—or to a computer, for that matter—as a sequence of symbols? That would certainly remove a lot of ambiguities and interpretation problems. When you watch a movie in a foreign language you understand but aren't that fluent in, you certainly appreciate the subtitles, the written symbolic form of the spoken words. That makes your comprehension of what's being said much clearer. Unfortunately, in the course of normal conversation, you don't have access to the written symbolic version of the words, but only to their acoustic, messy, noisy version: speech. Figure 4.1 is a representation of the noisy channel model from a computer's point of view.

What the computer perceives of an utterance, or to use the communication theorists' term, its *acoustic observation,* is the output of the noisy channel when fed with a sequence of symbolic representations of words. A speech recognizer searches for the most probable sequence of words as symbolic or textual representations that, going through the noisy channel, generated the acoustic observation corresponding to the utterance to be recognized. If you're familiar with probability theory, you can understand this notion in terms of the fundamental equation of speech recognition.[3] But even if you aren't and you don't want to go through the math, you may still be interested in the intuition behind the equation. Let me first

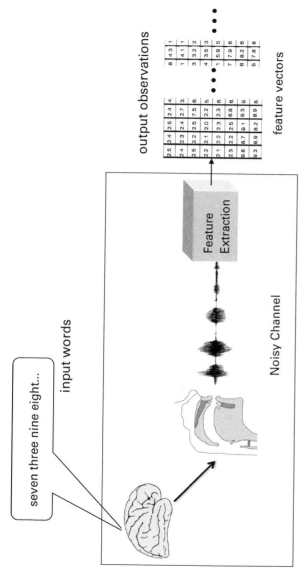

Figure 4.1
Noisy channel model.

explain that intuition with something simpler than language, a game involving dice and a prestidigitator.

A Game of Unfair Dice

Prestidigitators are sleight-of-hand artists who like to play tricks with cards, dice, and coins. In this game, you'll be dealing with a prestidigitator who likes to play with unfair or loaded dice. If you roll a regular or fair die, each of its six possible numbers will come up about one-sixth, or 16.67 percent, of the time (figure 4.2).

This corresponds to the most intuitive notion of probability, a number between zero and one, or a percentage between zero and one hundred, that reflects how often you expect to see a certain event occur in a large number of trials. A statistician would say that the six outcomes of a fair die are equiprobable. This is not the case with an unfair or loaded die, however, which has a bias toward one or more of the six possible outcomes, like the unfair die in figure 4.3.

If you roll this loaded die, you'll notice that sixes come up more often than fives—about 5 percent more often—and fives come up ten times more often than ones. Whereas there's only one possible fair die—one for which each number comes up about one-sixth of the time, there are many possible unfair dice, each one with

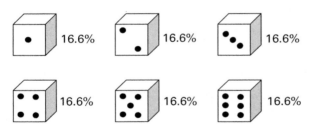

Figure 4.2
Probabilities of a fair die.

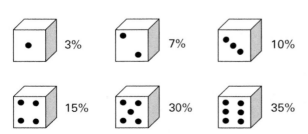

Figure 4.3
Probabilities for an unfair die.

a different level and kind of unfairness. In other words, fair dice are all alike; every unfair die is unfair in its own way.[4]

Our prestidigitator, Mr. P., uses his own set of unfair dice. He actually has boxes full of unfair dice. Let's say he has four boxes of dice, A, B, C, and D, and each box contains five dice. Each die in each box is unfair in its own way. Mr. P., being a prestidigitator, plays tricks with the boxes of dice, and he is extremely dexterous at changing boxes and dice between rolls without your noticing it. You're aware only of each roll's outcome; you don't know which die he used and from which box. Thus what you see, your observation, is a long series of numbers from 1 to 6,

1 2 5 1 4 5 6 4 2 3 4 1 6 6 2 1 4 5 6 2 3 4 5 1 3 6 5 1 2 4 5 2 6 1 3 5 . . .

The game consists in guessing which box he used for each particular roll. For instance, your guess might be

1 2 5 1 4 5 | 6 4 2 3 4 1 6 | 6 2 1 4 5 | 6 2 3 4 5 1 | 3 6 5 1 2 | 4 5 2 6 1 3 5 . . .

←   B   →←   D   →←   A   →←   C   →←   B   → . . .

Which is to say, you might believe that the first six outcomes (1 2 5 1 4 5) came from the dice in box B, the following seven (6 4 2 3 4 1 6) from the dice in box D, the next five (6 2 1 4 5) from the dice in box A, and so on.

At this point, you might also start to see a resemblance between the problem of guessing the dice boxes from a sequence of outcomes, and the problem of segmenting an input stream of feature vectors, or acoustic observations, into the words that generated them. Of course, with just the information you have, it seems quite impossible to guess the right sequence of boxes. Any guess is as good as any other. But imagine you know that Mr. P. chooses certain sequences of boxes more often than others. For instance, you may come to know that the probability of the sequence ABDABC is about 2 percent, that is, Mr. P. chooses it about once in every fifty games, whereas the probability of the sequence ACD is only 0.01 percent, that is, Mr. P. chooses it about once in every ten thousand games, and so on. Since there's no limit set by rules either to the number of boxes used in a single game or to the number of times dice are rolled from each box, there are infinitely many possible box sequences, each one with its own probability of being chosen, whether you know that probability or not.

So what would your strategy be, if you wanted to win as many games as you could and you knew only the probability of each possible sequence of boxes? Your strategy would be simple: always bet on the sequence with the greatest chance of coming up—the one with the highest probability. Even if that probability was only 2 percent, you'd win about two in every hundred games, which is twice as many as if you'd picked a sequence with a probability of 1 percent, and twenty times as many as if you'd picked a sequence with a probability of 0.1 percent. Note that, with the little knowledge you have, your actual observations don't help you at all. So you stick to your best bet regardless of any outcome you observe for any game. If you had more information, however, you could do better than that.

It's now time in our crash course on probability theory to talk about conditional probabilities. Whereas the unconditional probability of an event—also called its "marginal probability"—tells you how often it's likely to occur in a large number of trials overall, its *conditional probability* tells you how often it's likely to occur based on some other event that is correlated to it. For instance, if you know that the probability of rain on any given day in New York City is 7 percent, every morning, regardless of the season or the month, you'll wake up with a 7 percent chance of rain overall on that day. In other words, about seven out of every hundred days in the course of a year are rainy days in New York. But if you take into consideration the actual month, you could make a more accurate estimate of the probability of rain on that day. Thus, even though the overall unconditional or marginal probability of rain on any given day is 7 percent over the whole year, the probability of rain on a day in March may be as high as 9 percent, or as low as 4 percent on a day in June, a dry summer month. Conditional probabilities let you better estimate the chance of an event when you have evidence of one or more other events that are correlated with it. Let's go back to our dice and boxes game. When you didn't know anything other than the marginal probabilities of box sequences, your best bet was to choose the most probable sequence of boxes, regardless of any outcome you observed. But if you knew the probabilities of the box sequences conditional on the sequences you observed, by betting on the sequence of boxes with the highest conditional probability, you could significantly improve your chances of winning. To show you how this might work in our game, we need to get a little bit more specific about the dice in each one the boxes and about Mr. P's die selection statistics.

You may find it hard to believe, but the problem of winning the game of unfair dice as I've posed it closely resembles the problem of recognizing speech according to the noisy channel model. You've a hidden message, the sequence of words, in the utterance you want your machine to recognize, just as you've a hidden sequence of boxes chosen by Mr. P in the game you want to win. Recovering the message is the goal of speech recognition, just as recovering the sequence of boxes is the goal of the dice game. Unfortunately, you can't directly observe either the words in their symbolic form or the sequence of boxes, but only distorted, noisy representations of both. The noise added to the original message, in the case of the dice game, is the randomness of the choice of the dice and their outcomes; in the case of spoken words, it's the randomness and variability of speech, characterized by the sequence of feature vectors. What you want to do, for each dice game or each utterance, is find the sequence of boxes or words that has the highest probability. Not the highest probability overall, but the highest probability conditional on what you just observed: die roll outcomes in the case of the unfair dice game; feature vectors in the case of speech. But how would you solve this problem? With the dice game, you need to know all the probabilities that characterize the game: those of selecting a sequence of boxes, those of selecting dice in each box, and those of the outcomes for rolling each die in each box. You could compute, for a given observation of die roll outcomes, the conditional probability for all possible sequences of boxes, and all possible sequences of dice inside each box. But that would involve a lot of computation. Could you use dynamic programming here as well?

Statistical Language Models

Turning back to language and speech recognition, let's restate the problem in terms of probabilities. The sequence of words is the hidden message—analogous to the hidden sequence of boxes chosen by Mr. P. The sequence of words is what a speech recognizer doesn't know but needs to find. The recognizer "observes" a sequence of feature vectors corresponding to the frames of the utterance to be recognized—just as you observe a sequence of die roll outcomes. It has to recover the original message—the sequence of words—based only on what it's observed. Following the concept of the noisy channel and what you learned in the unfair dice game, a good strategy for your speech recognizer would be to find the sequence of words, among all possible sequences of words, that has the highest conditional probability, given the recognizer's observation of the feature vectors of the unknown utterance.

Not all sequences of words are equally probable: some are more probable than others. For instance, there's no doubt that, in general, you'd encounter the sentence "Lions are ferocious animals" more often than "Lions highway one telephone down." And unless you're a zoologist who specializes in African carnivores, you'd have a higher probability of hearing, "I need a flight to San Francisco," than something about lions and their behavior. And you'd definitely be more likely to hear the sentence "How're you doing today?" in your day-to-day communications with other people than something about flights and destinations, unless, of course, you happened to be a travel agent. Speech recognition scientists use the term *statistical language model* to denote a model that lets them rank all permissible sentences within a given set of words, a restricted vocabulary, in terms of probability. Traditional linguists make a hard and fast distinction between sentences that follow grammar rules and ones that don't, and they generally consider ungrammatical sentences not to be part of a language. On the other hand, language statisticians—often called "computational linguists"—generally *don't* make a hard and fast distinction between what is and isn't grammatical or permissible. To them, all sentences are permissible in a language, though some of them are more permissible than others. A statistical language model is a computational expression of this philosophy; it's a mathematical tool that, for any given sequence of words, will give you the probability of its occurring in a specific language.

Of course, the probability of a sequence of words in any given language depends on many factors. One of them is the context in which the words are used. In the context of a zoology lesson, for instance, you'd be more likely to encounter sentences involving lions, tigers, and other animals—they would have higher probabilities—than sentences involving home purchases, mortgages, and property rights. The opposite would be true if your context was a real estate sale. So anytime you hear about language probabilities, you have to think of them in terms of their particular context—their *language domain*. When IBM Research, the corporation's R&D division, developed one of the first statistical language models, it focused on the language domain of IBM's technical memos. That choice was no accident: it was dictated by the need to build a voice-activated typewriter, on the one hand, and by the availability of thousands of digitized technical memos, on the other, which IBM researchers could readily use to compute language probabilities. Creating a statistical language model, even in a well-defined language domain, is no easy task. There are so many possible combinations of words that, for all practical purposes, you can consider their number to be infinite. Even if you limit the vocabulary size of your speech recognizer to 1,000 words with sentences no longer than 10 words, you'd have $1,000^{10}$—that's 1 followed by 30 zeros—possible sentences: an impossibly large number. You couldn't list all the possible sequences nor even hope to find all of them at least once. Say you chose the language domain of documents about African carnivores. Although you could probably find "Lions are ferocious animals" in your collection of documents, you might not ever find "Lions are ferocious animals, but not as ferocious as hyenas," a perfectly legal sentence in the language domain of speech about African carnivores, with a reasonable nonzero probability. Counting is the basis of statistics; it's used to compute probabilities, but counting the occurrences of each of a practically infinite number of possible events is exceedingly hard, if not impossible. To arrive at the probability of every sequence, you'll have to infer it from some other set of events, a finite and countable one.

Words in utterances don't come completely haphazardly one after the other. Unless you're speaking complete nonsense, there's definitely a relationship between any given word in an utterance and the ones after it. Even though the outcome of the roll of a die won't tell you anything about the outcome of the next roll, that's not true with words in normal speech. If you listen to the first few words of an utterance, you can make a reasonable guess as to what the next words will be. Statisticians would say that consecutive outcomes of a rolled die are "independent events," whereas the consecutive words of a normal utterance aren't. They would also say that the probability of each word is "conditionally dependent" on the other words in the same utterance. Although the statistical dependency of all the words in an utterance on one another can be very complex, for the sake of simplicity and to make your calculations mathematically manageable, consider only the dependency between words that come one right after the other. For instance, if someone says the word "lion," there's a fairly high probability that the next word will be "roars," a lower probability that it will be "bikes," and very small probability that it will be "green." In 1948, Claude Shannon noticed that artificial sentences generated by his computer selecting words randomly more closely resembled normal English sentences when he made the probability of each word depend on the previous word, as the following example illustrates:

THE HEAD AND IN FRONTAL ATTACK ON AN ENGLISH WRITER THAT THE CHARACTER OF THIS POINT IS THEREFORE ANOTHER METHOD FOR THE LETTERS THAT THE TIME OF WHO EVER TOLD THE PROBLEM FOR AN UNEXPECTED.[5]

Though still nonsensical, the sentence reads much like a normal English sentence. Let's see what considering adjacent word probabilities means in practical terms, again using dice as an intuitive way to exemplify random events. Imagine that, instead of a computer, you have a bag of special dice. Each die has, not six faces, but as many faces as the number of words you may want to consider: one thousand, two thousand, even ten thousand. Imagine further that you've a large number of these special dice; that, on each of their faces, you've written one of the words from the restricted vocabulary of your speech recognizer; and that these are unfair dice, each in its own way. And each die is associated with a particular word: its "current word." Moreover, each is loaded—weighted—with the probability of each word to come out next after the die's current word. Imagine you take the die that has as its current word "the." Every time you roll it, you'll have a higher probability of getting faces with words that occur more often after "the," such as "lion," "red," and "man." Now and then, you may also get words like "that," "is," and "what," but that would be very seldom since the die would favor words that appear more often after "the." Among your special dice, you've one called "beginning" that's weighted with the probabilities of the words that appear first in a sentence. To arrive at the sentence quoted above, imagine that you are Shannon—but, again, you're using your special dice instead of a computer. You roll your "beginning" die and "THE" comes up. You go to your bag of special dice and find the one associated with the current word "THE." You roll it and "HEAD" comes up, by chance, although "LION," "HOUSE," or "SKY" might also have come up because they, too, are likely to follow "THE." You reach into your bag and pick the die associated with "HEAD," roll it, and "AND" comes up. You continue to roll die after die, picking a new die each time corresponding to the current word, until a face marked with a dot comes up—the period that typically ends a sentence in English. At this point, you stop. The result is the nonsensical sentence above, which looks rather like a normal English sentence. Of course, the real Shannon didn't use imaginary dice but a real computer that could simulate the rolling of a die by selecting words at random with different conditional probabilities, the probability of each word depending on the current word, the one just before it.

The results of Shannon's actual experiment suggest that, if you considered the statistical dependency of each word in a sentence with respect to the preceding one and did so for a sequence of preceding ones of reasonable length—a dependency may exist also with respect to not immediately adjacent previous words—you could create an extremely powerful mechanism that would function like grammar rules. Shannon did exactly that, calling his mechanism "*n*-grams," where *n* indicates the number of words considered in the probability calculation. In our imaginary replication of Shannon's computer experiment, you, in effect, used bigrams, the two words of the bigrams being the chosen and the preceding or, as we called it in the unfair dice toss, the "current," one. The *n*-grams most often used in practice, trigrams, take into account sets of three consecutive words: the dependency of a word on the pair of preceding ones.[6] To use trigrams, you'd need to have as many dice as there are possible pairs of words. So, if the restricted vocabulary of your speech recognizer was 1,000 words, you'd need 1,000 × 1,000 = 1 million dice. Since every one of these dice would have 1,000 faces, practically speaking you would need to store 1,000 × 1 million = 1 billion probabilities, in other words 1 billion trigrams.

Besides generating nonsensical but, for the most part, syntactically correct English sentences, you can use a full set of trigrams for a given vocabulary to compute the probability of any given sequence of words with a probabilistic mechanism called "the chain rule."[7] Assume you know the probability of any given word following any possible pair of words in the vocabulary. For instance, take the pair of words "the dog." You'd expect that the probability of "eats" being the next word to be reasonably high since "the dog eats" is a fairly common part of an English utterance, whereas you'd expect the probability of "computer," "green," or "the" being the next word to be rather low. If you had all the trigram probabilities for your speech recognizer's restricted vocabulary, you could, in principle, approximate the probability of any sequence of words, for instance, "My dog ate your sausage," by *chaining* all the appropriate trigrams:

Probability of "my" to start a new sentence multiplied by

probability of "dog" to follow "my" multiplied by

probability of "ate" to follow "my dog" multiplied by

probability of "your" to follow "dog ate" multiplied by

probability of "sausage" to follow "ate your" multiplied by

probability of "." to follow "your sausage."[8]

In practice, however, even though less than the number of all possible sequences of words, the number of trigrams is still large enough to be a challenge even for a modern computer. As you saw earlier, with a vocabulary of 1,000 words, a not uncommon, but actually quite small vocabulary for certain applications of a speech recognition system, there are $1,000 \times 1,000 \times 1,000 = 1$ billion possible trigrams—and, even after excluding low-probability trigrams, you'd still have nearly a billion probabilities to estimate.

Say you want to use your speech recognizer to build a voice-activated typewriter, or a "dictation" machine. Because digitized text is more available than transcribed speech, you can more readily estimate the probabilities of your trigrams from text, as the IBM researchers did. And you can reasonably assume, as again the IBM researchers did, that whoever uses your typewriter will speak in sentences like those in commercial or business letters. But if you want to find each one of your billion trigrams at least once, and assuming the least probable trigram is 100,000 times less probable that the most probable one—an extremely conservative assumption—you'd need to process more than 100 trillion words. And assuming that a document has on average 1,000 words, you'd need more than 100 billion documents—a number comparable to the total number of documents on the entire Web today. Even if you could somehow manage both to obtain 100 billion documents and to process them—and even though you restricted your recognizer to a modest vocabulary of 1,000 words—you might still not find some of the trigrams!

Thus, whatever reasonable number of documents you use to estimate your trigram probabilities, there'll be a lot of trigrams you'll never see in your collection and to which, at least in principle, you'll have to assign a probability of zero. But you can't honestly say that the trigrams you never see in your collection are impossible. Indeed, considering them impossible creates a real problem if your recognizer encounters one of these sequences of words in an unknown utterance. Since the chain rule multiplies all probabilities, and since zero times anything is zero, a single probability of zero will cause the final product to be zero, no matter how large the other probabilities are. Thus just one "impossible" trigram would make the whole unknown utterance impossible, which almost certainly isn't true. Nothing is ever zero in the world of probabilities. Even the most uncommon event has an infinitesimally small probability, but never zero.

So you have to come up with a nonzero number for all the trigrams you never see in your collection of documents. Luckily, statisticians have found ways to make more or less accurate guesses about events they've never seen before. They use different techniques that go under obscure names, such as "back-off," "interpolation," or "Good-Turing estimation."[9] To avoid the curse of zero probabilities, speech recognition scientists have tried all these techniques and found that, together with powerful statistical language models, they all work more or less fine, with different degrees of accuracy, even with vocabularies of many thousands of words.

You can now compute the probability of any possible sequence of words. As with the probabilities of the sequences of boxes in the unfair dice game, absent any other information, the best your speech recognizer can do is choose the most probable sequence of words, the one that would come up more often than any other possible sequence. But that would mean your speech recognizer would always guess the same sequence of words, no matter what the unknown utterance was, not at all the type of accuracy you want from a speech recognizer.

Luckily, you've information that your recognizer can use to make a better guess as to what was said; you have the observation of the sequence of feature vectors corresponding to the frames of speech in the unknown utterance. And your recognizer can use them to find the sequence of words that has the highest conditional probability given the very sequence of feature vectors your recognizer's just observed. Whereas computing the probability of a sequence of words is the job of a statistical language model, computing the conditional probability of a sequence of words, given the acoustic observation, is the job of a statistical *acoustic* model. Just as you needed to know the probabilities of the observed die roll outcomes in each box of dice in the unfair dice game, so you need to know the probabilities of the observed feature vectors for each chosen word of the unknown utterance. And like unfair dice favor certain number outcomes, each individual word is biased toward certain feature vector combinations. At this point, you need a powerful mechanism that correlates die roll outcomes with dice boxes and feature vectors with words of an unknown utterance so you can win the prestidigitator's unfair dice game most of the time and build a machine that correctly recognizes words most of the time.

The Hidden Models of Markov

The Russian mathematician Andrey Markov (1856–1922) developed a theory that's known today as "stochastic processes." A *stochastic process* is a mathematical model that characterizes—describes and predicts—the behavior of sequences of symbols based on their statistical properties. The Markov theory of stochastic processes is of particular interest when the symbols in the sequence show some sort of dependency on one another, like the words in a sentence. Markov extended his theory, known as the "theory of Markov chains," to the characterization of all possible sequences of events that depend on one another in a complex but often inscrutable way. A *Markov chain* can be thought of in terms of a finite state machine in which

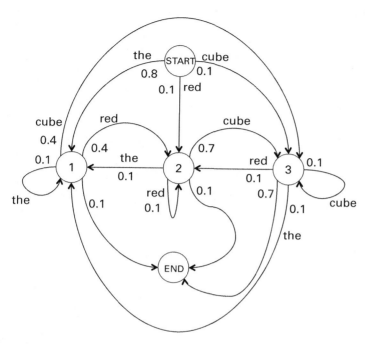

Figure 4.4
Language represented as a Markov chain.

there's a given probability for making a transition from each state to any other. The *n*-gram model you used to characterize sequences of words above can be represented by a Markov chain, like the one shown in figure 4.4, which characterizes the use of the words "the," "red," and "cube."

The numbers beside the transition arrows represent their probabilities: because all the transitions out of each state represent the set of all possible events out of that state, the sum of their probabilities is 1. The probability of starting with "the" is higher (0.8) than that of starting with "red" (0.1) or "cube" (0.1). Then, after "the," there's an equal probability of continuing the phrase with "red" (0.4) or "cube" (0.4), whereas there's a lower probability of adding another "the" (0.1) or ending the phrase (0.1). After "red," which corresponds to reaching state 2, there's a higher probability of continuing the phrase with "cube" (0.7) and a lower probability of ending the phrase (0.1). Following any path from START to END, you can determine the probability of each sequence of words, the most probable sequence being "the red cube."

To represent other complex aspects of speech such as sequences of acoustic feature vectors, however, you'll need more sophisticated mathematical tools than a basic Markov chain. When you speak, you generate sequences of acoustic events; your vocal tract changes its shape and acoustic properties. Each time it assumes a different configuration, with a different position of your tongue, velum, and the other moving parts of your vocal apparatus, it influences the probabilities of the sequences of acoustic events. You perceive the acoustic signal that's directly related to the feature vectors, but the exact configuration, or state, of your vocal tract for a given feature vector during the pronunciation of a word is hidden from you. You don't know what it is in much the same way you don't know which die the presti-digitator is using for any given die roll outcome. What you see is only the outcome. You can model the sequence of die roll outcomes or the sequence of feature vectors using a Markov chain, but you don't yet know how to represent the different hidden states that influence the probability of each observation.

The solution to this complex problem came in the 1960s and early 1970s from work by another mathematician, Leonard Baum, and some of his colleagues at the Institute for Defense Analysis (IDA) in Princeton, New Jersey. Baum extended the theory of Markov chains so as to characterize the dynamics of complex statistical phenomena, like the dice and boxes in the prestidigitator's unfair dice game or feature vectors and words in an unknown utterance. That theory came to be known as "hidden Markov models" (HMMs), where "hidden" refers to hidden states.

Let's go back to our prestidigitator and his unfair dice game. In particular, to get some idea about Mr. P.'s process of selecting and rolling once he's chosen a box, you need to make some assumptions. Let's say you're pretty sure that each box contains five dice, numbered from 1 to 5, and that Mr. P. selects them exactly in numeric order, always starting with die 1 and rolling each die until he's done with die 5. After that, he may change boxes or he may select the same box and start over again with die 1. Of course, since he may roll each die an arbitrary number of times, at any point in time, you don't know which box and which die is in use. What you observe are just the die roll outcomes—a long sequence of numbers from 1 to 6.

You can model the die-rolling process with a finite state machine or, better still, with a probabilistic finite state machine, like the Markov chain in figure 4.4. Each one of the five dice in a box represents a state of the machine. Unfortunately, the exact identity of the machine state at any point in time is hidden from you because you don't see which particular die is in use. However, you know that each one of the five dice is unfair in its own way, and you know exactly what the unfairness of each die is: the probabilities, which we'll call "observation probabilities," that char-acterize rolling each number on the die's six faces. How you got to know those probabilities is another matter, which we'll talk about later. For now, assume you simply know them. Moreover, assume you know another set of probabilities: the transition probabilities. For each state at each roll, you know the probability of

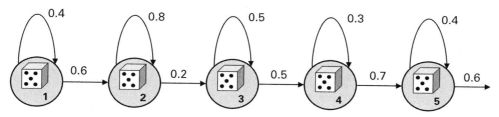

Figure 4.5
Unfair dice game represented as a hidden Markov model.

going back to the same state or moving to a different state—which is to say, you know the probabilities of Mr. P. using the same die again or putting the current die in the box and taking the next one. Figure 4.5 is a diagram of our probabilistic state machine, also called a "hidden Markov model."

Let's see how our new HMM can model Mr. P.'s game. You know the die-rolling process always starts with die 1, which is to say, in state 1. The prestidigitator picks die 1 and rolls it. Then he has two choices: roll the same die again or move to die 2. From the HMM's diagram in figure 4.5, you can see that the probability of rolling die 1 again—which corresponds to selecting the transition that goes back to state 1—is 0.4, meaning that, in a large number of games, 40 percent of the time Mr. P., having rolled die 1, selects the same die for the next roll, whereas 60 percent of the time he puts the die back in the box and moves on to die 2. Just as the observation probabilities are different from state to state, so are the transition probabilities. If all the probabilities are correct and truly reflect the probabilities of the prestidigitator's game, once you put this probabilistic finite state machine in motion, it starts generating sequences of outcomes that are very similar to those generated in reality by the prestidigitator.

But there is something more interesting that you can do with this machine than generating sequences of numbers. For any given sequence of observations, assuming they all are of die rolls for the same box, you can compute the most probable sequence of states that generated it. The mathematical details on how to do that are beyond the scope of this book, but know that you can use dynamic programming with your hidden Markov model to find, in an effective way, the most probable sequence of states that generated any given observation.[10] Thus, if you see a sequence of die roll outcomes, like

1 3 4 5 3 4 6 2 4 5 2 4 5 1 1 1 2 4 5 3 2 5 2 2 5 4 3

and you have an HMM representing the die rolls for a given box, and if you assume that the above sequence of outcomes comes from the same box, you'll be able to find the most likely sequence of states—or dice—that would have generated it. You'll also be able to compute the probability of the sequence among all sequences that might be generated by the same box—still assuming that the HMM is a true model of what happens. So, for instance, for the above sequence:

Outcomes: 1 3 4 5 3 4 6 2 4 5 2 4 5 1 1 1 2 4 5 3 2 5 2 2 5 4 3

States: ←   1   →←   2   →←   3   →←   4   →←   5   →

Probability: 0.0001245

Because hidden Markov models segment a series of observations into *hidden* states, you'll never know whether the segmentation performed by your HMM is correct. The only thing you can say is that, according to the probabilities of the HMM, and assuming it reflects the true probabilities, this segmentation is the most probable one among all possible segmentations. Again, it's a problem of alignment.

Hidden Markov Models of Speech

Let's see how can you use an HMM to represent speech units like words, syllables, or phonemes. Take a word, for example. What you observe of a word—or, better, what your speech recognizer "observes"—is a sequence of feature vectors: a sequence of columns of numbers representing spectral information. You remember from chapter 3 that this is what a spoken word looks like to a computer—or we could say, what it sounds like to a computer's ears.

2.5	2.4	2.5	2.4	4.8	7.9	7.7	7.6	5.8	4.3	1.2	1.1	0.9	0.5	0.2	0.1	0.2
2.4	2.3	2.4	2.7	3.9	7.4	7.1	7.2	6.1	4.1	1.3	1.2	0.7	0.3	0.1	0.1	0.1
2.5	2.2	2.5	7.5	6.9	7.2	3.2	2.8	3.3	3.2	2.6	3.1	0.8	0.4	0.3	0.2	0.1
2.2	2.1	2.0	2.2	5.3	6.5	5.8	5.3	5.4	3.5	3.7	3.5	1.1	0.3	0.1	0.2	0.1
2.1	2.2	2.3	2.3	6.1	7.1	6.5	6.7	6.1	5.9	5.5	52	1.2	0.6	0.4	0.4	0.3
2.3	2.2	2.5	6.8	6.2	7.8	9.9	9.9	8.7	7.9	6.1	2.1	1.5	0.2	0.4	0.2	0.4
9.8	8.7	9.1	9.3	9.1	9.7	9.9	9.9	8.6	8.2	6.3	2.8	1.1	0.3	0.3	0.3	0.3
9.3	8.9	8.2	8.9	8.7	9.5	8.7	8.5	8.5	7.8	8.1	8.3	7.1	6.6	4.2	3.9	2.8

Figure 4.6
Feature vector representation of an utterance.

Each column of numbers, each feature vector, in figure 4.6 is analogous to the outcome of a die roll. And just as you don't know what caused the six of a die to come up on a certain roll, so you don't know what governs the presence of each feature vector number in each column. Even if you knew the initial conditions of the roll of the die and everything else that might affect it, you'd find calculating the exact outcome of the die roll extremely difficult, if not impossible. So you rely on statistics. You take note of the outcomes of many rolls of the die, and you assign a probability to each number on the die. Turning back to speech, even if you knew the exact position of the tongue, velum, cheeks, and lips, the speed of the airflow, and the exact shape of the vocal tract of a speaker, you'd find it impossible to compute, from all that, the numbers in each column of the feature vector matrix of a specific instance of a specific word spoken by that speaker. So, again, you rely on statistics. You consider those feature vector numbers as random events governed by probabilities, much like the rolls of a die, and you characterize them statistically.

However, because you know that when you utter a word, your vocal tract moves from one configuration to the other, it's only reasonable to assume that whatever statistical property the feature vector numbers have, it would be different for each different configuration of a speaker's vocal tract. Looking at both in these terms, you can clearly see the analogy between the outcomes of the die rolls for a specific box and the feature vector numbers of a specific word. But, whereas each different die in the box is characterized by a different probability for each of all possible outcomes, which are only six, each configuration of the vocal tract can be characterized by the different probabilities of all the possible feature vectors, which, unfortunately, are infinitely many. But don't worry about that now; we'll deal with the problem of infinity later.

Each specific configuration of a speaker's vocal tract during the pronunciation of a word is analogous to the roll of an unfair die with infinitely many faces, each corresponding to one of infinitely many possible feature vectors. And just as you represented the sequences of die roll outcomes for a particular box as a hidden Markov model, where each of the states represented the statistics of a particular die, so you can represent a word as an HMM, where each of the states represents the feature vector statistics of a particular vocal tract configuration—and where each state transition represents the probability of drawing the next feature vector from the statistical properties of the current configuration or moving to the next one, as shown in figure 4.7.

As it did with the die rolls, knowing how to compute the probability of a feature vector in each state allows you to compute, for a given sequence, the most probable sequence of states that generated that sequence, and its overall probability: in

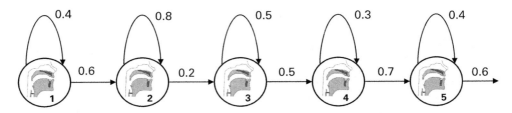

Figure 4.7
Hidden Markov model representation of a word where each state roughly corresponds to a different vocal tract configuration.

2.5	2.4	2.5	2.4	4.8	7.9	7.7	7.6	5.8	4.3	1.2	1.1	0.9	0.5	0.2	0.1	0.2
2.4	2.3	2.4	2.7	3.9	7.4	7.1	7.2	6.1	4.1	1.3	1.2	0.7	0.3	0.1	0.1	0.1
2.5	2.2	2.5	7.5	6.9	7.2	3.2	2.8	3.3	3.2	2.6	3.1	0.8	0.4	0.3	0.2	0.1
2.2	2.1	2.0	2.2	5.3	6.5	5.8	5.3	5.4	3.5	3.7	3.5	1.1	0.3	0.1	0.2	0.1
2.1	2.2	2.3	2.3	6.1	7.1	6.5	6.7	6.1	5.9	5.5	52	1.2	0.6	0.4	0.4	0.3
2.3	2.2	2.5	6.8	6.2	7.8	9.9	9.9	8.7	7.9	6.1	2.1	1.5	0.2	0.4	0.2	0.4
9.8	8.7	9.1	9.3	9.1	9.7	9.9	9.9	8.6	8.2	6.3	2.8	1.1	0.3	0.3	0.3	0.3
9.3	8.9	8.2	8.9	8.7	9.5	8.7	8.5	8.5	7.8	8.1	8.3	7.1	6.6	4.2	3.9	2.8

States: ←— 1 —→←— 2 —→←— 3 —→←— 4 —→←— 5 —→

Probability: 0.0000467

Figure 4.8
Segmentation into hidden Markov model states of a feature vector representation of an utterance.

other words, the overall probability for the HMM to generate the unknown word (figure 4.8).

In reality, when speech technologists build hidden Markov models of speech units—like words, syllables, or phonemes—they don't consider the actual number of different vocal tract configurations. They don't do so for two good reasons. First, because vocal tract configurations are complex, continuously changing phenomena, not simple, abrupt changes from one state to another, determining their exact number is extremely difficult, if not impossible. Second, and more important, the performance of HMMs simply doesn't depend much on either the exact number of their states or their exact correspondence with vocal tract configurations. As it turns out, a hidden Markov model with from five to ten states is enough to represent any possible word. The secret is in learning the probabilities of its states and transitions.

Training Probabilities

If you had hidden Markov models for each word in the vocabulary of your speech recognizer and good estimates of their probabilities, you could find which is the most likely to have generated any given sequence of feature vectors from an unknown utterance. But that's a big "if." Finding the right probabilities is at the core of what's called the "training problem." The solution to that problem emerged as one of the major achievements of Leonard Baum's theoretical work on hidden Markov models. In the early 1970s, Baum and his colleagues at the Institute for Defense Analysis developed a method that allowed them to estimate all the probabilities of HMMs from training data.[11] The IBM researchers then perfected Baum's training algorithm—known as the "Baum-Welch" or "forward-backward algorithm"—and used it to train HMMs of speech.[12] The training data consisted of lots of utterances of connected speech available in their feature vector representations. The forward-backward algorithm doesn't require any prior segmentation of an utterance into words, only the feature vectors of all words spoken in each training utterance. Being able to derive models of words, or of their phonetic units, starting from unsegmented, long lists of feature vectors might seem like magic. But it isn't; it's based on an iterative (repeating or looping) procedure that gradually converges to (arrives at) a segmentation that makes most sense from the probabilistic point of view: the optimal segmentation based on probabilities. I'll give you an intuitive description of how the algorithm can converge to an optimal segmentation later, but let's first see how hidden Markov models contributed to the creation of the first voice-activated typewriter.

Fred Jelinek at IBM and Jim Baker, initially at IBM but then at Dragon Systems, his own company, both wanted to build a machine, then called a "dictation machine," that would allow the user to dictate any kind of letter or document and have the machine type it out. To that end, the machine's speech recognizer needed quite a large vocabulary, one that would include all the words that a user might possibly use in a letter or document: thousands, even tens of thousands of words. But building a hidden Markov model for each of thousands of words was simply not practical for a commercial machine. It would have required far more memory and computation power than was available in the 1980s, even at IBM. More important, accurately estimating all the probabilities of each HMM for each word would have required a set of training utterances in which each word of the vocabulary appeared many times in as many different contexts as possible.[13] And for each new word added to your machine's vocabulary, the machine's designers would have had to collect new training utterances, create a new HMM, and train it.

Faced with the impracticality of using hidden Markov models for each of the words in a large vocabulary, the IBM and Dragon teams took another approach. They used HMMs of phonetic units and linked these together to form HMMs of words. This allowed them to add new words to their machines' vocabularies at any time without the need to create and train new HMMs for those words. By using the forward-backward algorithm, whose beauty was immediately evident to the followers of the statistical approach to speech recognition, the Jelinek and Baker teams were able to avoid the laborious manual segmentation of training utterances into the phonetic units they'd used for recognition: the algorithm converged to an optimal segmentation on its own.[14] They could feed it utterances covering all possible phonetic units of their choosing and let the computers crunch numbers until the algorithm figured out what the best segmentation of each individual utterance was for the purpose of estimating all the HMM probabilities.

But how does the forward-backward algorithm decide what a good estimate of the HMM probabilities is? It uses an overall optimization criterion. Its best estimate of the HMM probability is the one that maximizes the overall likelihood for the estimated HMMs to generate exactly the whole set of training utterances—or rather the sequences of feature vectors for all utterances in that set. But still, how can it segment utterances into phonetic units without knowing anything about them? Is there any segmentation information in a large set of utterances, assuming you know which words were spoken and you can therefore infer the sequence of phonetic units?[15] Yes, there's a lot of segmentation information in a large inventory of utterances, assuming that each segmentation unit appears in the inventory in a variety of different contexts.

To show you how a collection of strings of symbols can be segmented into units even if you know nothing about what constitutes each individual unit, consider the following example. I know practically nothing about the Thai language, except that, like Chinese, it doesn't use spaces between words. I went to Google Translate on the Web and asked it to translate the phrase "one man" into Thai for me. This is what I got:

I've no idea whether Google is right about the translation into Thai. Nor do I have any idea which Thai characters represent the word "one" and which the word "man." I don't even know whether "one" precedes "man" in Thai, as it does in English, or the other way around. Or whether the whole string of Thai characters represents "one man" as a single word that can't be broken into two words. Which is to say, I don't have any idea how to segment this string of characters into individual words. But now I ask Google to translate another phrase for me, "tall man":

ชะลูดมนุษย์

If I look carefully at both strings of Thai characters, I can see that the last four characters are exactly the same in both strings. I can therefore infer that those four characters correspond to the only word they have in common: "man." Making use of the fact that one of my words, "man," appeared in two different contexts, I can easily tease apart the Thai characters that correspond to it. I can now make a segmentation of the string of characters without knowing anything about Thai at all:

Let me try once more with a slightly a more complicated phrase, "one tall man":

ONE   TALL   MAN

Knowing what I know about "one" and "man," I can now try to spot these words in any string of Thai characters, even though the characters corresponding to the word "tall" are substantially different from those I saw before. If I believe that Google's translation into Thai is correct, I can assume that this version of the Thai word for "tall" differs from the previous one because of the different context in which it appears. So I've learned that "tall" in Thai can be written both as ชะลด and as สูง, depending on the context, even if I don't know why. Following the principle of the noisy channel, the principle of statistics as an ignorance model, I can just assume that the two versions of the word in Thai are statistical variations. I could go on to learn much more about the language, as long as I had a translation available for each phrase or sentence.[16] Given enough translated strings and enough patience, I could learn written Thai well enough to be able to decently translate any string of Thai characters into its equivalent in English words, without having read any Thai grammar book, and without the help of any dictionary. Which is to say, without having acquired any direct, explicit knowledge of the Thai language and based only on indirect, implicit knowledge derived from different contexts and a large amount of data. This is most likely the method that Jean-François Champollion used in the 1820s to decipher ancient Egyptian hieroglyphics with the Rosetta stone, which consisted of the same passage in three languages, one of which was ancient Greek.

Now you understand why, by using the forward-backward algorithm, your speech recognizer can find the best possible segmentation into phonetic units from a large number of sequences of feature vectors—as arcane to your recognizer as the hieroglyphs were first to Champollion or Thai characters were to me. You understand why, but understanding *how* would require delving into the mathematical complexity of the forward-backward method, which is beyond the scope of this book. However, even without doing so, I can give you at least a somewhat better sense of the method.

The forward-backward algorithm, as one of what are known as "expectation maximization" (EM) algorithms, works by *iteration*—by repeating a sequence of computer instructions a specified number of times or until a specified result is obtained.[17] In the case of a speech recognition machine, you can use the algorithm to iterate the processing of your training data, and you can revise and improve your initial segmentation model at any iteration (repetition), until you reach a certain desired outcome. For instance, you can take all the utterances in your training data and, starting with the easiest segmentation that comes to mind—dividing each utterance in equal time slices—you can use the algorithm to help you build an initial set of hidden Markov models for segmentation. You can then use these HMMs to perform a new segmentation—called the "expectation step"—which you hope will be slightly better than your first one. With the new segmentation, you can calculate a new set of HMM probabilities—called the "maximization step"—to make another segmentation, and so on. This iterative procedure converges to (arrives at) a set of HMMs that best capture the statistical essence of each segment and perform the best segmentation you can make, given the data you have.[18]

That said, there's something else you need to understand. If you work with dice or Thai characters, you've a finite number of symbols, and thus you can readily assign probabilities to all of them. Unfortunately, feature vectors are neither symbols nor finite, which makes working with them more complicated.[19] First, each feature vector consists of a dozen or more numbers, visually arranged in columns that mathematicians call "vectors." And, second, each number is not one of a finite set of distinct numeric outcomes, like the numbers on the six faces of a die, but one of an infinite number of continuously varying numeric values, like 1.3478 or 0.675. Mathematicians define the probability of such continuously valued vectors with what they call "probability densities," generally assumed to belong to categories of functions with defined structural properties, for instance, shape.[20]

Assuming you now have the mathematical tools you need to calculate the probabilities of feature vectors, let's proceed to how you choose the speech units each of your hidden Markov models must represent. English has roughly forty phonemes. So, in principle, with forty HMMs, your speech recognizer should be able to recognize every word in its vocabulary. But as you've learned, because of coarticulation between consecutive phonemes, each phoneme has different acoustic features depending on its phonetic context. Phoneticians speak of a "left" or "right context" referring to the position of a phoneme immediately before or after another in speech. Experimental work showed that forming HMMs to account for phonemes in all possible left and right contexts resulted in much higher speech recognition accuracy. But since the number of phonemes in all possible left and right contexts is, in principle, $40 \times 40 \times 40 = 64,000$, you'd never be able to find enough training utterances with enough combinations of words and phonemes to account for several instances of each possible phoneme in each possible context. To estimate hundreds of parameters for each phoneme in all possible contexts with a large, but always finite, set of training utterances turned out to be an engineering problem. Not surprisingly, engineers found ways to solve it by making assumptions, applying some approximations, and making things work in the best possible way, using the computers and the memory available at the time.

At this point, you've all the elements for building a machine that recognizes speech using a statistical method. What you did with word templates and finite state models of language, you can do with HMMs of phonemes and statistical models of language by putting them together, in pretty much the same way. You can represent statistical language models, trigrams, as special finite state machines consisting of words; you can represent words as finite state machines consisting of phonemes; and you can represent phonemes as finite state machines consisting of individual HMM states. And though these finite state machines, like the ones in Harpy, consist of states and transitions, unlike the ones in Harpy, they're characterized by probabilities. You can put all of it together in one giant finite state machine characterized by probabilities and use dynamic programming to find the path that produces the highest probability of having generated just the sequence of feature vectors that correspond to the utterance just spoken. That path corresponds to the recognized sequence of words.

You made it. The first time around, with word templates and finite state machines, your speech recognizer worked quite well. The second time around, with a complete statistical and mathematical framework, it works much better. You now have a machine that can crunch thousands and thousands of training utterances and produce thousands and thousands of parameters to compute the statistical probability of any possible utterance and that can give you the statistically most likely sequence of phonemes and words in the utterance just spoken.

The Invincible Approach

Although the hidden Markov model approach pursued by Fred Jelinek, Jim Baker, and their colleagues proved far superior to any other speech recognition technique ever attempted before, its dissemination and deployment in research centers around the world didn't take place immediately, even after IBM researchers decided it was finally time to start presenting their results at international conferences. For one thing, the mathematics and algorithms described in the IBM papers were hard to understand for researchers without a background in statistics and probability theory. Indeed, many in the field of speech recognition, as members of the artificial intelligence and linguistic communities, often had neither the preparation nor the confidence they needed to understand and believe in, much less to implement, the HMM approach. For another, many were skeptical that the problem of speech recognition could be solved by reducing the intelligent activity of speech to a bunch of probabilities, a mere matter of *counting*. Again, as with template matching and dynamic time warping, for a long time, linguistic and AI scientists alike considered the HMM–based approach to be little more than an exercise in engineering, having nothing seriously to do with accepted cognitive theories of human language understanding. "The brain doesn't use probabilities" was a typical remark among these skeptics on hearing about HMM theory for the first time. Not surprisingly, their interest in understanding and experimenting with the statistical approach was very limited, all the more so because the approach required large amounts of speech data, as well large amounts of computational memory and power, which only the largest and wealthier research centers like IBM's could afford. Finally, the many subtle implementation and engineering details not described in the IBM papers, especially those behind HMM training, weren't immediately obvious and were hard to reinvent.[21] All of this was more than enough to discourage even the most well intentioned researchers.

Larry Rabiner, who had worked at Bell Labs since his student days at MIT, joined the speech team headed by Jim Flanagan in 1962. After Pierce's ban on speech recognition research was lifted, Rabiner pursued active research on the template-matching approach, extending the dynamic time-warping technology to connected speech and speaker independence. In the early 1980s, Rabiner built the best-ever-seen digit recognizer and began to investigate IBM's hidden Markov model approach. After figuring out the math, he went on to write several papers about it. In 1989, as head of the speech research department at Bell Labs, Rabiner published a highly influential tutorial on HMM theory and its use in speech recognition.[22] By divulging the hidden Markov model approach in all its details in a clear and precise manner, Rabiner encouraged the speech research community at large to adopt what would become known as the "invincible approach" to the automatic recognition of speech.

Even though it was clear to many speech researchers in the mid-1980s that the statistical approach was the best approach yet, the performance of statistical speech recognizers was still not satisfactory. And even though different research institutions around the world embraced the statistical approach, the different tasks they undertook and the different settings, vocabularies, and languages they used made it impossible to determine whether real progress was being made in the field. Speech recognition scientists needed a common effort to raise the performance of their statistical machines to an acceptable level. That would come during the next era in speech recognition history, the era of incremental improvement and the struggle for higher performance.

5

There Is No Data like More Data

When researchers finally published the results of their template-matching and statistical methods in scientific journals and presented them at conferences, interest in speech recognition spread around the world like wildfire. In the early 1980s, in the United States, AT&T's Bell Laboratories, IBM, Bolt, Beranek and Newman, the Stanford Research Institute, MIT, Carnegie Mellon University, and Texas Instruments all established labs to actively pursue speech recognition research. In Italy, CSELT, the research laboratory of the national Italian telephone operating company (SIP) in Turin, built MUSA, one of the first real-time speech synthesizers, and went on to actively engage in speech recognition research. So did the University of Turin under the leadership of Renato De Mori, who then pursued a brilliant carrier first at McGill University in Montreal and then at the University of Avignon in France. In Germany, the Technical University of Munich and the University of Erlangen, as well as Siemens's and Philips's research labs in Munich and Hamburg, respectively, all conducted work in speech recognition. In Belgium, Philips's Brussels-based laboratory pursued both template-matching and statistical approaches and made important contributions to the field. In France, the France Telecom Laboratories in Lannion, the University of Nancy, and the national Computer Sciences Laboratory for Mechanics and Engineering Sciences (LIMSI) were among the French pioneers of the emerging technological research into human-computer spoken communication. In the United Kingdom, the defense research laboratory Royal Signal and Radar Establishment in the small town of Malvern and the Joint Speech Research Unit (JSRU) of the British Post Office in Cheltenham actively pursued advanced speech recognition research, as did the Swedish Royal Institute of Technology (KTH) in Stockholm, which had conducted extensive research in speech for many years. In Japan, Nippon Telephone and Telegraph (NTT) Laboratories and several Japanese academic institutions, like the universities of Tokyo and Nagoya, were precursors of modern speech technology research. In the 1980s and early 1990s, the research landscape of speech technology, and of speech recognition in particular, was rather broad and heterogeneous. Whereas, in the United States, IBM was achieving solid results with the statistical approach, and Bell Labs was tweaking its template-matching approach and making progress on statistical techniques as well, elsewhere around the world, different labs were pursuing many alternative approaches.

Leafing through the various volumes of the proceedings of the International Conference on Acoustic Speech and Signal Processing (ICASSP), you can get a glimpse of the history of speech technology.[1] For instance, whereas only ten papers on speech recognition were presented at the conference in 1981, ten years later, more than 100 papers were, at the conference in 1991. Between 1981 and 1985, roughly half of the papers discussed acoustic/phonetic rule-based techniques using the expert system approach; the other papers were dedicated to template matching—the brute-force engineering approach that had used dynamic time warping to produce the best results at the end of the 1970s. In the early to mid-1980s, only a very small, almost insignificant number of papers reported results on the statistical approach. After 1987, however, and especially after 1989 with the publication of Larry Rabiner's tutorial on the use of hidden Markov models in speech recognition, more and more researchers became interested in the statistical approach; the number of papers on template matching and rule-based expert systems quickly dwindled.

During the late 1980s, another approach to the speech recognition problem, one using what were known as "artificial neural networks" (ANNs), received quite a lot of attention for some time.[2] But, unfortunately, each research team tested its particular application of ANNs on its own test set, rarely compared its results with those of other ANN researchers, much less with those of researchers using other approaches, and tried to convince the whole speech recognition community that it had found the best solution to the problem. As in the decade before, so in the 1980s, the lack of rigor and comparability started to create a sense of dissatisfaction in the wider speech technology community.

It was not uncommon to find a large number of technical papers that didn't report any specific experimental results but instead offered vague qualitative assessments such as "We tried this technique and it worked." And even when the researchers followed the best tradition of scientific rigor, they performed their experiments in different languages, using different techniques, with different vocabularies, and on different tasks. How, for instance, could you compare 95 percent accuracy on speaker-dependent isolated-digit template-matching recognition in German with 85 percent accuracy on speaker-independent rule-based connected-word recognition in U.S. English with a 100-word vocabulary? Yet this was the situation with the experimental work on speech recognition in the 1980s. You could read hundreds of papers, go to a dozens of conferences around the world, and never learn which speech recognition technology actually worked best. A more rigorous approach was needed to compare different techniques. The missing link between theoretical research and practical results proved to be a common evaluation methodology based on a shared test set, or corpus.[3]

Sheep, Goats, and Digits

Among the first to take up the challenge of creating a rigorous way to compare different speech recognition systems, Texas Instruments had since its founding been involved in the mass production of semiconductors, such as transistors and integrated circuits, and their applications; indeed, transistor radios and hand calculators are only a few of the many low-cost electronic devices invented at its laboratories that reached virtually every household. The company had started to devote research resources to speech technology in the 1960s; in the 1970s, it developed chips for the production of synthetic speech, which it then deployed in 1978 in the first electronic toy with artificial speech.

Speak & Spell, which had a keyboard, a one-line display, a robotic speech synthesizer, and which played spelling games, was a big commercial success. It encouraged Texas Instruments to develop devices that operated at the other end of the speech chain: speech recognizers. Voice-activated calculators, household appliances, and toys were the most obvious applications of the new speech recognition technology. But, unlike a speech synthesizer, which needed only to speak with *one* voice, to be commercially successful, a speech recognizer needed to recognize a *variety* of voices. Thus, in the 1980s, Texas Instruments was one of the leading companies aiming to build *speaker-independent* machines, ones that could recognize the speech of any user at the same level of performance and with no need for specific tuning or training. Well aware of the difficulty of the task, George Doddington, a leading speech recognition researcher at TI, wrote in 1980:

Performance will continue to be inhomogeneous across various speaker subsets. The traditional, highly skewed distribution of performance among speakers will not be eliminated; recognition performance will always be better for men than for women; performance degradation will be experienced for unexpected dialects (in speaker-independent systems); and performance for experienced speakers will be better than for naïve, inexperienced speaker. However, improved recognition capabilities should provide greater ability for the user to self-adapt to the system to improve his recognition performance. . . . We at Texas Instruments symbolize the skewed distribution [of performance among speakers] by categorizing speakers as either "sheep" or "goats." The sheep, for whom the system works well, comprise the bulk of the population, say 80–90%. But the goats, despite their minority, have the greatest influence on the performance of the system, because most of the recognition errors are attributed to them.[4]

With the goal of creating a touchstone for comparing all the different techniques developed and experimented with around the world, in 1982, Texas Instruments compiled TI-DIGITS, a corpus of data for speech recognition experiments that would be used by laboratories for more than a decade.[5] The corpus was recorded with the highest possible acoustic quality and compiled with the utmost scientific rigor. Its speakers were selected to represent all basic categories of human speakers—adults and children, males and females—and all basic accents from twenty-one defined dialectal regions of the United States.[6] Each of the 326 speakers provided 77 utterances, which ranged from individual isolated digits—"zero" or "oh" to "nine"—to naturally spoken connected sequences of two to seven digits. In all, 25,102 utterances (77 × 326) were recorded and digitized between June and September 1982. Speakers were prompted, one utterance at a time, by a textual representation of the digit or digit sequence written in large characters on a computer monitor, for instance, "9 4 OH" or "ZERO 7 8 2."

TI researchers went the extra mile to make sure the corpus was error free—that the speakers uttered exactly what they were asked to and that the recordings were correctly labeled as such. Even a small number of mistakenly labeled recordings would undermine the accurate evaluation of speech recognition systems, some of which were reported to have already achieved recognition accuracies in the 99 percent range. So Texas Instruments verified the corpus by hiring twenty-six "listeners" to listen to all 25,102 utterances, one by one, and make sure that each utterance was exactly what it was supposed to be. Listeners were to transcribe what they heard, but because they, too, could make mistakes, TI researchers had each utterance independently assigned to three different listeners. The listeners were encouraged to produce accurate transcriptions by giving them a bonus if they made no mistakes. Only utterances for which the three listeners produced the same transcription, which had to exactly match the digit or digit sequence originally presented to the speaker, were considered correct. If even one transcription differed, the transcriptions and the utterance were inspected. In the end, the transcriptions made by the listeners differed for only 136 utterances: 30 because of speaker errors; the remaining 106 because of listener errors. That even well-motivated human listeners could make errors was used to set an acceptable error rate for machine speech recognition, in this case, a mere 0.4 percent (106 errors out of 25,102 utterances). Building a recognizer that would identify spoken isolated digits with that same low error rate was the ultimate challenge set by the TI-DIGITS corpus. Doing better than that was, well, superhuman.

The Accurate Definition of Accuracy

Measuring the performance of a speech recognition system is straightforward with isolated words. Anytime the recognizer correctly identifies the uttered word, that's a correct recognition; otherwise, it's an error. The percentage of correctly recognized words is called "word accuracy." So, for instance, if you test a recognizer with 1,000 utterances corresponding to isolated words drawn from the restricted vocabulary and it makes 995 correct recognitions and 5 errors, you can say that its word accuracy is 99.5 percent.

Unfortunately, measuring the word accuracy with connected speech—speech without pauses between words—is a bit more complicated. Imagine, for example, that someone speaks the following sequence of digits into a speech recognizer:

ZERO ONE THREE FIVE NINE

If the recognizer doesn't make a mistake, it will return exactly the same sequence. At least, that's what every speech recognition scientist hopes will happen. But, unfortunately, a recognizer sometimes does make mistakes. And its mistakes come in different forms. For instance, the recognizer can return the same number of digits as the original string, five to be precise, but one of them may actually be different, such as

ZERO ONE THREE NINE NINE

Here you can plainly see that the recognizer has wrongly substituted a NINE for the FIVE.[7] In fact, this is called a "substitution error." But that's not the only type of error it can make. For instance, one of the spoken digits can disappear in the the recognizer's output:

ZERO THREE FIVE NINE

Here the digit ONE after the ZERO is missing. In this case, we say that the recognizer made a "deletion error." Remember that the recognizer doesn't know how many words have been spoken, and there are no clear signs in the speech signal to help it detect with 100 percent accuracy how many words are in an unknown utterance. And, of course, not only can the recognizer substitute or delete digits; it can also *insert* digits that weren't actually spoken, as the OH in

ZERO ONE THREE FIVE <u>OH</u> NINE

Thus substitutions, deletions, and insertions are the three kinds of errors a recognizer of connected words can make. You no doubt found it easy to spot those errors in the above examples because there was only one error per utterance. See what happens when the recognizer makes more than one error in an utterance:

ZERO ONE ONE SIX FIVE NINE

Remember that the original string was ZERO ONE THREE FIVE NINE —five digits in all—and the recognizer returned a string of *six* digits. So there has to be at least one insertion error. And that's not all. Where has the THREE between the ONE and the FIVE gone? Did the recognizer substitute a ONE for the original THREE, or did it delete the THREE and then insert a ONE—and a SIX—instead? Which errors did the recognizer make: one substitution and one insertion or one deletion and two insertions? A scientific evaluation requires a certain degree of precision, even in the classification of errors. So let's consider all obvious possibilities for errors in the string returned by the recognizer:

ZERO (ONE inserted) ONE (SIX substituted for THREE) FIVE NINE

ZERO ONE (ONE inserted) (SIX substituted for THREE) FIVE NINE

ZERO ONE (ONE inserted) (THREE deleted) (SIX inserted) FIVE NINE

ZERO (ONE inserted) ONE (THREE deleted) (SIX inserted) FIVE NINE

The first two possibilities seem to be the most reasonable, and they are pretty much equivalent for the purpose of counting the errors. In both cases, the speech recognizer made one insertion error (the digit ONE was inserted) and one substitution error (the digit SIX was substituted for the digit THREE). The second two possibilities are somewhat redundant: both involve two insertion errors and one deletion error. So we choose the simplest possibility, which involves the smallest number of insertions, deletions, and substitutions (either the first or second possibility).[8]

Since counting the word errors of a connected-word speech recognizer isn't a completely trivial exercise, if you plan to conduct a lot of experiments, you need to automate the process of counting errors. As it turns out, counting the number and types of errors is an alignment problem: finding the best alignment of the recognized string with the string of words that was actually spoken. If you put the two strings on an alignment grid such as the one in figure 5.1, just as you did with a template and an unknown word on the alignment grid in figure 2.20, it becomes clear that you can also solve this problem with dynamic programming:

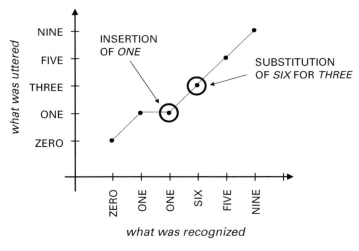

Figure 5.1
Dynamic programming alignment of a recognized word string with the correct one for the identification of errors.

If you remove all substitution, insertion, and deletion errors in a speech recognition experiment, what's left are the words that have been correctly recognized. That number gives us a measure that is now universally known as "word accuracy": the ratio between the number of correctly recognized words and the total number of words spoken in all test utterances, expressed as a percentage. For instance, in the above example, four words were correctly recognized out of a total of five uttered words: the word accuracy in this very limited experiment is thus $(4/5) \times 100 = 80$ percent.

Although word accuracy is the standard measure of the accuracy of a speech recognizer, depending on the type of application, it may not be enough by itself to correctly predict performance: other measures may be needed as well. For instance, for some applications, even a single word error in a recognized utterance may lead to failure. Voice dialing, placing a phone call by simply speaking the telephone number, is one example. If the recognizer substitutes just one digit for another, you'll be dialing the wrong number, even if the other digits are correct. And word accuracy by itself doesn't tell you how often you'll be dialing the correct number. Other applications where word accuracy alone doesn't tell you how often the application will perform correctly are, for instance, collecting an address and commanding a robot to move to a precise point. In all these applications, a more meaningful measure, called "string accuracy," is the percentage of utterances in which every word is correctly recognized. And when a speech recognizer is used as a component of a conversational system, another more meaningful measure is how often it gets the correct meaning, rather than every word that was spoken. That's called "semantic accuracy," and we'll discuss it when we talk about dialog systems.

Digit Wars

But let's go back to TI-DIGITS and the early years of speech corpora. When Texas Instruments decided to share TI-DIGITS with other research centers like AT&T's Bell Laboratories, Larry Rabiner, who had become more and more convinced of the superiority of the statistical approach, took up the challenge, armed with his great enthusiasm for conducting rigorous experimentation and for exploring nearly all the possible configurations of parameters. This is how he remembers those times:

Bell Labs had started to look seriously at connected-digit recognition and TI decided that a world-class database was essential to compare and contrast the various speech recognition systems that were being created at Bell Labs, TI, BBN, and other places. The choice of a standardized database won over a standardized testing procedure since there were just too many free variables for recognition testing to have any real meaning. In any case, TI graciously decided to make the TI connected-digits database freely available, and it became one of the driving forces for many of the improvements in speech recognition systems of the 1980s. Many labs used the TI connected-digits database as a bellwether of how well their systems worked. . . . The best working system [developed at AT&T and based on a segmental characterization of the digits] achieved digit error rates on the order of 0.2%. . . . [T]he DARPA community devoted a lot of time and effort to create a series of standardized databases including TIMIT, RM [Resource Management], ATIS [Air Travel Information System],WSJ [Wall Street Journal], etc., and the ASR [automatic speech recognition] community followed that for all common evaluations and tests. . . . Most groups used the TI-DIGITS database to show that their recognition technology worked on this common database and was scalable from small vocabulary digits to large-vocabulary natural speech recognition. Even today, almost every available system has some hooks to test the TI-DIGITS database to show that things are basically working correctly. . . . Perhaps the only negative aspect of the TI-DIGITS database is that it was recorded in a very clean environment.[9]

Yes, the TI-DIGITS corpus was recorded in an acoustically controlled—"clean"—environment, and, as such, it didn't represent the typical working conditions of a speech recognizer in everyday situations with background noise and other disturbances. But a few years had to pass before the speech recognition community started to look at spontaneous speech in less than perfect acoustic environments.

The Age of the DARPA Evaluations

The success of TI-DIGITS prompted the Defense Advanced Research Project Agency (DARPA) to reconsider speech recognition research again after the perceived failure of the Speech Understanding Research program in the 1970s. In 1983, DARPA launched a new, $1 billion, 10-year program to foster innovation and research in all technological areas related to machine intelligence and to transfer whatever technology advances were achieved to the defense industry. Naturally, speech recognition was one of the targeted areas. This time, however, DARPA set more realistic goals than those of the SUR program and, more important, seriously addressed the problem of evaluation. Thus, around 1985, following TI's example and with the help of Texas Instruments and Bolt, Beranek and Newman, DARPA started to compile a new corpus to train, test, and improve connected-speech recognition. With more than 25,000 connected-speech utterances using a restricted vocabulary of 900 words spoken by 160 different speakers representing a wide variety of U.S. dialects, DARPA's corpus came to be known as "Resource Management" because all the utterances were in the military domain of naval battleship resource management.

To create the corpus of utterances, the participating research groups defined a set of 990 basic sentence types from which you could generate a larger number of sentences simply by replacing some of the key words. For instance, by taking a sentence in a basic sentence type such as

WERE THERE MORE THAN <u>EIGHTY</u> <u>SUBMARINES</u> EMPLOYED IN <u>EIGHTY-TWO</u>[10]

and replacing the content words EIGHTY, SUBMARINES, and EIGHTY TWO with comparable words, you could produce many other sentences in that same sentence type, such as

WERE THERE MORE THAN <u>TWENTY-FIVE</u> <u>CRUISERS</u> EMPLOYED IN <u>SEVENTY-NINE</u>

and so on.

This time, DARPA asked the National Institute of Standards and Technology (NIST) to be in charge of the evaluation process to guarantee its fairness. Every six months or so from March 1987 to June 1990, NIST conducted formal evaluations, taking all possible precautions to ensure that conditions were identical at all the participating sites.

For each one of the six official and all subsequent evaluation rounds, NIST prepared and validated secret test sets, each consisting of a few hundred utterances that conformed to the same construction rules used for the rest of the corpus, which was considered to be the "training set." The content of each test set was kept secret until a few days before each established evaluation date, when NIST distributed the digitized audio files of the test utterances—*without* the correct transcriptions—to each of the participating labs. Of course, each lab could, had it chosen to, listen to and transcribe each utterance, but there was mutual trust among the competing sites that nobody would do that, reinforced by the fact that there was very little time between the distribution of the test utterances and the deadline for presenting the systems' transcriptions.

Each participating lab's speech recognition machines had to produce automatic transcriptions of the test utterances before the evaluation deadline, if they could. The test days were hectic and filled with anxiety as the labs mobilized all available computing power and asked people not involved in the DARPA contest to kindly stay off the computers. The labs tuned their recognizers to get the best performance, no matter how long it took the systems to recognize each utterance. Unlike the SUR project in the 1970s, Resource Management set no requirement for recognition speed. So there was no reason to cut corners to make the speech recognition machines faster and faster. The labs' systems could take as much time as they needed to get it right. The only time constraint was returning the transcriptions to NIST before the evaluation deadline, which was generally set a few days after the distribution of the test data. The best-performing systems often ran at a speed of a few utterances per hour on the most powerful computers of the time. At that speed, the test lasted for days of uninterrupted number crunching.

Upon receiving the transcriptions generated by the participants' recognizers, NIST used the correct transcription of each utterance to automatically evaluate the performance of each recognizer; it then reported the recognizer's performance scores for word accuracy and error rates by individual error type. A few weeks later, all the participants met to discuss the results, brag about their best accuracy, downplay their failures, lick their wounds, and, above all, share useful technical information.

NIST's evaluation results included many details for each competing system. Not a few labs submitted the transcriptions for more than one system. Table 5.1 is a copy of a summary table of test results as reported by NIST; it includes word accuracy ("Corr"); error rates for word substitutions ("Sub"), deletions ("Del"), and insertions ("Ins"); total error rate ("Err"); and sentence—or string—error rate

Table 5.1
NIST scores for different speech recognition systems in DARPA Resource Management evaluation

NIST-ID	Corr	Sub	Del	Ins	Err	S.Err	Arr. Date	Description
sys1	95.9	3.0	1.0	0.8	4.8	26.0	Jan-31	SRI Spkr-Indep Word-Pair
sys2	93.3	6.0	0.7	1.2	8.0	33.7	Feb-4	MIT Spkr-Indep Word-Pair
sys4	96.8	2.5	0.8	0.4	3.6	19.3	Feb-5	CMU Spkr-Indep Word-Pair
sys6	96.2	2.8	1.0	0.6	4.4	23.3	Feb-6	MIT-LL Spkr-Indep Word-Pair
sys7	95.7	3.3	1.0	1.2	5.6	27.0	Feb-6	BU-BBN Spkr-Indep Word-Pair
sys8	95.5	3.5	1.0	0.7	5.2	28.0	Feb-6	AT&T Spkr-Indep Word-Pair
sys10	96.7	2.3	0.9	0.5	3.8	21.0	Feb-7	BBN Spkr-Indep (109) Word-Pair-LATE
sys11	96.7	2.8	0.6	0.5	3.8	23.0	Feb-7	BBN Spkr-Indep (12) Word-Pair-LATE
sys12	95.7	3.3	1.0	1.1	5.4	27.7	Feb-8	BU-BBN (W/O BU SSM) Spkr-Indep Word-Pair-LATE
sys13	93.0	5.3	1.8	2.6	9.7	47.3	Feb-12	BU Segment Model Spkr-Indep Word-Pair-LATE
sys14	96.1	3.0	0.8	0.7	4.5	25.7	Feb-28	AT&T Sex-Modeled Spkr-Indep Word-Pair-LATE

("S.Err"). Note that the table also reports the arrival date of the results. Late results, marked "LATE" in the "Description" column, were deemed "suspicious" and generally not taken as "official" results.

The DARPA evaluations became the equivalent of beauty pageants for the speech recognition community. All labs wanted their systems to look good, and getting the lowest word accuracy made your lab an object of scorn. The entry bar kept rising at each evaluation, and it was more and more difficult to keep up with the best performance obtained by sites with a longer history in speech recognition.

With the Resource Management project, DARPA funded speech recognition research at places like Carnegie Mellon University, Bolt, Beranek and Newman, Stanford Research Institute, and MIT and used the NIST evaluations to gauge their progress. Other sites, like AT&T's Bell Laboratories, chose not to accept external funds, with the strategic intent of remaining independent of external forces, like the government. As strange as it may seem, the managers at Bell Labs didn't tell their researchers what to do but rather let them follow their natural curiosity. At the end of each year, they evaluated the researchers' performance by the number and the quality of their publications, the number of patents they filed, and their standing within the scientific community. So, out of this "spirit of independence," Bell Labs didn't take part in the Resource Management project, at least not at first. Highly impressed with the work done on connected digits by Larry Rabiner and his Bell Labs team, however, DARPA's managers felt that having them on board would give a burst of energy to the other project participants. So, in 1988, DARPA invited Larry Rabiner to one of the Resource Management postevaluation workshops and asked the Bell Labs team to join the project. The team members agreed to participate but declined to take any funds from DARPA and retained the right to pull out at any time and change the course of their research if they wanted to. Meanwhile, the other giant research laboratory on the East Coast, IBM's T. J. Watson Research Center, refused to engage in the DARPA contest altogether, although a few IBM scientists did participate in the postevaluation workshops from time to time.

The Kai-Fu Effect

Raj Reddy, the unsung hero of DARPA's Speech Understanding Research program in the 1970s, saw his team at Carnegie Mellon University achieve the highest accuracy scores in the Resource Management project. Since the end of the SUR program, Raj Reddy had devoted a considerable amount of his lab's resources to the problem of speech recognition. Some researchers in Raj's team continued to pursue the classical artificial intelligence approach, with rules and hand-coded phonetic and linguistic knowledge; others pursued new approaches such as artificial neural networks. In the mid-1980s, with a long tradition and vast wealth of knowledge in the field of artificial intelligence and expert systems, and despite the partial success of the brute-force engineering approach with Harpy in the 1970s, Carnegie Mellon University was drawn to the apparently more sophisticated knowledge-based techniques. Many scientists there and elsewhere, convinced that nothing of any scientific value could be learned from brute-force engineering approaches using dynamic time warping and hidden Markov models, believed that artificial intelligence approaches would eventually give rise to a speech recognition system with humanlike capabilities and perhaps even to a sound scientific model of some of the mysterious human cognitive processes.

Because Raj Reddy believed in hedging his technology bets with a wide diversification of his research portfolio, when a young Chinese graduate student named Kai-Fu Lee joined his group with the intention of writing a Ph.D. thesis on statistical methods for speech recognition, Raj Reddy took this as an opportunity to catch up with the bigger laboratories. He set as the goal of Kai-Fu's dissertation work (to be completed in 1988) achieving the best possible speech recognition results ever obtained using statistical methods. Called "SPHINX," Kai-Fu's system is still distributed today as an open source by Carnegie Mellon University.[11]

After making a thorough survey of all statistical techniques that had been used before, Kai-Fu diligently reimplemented and tested any he thought could yield significant improvements over the basic hidden Markov model technique. No one had ever compared all these techniques on the same system under the same experimental conditions. By intelligently combining any that showed significant incremental improvements, Kai-Fu achieved better and better results on the DARPA Resource Management corpus. He was reaping the benefits produced by the work of the whole statistical method community; along the way, he introduced new ideas and worked out the details for improvement. He entered SPHINX in every Resource Management evaluation, and his system quickly moved to the top rank.

At each new evaluation meeting, Kai-Fu Lee reported improved results, which created a renewed optimism among statistical speech researchers and an increased sense of confidence in the statistical methods. Kai-Fu's tangible and reproducible results convinced several labs to adopt his rigorous engineering process and compete with Carnegie Mellon in a race for the most accurate system. The competition pushed the HMM technology to higher and higher levels of performance. In less than three years, the total word error rate—the sum of substitution, insertion, and deletion error rates—was more than halved: from about 7 percent to about 3 percent.

The DARPA Resource Management task became, at the end of the 1980s, the new touchstone of speech recognition after the TI-DIGITS. If you wanted to prove how well your speech recognition system worked, you had to try it on one of the Resource Management test sets and compare your results with DARPA's official published results. Otherwise, whatever accuracy claim you made would simply not be taken seriously. Indeed, if you didn't publish your results on the Resource Management corpus, you could easily see your paper rejected at a major conference. That tangible and scientifically comparable improvements in speech recognition were plain to see prompted more labs and individual researchers—both funded and unfunded—to take up the DARPA challenge. Soon DARPA's postevaluation meetings became the place to be, the trendiest beauty contests for the speech recognition research community in the United States, and anywhere else for that matter.

The United States was not, of course, the only country to undertake advanced speech recognition research. To foster a greater exchange and dissemination of technological advances within the global speech research community and to accelerate improvements in speech recognition technology, DARPA decided to share its precious data with a number of foreign research institutions. Three European researchers in particular embraced DARPA's initiative: Jean-Luc Gauvain, a computer speech scientist from the French National Center for Scientific Research (CNRS); Hermann Ney, who was leading the Philips speech research lab in Hamburg; and Steve Young, who was working on his doctoral thesis on speech at the University of Cambridge and soon to become professor there.

Both Jean-Luc Gauvain and Hermann Ney had briefly worked at Bell Labs with Larry Rabiner and his team on the Resource Management project. Steve Young had been mentored by Frank Fallside, one of the most respected and well-known speech scientists of the United Kingdom. Gauvain, Ney, and Young, the new kids on the block, posed a serious challenge to the U.S. labs that had worked for years on the DARPA data. While the sponsors of the speech research program were trying to show their DARPA managers that the money spent on U.S. research was worthwhile, the young and unfunded Europeans were achieving increasingly better results than most of the funded U.S. labs. But, evidently, Charles Wayne, the DARPA officer responsible of the Resource Management task, managed that challenge quite well. So well that, at the end of the Resource Management project, DARPA would embark on a new and more difficult endeavor that would involve not only speech recognition, but also speech *understanding*—a revised and improved version of the not-so-successful SUR project of the 1970s.

Flying from New York to Denver

After a few years of continuous incremental improvement the speech recognition research community and DARPA lost interest in the Resource Management project. European researchers and a few others were consistently getting the top results and driving innovations. Everyone was doing pretty much the same thing, and, as the improvement curve leveled out, so did the difference in results achieved by the various laboratories. More and more work was needed to gain smaller and smaller fractions of a percent in accuracy; the technological improvements to achieve infinitesimal increments of performance were of little scientific value. The Resource Management task was a fairly constrained and contrived one, and getting closer and closer to 100 percent accuracy didn't bring the research community any closer to solving the general speech recognition problem. Moreover, it was clear that the Resource Management task was far from representative of a real speech recognition application. All the utterances in the corpus belonged to a well-defined, limited set of very predictable sentences defined beforehand by a small number of rules and carefully read by the same set of speakers. The words, the grammar, the speaking style, and the acoustic conditions were completely controlled, a situation almost never encountered in real life. Besides, the task did not represent an interesting application. Reading a sentence from a predetermined list and having the speech transcribed by a computer to obtain the original sentence, though impressive at first, certainly wasn't very useful.

Based on these considerations, DARPA decided it was time to move on to a new and harder speech recognition project, one closer to a more realistic application than that of accurately transcribing sentences read from a predetermined set. The new project, which DARPA funded from 1989 to 1995, was called "ATIS" (*Air Travel Information System*).[12] At its core were two concepts that differentiated it from Resource Management: *understanding,* not just recognizing, spoken words; and having those words be part of *spontaneous,* as opposed to read, speech.

The goal of the ATIS project was that of building a machine that would provide answers to spoken requests about commercial flight travel such as departure and arrival times, itineraries, fares, and anything else in a typical database used by travel agents. People in need of travel information would speak naturally to a computer and receive answers to their requests on its display. Imagine, for instance, you're a traveler who wants to fly to Denver from New York; you approach an ATIS–equipped computer and say,

I'm looking for a flight from New York to Denver, tomorrow, early in the afternoon.

ATIS can't talk to you nor can it ask you questions since neither of those capabilities was required by the project. The only thing it can do is display simple yes or no answers, numbers, or tables that include all the information—and only that information—related to your requests (table 5.2).

Not being familiar with the abbreviations in table 5.2, you might ask a follow-up question like

What do LGA and JFK mean?

Table 5.2
ATIS machine response to "I'm looking for a flight from New York to Denver, tomorrow, early in the afternoon."

DEP_CITY	DEP_AIRPORT	ARR_CITY	ARR_AIRPORT	AIRLINE	FLIGHT_N	DEP_TIME
NNYC	JFK	DDEN	DEN	CO	156	12:37
NNYC	LGA	DDEN	DEN	DL	8901	12:58
NNYC	LGA	DDEN	DEN	DL	8903	13:45
NNYC	JFK	DDEN	DEN	AA	578	13:57
NNYC	LGA	DDEN	DEN	UA	187	14:15
NNYC	JFK	DDEN	DEN	DL	987	15:27

Table 5.3
ATIS machine response to "What do LGA and JFK mean?"

Airport ID	Airport Name
JFK	John Fitzgerald Kennedy International Airport
LGA	La Guardia Airport

Table 5.4
ATIS machine response to "What's the distance between them and New York City?" based on the context of examples in tables 5.2–5.3

Airport ID	City Name	State Name	Distance
JFK	New York	New York	25
LGA	New York	New York	35

And a properly built ATIS machine would come back with the proper answer, as shown in table 5.3.

Not yet satisfied, as a traveler who knows that both La Guardia and JFK are in New York, you may want to find out which one is closer to downtown:

What's the distance between them and New York City?

And the ATIS machine would come back, promptly, with another table (table 5.4):

And so on, until you're finally satisfied with the responses to all your travel requests.

To make the problem more challenging and not artificially constrained, DARPA didn't impose any limitations on what users could say and how they said it as long as their requests were relevant to the information in the flight database. If a request could be answered with that information, any machine built by the labs participating in the ATIS project had to understand it and generate an appropriate answer. If it didn't, that was considered a negative point.

Say you want to build an ATIS machine. The first task your machine needs to perform is straightforward: it needs to recognize the words spoken to it. However, the ATIS project posed a much greater challenge than the Resource Management project: the users' vocabulary and grammar are neither fixed nor defined in advance, the users' sentences are spontaneous and neither read nor drawn from a finite set of possibilities. And your machine needs not only to get all the spoken words right; it also needs to provide the right answer to every request. Which is to say, your ATIS machine needs to *understand* the words spoken to it. Understanding is complex, and it's often unclear what it means in general terms. But, in the well-defined and restricted context of the ATIS project, *understanding* means being able to use the words in the uttered sentence to form a query to the flight information database, extract an appropriate yes or no answer, a number, or a table, and present it to the user. Though simpler than understanding in general terms, understanding in this narrower sense isn't trivial at all.

Formally, a database is a collection of data typically divided into many tables that capture different aspects of a domain. For instance, in the air travel domain, there's one table with flight times, another with information about airports, still another with fares, and a fourth with on-board services, such as what type of meal is served on each flight. To extract the proper data from a database, your machine needs to first select the right tables and link them with an operation called "join," then extract the required information. For example, asked to find the cheapest flight from New York to Denver that leaves before eight in the morning and serves breakfast, your machine needs to search the table with flight times and find the flights from New York to Denver that leave before 8 a.m. Then it needs to search a different table to see which of the flights leaving before 8 a.m. and going from New York to Denver serve breakfast. And, finally, it needs to search the fare table and find the flight on its now-reduced list that has the lowest fare. Using modern database technology, your machine can perform all these operations with a single command in a computer language called "SQL" (Structured Query Language; pronounced like the word "sequel").[13] SQL may look quite cryptic to the nonspecialist:

SELECT DEP_CITY, DEP_AIRPORT, ARR_CITY, ARR_AIRPORT, AIRLINE, FLIGHT_N, DEP_TIME, FARE **FROM** FLIGHT, FARE, SERVICE **WHERE** FLIGHT.DEP_CITY = "NNYC" **AND** FLIGHT.ARR_CITY = "DDEN" **AND** FLIGHT.DEP_TIME < 800 FLIGHT.FLIGHT_ID=SERVICE.FLIGHT_ID **AND** SERVICE.MEAL=BREAKFAST **AND** FLIGHT.FLIGHT_ID=FARE.FLIGHT_ID **AND** FARE.CLASS="ECONOMY" **AND** FARE.PRICE=MIN();

but any computer expert with minimal training in databases and SQL can easily translate an English sentence like

Find the cheapest flight from New York to Denver that leaves before eight in the morning and serves breakfast

into the above SQL command. Well, your ATIS machine has to be able to do the same. So *understanding,* in the context of the ATIS project, means being able to translate a sequence of words in natural spontaneous English into the appropriate formal SQL command that will retrieve the information needed to provide the right answer. Although it may seem contrived, this definition of understanding is quite general. Indeed, understanding, in general terms, may be seen as an act of translation between two languages. In the case of your ATIS machine, the input is natural language, the language spoken naturally by humans. The output is a formally defined language, like SQL. There are many ways, perhaps infinitely many ways, to phrase the above request in English, but there are only one or a few ways to express the same request in a formal language like SQL. To convert natural language, no matter how imprecise, vague, or ambiguous, into a precise, inflexible, unambiguous formal language—the language spoken by machines— requires your machine to understand the meaning of the former and translate it into the latter. That's what the speech understanding module of an ATIS machine is meant to do.

It became immediately clear to everyone in the ATIS community that the lack of any linguistic restrictions on the utterances and their spontaneous nature posed serious problems for both the speech recognition and the speech understanding modules. But the challenge for ATIS machines wasn't just to translate each individual natural language sentence into SQL, but to follow entire conversations with their users through several exchanges, as in a dialog between humans.

We humans are very efficient at dialog. We—at least most of us—tend to avoid repeating the same information over and over. There's no need to repeat things we've already said in previous exchanges; and we remember what we've heard—at least most of us do—and use that as a context to interpret subsequent exchanges. ATIS machines were supposed behave in the same way. For instance, at a certain point, after the initial request you made earlier, you might say:

Show me the cheapest one from the closest airport

It would be immediately obvious to a human listener that your request actually means

Show me the cheapest flight among all flights that go from New York to Denver tomorrow early in the afternoon and leave from the airport closest to New York City.

But, of course, there's no need for you to say all that because you've said it once already. That information—what you've said already—is what's known as "context." There are many linguistic theories about how we humans use and maintain the context of a conversation, but building a machine that uses it as well as we do was yet another ATIS challenge.

Thus, after recognizing and understanding spontaneous speech while taking into account the context of the whole conversation, the final challenge for the ATIS machines was to correctly translate all that into SQL to extract the needed information from the database. It turned out that the exact definition of this problem was so complex it required a committee of experts working together for the whole duration of the project to solve.

Searching for the Right Metrics

TI-DIGITS and Resource Management projects had clearly shown the advantage of having a common evaluation corpus in achieving accurate word recognition. That advantage was clear for ATIS, but word accuracy was not the only measure of performance. Understanding each user request—not simply recognizing each of its words—and providing the right answer to it were the ultimate goals of ATIS. In principle, you can think of an ATIS machine as composed of two distinct modules: the speech recognizer and the natural language understanding module (figure 5.2).

As you know, the speech recognizer transforms speech into text, a word-for-word transcription of each input utterance.[14] The second module, again in principle, takes the transcribed speech and understands its words in the context of what the user previously said to arrive at an appropriate answer. So, still in principle,

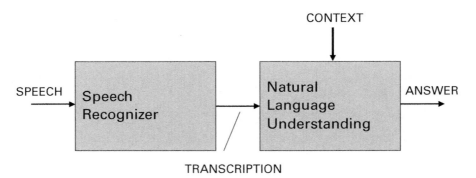

Figure 5.2
Schematic diagram of a spoken language understanding system.

although the overall performance of your ATIS machine is how accurately it answers spoken user requests, you can also measure the individual performance of each module:

• Speech recognition alone: how accurately does your machine's speech recognizer module recognize speech, that is, what's its average word accuracy?
• Natural language understanding alone: how accurately does your machine's natural language understanding module understand input text (assuming that text is a faithful word-for-word representation of what the user said)?

Breaking down the speech understanding process into two distinct modules, one feeding its result to the other, is a somewhat arbitrary design choice. Indeed, there's no guarantee that building a speech understanding machine with two separate modules—a speech recognizer followed by a text understanding system—is the best approach, but doing so certainly simplifies the design, or at least the conceptual architecture, of the machine. On the other hand, when it comes to us humans, recognizing speech and understanding it, far from being separable, distinct activities, are almost certainly intermingled in our brains. As a proof of that, we find it extremely difficult, if not impossible, to accurately transcribe words we don't understand, such as words in a foreign language we don't speak. This is because we can't recognize speech we don't understand, thus recognition can't be fully separated from understanding. In contrast, separating speech recognition and speech understanding into two distinct modules makes it easier to build a machine where the two activities must work together.[15]

Although the speech technology community had learned how to use word accuracy to characterize the performance of a speech recognizer, it had had almost no experience in formally measuring understanding accuracy. To do that, in principle, you had to compare the output of your machine's second module with a reference representation of the *meaning* of the input utterance. But whereas the symbolic representation of words, the written or textual form of an utterance, is a universal concept about which we can all easily agree, there's no universal concept of the meaning representation of words, and no universally accepted way to express that representation.

Mad Cows in the Speech Understanding Field

Clearly, the ATIS project needed data, lots of data. To collect it, a working group called "MADCOW" (Multi-Site *A*TIS *D*ata *CO*llection *W*orking Group) was formed in 1991, which included all the major participating ATIS sites: AT&T's Bell Laboratories, Bolt, Beranek and Newman, Carnegie Mellon University, MIT, Stanford Research Institute (SRI), and Paramax (formerly Unisys).[16] The MADCOW group also included the National Institute of Standards and Technology (NIST), which, as it had been in the Resource Management collection effort, was to be responsible for data validation and distribution and for supervising and running the whole evaluation process in a fair and scientific fashion. A separate group at the Stanford Research Institute was responsible for the annotation of data.

Most MADCOW sites contributed directly to data collection. On February 1992, there were more than 15,000 utterances available; by the end of the project in 1995, the number had grown to more than 25,000.[17] Unfortunately, however, each site implemented its own collection procedure. Although MADCOW was aware of the importance of standards and consistency, the difficulty of creating, agreeing upon, and enforcing such standards within the aggressive timelines of the project meant giving the collecting sites a lot of latitude. Although all subjects at every collection site were led to believe they were talking to a fully automatic system and some sites did indeed use intermediate versions of their fully automated ATIS machines without any human intervention, others used human operators who acted in real time as if they were speech recognizer and speech understanding systems. At some sites, the human operators transcribed the utterances in real time and then fed them to automated natural language understanding modules that provided the answers back to the subjects. At other sites, the operators listened to the utterances spoken by the subjects and quickly interacted with the database in order to show the correct answers on the subjects' displays.

The MADCOW team took the data collection task very seriously. They even instituted a prize for the *worst,* most ungrammatical and disfluent utterance in the whole corpus. That utterance received the honor of being printed on the back of the MADCOW T-shirt distributed to all the participants in the ATIS program (figure 5.3).

Human-machine interaction researchers had long used humans in the collection of data while making their experimental subjects believe they were interacting with machines. Researchers often needed human-machine interaction data even before they could actually build a machine, to get useful information about how to design it or about how humans would react to certain design choices. Because they didn't have the machine ready, their only choice was to use humans to replace it or part of it in a methodology known as the "Wizard of Oz" (WoZ).[18] Subjects were given a scenario with a problem to solve, for instance:

You want to fly from Boston to San Francisco on the first weekend in December (Saturday, December 5 or Sunday, December 6). You'd like to return to Boston on the following Wednesday, in the evening if possible. Your main concern is that all the flights be on Continental, since you're trying to maximize your frequent-flyer miles. Identify one flight in each direction that you can take.

Figure 5.3
ATIS T-Shirt. Artwork by Lynette Hirschman and David Goodine; photo courtesy of Richard Schwartz of Bolt, Beranek and Newman.

In writing the scenarios, researchers made every effort to avoid leading the users. The idea was not to suggest to users *what* to say, but to give them a problem to solve, and hope they'd express themselves naturally and in their own language.

That turned out to be difficult when scenarios were presented textually, as they were in ATIS. And, indeed, after a thorough analysis of the recoded interactions, one of the participating sites found that there were sequences of ten or more words that appeared with an improbably high frequency. Those sequences matched exactly one of the sentences used in the scenarios.

While the subjects tried to solve their travel problems with successive requests, the experimental systems, or rather the human Wizards in the other rooms, provided answers that were sent to the subjects' displays. Eventually all the utterances in all the interactions with the subjects were recorded, transcribed, and annotated by human listeners with their corresponding meaning representations. But to understand what the correct meaning representation of each utterance was, we need to talk first about how ATIS researchers set about defining the air travel domain.

The Principles of Interpretation

Evaluating speech recognition accuracy is intuitively obvious because it's easy to agree on what words were actually spoken, what words a recognizer came up with, and the difference between the two. On the other hand, evaluating how well a system decodes the meaning of spoken words can generate a lot of arguments because the meaning of what we say is often quite ambiguous. But it all goes back to understanding what understanding is. Take a typical ATIS request:

I'm looking for a flight from New York to Denver, tomorrow, early in the afternoon.

Ask someone what this sentence means, and most likely the answer will be another sentence, usually much longer, where some of the original words are replaced with others to make their meaning clearer. For instance:

It means that the person asking wants to find a way to fly from a New York airport to one in Denver, and wants to travel tomorrow after twelve noon, but not much after that, say no later than 3 p.m.

It turns out it's not easy to describe the meaning of a simple sentence without making it longer and more complex.[19] If you want to do better than that, and if you know that most of your sentences are in the same domain (for instance, the air travel domain), you can establish a set of conventions to define the meaning of each sentence. Of course, you and whoever's going to use these conventions have to agree on them, and getting a large group of people to agree can take a long time, especially when they have different interests and agendas. To establish this set of conventions, you have to first define the objects of the world you're talking about and all the possible relationships between them. And of course you have to convince your peers that these are the right objects and relationships. Once that's done, you can describe any sentence by specifying the objects and the relationships between them that it establishes. So, for instance, you could formally represent the above sentence and many others with the same meaning with a formal expression such as

ACTION: SEARCH FLIGHTS

FLIGHT_DEPARTURE_CITY: NEW YORK

FLIGHT_ARRIVAL_CITY: DENVER

FLIGHT_DEPARTURE_TIME: LATER THAN 12PM

FLIGHT_ARRIVAL_TIME: EARLIER THAN 4PM

But, of course, you have to clearly define, without any ambiguity, what you mean by ACTION, FLIGHT_DEPARTURE_CITY, and all the other elements of the formal representation above, as well as how they relate to natural language expressions. And that has to be done in such a way that anyone looking at a natural language sentence and its formal representation can say without any doubt that the sentence means exactly what the representation says it means.

So, let's start by defining the main objects of ATIS: cities, airports, and flights.

Cities and Airports

Cities are identified by names. Cities are served by airports. A city may have more than one airport, and an airport may serve more than one city. Airports have names, too.

Flights

Flights transport people between a departure and an arrival airport. Flights are identified by the name of their operating carrier (the airline) and by a number that may or may not be unique. Flights transport people with aircrafts. Flights can be nonstop, direct, or connecting. Nonstop flights don't make any intermediate stops, whereas direct flights can make some stops, but usually don't change their flight numbers. All other flights are called "connecting flights." Sometimes meals, such as breakfast, lunch, a snack, or dinner, are served on flights.

Of course, this is just the beginning because you still have to define, clearly and without any ambiguity or vagueness, what a flight number is, what a carrier is, what ground transportation is, and so on. As you can readily see, it's extremely difficult to cover all the possibilities and exceptions, even in a restricted and well-defined domain like air travel. What about flights that are served by one carrier but have two different carrier names and two different numbers? Or multiple-leg flights? Or flights with different itineraries that happen to have the same flight number? The list of needed definitions and of exceptions to them, although certainly finite, seems endless. Indeed, trying to define everything in a clear, formal, and unambiguous way seems very much like opening a can of worms.

Clearly defining the objects and relationships of the air travel world requires the same skills that lawyers employ when writing legal agreements and contracts. All of this has to be done in a precise language that leaves little or no room for doubt or ambiguity: a formal language as opposed to intrinsically ambiguous natural language. Just like legal language, it has to be clear, almost pedantic, using terms that require no further explanation and are agreed upon by all the parties involved. But just as contracts, legal agreements, and laws, whether on purpose or not, can leave some room for ambiguity and can be interpreted in different ways, so can air travel definitions be interpreted in more than one way. And if you want to come up with a process that leads to an objective assessment of the understanding capabilities of an automatic system, you have to do the best you can to rule out ambiguities and cover all possible exceptions knowing that arguments will always be possible.

The researchers involved in the ATIS project soon realized that, to accurately evaluate and compare the understanding capability of systems built by the various labs, they had to define the air travel domain with the utmost lawyerly precision. To that end, they put together an ad hoc committee to create, maintain, and update the Principles of Interpretation (PofI) document. It took the committee more than two years of weekly conference calls and more than eighty interpretation rules to bring the PofI document to a final acceptable form.

Reading this document gives you an idea of how much what you say depends on conventions you almost never define explicitly. For instance, if you say something like

I want to fly from New York to Washington tomorrow, early in the afternoon,

you're making an underlying assumption that your listeners share most of your linguistic conventions. You assume that "to fly" means "to take a commercial flight," and not, for instance, "to fly by hang glider." Moreover, the common expressions "from New York" and "to Washington" are conventions that actually mean "from an airport reasonably close to New York" and "to an airport reasonably close to Washington." Flights aren't between cities but between airports. Everyone knows that. But what about "early in the afternoon"? What does that mean? Is 2 p.m. early in the afternoon? Is 3 p.m.? And, on the other hand, what about a flight scheduled for 12:00 noon sharp? Does it qualify as "early in the afternoon"? Afternoon starts "after" noon, which is, technically speaking, any second after 12:00 noon. Well, go ahead (as the ATIS project did) and consider 12:00 noon early afternoon, even though it's not really after noon. What about a flight that leaves La Guardia Airport in New York at 1:45 p.m., then lands in San Francisco at 4:20 p.m., then connects to a flight that leaves San Francisco at 5:10 p.m., makes a 40-minute stop in Denver and finally lands in Washington at 1:30 a.m. the day after. Well, technically, that's a flight from New York to Washington that leaves early in the afternoon, but who would ever choose it to get from the Big Apple to D.C.? Wait a minute, you said "Washington," not "D.C.," didn't you? Do you mean some airport in Washington, the capital of the United States, or one somewhere in the state of Washington?

The PofI document tried to answer most of these questions as best it could with a set of rules that may seem obvious but that are necessary to formally define the domain, such as

Rule 2.2.1   A flight "between X and Y" means a flight "from X to Y."

or

Rule 2.2.8   The location of a departure, stop, or arrival should always be taken to be an airport.

Others rules were clarifications of common expressions that, if not properly defined, might be ambiguous, such as

Rule 2.2.3.3 "Stopovers" will mean "stops" unless the context clearly indicates that the subject intended "stopover," as in "Can I make a two-day stopover on that flight?" In that case, the query is answered using the stopover column of the restrictions table.

Other rules try to define commonly used idioms and jargon terms:

Rule 2.2.6 A "red-eye" flight is one that leaves between 9 p.m. and 3 a.m. and arrives between 5 a.m. and 12 noon.

And other rules tried to handle inherently ambiguous questions:

Rule 2.2.16 "The times for that/those flight(s)" may be ambiguous between departure and arrival time. If the subject is clearly asking for more than one time for a flight, as in "What are the times for that flight?," both departure and arrival times will be given (ala "schedule"). If just one time for a flight is asked for, as in "What is the time for that flight?," only departure time will be given. And if this distinction is unclear, as in "What are the times for those flights?," there is an ambiguity, and either type of answer may be given.

And what about those fuzzy time expressions that we all use but don't have a precise definition for, such as "late morning," "early afternoon," and so on? The PofI committee members—or "PofIers," as they were called—used tables such as table 5.5 to define them.

And if you say "between 7 and 8 in the morning," does the time interval include 7:00 and 8:00, or does it start at 7:01 and run to 7:59? Of course, the PofIers had another table (where "T1"= "only or first time referred to" and "T2" = "second time referred to") to unambiguously answer that and similar questions:

Table 5.5
Principles of Interpretation definition of periods of the day

TERM	START	END
morning	0000	1200
afternoon	1200	1800
evening	1800	2200
day	0600	1800
night	1800	0600
early morning	0000	0800
mid-morning	0800	1000
. . .	. . .	. . .

Table 5.6
Principles of Interpretation definition of time intervals

TERM	INCLUDES END-POINT
before T1	No
after T1	No
between T1 and T2	Yes
arriving by T1	Yes
departing by T1	Yes
periods of the day	Yes

Members of the ATIS community still remember defining the Principles of Interpretation as a nightmarish experience. Endless discussions on whether you should or shouldn't include the end-points in "between X and Y" expressions, or whether the 5 in "from 5 to 9 in the evening" was to be considered ambiguous (either 5 a.m. or 5 p.m.) filled the hours of weekly teleconferences among the dozen or so committee members and jammed their e-mail inboxes. But that wasn't all. There were other issues, more general and philosophical, to be discussed. For instance, were all the collected utterances, even those just outside the domain of the database, to be considered valid for the ATIS project, and should the competing systems even attempt to understand them? What about the utterances clearly outside the domain? For instance, "How much fuel does a Boeing 747 need to fly from New York to Caracas?" Should systems that can't answer such utterances receive penalty points? What's a valid answerable ATIS utterance? How much of the common, general knowledge should an ATIS machine be required to include?

Finally, there was the most difficult problem of all: that of defining and computing a number that would measure how well a system understands and allow the different systems to be compared and ranked. At first, the Poflers tried to define a formal meaning representation to use as a reference for each utterance, to be used by each system. This would allow the evaluation committee to measure how accurate the systems were based on how closely the meaning representation they generated matched the reference one. But the Poflers could never agree on a formal meaning representation. They then tried to standardize symbolic expressions of the meaning representations of the ATIS utterances but soon gave up on this as well. They agreed, instead, on a much simpler, but quite effective mechanism. Rather than representing the meaning of each utterance in a formal way, they decided to associate the meaning of each utterance with a correct answer: expressed as a yes, a no, a number, or a table. Then the Poflers defined a mechanism to compare the reference answers with those generated by the ATIS machines, and NIST distributed a computer program that automated the comparison.

Defining the Principles of Interpretation and the comparison between the correct answer and that of the research systems was certainly hard work, but it made a formal evaluation of the systems possible. The formal ATIS evaluations took place from 1989 through 1994. As with the previous projects, having a common corpus and evaluation methodology served to push the performance level of the systems higher and higher. The first results were quite disappointing: measured separately, the speech recognizer module of the best system achieved only 80 percent word accuracy and its natural language understanding module only 50 percent. The results were even more disappointing when the two modules were actually connected: the understanding accuracy of the best performing system fell to a mere 39 percent. The ATIS machines' performance would improve dramatically by the end of the program in 1994, however, with accuracy rates exceeding 90 percent for system modules measured both separately and together. That was another tangible proof of the power of frequent, reliable evaluations.

Statistics . . . Again

The most important lesson learned in the five years of the ATIS program was how different spontaneous speech is from read speech. The Resource Management task was performed under unrealistically controlled conditions, with subjects reading utterances from a predetermined list using a tightly restricted vocabulary and well-defined grammar. In contrast, for the ATIS project, subjects could, and did, say what they wanted. There was no control over the vocabulary and the grammar. The words and expressions that came up were unpredictable, with ungrammaticalities and disfluencies—the ums and uhs and ers—false starts, changes of subject, word repetitions, and everything that happens when we speak normally. The worst ATIS utterance, the one on the back of the MADCOW Tshirt, was a not-so-uncommon example of that.

Indeed, the unpredictability of spontaneous speech was the main cause of the initial setback in the speech recognizers' word accuracy, which declined to 80 percent or less from the 95 percent or more it had been in the Resource Management project. How could the ATIS research labs get back to higher word accuracy? The answer was simple: "There is no data like more data!"[20] And as more data became available through the MADCOW collection, all sites started to achieve word accuracies in the 90 percent range. But the answer to improving the natural language understanding part wasn't so simple.

Years before the ATIS project, natural language processing was a branch of research mostly devoted to understanding text sentences, not spontaneous spoken utterances. And, of course, text sentences, such as those written in books, are generally free of the ungrammaticalities and disfluencies of spontaneous speech. At the beginning of the ATIS project, the speech research teams, with little or no experience in speech understanding, asked their colleagues working in natural language processing for help, which they provided by using what they'd learned from understanding text sentences. But, as soon as the first NIST evaluation results came back, it was painfully clear to everyone that spontaneous spoken language simply couldn't be approached in the same way as written text. The language understanding systems the natural language scientists had used for years, and which had worked so well with well-formed sentences, failed miserably with spontaneously spoken utterances.

Like the speech scientists of the 1970s, the natural language scientists had not taken into account the huge variability of spontaneous language. They tried their rule-based systems on ATIS, and failed. A novel idea, that of *robust parsing*, thus emerged as a way to cope with the issues of spontaneous speech. There was no way to handcraft grammars that could cover all possible spontaneous utterances, and take into account all the disfluencies. Consider the following quite realistic spontaneous utterance:

Hmm . . . I need to . . . I—do you have a flight to San Francisco? . . . I—departing on May 15th?. . . I—it should be a Saturday . . . I need to go from New York to San Francisco . . . I'm not sure about the departure time, but I need to be there before 8 p.m.

The idea behind robust parsing is that we actually don't need a grammar that covers all possible long and disfluent sentences. However, you may have noticed that, although the sentence above is not grammatical as a whole, some parts of it are perfectly grammatical:

do you have a flight

to San Francisco

departing on May 15th

from New York

be there before 8 p.m.

The other parts of the utterance, the disfluencies and ungrammaticalities, are actually not very interesting, don't carry useful information, at least for the task at hand, and they can be disregarded without modifying the meaning of the whole sentence:

Hmm

I need to

it should be a Saturday

I'm not sure about the departure time

Some speech engineers realized that, in order to understand the meaning of a whole utterance, the natural language understanding module doesn't have to analyze it as a whole, but just the individual segments that make sense within the defined task. They called these semantic segments "concepts."

Concepts in this narrow sense need to be interpreted in the context of the defined task, which, for ATIS, usually means flights, times, dates, airports, airlines, and so on. In fact, concepts—those little semantic segments of an utterance—may not mean much if the context isn't well defined. If you go to Starbucks instead of your travel agent's office and say, "Departing on May 15th," what you'll get from your barista is a puzzled look. Within a well-defined context, however, you can assign a precise meaning to concepts that are relevant to that context, and, for ATIS, the context was extremely well defined by both the database of flight information and the Principles of Interpretation. For instance, in the ATIS context, the word "departure" can't mean anything else but the departure of a flight, while the word "meal" can't mean anything else but a meal served on board an airplane. So, given the structure of the flight database and the Principles of Interpretation, you can assign a formal symbolic meaning to each concept taken in isolation. For instance:

do you have a <u>flight</u> → *REQUEST: FLIGHTS*

to <u>San Francisco</u> → *FLIGHT_DESTINATION: SAN FRANCISCO*

departing on <u>May 15th</u> → *FLIGHT_ DEPARTURE_DATE: MAY 15*

from <u>New York</u> → *FLIGHT_ORIGIN: NEW YORK*

be there <u>before 8 p.m.</u> → *FLIGHT_ARRIVAL_TIME: < 8PM*

Your ATIS machine can then transform the formal expression of the meaning of each concept, the elements on the right-hand side of the above examples, into a formal request for the database, which in an English-like formal language would sound like

FIND ALL <u>FLIGHTS</u> FROM ALL THE AIRPORTS SERVICING <u>NEW YORK</u> TO ALL THE AIRPORTS SERVICING <u>SAN FRANCISCO</u> DEPARTING <u>MAY 15</u> AND ARRIVING <u>BEFORE 8 PM</u>[21]

and, expressed in the database language of SQL, would look like

SELECT AIRLINE_CODE, FLIGHT_NUMBER **FROM** FLIGHT **WHERE** ORIGIN_CITY == "NEW YORK" **AND** DESTINATION_AIRPORT == "SAN FRANCISCO" **AND** DEPARTURE_DATE == "05/15/1991" **AND** ARRIVAL_TIME < 2000.

So, what does "understanding" mean? All your ATIS machine has done is translate a vague, confusing, ambiguous natural language expression—one that only humans can reliably make sense of—like "Hmm . . . I need to . . . I—do you have a flight? . . ."—into a precise, unambiguous, formal statement that can be processed by computers, like SELECT ORIGIN_AIRPORT, DEPARTURE_TIME . . . So you now have a clearer understanding of what understanding is. Understanding looks very much like translating from one language to another: from a confusing, highly variable, and free-form language—the natural language—to a more precise, schematic, formal language, a language so unambiguous that even computers can understand it.

But let's take a closer look at the structure of the requests in ATIS. You can break down every request made to ATIS into three elements: what you're asking ATIS to do (or the action), the objects of the action, and a set of constraints. For instance:

ACTION:
  FIND
OBJECTS:
  AIRLINE_CODE, FLIGHT_NUMBER,
CONSTRAINTS:
  ORIGIN_CITY == "NEW YORK"
  DESTINATION_AIRPORT == "SAN FRANCISCO"
  DEPARTURE_DATE == "05/15/1991"
  ARRIVAL_TIME < 2000.

Finding the action, the objects, and the constraints in the natural language requests is all your ATIS machine needs to do to translate their meaning into a formal, rigid language, at least for all requests that fall within the limited air travel context of ATIS. Speech researchers have known this for a long time. In fact, both the traditional analysis techniques and the new, robust parsing aimed to find these elements in each utterance. Some ATIS researchers, however, thought to use statistical methods to describe the semantic segments of speech in the same way that other speech scientists, almost twenty years earlier, had used them to describe the phonetic segments of speech.

Esther Levin and I, at AT&T's Bell Laboratories, began to explore the idea of statistical modeling of concepts in the early 1990s.[22] The result was a system we called "CHRONUS" (*Conceptual Hidden Representation Of Natural Unconstrained Speech*).[23] CHRONUS used hidden Markov models to represent concepts such as OBJECT, ORIGIN, DESTINATION, DEPARTURE_TIME, and AIRLINE. Conceptual HMMs can find the most probable concepts represented by a sequence of words, just as acoustic HMMs can find the most probable phonemes for a given sequence of acoustic observations. So, you might expect, the hidden Markov model that represents the concept ORIGIN, for instance, would assign high probabilities to sequences of words such as "from New York" and "leaving out of Boston," whereas the HMM representing the concept DEPARTURE_TIME would favor sequences of words such as "leaving at 10:30 p.m." and "departing in the morning."

The big advantage that statistical conceptual models had over more traditional methods of language understanding was that they could learn from data without the need for hand-coded rules. Moreover, as with the acoustic modeling approach twenty years earlier, the statistical approach showed once more that "there is no data like more data," not only for speech recognition, but also for language understanding. In fact, at the final evaluation of the ATIS project in 1994, much to the surprise of all the other participants, the AT&T CHRONUS system achieved the highest accuracy (lowest error rate) on the "natural language understanding alone" task, where the natural language understanding module was directly fed the test utterances, and not the speech recognizer output. Using the Principles of Interpretation, CHRONUS correctly understood more than 94 percent of the test utterances. Figure 5.4 shows a graph of the final error rates for the three tests for each participating laboratory:[24]

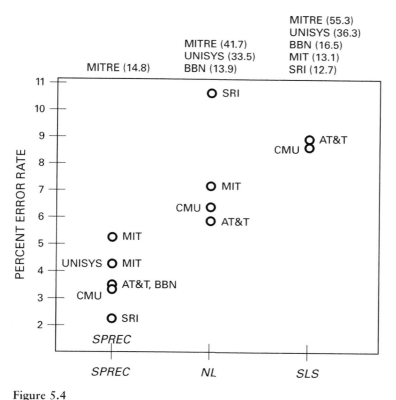

Figure 5.4
DARPA ATIS final error rates for the speech recognition (SPREC), natural language (NL), and full spoken language system (SLS) tests.

For the first time, ATIS showed the world that it is possible to achieve quite high levels of accuracy in the recognition and understanding of spontaneous speech. Unfortunately, systems like the ATIS machines were a purely academic exercise. They had no commercial potential for the simple reason that, even though they could give answers, they couldn't ask questions. And asking questions is an essential part of communication. Something else was needed, something called "dialog."

6

Let's Have a Dialog

Although the Air Travel Information System task was much closer to real-world human-computer communication than the Resource Management task was, the sophisticated and high-performing ATIS machines were far from commercially usable, even by the end of the project. Most could answer any relevant spoken question with a high degree of accuracy, but what they couldn't do was ask questions.

The ability to ask questions, the right questions, is essential for any type of conversation. Imagine going to see a travel agent, let's call him "Tom," who can't ask questions but can only provide answers: tables, yeses and nos, or numbers. You say, "Hi, I need to fly to San Francisco," and Tom responds by showing you a table on his computer that lists *all* flights to San Francisco from all possible airports, on all possible airlines, at all possible times.[1] Of course, that's the correct "answer" to what you said according to the ATIS Principles of Interpretation—you mentioned no departure point and no time either to leave or to arrive—but it's mostly useless: there are hundreds, if not thousands of flights listed on Tom's computer. A normal travel agent would have responded to what you said with something like "I can certainly help you with that. Where are you leaving from and when do you need to get there?"

The spoken interaction between two humans, in most cases, is said to be of the "mixed-initiative" type because both parties can take the initiative at any time and change the course of the conversation. Each party gives answers to posed questions, provides additional information, and asks more questions until the conversation runs its natural course or ends for some other reason. To see why people whose job is to provide answers, like travel agents, also need to ask questions, let's go back to our previous situation where you, as a traveler interested in booking a trip, started with the very general request "I need to fly to San Francisco." A normal human agent, let's call her "Tess," before going ahead, would ask you a few questions to narrow down her search. What date do you need to travel? Where from? What time do you need to get there? At this point, it's not you the traveler who'd be asking questions, but Tess the travel agent, and you'd be the one answering. When Tess has gathered enough information, she can tell you about a small number of flights that, at least in principle, meet the constraints you've set. If you don't like the choices she's giving you, you can ask further questions, such as "Do you have an earlier flight?" or "How about a cheaper fare?" You can also change your mind and say, "What if I leave two days later?" or "Forget about San Francisco; I'd rather go to Los Angeles." But it can also happen that the flight you want is simply not available: "Sorry, there are no available flights tomorrow with United, but there are with Delta, would that be okay?" In this case, the agent needs to take the initiative and ask more questions, trying to find a satisfactory alternative.

During the ATIS project, the MIT speech research group was led by Victor Zue, who had first showed the world how to read a spectrogram twenty years before. Realizing that a useful system would need to ask questions as well as give answers, Zue and his group aggressively explored the idea of mixed-initiative systems. They actually built a real-world dialog system, which all the members of their department at MIT could use to plan for their real flights, and they went so far as to "kindly" ask them to use the system if they wanted to be reimbursed for their business trips. By doing so, Zue's researchers collected and recorded thousands of interactions that they regularly used to test and improve all the aspects of their system. That was just the beginning. They built many other systems besides their ATIS machine, which they used as a test bed for their research.

There are several degrees of initiative in a dialog system. At one extreme is the pure *user-initiative* dialog system, like an ATIS machine, in which the user has all the initiative, and the machine none. The machine interprets all user utterances as requests, which it immediately answers. The machine never asks questions. At the other extreme is the pure *system-initiative* dialog system, where the machine has all the initiative and the user none. The machine asks all the questions, and users can only give answers; they can neither change their minds nor ask follow-up questions. Although pure user-initiative dialog systems, like the ATIS machines, may not work in the real world, pure system-initiative systems, later known also as "directed-dialog" or "menu-based" systems, turn out to be very useful in many applications. Between the two extremes are various degrees of mixed initiative. Although we don't know what the optimal working point, the perfect degree of initiative, for human-machine communication is, the art of finding that point is the art of voice user interface (VUI) design, which will have an important place in the development of commercial systems discussed in chapter 8. But for now, let's get back to research on dialog systems.

While the rest of the speech recognition community was mostly busy with ATIS and the Principles of Interpretation, the MIT speech research group built several sophisticated and sleek mixed-initiative spoken dialog systems. VOYAGER was the first one:

The system, which we call VOYAGER, currently focuses on the city of Cambridge, Massachusetts, between MIT and Harvard University. . . . It can answer a number of different types of questions about certain hotels, restaurants, hospitals, and other objects within this region. At the moment, VOYAGER has a vocabulary of 324 words. Within this limited domain of knowledge, it is our hope that VOYAGER will eventually be able to handle any reasonable query that a native speaker is likely to initiate. As time progresses, VOYAGER'S knowledge base will undoubtedly grow.[2]

VOYAGER, like ATIS, used a display to present the answers in textual form and to show itineraries and locations on a map of Cambridge. Its dialog capabilities were limited, but functional. Here's an example of a conversation with VOYAGER:

User: Can you tell me how to get to the Chinese restaurant?
VOYAGER: Where are you?
User: I am near a bank.
VOYAGER: I know of many banks. Can you specify which one you mean?
User: The one on Main Street
VOYAGER: The only bank on Main Street that I know of is the Baybank at 226 Main Street in Cambridge. The Chinese restaurants that I know of are Hong Kong and Royal East. Can you specify which one you mean?
User: The one nearest me.
VOYAGER: The nearest Chinese restaurant to the Baybank at 226 Main Street that I know of is the Royal East. I will try to find the best way to go from the Baybank at 226 Main Street to the Royal East. (Directions)

Among those who built VOYAGER were two young researchers who would later play key roles in the development of speech technology. One of them, Jim Glass, would take Victor Zue's place at the helm of the MIT speech research group. The other, Mike Phillips, would in 1994 create one of the two start-ups that energized the dormant speech industry of the early 1990s. Glass, Phillips, and the other researchers in the MIT speech research group, including Stephanie Seneff, Zue's wife, started exploring the many aspects of spoken dialog technology by creating a series of systems with higher and higher degrees of sophistication, including weather forecast systems such as Jupiter, airline scheduling systems such as Pegasus, and flight planning systems such as Mercury. Publicized and deployed on the public telephone network, some of the systems received thousands and thousands of calls, which allowed the group to gauge and improve their performance. After having built a few systems, the MIT researchers felt the need to create a software infrastructure that would allow them to easily reuse previously developed modules and build other systems by simply putting those modules together as if they were Lego blocks. Given their penchant for astronomy names, they called that infrastructure "Galaxy."[3]

A Communicator's Galaxy

Sophisticated computer programs aren't built as huge, monolithic, indivisible, and amorphous masses of programming code. Rather, following the basic engineering rule of divide and conquer, they're made up of different *modules,* simpler programs that interact with one another to give the main program the necessary functionality. In general, the more complex the program, the larger the number of modules and the more complex their interactions are. Spoken dialog systems are fairly complicated programs that require several modules. For instance, most of the ATIS machines can be broken down into at least two modules: the speech recognizer and the natural language understanding module. A conversational—or dialog—system needs quite a few more.

Figure 6.1 shows a simplified schema—or *architecture*—of a spoken dialog system. You already know the functions of the speech recognizer and natural language understanding modules. Together, they try to produce a symbolic representation of the meaning for each input utterance. However, as you saw in our ATIS discussion, some utterances such as "I want to go there tomorrow," "Book it," and "Do you have anything cheaper?" are meaningless outside the context of what's been said before.[4] It's the function of the *discourse analyzer* to interpret individual utterances in the context of the previous ones.

As its name suggests, the *dialog manager* governs the behavior of the whole system. It decides what to do at each turn of a dialog, based on what the speaker said, or other conditions, such as the information retrieved from the *knowledge database,* which includes the facts of the domain, like the flight database in the case of ATIS. The dialog manager decides whether to ask another question, retrieve data, or conclude the dialog; it creates the intention of doing something, and this intention, be it to speak, listen, or retrieve data, is then put into practice by the other modules.

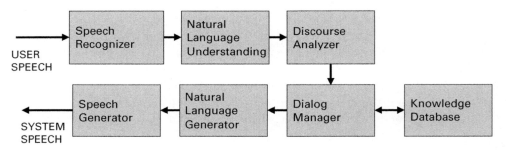

Figure 6.1
Simplified architecture of a spoken dialog system.

The *natural language generator* realizes the dialog manager's intention to say something. Whereas the natural language understanding module starts from a sequence of words and generates a meaning, the natural language generator starts from a meaning and generates a sequence of words that need to be spoken. Of course, this can be done at different levels of sophistication, with the simplest language generator being nothing more than a list of recorded utterances to choose from, generally called "prompts."

A slightly more sophisticated natural language generator can handle lists of sentences in textual form. Once the dialog manager requests that a sentence be spoken, the language generator retrieves the corresponding string of words, and sends it to the *text-to-speech synthesizer* (TTS). Just as the language generator's function is the exact opposite of the language understanding module's, so the text-to-speech synthesizer's function is the exact opposite of the speech recognizer's: it goes from sequences of words in textual form to speech. We'll discuss TTS systems in chapter 7.

When creating a program with many modules such as a dialog system, you need to establish the functionality of those modules and to precisely determine the way they communicate with one another. This is important for many different reasons. First of all, a complex program like a spoken dialog system is generally not built by a single person. When people collaborate, each building one or more modules, they have to specify beforehand what each module does, which data it expects as input, and which data it expects as output. If they don't do this beforehand, the various pieces they build won't fit together, like pieces from different jigsaw puzzles. Software engineers call the specification of what a module does and how it talks to the other modules an "application programming interface" (API). Following an API, different programmers build the modules assigned to them. When all their modules are ready, fully functional, and tested, they'll put them together to build the whole system. If the API was well designed, that system should, at least in principle, work.

A well-designed API not only breaks a complex system into modules that can be individually programmed by different people, but also makes those modules reusable and interchangeable. Indeed, with a well-designed API, you can take a module from one system and reuse it in a different system, or exchange one module for another with the same functionality but a different implementation or better performance. Moreover, again with such an API, different people or different companies can build different, but fully interchangeable, versions of the same module.

By allowing researchers to exchange or mix and match modules, a well-defined application programming interface can promote collaboration and sharing in a research community and can potentially help accelerate and foster innovation. When the speech research group at MIT realized that, by defining an API for the various components of the different systems they had built, they could easily reuse them to quickly build other systems, they opted for a very simple and general interface. In fact, the MIT dialog system API was so general that it turned out to be the same for all the modules. Each module, whether it was a speech recognizer, an audio player, a text-to-speech synthesizer, or a natural language understanding module, communicated with the other modules in a standard data format that was called a "frame."

A *frame* is a container of data arranged in a hierarchical manner.[5] For instance, a flight itinerary returned by the database of flights is represented by pieces of data, such as the departure time and the arrival airport. But since there's a hierarchical relationship among all the pieces of data, each one of them is part of a higher-level frame and includes other data from lower levels. In our simple example, an ITINERARY may include DEPARTURE, ARRIVAL, and flight identification, which we'll simply call "FLIGHT." Both DEPARTURE and ARRIVAL include an identifier of the AIRPORT, for instance, its full name or its three-letter airport code, the DATE, and the TIME, which in turn represents the date and time of the departure or arrival. FLIGHT includes the AIRLINE identifier and the NUMBER. Figure 6.2 shows what a typical ITINERARY frame might look like.

As a general data container, a frame can include all types of data like the bits of the digitized speech waveform, its feature vector representation, the textual transcriptions of an utterance, the formal representation of meaning, and all the other

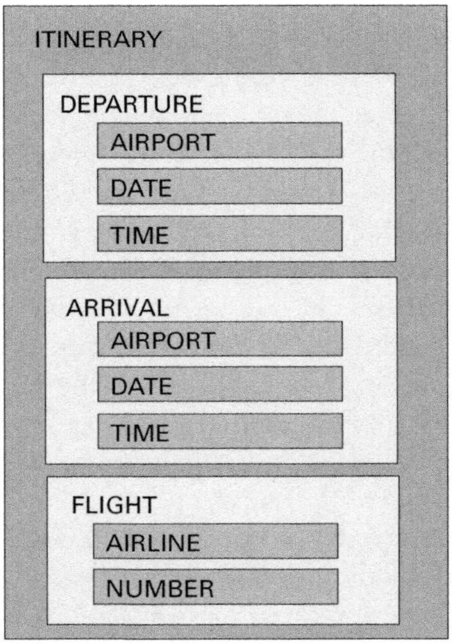

Figure 6.2
Frame representing the definition of an "itinerary."

numeric or textual pieces of information that are exchanged by the modules of a spoken dialog system.[6] The MIT researchers decided that every module was to both receive input and generate output as frames, leaving to each individual module the responsibility to interpret the input frame and to generate the output frame according to its function.

Since their main interest was research on dialog systems, the MIT researchers didn't want a fixed architecture like the one in figure 6.1, where the connections between modules are established once and for all. They wanted to have the freedom to add additional modules, remove old ones, redefine their functionality, and connect them in different ways. So they created an architecture that could be rewired at will. Based on a central element, called the "HUB," Galaxy could be programmed to route frames between the different modules—called "servers"—that were connected to it. The HUB worked as a sort of traffic cop for frames: it would intercept all incoming frames and decide where to send each one based on a set of "dispatching" rules. So, rather than a traditional architecture of successive modules, each feeding into the next, the architecture of a dialog system looked more like a wheel with the various server modules on its spokes, each feeding into and from a central module, the HUB, as shown in figure 6.3.

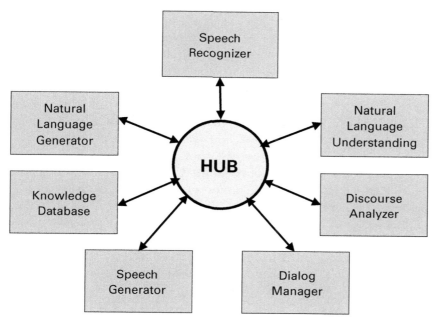

Figure 6.3
Galaxy architecture.

The HUB could be programmed either to react to the content of each frame it received, change it, and reroute it to one or more servers or, after having shipped a frame, to wait until a particular response was received and to continue to route frames in the meantime. For instance, the following HUB program would cause Galaxy to simulate the traditional architecture shown in figure 6.1:[7]

• Send frames without a meaning interpretation to the natural language understanding module;

• Send frames with an interpretation and unresolved contextual references to the discourse analyzer;

• Send frames with a complete interpretation and no selection of the next dialog action to the dialog manager;

• Send frames with database requests to the knowledge database;

• Send frames with data from the knowledge database to the dialog manager;

• Send frames with requests to prompt the user to the natural language generator

• Send frames with textual prompts to be played from the natural language generator to the speech generator.

You can use a larger set of servers, or even multiple servers for the same role, and add rules to manage new capabilities. For instance, you can have two speech recognizers, one returning a transcription, and one returning a full interpretation. The HUB sends the result of the first recognizer to the natural language server, and the result from the second one to the discourse analyzer. It can then wait to receive both answers and send them to a comparison module that selects the more likely interpretation.

By the end of the ATIS project, DARPA realized that the research community needed to move toward more usable, mixed-initiative dialog systems. Allen Sears, a DARPA program manager for speech research, took the initiative and created an advisory committee composed of researchers from MIT, AT&T, Stanford Research Institute, and MITRE. The goal of the committee was to set the agenda for the new DARPA project: the Communicator.

Officially launched in 1997 with a budget of several million dollars, the Communicator project had as its goal the creation of a computer program that would help users solve any general, arbitrarily complex travel problem using a mobile voice-activated device with display. Sears vividly described the challenge facing the Communicator during the project's first meeting:

You are in Denver, Friday night at 8 p.m. on the road to the airport after a great meeting. As a result of the meeting, you need to attend a group meeting in San Diego, on Punta Loma on Monday at 8:30, a meeting Tuesday morning at Miramar at 7:30, then one from 3 to 5 p.m. in Monterey; you need reservations (car, hotel, air). You pull over to the side of the road and whip out your Communicator. Through spoken dialog (augmented with a display and pointing), you make the appropriate reservations, discover a conflict, and send an e-mail message (dictated) to inform the group of the changed schedule. Do this in 10 minutes.[8]

The Communicator's domain was an extension of ATIS, including multiple-leg flights, hotels, and car rental agencies. The usual research laboratories such as Bell Labs and those at AT&T, Stanford Research Institute, Carnegie Mellon University, and even IBM joined the project, together with a number of small companies including SpeechWorks, which would go on to play an important role in the development of the speech industry.[9] DARPA gave the Massachusetts-based nonprofit MITRE Corporation (chartered to counsel the government on scientific and technical matters) the task of engineering the Galaxy infrastructure, distributing it among the project participants, and providing them with documentation and training. In fact, one of the requirements for participating in the Communicator project was to use the Galaxy architecture; all systems developed within the Communicator project had to be HUB compliant.

From Hell to PARADISE

Having already developed systems using their own architecture, most Communicator participants regarded making them "HUB compliant" to be an unnecessary burden, at least at first. Reprogramming these systems to fit into the new common framework was a lot of work that didn't seem to be directly related to technological improvement and innovation. Once they had done so, however, the benefits of Communicator's collaborative plug-and-play architecture became apparent. A few labs, such as those at MIT, Carnegie Mellon University, and the University of Colorado–Boulder made some of their modules available to the smaller groups so they could focus on those modules they were particularly interested in. Most of the Communicator systems ended up being quite sophisticated and often very chatty, as you can see from the following real conversation with one of them:

Computer: Welcome to the initial development version of the MIT air travel system. This call is being recorded for system development. You may hang up or ask for help at any time. Please say your PIN number.

Caller: One three nine zero.

Computer: I'll enroll you temporarily as a guest user. How can I help you?

Caller: I'd like to travel from Atlanta, Georgia, to London on September 25th.

Computer: Okay, from Atlanta to London on Monday September 25. Can you provide the approximate departure time or airline?

Caller: Uh, uh . . . during daytime.

Computer: Sorry. I'm not sure what you said.

Caller: During the day.

Computer: I'm sorry. I'm having trouble understanding you. Try a shorter sentence.

Caller: I'd like to depart at 10 a.m.

Computer: What about a Delta flight connecting in New York's La Guardia leaving at 10:30 a.m.? Would that work? I also have a Continental flight connecting in Newark leaving at 8:30 a.m.

Caller: Do you have any direct flights?

Computer: What about a British Airways leaving at 4:10 p.m.? Would that work? I also have a Delta flight leaving at 5:40 p.m.

Caller: Uh, British. I'd prefer the British Airways Flight.

Computer: I have two nonstop flights arriving in London: a flight leaving at 4:10 p.m. and a flight leaving at 6:20 p.m. Are any of these okay?

Caller: Yes, the 4:10 p.m.

But, in the spirit of the later DARPA projects as well as that of the best scientific tradition, showing that the Communicator system could converse with a user only showed that the system could work, not that it worked well or better than other equivalent systems. As the dramatic improvements in speech recognition and spoken language understanding of the previous projects demonstrated, common evaluation was the main promoter of continuous improvement. Unfortunately, evaluating full dialog systems is far more difficult. You can test a spoken language understanding system on a corpus of utterances, one at a time, compare your results with the desired outcome, and see how well you're doing. Then you can improve your system, do the same test, and see how much better you're doing. But you can't do this with a dialog system. As an interactive activity, dialog eludes any corpus evaluation paradigm. The user's response at each turn of a dialog depends on what the system said in the previous turn, which depends on what the user said before that, and so on. Thus each user utterance depends on the whole history of the interaction, from the first exchange to the current one. Assume you store a corpus of sets of utterances, each set representing a whole user interaction with a "reference" dialog system. You feed your system with the interactions stored in the corpus, one utterance at a time, and see if its response is correct. But that won't work because, at a certain point, if your system is different than the reference one, it may ask a question not expected by the next utterance in the corpus. And from that point on, your system's dialog and the reference one will rapidly diverge. Thus corpus-based evaluation doesn't work with dialog systems. To evaluate a dialog system, you'd need a program that would behave like a user, in a reactive manner, and respond with the appropriate utterance to any system request. But that's too complex for an evaluation plan. Besides, who'd evaluate the system that simulates the user? Although, as you'll see later, the idea of building an artificial user to test and train a dialog system isn't all that far-fetched, it was too "before its time" to be used to establish a common evaluation criterion in the DARPA Communicator project.

But there was a more fundamental issue looming over the DARPA Communicator. Considering that spoken dialog systems are generally designed to help users achieve a goal, what type of measure would tell a good dialog system from a bad one? That the goal of the Communicator systems was to solve traveling problems suggests a straightforward measure: has the goal been reached or not? For instance, if you as a user, after communicating with a system, find a satisfactory travel plan, one that matches the original constraints you had in mind, we can say that your goal was attained. In a large number of trials, the average number of times a system reaches the user goal would determine what's called the "task completion rate." Unfortunately, the task completion rate alone doesn't tell us whether a system is good. Say you have two systems with the same task completion rate, but one of them takes less time to reach the goal. Everything else being equal, you could consider the faster system to be better. Thus you could use the average time to reach the goal, or *time to completion*, as an additional evaluation measure.

But here we should note that the fastest system is not always the best. Imagine two human travel agents. The first one is a very good agent who always performs thorough searches on the database, knows what you want, and always finds the best overall solution for your travel problems. The second, faster agent, always finds a reasonable solution for your travel problems, too, but because this agent tries to spend as little time on the phone with you as possible, that may not always be the best solution, not the cheapest option nor the one that best satisfies your time constraints. Both agents have the same high task completion rate, but you can't really say that the faster agent is better simply by virtue of being faster. So a fair evaluation of dialog systems needs to include, besides the average task completion rate and the average time to completion, the quality of the solution proposed to the user as one of its criteria. But the quality of a travel planning solution, because of its inherently subjective nature, can't be assessed in an easy and objective fashion. Some users would rather get a more expensive option but one closer to their time constraints; others would rather get the cheapest option of all, even it's not the one closest to their time constraints.

Unfortunately, that's not all. You can't assess the quality of a dialog only by considering whether the goal was reached, how long it took, or whether the solution found was satisfactory to the user. You also have to consider whether the user's experience was a positive one. Even when you speak to human agents, though you may finally reach your goal, your experience may not always be a positive one. Some human agents may be rude or difficult to understand. They may speak too fast or too slow, or they may keep asking you to repeat what you just said. The same is largely true for machines. For instance, if, as a user, you have to repeat every utterance because the speech recognizer gets each one wrong, if you can't make out what the machine's telling you, if what it says doesn't make much sense, or if you're led through long, elaborate menus in order to reach your goal, then you can't say you've liked interacting with the machine. And, if that's so, you may not be inclined to use it again and may opt to talk to a human agent after all. Unfortunately, the user experience is highly subjective. Except in extreme cases, when users express their frustration verbally—curse words and imprecations can be detected automatically by a speech recognizer—the quality of the experience may be assessed only by surveying users after they have finished interacting with the system. Of course, surveys can be automated using speech recognition by adding a few questions at the end of each transaction. The problem is that automated surveys generally have a positive bias because they're answered only by those users who have reached the end of a transaction.[10] What about those users who are so exasperated they hang up before reaching the survey? To obtain unbiased surveys, you need to get in touch with an unbiased sample of all users, including both those who completed the task and those who didn't—and you need to do so shortly after their interactions, when they still vividly remember what they experienced.[11] This is often impractical and expensive, especially for systems used by the general public.[12]

So, to evaluate dialog systems, you need to use both objective and subjective measurements. But whereas you can generally automate objective measurements using recorded data, you can't completely automate subjective evaluations, which are expensive and take time to do properly. But could you perhaps guess what a subjective evaluation might be from the objective measurements? Yes, you could definitely establish a cause-and-effect relationship between them. For instance, a low-accuracy recognizer may well be a principal cause for a bad user experience. Lyn Walker and other researchers at AT&T Laboratories developed a dialog evaluation paradigm that correlated objective and subjective measures, one they called "PARADISE" (*PARA*digm for *DI*alog System Evaluation).[13] The goal of PARADISE was to reliably predict user satisfaction based on objective measurements of the systems in use.

This is how PARADISE works. You run several interactions of the dialog system with a set of users. For each interaction, the system takes note of a large number of objective measurements, such as task completion, average turn duration, speech recognition word accuracy, and sentence error rate. Then you politely ask the same users to provide a subjective evaluation of the system. The subjective evaluation includes the level of user agreement with different statements regarding several perceptual dimensions of the systems. The level of agreement is expressed on a 5-point scale, known also as a "Likert scale."[14] We've all seen this scale many times in the marketing questionnaires for evaluating the service provided in restaurants

	1	2	3	4	5
	Strongly Disagree	**Disagree**	**Neither agree nor disagree**	**Agree**	**Strongly agree**
I was able to successfully complete my task	☐	☐	☐	☐	☐
It was easy to get the information I wanted	☐	☐	☐	☐	☐
The system was easy to understand	☐	☐	☐	☐	☐
I knew what I could say at each point in the dialog	☐	☐	☐	☐	☐
The system worked the way I expected	☐	☐	☐	☐	☐
Based on my experience, I would use the system regularly	☐	☐	☐	☐	☐

Figure 6.4
Subject questionnaire used in the DARPA Communicator project.

or hotel rooms or by the flight crew on an airplane, but instead of statements like "My room was clean" or "The service was courteous," in questionnaires for dialog systems, the statements would look like the ones in figure 6.4.

The sum of the Likert scale points for all the answers is a global subjective evaluation of user satisfaction for that particular user and system. Given the six statements in our sample questionnaire, the maximum user satisfaction is $6 \times 5 = 30$ (if the user strongly agrees with all statements) and the minimum is $6 \times 1 = 6$ (if the user strongly disagrees with all of them). By doing this for a reasonable number of users, you end up with a collection of values that represent the subjective measurements of user satisfaction. At the same time, you need to collect, for each interaction, the corresponding values of the objective measurements mentioned above. Using an appropriate statistical formula, you can correlate the degree of user satisfaction with the values of the objective measurements. You can then use another appropriate formula to approximate user satisfaction given those objective measurements. And you can use it to predict user satisfaction from the values of the objective measurements, without having to run the survey again for each modification and upgrade of your system.

The DARPA Communicator project conducted two large-scale evaluations, one in 2000 and one in 2001. For each evaluation, subjects were given travel scenarios and asked to interact with each of the nine complete systems built by AT&T, Bolt, Beranek and Newman, the University of Colorado–Boulder, Carnegie Mellon University, IBM, Lucent Bell Laboratories, MIT, MITRE, and Stanford Research Institute. The evaluations produced more than 1,900 dialog records and a lot of measurement data. The task completion rate of similar simple scenarios involving one-way and round-trip travel plans, averaged over all the nine systems, was around 60 percent for the tests in 2000, and increased to about 80 percent in 2001, when the evaluation team also introduced more complex travel scenarios with multiple trips. For those particular scenarios, the average task completion rates dropped to less than 40 percent! PARADISE was applied to the 2001 Communicator evaluation, and the result of the analysis confirmed a reasonable hypothesis: the main factors influencing user satisfaction were task duration, average number of words spoken by the system at each turn, and both task completion and speech recognition sentence error rates.

Although considered statistically significant, the Communicator evaluation tests were not based on a large number of calls. Nonetheless, all the teams tried their best to build systems as if they were commercial applications exposed to much larger populations of users. For instance, the flight information provided by all systems was correct and updated in real time. Some of the research sites made their systems available internally to generate actual flight plans for their employees and students, often forcing them to use the system for all their business trips. But the reality is that the Communicator systems were, over all, used very little: at most, a few hundred calls per month. Moreover, the testing conditions did not reflect real-world situations. The scenarios were predetermined; the subjects were not real users but people recruited just to test the systems. That alone diminished the value of the assessment: experimental users are typically not as deeply motivated as real users, and the experimenters often observed that, when in trouble, their users changed scenarios and accepted wrong itineraries if that would bring the test to an end so they could leave and collect their compensation. Moreover, although the evaluations performed within the DARPA Communicator project provided useful insights to the researchers, the small number of tests didn't provide sufficient feedback for the researchers to improve their systems' technology. Indeed, improving dialog systems proved to be much harder than improving speech recognition systems in the Resource Management and ATIS projects.

On top of these difficulties, there was another issue that started to push DARPA away from interactive speech systems. Early in 2000, the U.S. spoken dialog industry was starting to gain momentum. A few companies were building real-world systems deployed for large companies that were handling hundreds of thousands of real-world users every day, as opposed to the few thousands of calls that the Communicator systems handled over their entire lifetimes. Nor could the Communicator systems benefit from the results achieved by these real-world systems: the firms that built them participated only marginally in DARPA's scientific projects, and the industry itself was evolving on its own path, with its own standards, architectures, and paradigms, which often differed—and with good reason—from those of the research community. Deciding after 9/11 that spoken dialog research was far less important than research more directly related to homeland security, DARPA terminated the Communicator project at the end of 2001 and did not renew it.

Exploration and Exploitation

Besides deepening our understanding of the complex issues involved in building and testing sophisticated mixed-initiative dialog systems, the DARPA Communicator project also fostered the evolution of machine learning to automatically determine an optimal interaction strategy. It did so with what's known as "reinforcement learning," which allowed speech researchers to solve problems they couldn't solve with more traditional supervised learning.

Before considering the difference between the two types of learning, however, let's look at what's involved in machine learning, one of whose bare-bones tasks is learning how to give names to unnamed things or, as scientists would say, how to "classify unknown patterns." When you come across a dog, for example, you immediately give it a name according to what breed you think it is: a golden retriever, a Labrador, a poodle, and so on. If the dog doesn't have the clear characteristics of any breed you know, you name it anyway: mixed-breed, mutt, mongrel. Or you simply say, "I don't know what kind." Your ability to recognize the breed of a dog is based, first, on your ability to detect its characteristics or features, what computer scientists call "feature extraction." For a dog, those features might be its size and height, the size and shape of its muzzle and ears, the color and type of its fur, and so on. And, second, your ability to recognize the dog's breed is based on your ability to match those features with the features of all the breeds you know. If you're good at recognizing dog breeds, it means that you've learned, in more general terms, how to assign predetermined categories to sets of features. Machine learning is about that: associating sets of features with predetermined categories. So an intelligent machine should be able to assign a category, a name, a label, even a specific breed to any set of features presented to it, or, failing that, to return an "I don't know" type of response, and, ideally, it should be able to do all this while making the fewest possible mistakes.

Now, assuming the machine has some ability to learn, how do you teach it to make associations between sets of features, or patterns, and categories? Up till now, we've considered several instances of what machine learning scientists call "supervised learning," such as template-matching speech recognition and hidden Markov models. Basically, with supervised learning, you present a machine with samples of patterns, such as sequences of feature vectors corresponding to utterances, each categorized with the correct label, for example, the word or the words that were actually spoken. The set of samples is called a "training set," and the learning is said to be "supervised" because you provide, for each sample, the correct category. Based on that, the machine should learn how to assign a category label to patterns that were not part of the training set, as long as they belong to the same predefined categories. This is called "generalization ability."

Let's consider a different learning situation. Do you remember how you learned to play games like chess, backgammon, checkers, or poker? First, you learned the rules of the game, of course. And, at least when you were starting out, an older relative or friend may have given you a few pointers. But, almost certainly, no one ever told you what the right thing to do was in every possible situation, or even in most situations, what piece to move and where, what cards to keep or discard, and so on. Instead, you simply started to play. Sometimes you won, and sometimes—more often than not at the beginning—you lost. And each time you won, that was a reward. If you played a lot of games, and if you paid attention to what worked and what didn't, you won more and more often. You learned what moves to make and what moves to avoid in order to win again. You learned when you won, and even when your opponent won. Well, what you were doing is known as "reinforcement learning," and it's a learning situation we humans often find ourselves in.[15]

Among scientists taking interest in a mathematical model of reinforcement learning was Gerald Tesauro, from the IBM's T. J. Watson Research Center, who began in the early 1990s to develop algorithms that would use the reinforcement learning paradigm. Board games, such as backgammon, were a perfect sandbox for these algorithms. In fact, the scientific world started paying attention to the power of reinforcement learning algorithms when Tesauro published his results on the computer game TD-Gammon, whose program could play better than all previous backgammon programs, to include Neurogammon's, built by Tesauro himself a few years earlier, and better, or almost better, than some of the best human players in the world. The success of TD-Gammon was, in a way, paradoxical. Although previous backgammon programs such as Neurogammon's had a lot of knowledge about the game and were often trained on extensive corpora of sample moves performed by champions, TD-Gammon's had none. TD-Gammon was given only the rules of the game and then allowed to play against itself in hundreds of thousands of computer-simulated matches. At the end of each match, TD-Gammon *reinforced* the strength of the moves that led one of the two parties to victory by using an algorithm called "TD-lambda." After 300,000 matches, selecting the strongest moves in each situation, TD-Gammon was playing at least as well as any previously built backgammon computer program. After 1,500,000 matches TD-Gammon was superior to any other program and stopped improving. No matter how many more matches it played after that, its strategy didn't change. It was so good it couldn't play any better!

At the time of the Communicator project, my colleague Esther Levin and I at AT&T Laboratories were working on spoken language understanding and dialog systems. We had built CHRONUS, the best-performing ATIS project system for natural language understanding. A statistically based system, CHRONUS is a typical example of well-engineered supervised learning. But, unfortunately, the problem of spoken dialog couldn't be successfully tackled by any form of supervised learning.

During the winter of 1996, Esther participated in "Machines That Learn," a small workshop that was held every year in the snowy mountains of Utah to bring together the world's leading experts in statistical machine learning—most of whom are also excellent skiers. There she met Gerald Tesauro, who discussed, among other things, some of the most recent results on TD-Gammon and reinforcement learning. Esther returned home with a striking insight: a dialog is pretty much like a board game, except that, at the end, there's no winner or loser: both parties collaborate to reach the goal. In fact, reaching the goal in a dialog can be regarded as winning for both; if the goal isn't reached, both parties lose. Reaching the goal seems like a good reward for a reinforcement learning machine. But, as you now know, just reaching the goal isn't enough to determine whether a dialog's actually good. Thus the reward function for a dialog would need to be more complex than simply winning or losing. It would need to use a continuous range of values that corresponded to the quality of the dialog. For instance, a shorter dialog that reached its goal would get a higher reward than a longer dialog that reached the same goal.

Focusing on flight information learning machines, let's consider a reinforcement reward based on two components. One component is related to the duration of the dialog: the shorter the dialog, the greater the reward. That will teach a machine to favor short dialogs over long ones. Another component is related to the number of flight solutions found that match the user requirements. The dialog machine is given a reinforcement reward, a nonzero value, for finding a reasonable number of flight solutions, say between one and five, and penalized—given *no* reinforcement reward, or zero—if it finds either no solutions or too many solutions (for instance, more than five), which is probably just as bad.

Most reinforcement learning methods are based on the concept of Markov decision process (MDP), which is a close relative of the hidden Markov models used in speech recognition. Without going into the math of MDPs, it's enough to know that interactive processes, like games, lend themselves quite naturally to an MDP representation. Markov decision processes take note, continuously, of any change of state in everything that's of interest to the system, which is called the "environment" in reinforcement learning jargon. For instance, in the case of backgammon and other board games, the environment is the board, and only the board. There's nothing else of interest to a backgammon player while playing. Anytime a backgammon player makes a move—performs what's called an "action"—the opponent will make another move, thus changing the state of the environment, the configuration of the pieces on the board. How many possible states of the environment or board configurations are there? Backgammon has some billion trillion (10^{20}) possible configurations—far too many to consider all of them. To successfully play backgammon, a model like a Markov decision process must therefore do something besides finding the best action for each possible state, the action that will give it the greatest chance to acquire the maximum amount of rewards. The large, sometimes infinitely large, number of states in any practical problem worth solving with reinforcement learning creates a challenge for mathematicians and computer scientists, one they rise to time and again, however. So that, even though an MDP can't find what's called its "optimal strategy" or "optimal policy" when dealing with as large a number of states as they are in backgammon, with certain algorithms, it can find a *suboptimal,* but still useful solution.

Most of the solutions to reinforcement learning problems are based on assigning a value to every action in every state or set of states. That value represents how good any particular action is for that particular state of the environment in getting rewards in a large number of games. Each time the system wins a game, the value of any action taken during that game increases. In any game, for every state, the system chooses the action with the currently highest value. However, from time to time and at random, the system also tries some new actions to avoid getting stuck in old ones that happen to have received high values just by chance. This is called "exploration and exploitation" and is basically following a known principle of learning: if you don't try something new now and then, you'll never learn anything new.[16] Or, as Alexander Graham Bell put it in a famous quote, inscribed on his bust at the entrance to Bell Telephone Laboratories in Murray Hill, New Jersey:

Leave the beaten track occasionally and dive into the woods. Every time you do so you will find something you have never seen before.

So, acting on her insight from the snowy mountains of Utah, Esther and I tried to model dialog as a Markov decision process. To see how we did that, look at a dialog as if it were a game between a machine player trying to learn the best dialog strategy and a human player, who presumably knows how to converse— and do this from the perspective of the machine. Imagine the virtual game board as a blackboard where, at any point in time, the information exchanged by the two players is written. So, the human player starts first and says something. The pieces of information extracted from the human's sentence are noted on the board. As the machine player, you look at the board and, based on what's written there, you select a possible action, following an exploration and exploitation strategy. That action might be a question, the retrieval of some information from a database, or the presentation of certain pieces of information. As a result of your action, new pieces of information are generated either by a query to the machine's database, such as the flight information database, or by a response of the human player. The new pieces of information are written on the board, and again you analyze them, select another action based on that analysis, and continue to the next step. The information written on the board represents the state of the environment. The assignment of the best action to take for each state is the *dialog policy*, which is eventually optimized by the reinforcement learning method.

Now, staying in the domain of flight information, as the machine player, you formally define specific possible actions in a dialog. One action might be asking a general question such as "How may I help you?" Another might be looking at the board and presenting to the human player (the user) any flight information written there. A third possible action might be converting available constraints from the board, such as origin and destination airports, departure and arrival times, and airlines, into a database query. You formally define constraining actions, too, such as asking about a particular flight constraint: "When do you want to leave?" or "Which airline do you like to use?" And relaxation actions such as asking the human player (the caller) to remove a constraint: "Do you mind flying on other airlines?" or "Do you mind leaving from somewhere else?" Finally, you formally define a closing action, such as saying something like "Good-bye, and thank you for using our services," which brings the dialog to an end.

Once you've formally defined the state space and the actions, you can try to interact with the human player. Since, at the beginning, there's no strategy, you'd start by selecting actions at random at each state. Your first few dialogs would sound a bit strange, to say the least:

Machine: Do you mind considering other departing times?
Human: What? . . . I want to go to Boston.
Machine: Do you mind considering a different airline?
Human: Uh . . . I said I want to go to Boston
Machine: There are 1,527 flights to Boston, Flight 1 is . . . flight 2 is . . . flight 1527 is . . .
Human: . . . I need to leave tomorrow. To Boston tomorrow, from San Francisco!
Machine: Thank you for using our services. Please call again.

Note that, as the machine, you're just exploring at this point, so you're choosing each action at each turn in a completely random manner. But sometimes, in a large number of these strange-sounding dialogs, you get lucky and happen to do something right, and you may even collect some reward. With a lot of these dialogs, and with rewards now and then, you'll actually learn to do the right things more often than the wrong ones. Unfortunately, depending on the system parameters, such as the number of states and actions, reinforcement learning algorithms may converge very slowly to a possible solution, and it may take you tens, or even hundreds, of thousands of inconclusive dialogs to come to something that may actually make sense, like the following dialog:

Machine: Hello, this is the automated flight information system. How can I help you?

Human: I want to go to Boston tomorrow.

Machine: Where are you leaving from?

Human: San Francisco.

Machine: There are thirty-two flights from San Francisco to Boston. Which airline do you want to use?

Human: Hmm . . . I don't care about which airline, but I want to take the latest flight.

Machine: Sure. Flight AA 123 leaves San Francisco at . . .

But eventually, in a long but finite time, you, as the dialog machine, will learn how to conduct a normal-sounding, proper dialog. That's guaranteed by the convergence properties of the reinforcement learning algorithm. The system will eventually converge to the strategy that would collect the most rewards, or what's called the "optimal strategy."

Even though our dialog machine would eventually learn how to properly interact with users, Esther and I knew we couldn't recruit users with enough patience to go through the tens of thousands of inconclusive dialogs needed for that to happen. So we came up with another idea: an artificial user machine that would provide questions and answers, as a real user would, to the learning dialog machine for as long as we wanted, tirelessly, with infinite patience, and at practically no cost. The artificial user machine would start with a random selection of an itinerary and goals, such as finding the cheapest, the latest, the earliest flight, or one with a specific airline. Then it would patiently provide the answers to the learning machine, sometimes giving more answers than was requested, sometimes providing no answer at all, sometimes asking other questions or changing its mind, in the same ways and with the same frequency as a human user would. Indeed, we built an artificial user machine by taking samples from the behavior of the real human users of DARPA Communicator systems. We made the artificial user machine interact, at the symbolic level, with the learning dialog machine. And, eventually, after hundreds of thousands of inconclusive dialogs, the dialog machine learned to interact in the proper way and with an optimal strategy, which can be summarized by the following six steps:

1. Greet with an open prompt and collect the user's initial constraints on the flight, typically origin and arrival airport.

2. Go find all flights that match the constraints collected so far.

3. If there are too many flights, explicitly ask for further constraints, such as departure time and airline.

4. Go find all flights that match the additional constraints.

5. If no flights are found, try relaxing some of the constraints, such as departure time or airline.

6. When a reasonable number of flights are found, present them to the user, and conclude the dialog.[17]

Of course, any good designer of user interactions wouldn't need to go through the process of running hundreds of thousands of reinforcement learning experiments with an artificial user and a reinforcement learning dialog machine to arrive at this, quite reasonable strategy. But our experiment, as a proof of concept, was intended only to show that it's possible to build a machine that can learn dialog just by interacting. And it succeeded admirably; indeed, it was the beginning of a new line of research in automatic spoken dialog systems.

Steve Young, a professor at the University of Cambridge who'd challenged the DARPA evaluations a few years earlier with his excellent results on the Resource Management task, has continued the research started by Esther Levin and me. With a theory of learning dialog based on the concept of partially observable Markov decision processes (POMPDs), Young has taken into account the natural uncertainty caused, for instance, by the possible errors of the speech recognizer.[18] Young's team and other teams around the world, like those led by Oliver Lemon in Edinburgh, Jason Williams at AT&T Laboratories, and Olivier Pietquin first in Belgium and then in France, are carrying forward one of the most promising endeavors in human-machine spoken language communication—that of building systems that can learn to talk and interact with humans by experience.

Diminishing Returns

DARPA's Resource Management, ATIS, and Communicator projects were not alone in pushing the envelope of speech recognition technology. To focus on large-vocabulary speech recognition, Texas Instruments' laboratories used passages from the *Wall Street Journal* read by selected speakers to compile a corpus known as

"WSJ." With NIST distributing the data and evaluating the results, the WSJ project was expanded to include several other laboratories and corpora with vocabularies of 5,000 and 20,000 words. Well-managed evaluations drove down the word error rate from more than 15 percent to just a few percent in as many years.

In the early 1990s, Texas Instruments compiled another corpus, called "Switchboard," of people talking on the telephone about topics selected at random, which TI made available for research, as it had with other corpora. Initial results were quite disappointing, however, with some sites reporting a word error rate of 90 percent! The Switchboard corpus presented speech recognition scientists with their most difficult task ever. Using an unrestricted, unknown vocabulary, both parties in the recorded conversations spoke in an unconstrained, casual manner and in the presence of considerable background noise; their speech often overlapped and was filled with disfluencies. Further work on the conversational speech recognition task pushed the word error rate down to 48 percent in 1995 and to 19 percent in 2001, where it leveled out.

Another challenging speech recognition task was based on a corpus called "Broadcast News," compiled from recordings of *Marketplace* broadcasts on National Public Radio. The challenge here was to recognize speech in the presence of noise, music, and frequent changes of topic. But broadcast speech was much better formed than the conversational speech of the Switchboard corpus, and thus easier to recognize. The speech recognition community was able to reduce the error rate from 31 percent in 1996 to 13 percent in 1998.

NIST tracked the accuracy levels reported by the various speech recognition projects, most of which were funded by DARPA. The graphs in figure 6.5 plot the word error rate through the years by type of speech.

The easiest tasks were the recognition of read speech with restricted vocabularies, as in the Resource Management and Wall Street Journal projects, and interactive spontaneous speech, as in the ATIS project. Conversational speech over the telephone, the broadcast speech of newscasters, and meeting speech posed more serious and still unresolved recognition issues. Each project shows the same evolution in terms of word error rate. At the beginning, when the task is new, the word error rate is high. As more data is collected and the researchers become more and more familiar with the task, the error rate falls until it reaches the point of diminishing returns. It's interesting to note that, except for the Resource Management and the ATIS tasks, which can be considered quite simple from the speech recognition point of view, machines have never exceeded the level of the accuracy of human transcribers.

Did these challenges bring any substantial groundbreaking innovation to the speech recognition field? Although several improvements were made to the statistical modeling algorithms in the 1990s and early 2000s, most did not result in any

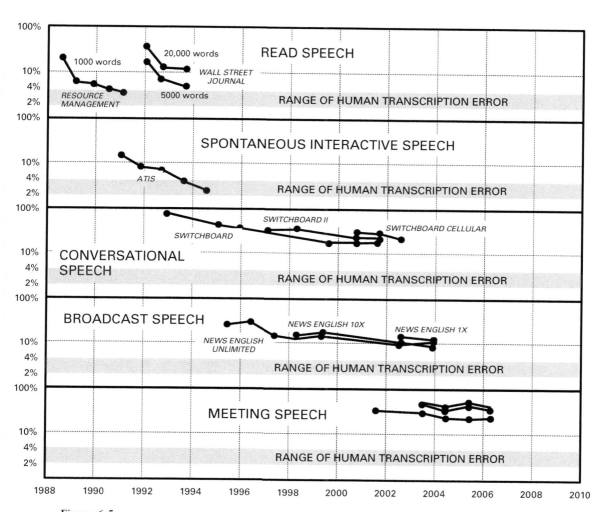

Figure 6.5
Evolution of the word error rate through the years in various projects evaluated by NIST.

significant advance beyond the basic hidden Markov model paradigm of the 1980s. Indeed, the feeling among researchers was that tweaking the algorithms and using more data were the only ways available to reduce the word error rate. DARPA sought to encourage innovation among the different labs that participated in its projects by competition for funding, on the one hand, and by collaboration through the sharing of data and technology, on the other. This two-pronged policy had both a positive and a negative effect: it sped up the rate of improvement of the speech recognition technology, but it also eliminated any significant technological differences between the various laboratories. Their speech recognizers looked more and more alike. Everybody was using the same tricks, the ones that worked best to improve accuracy and thus lower the word error rate. Whichever laboratory had the lowest error rates was publicly praised and had the best chance to see its funding renewed the following year. Trying a new technique was considered risky since it could produce a higher error rate than the best performing sites and jeopardize next year's funding. Thus the story was always the same. New tasks, new challenges, tweaking, more data, and applying more tricks, until everyone reached a plateau of performance, the point of diminishing returns, when the research community started to lose interest and turned to a new, more difficult problem. And the cycle would begin again.

The events of September 11, 2001, profoundly changed the way DARPA looked at the challenges facing the nation. The U.S. government began to recognize the importance of technology in fighting terrorism and enhancing national security through improved intelligence. Building speech recognition machines for making flight reservations was no longer considered either interesting or useful. But there was another development that contributed to DARPA's reduced support for research on talking machines: the birth of an industry, the "speech industry," as many called it, which started to gain momentum around the mid-1990s and was building speech recognition systems for millions of users by the year 2000. The industry's systems didn't attempt to solve the general problem of natural language understanding, yet they outperformed those built by the DARPA project researchers. And so it was that the funding agencies, both private and public, turned their attention toward other problems that required advanced speech technology, though not to understand speech and interact with humans.

7

An Interlude at the Other End of the Chain

Referring to the tasks of intelligent talking machines at a speech technology conference a few years ago, a famous scientist remarked that generating synthetic speech is as easy as squeezing toothpaste out of a tube. On the other hand, the scientist continued, recognizing and understanding speech is as difficult as putting the toothpaste back in. This remark was not well received by those involved in automatic speech synthesis. And they were right to object. Both speech synthesis and speech recognition and understanding are extremely difficult tasks. True, building a speech recognizer that recognizes a few words in a well-defined acoustic context is relatively easy. An undergrad student with a knack for signal processing and a copy of MATLAB programming language can do it in a few hours. But building a speech recognizer with near-human accuracy that can understand speech in all sorts of adverse conditions, from all possible speakers, and with all possible words and nonwords is still beyond the reach of our technology. Likewise, the same talented student can build a program that generates speech-like acoustic signals in the same few hours. But building a machine that speaks with near-human naturalness, expressivity, emotion, and intelligibility is also still beyond the reach of our technology, although speech technologists have made tremendous strides in the fields of both speech synthesis and speech recognition and understanding. As a brief interlude from our main concern, this chapter gives credit to the thousands of scientists who've made building machines that can speak as much as possible like humans the principal goal of their careers, and often of their lives. It's also intended to give you an idea of the technology issues at the other end of the speech chain: the generation of speech from text, or "text-to-speech," as it's often called.

We started our speech technology journey at the turn of the eighteenth century with Wolfgang von Kempelen's invention, a mechanical speaking machine that, with bellows, pipes, and a rubber mouth and nose, could simulate the production of simple speech sounds by the human vocal apparatus. We then jumped ahead to 1939 and a more advanced invention, by Bell Labs scientist Homer Dudley, an electronic talking machine that, with the help of a carefully trained operator, could speak actual words, phrases, and sentences. Those inventions were definitely the first attempts to give the gift of speech to inanimate devices of wood, rubber, metal, and electronic circuitry, to artificially create human speech in a machine—or to perform what's commonly known as "speech synthesis." Then we moved to the other end of the speech chain, the inverse problem, that of building machines that recognize and understand human speech, which is the central topic of this book, and we followed the struggle for a mathematical representation that would allow machines to recognize the words in a spoken signal with higher and higher accuracy. Building a near-perfect speech synthesizer is as challenging and complex as building a near-perfect speech recognizer. And you'll soon see why.

Back to 1939

Homer Dudley's 1939 invention, the Voder, is an ahead-of-its-time example of what today is called a "text-to-speech system" (TTS). Seen from a distance, the only difference between the Voder and a modern TTS system is that, lacking a computer, Dudley had to use a human operator to process text and execute commands.

Let's see how the Voder actually worked.[1] Its synthetic voice box used electronic circuits to generate the two basic sounds of human speech: a periodic tone for the voiced sounds, vowels and voiced consonants, such as /z/, /v/, and /l/, and a hissing noise for the unvoiced consonants, such as /sh/, /f/, and /k/. The tone and hissing were then filtered to produce the different vowel and consonant sounds. But, of course, that wasn't enough. The operator had to put together the sequences of sounds with the right characteristics to generate full words, phrases, and sentences by using the machine controls: ten white keys for generating the vowel and some consonant sounds, three black keys for generating the stop consonants, a wrist bar to switch from voiced to unvoiced sounds, a knob to select male or female voice, and a pedal to change the intonation or pitch.

Say you wanted to hear what "My dog ate the sausage" sounded like in the Voder's electronic voice. You'd write the sentence on a piece of paper and give it to the operator, let's call him "Toby." After reading the sentence, Toby would have to create a mental translation of it into a sequence of phonemes, the basic speech sounds:

My dog ate the sausage → /mə dog et də sosəj/.

That would be the first step, which relied on Toby's knowledge of the phonetics of spoken English and its rules of pronunciation. At this point, Toby would push the keys corresponding to each individual sound—a key for /m/, one for /ə/, one for /d/, and so on—making sure that each sound was generated using the correct voiced or unvoiced sound. For instance, for the /d/ initial stop consonant of the word "dog," he would need to push the correct black key, and at the same time push the wrist bar in order to generate a voiced sound. If the wrist bar was in the unvoiced position instead, the Voder would generate a /t/, and not a /d/, sound. Now, while Toby was generating the correct sequence of sounds, he'd have to take care of the intonation, too. Unfortunately, you didn't indicate the correct intonation on the piece of paper you gave him. No surprise there: we don't normally use intonation marks when we write; intonation has to be inferred from the context, the punctuation, and the meaning of the sentence in general. Seeing a period and not a question mark at the end, Toby would realize that the sentence was a simple statement. Perhaps he'd decide to stress "my," as in

<u>My</u> dog ate the sausage,

to convey the meaning that it was *my* dog and not someone else's that ate the sausage. So while he was pushing keys and working the wrist bar, he'd also have to push the pedal and raise the pitch on "my." Or perhaps he'd decide to stress—raise the pitch on—"ate" instead, as in

My dog <u>ate</u> the sausage,

to convey the message that my dog *ate* the sausage rather than knocked it off the grill or simply ignored it. And, of course, either way, Toby would also have to maintain the right rhythm and speed for the sequence of phonemes to make the spoken sentence sound natural and neither too fast nor too slow, and he'd have to make sure each phoneme sounded natural as well, and not like

My do-o-o-o-o-g a-a-a-a-ate the sausage

Now you understand why operators required a full year of training before they were able to make the Voder speak fluently. Learning to play its keyboard, wrist bar, and pedals with the right rhythm and speed was pretty much like learning to play a musical instrument, an organ, say, but instead of having to read music, they had to learn the ins and the outs of English phonetics and pronunciation.

The system comprising the operator and the Voder was indeed a text-to-speech machine, one that transformed any text into speech for a given specific language. You'd give the operator a piece of paper with some text on it, and, after a short time, you'd hear the synthetic, artificial machine voice of the Voder reading out loud exactly what you'd written. Today you don't need an operator to generate speech from text. The operator's function is performed by a computer program.

Creating Sounds That Sound like Speech

Speech synthesis, the artificial generation of speech-like sounds, was the challenge that Wolfgang von Kempelen and his contemporaries tried to meet by building mechanical devices that imitated the human vocal apparatus, whereas Homer Dudley and other scientists of his time approached the same problem with electronic devices that used generators and filters, pedals and keys. Even before Kempelen, the Russian professor Christian Kratzenstein, aware of the physiological differences in how humans produce the various vowel sounds, experimented with acoustic pipes of different shapes that reproduced those sounds when air was blown into them.[2]

Both Kratzenstein and Kempelen helped improve our general understanding of human speech. In the nineteenth century, others such as Hermann von Helmholtz, Sir Charles Wheatstone, and later Robert Willis would build speaking machines based on Kratzenstein's and Kempelen's work and would make further discoveries about the relationship between the geometry and mechanics of the vocal apparatus, on the one hand, and the perceived quality of individual speech sounds, on the other.[3] Even Alexander Graham Bell built a speaking machine and, it's said, went so far as to perform speech experiments on his dog, forcing changes in its vocal tract by pushing and pulling its jaws while it was growling to make it produce humanlike sounds.[4]

Although there were several attempts to create speech sounds by using electronic devices such as buzzers and resonators in the 1920s and early 1930s, it wasn't until Dudley's Voder that sounds comparable to the human voice would come out of a machine. The Voder drew the attention of the scientific world to the problem of speech synthesis. Several other labs besides Bell undertook significant research in that regard, most notably, Haskins Laboratories, a private nonprofit research institute founded in 1935, affiliated with Yale, and located in New Haven, Connecticut. There, in 1950, Franklin Cooper and his colleagues invented a machine called a "pattern playback synthesizer" that converted images of spectrograms printed on a transparent film into speech by using a moving belt and light sensors.[5]

As you may recall from chapter 1, formants are the characteristic resonation peaks in the speech spectrum that appear as dark, up-and-down horizontal lines in spectrograms. As you may also recall, the precise position of these formants on the frequency scale, determined by the particular configuration of the vocal apparatus at a precise instant during the pronunciation of a speech sound, characterizes which speech sound you actually perceive. F1 and F2, the first two formants in the lower part of the speech spectrum, determine whether you perceive a speech sound as an /a/, /e/, /u/, or any other voiced phoneme. This is graphically represented in figure 7.1, a familiar figure now, where the two axes represent the frequencies of F1 and F2, respectively, and where circles show the variability of the formant frequencies across different speakers and contexts.

So, for instance, if the first formant is around 300 Hz and the second around 2,000 Hz, you perceive an /i/ sound, as in "bit." If the first formant is around 250 Hz and the second around 900 Hz, you perceive an /u/ sound, as in "boot," and so

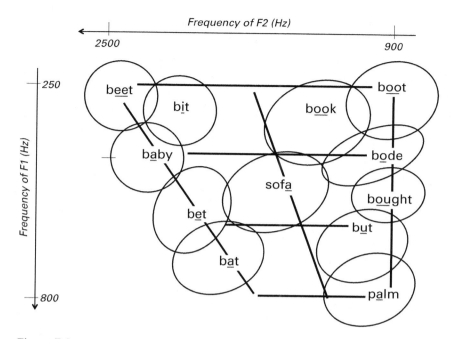

Figure 7.1
Across-speaker variability of the first two formant frequencies for the vowel sounds of U.S. English.

on. This is the idea behind what researchers call a "formant-based synthesizer," which starts with an electronically generated periodic signal, corresponding to the excitation of the vocal cords, and an electronic filter that resonates at the frequency of the first two or three formants. If the resonation peaks are placed at the right frequencies, as in figure 7.1, you perceive the resulting acoustic signals as an /a/, /u/, /i/ or other voiced phoneme. With a noise-like signal and some manipulations of its filter, the synthesizer can generate sounds you perceive as unvoiced consonants and nasals. And, finally, when the duration of all these parameters is carefully controlled, the synthesizer produces sounds you perceive as words, phrases, or even full sentences. This idea was pursued both by Walter Lawrence in the United Kingdom and Gunnar Fant in Sweden, who, independently, built the first formant synthesizers in 1953.

Lawrence's synthesizer, called "PAT" (Parametric Artificial Talker), had three formant resonator filters connected in parallel, excited either by a buzz or by a noise-like signal.[6] At the same time, Gunnar Fant, at the Royal Institute of Technology in Stockholm, built a formant synthesizer called "OVE" (Orator Verbis Electris), which also had three filters to simulate the first three formants.[7] The difference between PAT and OVE was in the details of the composition of their filters, but both were based on the same basic principle: control of fundamental speech parameters by a set of rules derived from expert knowledge of human speech, a principle later called "synthesis by rule."

During the time Lawrence and Fant were first working on rule-based speech synthesis, several other scientists were trying to do exactly the same thing the other way around, with speech recognition: derive a set of rules that would identify phonetic and linguistic elements from the values and variation of fundamental speech parameters such as formants. But, whereas rule-based speech synthesizers succeeded in producing intelligible and at least somewhat natural-sounding speech, rule-based speech recognizers consistently failed to recognize natural speech with any reliability. One of the reasons for this is that both inputs and targets at the opposite ends of the speech chain are themselves opposite in nature.

Thus, on the one hand, speech-to-text or speech recognition takes an immensely variable input, natural speech, and tries to reach a precise target: the words that were spoken. On the other hand, text-to-speech or speech synthesis takes a precise input, the words to be spoken, and tries to reach an immensely variable target: natural speech. Since there are many possible ways to pronounce a word or a phrase in natural speech, listeners don't have an ideal target pronunciation in mind, and thus a synthesized utterance doesn't have to sound precisely one way to be intelligible; indeed, it can sound quite strange and still be understood as long as it falls within the variations of speech that listeners are accustomed to hearing. The problem with speech synthesis is that there's no formal, objective way of determining whether a synthetic voice is a good one. It can only be assessed subjectively. To arrive at reliable subjective assessments, speech synthesis technologists have a statistically significant number of subjects listen to a statistically significant number of samples of synthesized speech and rate them on their intelligibility and speech-like quality.

Rule-based speech synthesis is still used today and actually works quite well in several commercial applications. Even though it hasn't produced the naturalness and the humanlike feeling that other speech synthesis methods have, it's highly intelligible and often the preferred method in applications where speed and intelligibility are at premium. For instance, blind people prefer to use ruled-based speech synthesis readers when they read documents and books. Such readers allow them to listen to a read text at a few times normal speed yet maintain high intelligibility.

In 1962, Gunnar Fant, still at the Royal Institute of Technology in Stockholm, built OVE II, an improved version of OVE I, followed by other versions in the subsequent years, which, in the 1980s, led to Infovox, one of the first widely adopted, commercially available multilingual speech synthesizers. Inspired by the success of PAT and OVE, John Holmes developed a similar formant-based synthesizer at the Joint Speech Research Unit in the United Kingdom; indeed, he manually tuned his synthesizer so well that listeners couldn't distinguish its sentences from natural human speech.[8]

Among many other experimentally successful rule-based and formant-based systems, probably the most sophisticated was MITalk, built by MIT researchers Jonathan Allen, Sharon Hunnicutt, and Dennis Klatt and first demonstrated in 1979.[9] Dennis Klatt went on to develop an improved version, called "KlatTalk." MITalk and KlatTalk gave rise to many commercial rule-based speech synthesizers, including DECtalk, produced and marketed by the Digital Equipment Corporation.

About this time, another school of speech technologists embarked on an ambitious project known as "articulatory synthesis," whose goal was to generate speech using a mechanical simulation of the human articulatory organs and vocal cords. Although the Kempelen speaking machine might well be considered an early example, the first modern example of articulatory synthesis was a machine invented in 1958 by MIT researcher George Rosen, who introduced the term. DAVO (Dynamic Analogue of the VOcal tract) was a mechanical reproduction of the human vocal apparatus whose different sections were controlled by impulses on a tape recorder.[10] With the advent of the digital computer, however, DAVO and other mechanical synthesizers would soon became obsolete.

Computers are often used today to simulate mechanical systems by encoding and solving in real time equations related to the laws of physics. Most video games are excellent examples of this. Take the Nintendo Wii, which solves motion equations of physics in real time to re-create not only the visual effect of a ball bouncing around on a tennis court, but also the sensation of its mechanical impact and feedback on the player's hand controller. All of this is achieved by encoding the laws of motion into a program that can compute, at any point in time, the position and velocity of every object on the display and take into consideration both collisions and friction between the objects. Articulatory synthesis of speech starts from the same premise. Assuming that the configuration of the vocal apparatus at each point in time is completely determined by its size and shape, the amount of lip aperture and protrusion, the position and the height of the tip of the tongue, and the position of the velum, and using the equations of acoustics and the motion and dynamics of fluids, you can compute, for any set of values, the frequency content of the sound that's generated.

By using X-ray techniques, acoustic linguists collected enough data about the position and shape of the vocal apparatus to create a fairly accurate mechanical model; they then extracted the values of the model that corresponded to the production of each sound. Unfortunately, being quite complicated, the movements of the tongue and of the other parts, like the jaw and the lips, could not be modeled in a simple way. Moreover, the solution of the motion equations in real time required a lot of computational power, which wasn't available until a few years ago. Thus, even though the articulatory approach has the potential to produce high-quality synthetic speech, it's never succeeded in doing so, although it's still pursued by some researchers for its potential to model human speech in an accurate way.

Even as rule-based speech synthesizers were becoming known around the world, a different technique was being developed that would again oppose the elegance and flexibility of the phonetic linguistic approach to the brute force of engineering.

Build Your Own Speech Synthesizer at Home

Even if you're not an expert in speech synthesis, you can build a rudimentary speech synthesizer using your home computer. The first thing you need is a sound editing program, which will allow you to open up an audio file, display the waveform, and cut and paste segments of it. There are many such programs you can download from the Web. Then you need to record a few hundred words. You may want to choose common words, like

a, the, this that, of, house, garden, horse, dog, sausage, eat, eating, ate, my, your, our,

and so on. With that collection of recorded words, you can now build a number of synthetic sentences, sentences that you've not directly recorded, for instance, "My dog ate the sausage," or any other utterance you want, as long as you have recordings of all its words. You can do that by *concatenating*—linking together in a series—the available words one after the other, using your sound editing program. You can also perform the same trick with an existing recording of a long speech by someone else. Use the audio editing program to cut it into individual words, and you can have the speaker say whatever you like, provided you have all the words you need. With some more work, you can also try to make your speaker say a word that's not in the recording. For that, you need to find parts of the word in other words, link the parts together, and create the word you need—a process that's called "concatenative speech synthesis." With enough recorded material, you'll have all the parts you need to build any possible word.

However, even though this process may seem quite simple and easy to perform, there is a whole range of technology issues to be resolved in order to produce good-sounding and intelligible speech. Most likely, the utterances you build by concatenating pieces of speech will sound awful, like a bunch of words or sounds cut and pasted together, which is exactly what they are. You can hear the discontinuity between words, the intonation would be completely off, and, in many cases, no one except yourself would be able to understand what was said, especially the words built from parts of other words. The rudimentary approach of cutting and pasting pieces of recorded speech won't bring you very far. You need additional work and knowledge to make the cut-and-paste approach to speech synthesis generate speech that is both intelligible and natural sounding. First of all, you need to record enough speech to have examples of all possible sounds in your language so that you can build virtually any word there is to build. But having all the possible sounds won't be enough. As you've seen, speech is a highly dynamic phenomenon. Thus, when your vocal apparatus is generating the sound /m/, as in the word "ambitious," it's just moved out of a configuration that made it generate the preceding /a/ sound and it's already moving toward one that will generate the /b/ sound. So the sound that everyone would perceive as /m/ is acoustically a /m/ that's in transition from an /a/ sound to a /b/ sound. And if you speak fast, the transition from the /a/ sound to the /b/ sound may never reach a point where it's just a pure /m/. But, of course, you'll always perceive it just as a /m/ sound.

So, if you want to build a real concatenative speech synthesizer, you'll need quite a large set of recordings, one that includes all speech sounds in all possible contexts. As you may remember, we did the same calculation earlier for the hidden Markov models of phonetic units. If you consider that the English language has about forty different phonemes, than you've $40 \times 40 \times 40 = 64,000$ possible sounds in left and right contexts—and that's disregarding the effects that other sounds beyond the immediately adjacent ones may have. Of course, not all of the 64,000 "possible" contexts are actually possible. For instance, the sequence of phonemes /ktg/ is quite unpronounceable in English. Besides, vowel sounds in normal speech do reach a point of stability in the middle, which may be considered a neutral point that doesn't depend on the preceding or following sounds. But, even after some reduction in the total number of basic sounds, you still need a lot of recorded speech

At this point, you have to cut or segment the sounds in context on your recording into individual snippets and save them as audio clips. But, again, that's not enough to get a decent synthetic voice. If your artificial speech is to sound like natural speech, the right stress and intonation are critical. Stress on the wrong syllable makes words sound strange and often even unrecognizable. Without intonation, phrases and sentences sound flat, inexpressive, and unnatural, and, with the wrong intonation, they can't readily convey the right meaning. To achieve the right stress and intonation in synthesized speech, you need to properly set the three fundamental parameters of pitch, duration, and intensity, also called "suprasegmental parameters." But, even though you've collected samples of all the sounds in context you need to build any pronounceable word in your language, you can't easily change their suprasegmental parameters and create the right pattern of intonation for your reconstructed speech. Though today you can push the limits of the brute-force approach and store many instances of those sounds in context, with different degrees of stress and different durations, pitches, and intensities—and though doing so is actually one of the most effective approaches to concatenative speech synthesis—it wasn't even conceivable in the 1970s, when computer speed and storage were very limited.

Back then, speech synthesis labs around the world built concatenative synthesis systems by representing all those recorded snippets of speech parametrically, so that they could re-create them with any duration, pitch, and intensity, and could model the overall intonation of any utterance according to the intended meaning. Further advances in speech technology allowed researchers to concatenate recorded snippets and change their duration and pitch without having to represent them parametrically. That gave rise to the corpus-based forms of speech synthesis in use today.

From Text to Speech

Although modern concatenative text-to-speech synthesizers don't fundamentally differ from the simple machine you can build at home, they do differ in smaller ways that make them sound—and work—much better. So that, if your machine starts from a set of large chunks of speech, like words or phrases, it can generate only a limited number of messages by concatenating them. To push beyond that limited number, it needs a set of smaller units, the basic sounds or phonemes. So why not have a professional speech recorder, a "voice talent, record all possible phonemes and then concatenate them to have your synthesizer speak any possible text? In principle, you could do that but, in practice, you need to deal with several issues. First of all, as you've seen, when individual basic sounds are pronounced in conjunction with other sounds (and they almost always are) to form speech, their acoustic characteristics change depending on the previous and following sound—a phenomenon known as "coarticulation," which we discussed at length in previous chapters. So asking your voice talent, let's call her "Tara," to record the phonemes as isolated sounds won't work. The best you can do is to first have Tara—whose voice will become the voice of your machine—record a large number of phrases that present a lot of phonetic variation and to then surgically isolate all the individual sounds using a sound editing program. And, as I've pointed out repeatedly, you'll need to have samples all the possible phonemes in all the possible contexts and, since the number of such samples is exceedingly large, you'll need to reduce that number by pressing statistics and certain useful algorithms into service.

Let's assume you've extracted all the speech chunks you believe you need to synthesize any possible spoken message in your language. Have your synthesizer take the speech chunks it needs to form a sentence, say, "My dog ate the sausage," from its inventory and concatenate them—assuming it knows how to make the concatenated chunks sound as smooth as possible.[11] Most likely, the resulting utterance will be intelligible to an English speaker, but, without intonation, it will sound toneless, robot-like, unnatural. By applying the right intonation to the utterance, your machine can make it sound more natural—and more meaningful as well. For instance, the right intonation distinguishes a statement from a question; just as lexical stress allows the listener to distinguish between similar words having different lexical stress, by introducing what linguists call "intentional focus," the right intonation allows the listener to understand what distinctions the speaker intends, as you saw in the examples above. So, whereas intelligibility depends mostly on phonetic context, naturalness depends mostly on intonation. Indeed, the history of synthetic speech is one of trade-offs between intelligibility and naturalness—and the struggle to achieve both.

As you've seen, you obtain intonation by changing three characteristics of the speech signal: intensity, duration, and pitch. For instance, you obtain the typical intonation of a question by raising the pitch at the end of a sentence. And just as you produce the lexical stress of a word by increasing the loudness, duration, and pitch of the stressed syllable, so you obtain intentional focus, or intonational stress, on one part of a sentence by increasing its intensity, duration, and pitch—alone or in combination—with respect to the other parts of the sentence. But, unfortunately, even though you can easily change the intensity of a recorded chunk of speech, you can't easily change its duration and pitch.

And so it was that the most advanced text-to-speech systems developed in from the 1960s into the1990s did not concatenate recorded chunks of speech. Instead, they concatenated models of phonetic units in context extracted from large amounts of recorded speech and then parameterized these in such a way as to let them control their duration, pitch, and loudness. The two major schools of speech synthesis in those decades were rule-based synthesis, which relied mostly on rules determined by speech scientists to control the formants and the other characteristics of speech sounds, and parametric synthesis, which leaned toward the engineering, brute-force approach. The experts used to say that rule-based synthesizers sounded more intelligible, whereas parametric synthesizers sounded more natural.

But, even before learning how to speak, your speech synthesizer has to learn how to read. In order to read, it needs to perform what's called "grapheme-to-phoneme transcription" or "phonetic transcription," that is, to translate the text's sequence of alphabetic symbols, called "graphemes," into a sequence of phonetic symbols for the corresponding phonemes—this step was one of the mental processes performed by the operators of Dudley's Voder. At the same time, your machine needs to identify the text's intonation patterns and assign the correct lexical stress to its words. But before all of these steps, before it performs the actual speech synthesis, before it produces the speech sounds, including short or long pauses according to the punctuation and the syntactic structure of the text's sentences, the machine needs to perform some sort of text preprocessing, something we do in our minds without thinking about it when we read. This is a necessary step because, even though most normal text looks simple, there are a lot of ambiguities that need to be resolved before reading it. Take, for instance, the following paragraph:

Yesterday, I went to the bank at the corner of St. James St. to deposit a check for 1,983 dollars. I remember when, in 1997, I went to the same bank to deposit my first paycheck of $300. The date was 5/25 and the amount was 1/10 of my paycheck today. As soon as I reached the window, the teller gave me a piece of paper to read. I read it, and it said . . .

None of us would have a problem reading this, but think about the many issues involved. For instance, you'd read the first "St." as "Saint" and the second one as "Street." You'd read the number "1,983," as "one thousand nine hundred and eighty-three" because it's clearly an amount, but the number "1997" as "nineteen ninety-seven" because, from the context, it's just as clearly a year. You'd read "$300" as "300 dollars" and not "dollars 300" even though the dollar symbol comes before the number. And you'd read "5/25" as "five twenty-five" or "May twenty-five" because the context tells you it's a date and not a fraction, whereas you'd read "1/10" as "one-tenth" because the context tells you it's a fraction and not a date. And, of course, you'd pronounce the two "reads" differently because the first "read" is an infinitive and the second one's in the past tense. Clearly, we have to make many decisions based on context and on our interpretation of the words and numbers in a text when we read. A text-to-speech synthesizer needs to make the same decisions in the text preprocessing phase.

Punctuation marks are another problem, especially for the assignment of the right intonation. Your machine needs to understand how these break the text into sentences, how they indicate whether a given sentence is a statement, question, or exclamation, and what pauses are implied by commas, colons, and semicolons. It further needs to know how punctuation marks are used to resolve ambiguous phrases and sentences, as shown in this joke from the bestseller *Eats, Shoots & Leaves: The Zero Tolerance Approach to Punctuation* by Lynne Truss:

A panda walks into a café. He orders a sandwich, eats it, then draws a gun and proceeds to fire it at the other patrons.

"Why?" asks the confused, surviving waiter amidst the carnage, as the panda makes towards the exit. The panda produces a badly punctuated wildlife manual and tosses it over his shoulder.

"Well, I'm a panda," he says, at the door. "Look it up."

The waiter turns to the relevant entry in the manual and, sure enough, finds an explanation. "Panda. Large black-and-white bear-like mammal, native to China. Eats, shoots, and leaves."[12]

But punctuation marks and their relationship to sentences and phrases aren't always obvious. Take periods. Singly, of course, they indicate the end of a sentence or phrase. But when they appear in groups of three as ellipsis points, they can indicate missing words, hesitation, a pause, or trailing off. And they're also used to end certain abbreviations, as in "chap." or "pp." or "no." or "vol." and elements within abbreviations, as in "a.m." or "B.C." or "m.p.h." or "Ph.D." (although most abbreviations are now spelled without periods). Sometimes these abbreviations need to be read as the words or phrases they represent, like "chap." or "m.p.h.," and sometimes not, like "a.m." or "Ph.D." Sometimes the same abbreviation needs to be read as different words, like "St." in the example above; other times an abbreviation needs to be read letter by letter like "IBM" or "IPA," or as a single word, like "NATO" or "AIDS." Numbers are clearly another problem for text-to-speech synthesizers. Numbers are read differently depending on whether they indicate a date, a year, a quantity, a telephone number, or the model of a machine, like a "747 airplane." These and many other problems make the task of preprocessing a text highly complex and language dependent; each language has special rules that need to be coded.

Phonetic transcription itself can be very complex for a language like English, whose pronunciation and spelling are highly irregular, with the same letters or clusters of letters pronounced differently and the same sounds spelled differently depending on the context. Just how irregular is often illustrated with the famous coinage "ghoti," which, if you take the "gh" in "tou_gh_," the "o" in "w_o_men," and the "ti" in "na_ti_on," you need to pronounce as "fish." Moreover, not only are there words in English that are spelled the same but pronounced differently depending on their grammatical function, like "read" in the example above. There are also quite a few that are spelled the same but have both different pronunciations and different meanings, all of which becomes clear in context: "you shed a tear," but "you tear your shirt," "you wind a clock," but "you brave the wind," "your dove flew high," but "you dove deep," and so on. Thus, to automatically assign the correct phonemes in their correct sequence to any string of text, a program needs to take into consideration not only a set of general pronunciation rules, a large list of exceptions, and the syntax of the phrases or sentences, but also the grammatical function and context of each word in the input text.

Brute Force and Statistics . . . Once Again

As it happened for speech recognition, brute force together with the speed and the memory capacity of modern computers eventually prevailed in speech synthesis, too. Imagine that your speech synthesizer has a substantial corpus of snippets of recorded speech from your voice talent, snippets of all types and sizes, phonemes in context, words, phrases, and even full sentences. And imagine it has so many of them that it can find snippets of the same speech sounds with many different intonations. To synthesize a text sentence, your machine looks into its corpus to find the largest chunks of speech with the context and intonation closest to those of the text sentence. If it's lucky, it'll find some of the words or phrases in the sentence there; if not, it can always create them from smaller snippets. When it concatenates all the snippets needed from its corpus and does so seamlessly, with no perceptible acoustic discontinuity between them, to speak the text sentence in its synthetic voice, your machine's become what's known as a "corpus-based text-to-speech synthesizer."

One of the first such synthesizers, called "Festival," was built in 1997 by Alan Black and Paul Taylor at the University of Edinburgh;[13] most of today's commercial text-to-speech systems are based in its architecture. With a very large corpus of a few hundred megabytes (or some hundreds of thousands phonetic elements in various contexts), the quality of a synthesizer's voice can be astonishing; indeed, you can barely tell whether it's synthetic or human. In the early 2000s, a small company named "SpeechWorks" acquired the necessary technology from AT&T to produce a high-quality corpus-based synthesis system called "Speechify." The intelligibility and naturalness of Speechify's synthetic voice were so impressive—indeed, the voice seemed to have its own personality—that SpeechWorks put a dozen audio clips on its Web site and challenged anyone to guess which of the clips were human recordings and which were synthetic ones. Although almost a thousand people accepted the challenge, most of their guesses were no better than chance.[14]

As corpus-based synthesis systems became better and better, their voices seemed to take on more personality and even emotions. To make the synthetic voices sound more natural, speech technologists added the various "er," "um," "oh," and "uh" as well as giggling, chuckling, or laughing sounds we make when we speak naturally. They created different voices from extensive recordings and enlisted famous actors and singers to lend their voices to the machines.

Speech synthesis and text-to-speech have come a very long way from the initial prototypes. Today it's possible to build a custom voice in a few weeks and to have the voice of your favorite voice talent say whatever you want it to. As one of the most pervasive uses of text-to-speech, car navigators let you choose which of a variety of male and female voices you'd like to give you directions—and in which of a number of available languages. You can have synthetic voice of your choosing read your book or your e-mails or SMS messages to you on your Kindle or cell phone or have it warn you about your appliances or let you know when they're done by speaking loud and clear.

That said, however, speech synthesis has not yet been broadly applied in dialog technology, which, as you'll see in the next chapters, has evolved mainly through improvements in automated telephone systems, such as those you most likely talk to when you dial an 800 number for a large service company. The voices of those systems are generally quite good simply because they aren't artificial. Their prompts and most of their responses consist of full recordings of each sentence made by voice talents and stored as a large number of audio clips, which are appropriately selected by the dialog system. And when their voices have to say something specific, like a name, an address, or a number, the response is composed by splicing together snippets of recordings or even small portions of speech spoken by the same voice talent who recorded the full sentences. So why hasn't speech synthesis found its way into the commercial dialog systems despite the tremendous improvements in quality it's made in the past few years? More often than not, the large companies that commission the development of an automated telephone system want to have the highest quality for the system's voice, and because such systems have a limited, though often quite large, number of things to say, that's still obtained by using high-fidelity recordings rather than text-to-speech synthesis.

In reality, today's speech synthesis systems fall somewhere along a continuum between pure full-sentence recordings and pure text-to-speech synthesis. Concatenative text-to-speech systems, as you've seen, let you create synthetic speech from large corpora of snippets ranging in size from phonemes in context or syllables, to words, to phrases and even full sentences. If you know the domain where your speech synthesis system's going to be used, you can have your voice talents record more and more words, phrases, and even full sentences in that particular domain. Take car navigators, for example, where a number of words and expressions are used over and over again, such as "Turn right," "Prepare to turn left," "Merge," and "Your destination is on the left." You can have your voice talents record those words and expressions in full and store them in your system's corpus. When your car navigator system needs to speak a sentence that contains one or more of those words or expressions, rather than synthesizing the full sentence from smaller units, it can use the recorded full words or phrases and synthesize the remaining parts of the sentence in a process called "domain adaptation," which can provide speech of exceptional quality.

Although not yet indistinguishable from human speech, synthetic speech has reached a point where it can be used pretty much as we might use a computer display, but in situations where, for one reason or other, we can't or don't want to use our eyes and would rather listen than look.

8

Becoming Real

In the early 1990s, much of speech technology in the United States was being developed in large corporate research centers such as AT&T's Bell Laboratories, IBM's T. J. Watson Research Center, and Texas Instruments' laboratories. Microsoft and Apple had just started to pay attention to speech technology. Funded in large part by DARPA through projects like ATIS and the Communicator, universities such as MIT and Carnegie Mellon, and research institutions such as Bolt, Beranek and Newman in Boston and Stanford Research Institute in Menlo Park, California, were also pursuing research into both speech recognition and speech technology in general.

Europe had its own programs for the advancement of speech technology, funded mostly by the European Union, which included companies like Siemens and Philips, national telecommunication organizations like France Telecom, Telecom Italia, the Spanish Telefonica, and academic institutions in almost every Western European country. In Japan, industrial research in speech flourished at Nippon Telephone and Telegraph (NTT) and Mitsubishi, among other companies. The prestigious and independent Advanced Telecommunication Research (ATR) institute in Osaka attracted speech scientists from all over the world. And in China and India, important universities also offered research programs in speech technology. The world seemed poised for a speech revolution, with researchers across the globe pushing the limits of speech technology to find new and better ways of solving known problems. Despite their efforts to make vocabularies ever larger, improve both the handling of different speakers and spontaneous speech and the methods for training acoustic models, and achieve greater robustness of recognition in noisy environments, and despite even the attractive potential of many applications of speech technology, its commercial development lagged behind. Indeed, it seemed as though the "business of speech-understanding computers" simply couldn't get started. Then a few, relatively unglamorous applications caught the attention of the world outside the research laboratories.

Automatic Speech Recognition Takes Off

On a morning in March 1992, AT&T heralded a new technology that could "respond to the voice during collect and billed-to-third-party long-distance calls," and that, through automation, would allow the telephone giant to lay off more than 6,000 operators. One of the technology's main developers, Jay Wilpon, from Larry Rabiner's team at Bell Laboratories, made the trip to AT&T's corporate headquarters in Manhattan to respond to questions from the media. "AT&T's deployment of [the new technology] convinced the world that ASR was . . . capable of doing real work," Wilpon would later recall. "This jump-started the speech recognition market. We heard from many companies working on speech, thanking us for our deployment as it validated their work in the minds of their management."[1]

The new technology deployed by AT&T on its nationwide network represented the first successful large-scale commercial application of speech recognition technology. Known as "voice recognition call processing" (VRCP), and experienced at least once by virtually all AT&T customers, it's been in continuous use for nearly two decades handling record volumes of 3 million calls a day, or more than 1 billion calls a year. This is how VRCP works: whenever callers dial 0 followed by a telephone number, instead of a live operator, they hear a recorded message that, after a short explanation, prompts them to speak one of five simple responses corresponding to the different ways they can place and bill a call: "calling card," "collect," "third-party," "person-to-person," or "operator." If the callers correctly speak one of the five responses, their calls proceed as requested.

Back in 1992, when most speech recognition research in the United States was devoted to the recognition of thousands of words, such a simple application might certainly have seemed to be of little interest. Yet it was clear to AT&T managers that providing those five options to all their customers automatically would yield huge savings for the company.

But why ask callers to use an error-prone and complex technology like speech recognition to select one of five options when you could have them simply press keys on their telephone pads: 1 for calling card, 2 for collect, and so on? "Press 1, press 2" systems, though already deployed in the early 1990s, had one unavoidable drawback, however: they required callers to use touch-tone telephones—telephones that *had* push keys and telephone pads; they wouldn't work with rotary dial telephones. And, unfortunately, there were a great many of these older telephones still in use at the time, to include especially public telephones, from which callers were most likely to choose the automatic service. Thus, to reach virtually everyone, speech recognition was the only solution for AT&T.

With speech recognition systems of the research community successfully recognizing thousands of words, you'd think that recognizing any of five simple responses—

two single words and three short phrases—would have been easy. Instead, the problems hidden in this apparently simple application would challenge the research and development team at AT&T's Bell Laboratories for years on end. How could that be? Just as the devil is in the details, so the answer to this question lay in the differences between research, on the one hand, and product development, on the other.

Making Things Real

In *The Mythical Man-Month*, his classic book on software engineering, Frederick P. Brooks states that converting a computer program written by "two programmers in a remodeled garage" into a commercial "product" was nine times harder than designing and building the original prototype.[2] Whether you're a young programmer starting a new company in your garage or a highly paid scientist in an ivory tower of corporate research, transforming a prototype into a real product does indeed take much more effort than inventing one. And this is because the product has to be much more than the invention it's based on. It has to be used flawlessly by thousands and thousands of different customers under different, real-world conditions, and that requires a lot of problem solving, engineering, discipline, and sometimes other inventions.[3]

The researchers at AT&T's Bell Laboratories had little trouble building a demonstration model of a speech recognition system that could recognize thousands of words under laboratory conditions, one that challenged the systems built by other prestigious research centers in DARPA and other competitions. But when it came to developing a real-world system that could recognize any of AT&T's five customer options with more than 98 percent accuracy from any telephone, in any situation, by any of millions and millions of callers, they found they had to go back to the drawing board and solve a number of additional problems.

The first problem was caused by the great variety of dialects and accents of the callers. To cope with that, and to build the best possible models of the five responses that would guarantee the highest accuracy, AT&T needed to collect enough speech samples to represent all possible acoustic, phonetic, and dialectal variations, which it did with the help of an experimental system. When, however, the researchers analyzed the tens of thousands of recordings of the five responses, they encountered a few unexpected phenomena. Telephone speech recognition systems in those days usually instructed callers to "speak after the beep," like the answering machines we're all familiar with. Unfortunately, a good percentage of the callers started speaking right at the beep or even before it. Since the recognizer would start collecting speech only after the beep, however, if the caller started speaking earlier than that, the system would hear only the last portion of the utterance, if anything at all. "Calling card" might be perceived by the recognizer just as "—rd" and "collect" just as "—ct." Thus the recognition accuracy for those "chopped" utterances was quite poor.

But, of course, that wasn't all the researchers found. Even though callers were instructed to say only one of the five responses and nothing more, they often added extra words of their own. Instead of just saying "collect," for instance, some would say things like "I'd like to make a collect call," or simply "Collect please" or "Yes, a collect call." As long as the system's grammar permitted it to recognize only the five responses mentioned in the prompt, speech recognition would fail for almost all of these variations.

To build a real-world application, and not just a proof of concept or a laboratory demonstration, these problems needed to be solved. And the solutions came with the invention of two powerful new algorithms, patented by Bell Labs.

When conversing, we humans tend to interrupt one another—we "barge in"—at any time, even when it's not considered polite. That's just the way we are. Since computers don't have feelings, when interacting with humans, they should *let* us barge in. To allow callers to speak over the prompt if they chose not to wait for the beep, and to stop the prompt as soon as they did, Bell Labs researchers invented a *barge-in algorithm*. For the new algorithm to work, however, they had to solve another problem first. The speech recognizer needed to start listening as soon as the prompt started to play. But if it was listening while the prompt was playing, it would hear the prompt as well, partly because of the echo always present on telephone lines, but mainly because of the acoustic coupling between the mouth- and earpieces of telephone handsets that lets callers hear themselves speak so they can control the articulation and loudness of their voices through feedback, as most all of us normally do when we speak. Hearing the prompt, whether through the line echo or feedback loop, would trigger the end-point detector, and the system would start to recognize its own voice rather than the caller's. Thus, to allow the barge-in algorithm to work, the speech recognizer needed to ignore the prompt that was being played. Researchers got it to do this quite effectively through a process called "echo cancellation." Because the system knew the prompt, sample by sample, having generated it either by text-to-speech or by playing a recorded message, it could also remove the prompt, sample by sample, from the incoming signal. When the prompt echo was properly canceled, the speech recognizer heard almost perfect silence while the prompt was being played. It could therefore activate an internal mechanism that would stop the prompt from playing as soon as it detected speech from the caller and start to recognize the caller's voice. In practice, just by speaking, the caller would be able to barge in and interrupt the prompt. Today, all speech recognizers use a form of the original barge-in algorithm developed at Bell Laboratories for the voice recognition call processing system.

Since many callers didn't stick to one of the five responses, as instructed by the prompt, but said other things along with it, the researchers also invented a *word-spotting algorithm* to allow the recognizer to spot a particular keyword in a longer utterance, while ignoring the extraneous words. Thus, if someone said, "I want to make a collect call, please," the word-spotting algorithm would ignore the words "I want to make a," "call," and "please," and spot the keyword "collect." Word spotting doesn't require a specific grammar to describe all the possible sentences. Instead, it treats all words extraneous to the keywords as noise or as what speech scientists call "garbage words." So it lets callers say whatever they want as long as a keyword is included in their utterance. Of course, if a caller says, "I don't want to make a collect call please," the algorithm will recognize the caller's response only as "collect." Although that's definitely a limitation, the word-spotting technology works very well for the vast majority of calls.

Indeed, both of the new algorithms worked so well they were incorporated into the production version of the VRCP speech recognizer that would serve millions and millions of customers for AT&T. The Bell Labs' speech research group gained credit and recognition throughout the whole company for having developed the technology of this extremely successful system, which helped save AT&T millions of dollars every year. As the first real-world deployment of speech recognition technology on a major telephone network, voice recognition call processing demonstrated that speech recognition was useful even for apparently simple tasks like recognizing one of five short responses. Its success served as a clear inspiration for the future of the speech industry.

An unusually interesting but unintended consequence of progress in speech recognition and text-to-speech technology was the creation of systems that allowed machines to talk to other machines using human spoken language. These systems proved highly useful both to AT&T and to NYNEX (the larger of the two northeastern "Baby Bells") for the completion of telephone directory assistance calls. Before these systems were deployed, directory assistance operators would look up the listing you requested on their computers, and when they found it, rather than speaking the number to you, they'd push a button, and the number would be read to you by a text-to-speech system. That would allow the operators to immediately move on to new calls and to serve new customers. After having spoken the telephone number you requested, the system would ask you whether you wanted to have that number dialed automatically for an additional small fee, an option you might welcome if you didn't have a pen and paper handy, were in a noisy environment, had a listening problem, or were just lazy. Since, after the AT&T divestiture, neither company was able to pass the number to the actual switch that would dial it if that number belonged to a different carrier, they resorted to installing a speech recognizer on the switch that would recognize the synthetic speech played at the other end. And since the telephone numbers would always be spoken by the same synthetic voice, with no variations, no extra words, no false starts, no "ums," "uhs," or "ohs," and no accent, the speech recognizer could recognize and dial the correct number virtually 100 percent of the time. Paradoxically, this uncommon example of machines talking to other machines using human speech is probably still the most widely used application of the speech recognition technology.[4]

Speaking to Your Personal Computer

Without any doubt, discovering the advantages of hidden Markov models, the statistical models widely known as "HMMs," marked a major turning point in the history of speech recognition technology. Jim Baker had built his first statistical speech recognizer, called "Dragon," in the early 1970s while working on his Ph.D. thesis at Carnegie Mellon University, where during the summers he'd also worked with Leonard Baum, who first developed the theoretical framework of HMMs at the Institute for Defense Analysis in Princeton back in the mid-1960s. After receiving their doctorates at CMU in 1975, Jim Baker and his wife, Janet, started working with Fred Jelinek, the head of the speech research group at IBM's T .J. Watson Research Center, where they built an isolated-word speech recognizer on an IBM System 370 computer that could recognize 1,000 words. Unfortunately, even the most powerful computers of the time couldn't achieve real-time recognition with the complex statistical methods Jelinek and the Bakers were using. Although much simpler systems with smaller vocabularies, such as those being developed by AT&T, would certainly run in real time, IBM wasn't interested in them, having directed its research efforts toward building a far more complex device, a fully operational voice-activated typewriter that it felt would one day replace the common typewriter. Convinced that the time had come to exploit the commercial potential of speech recognizers, the Bakers left IBM in 1979 for Verbex Voice Systems, a subsidiary of Exxon, where they worked on a telephone data collection system based on speech recognition. When Exxon shut down speech research in 1982, they decided to start their own company, called "Dragon Systems."

In the beginning, Dragon Systems survived on small projects and government funds. It built a simple voice-based command and control interface for Apricot, a short-lived British personal computer; it even built a Klingon speech recognizer for a U.S. toy company.[5] In 1988, DARPA awarded Dragon Systems the first of many contracts to pursue research on large-vocabulary continuous-speech recognition technology. That same year, Dragon Systems demonstrated the first real-time isolated-word recognizer with an 8,000-word vocabulary, followed, two years later, by the first continuous-speech recognizer with a 5,000-word vocabulary.

Then, in July 1997, the company announced the commercial release of its Dragon Naturally Speaking™ software for personal computers, a continuous-speech recognizer with a 23,000-word vocabulary. Spurred by the immediate success of the Dragon product, IBM released its own continuous-speech recognizer for dictation, ViaVoice™, the very next month. By the end of the year, the two companies had sold more than 75,000 copies of their recognizers. Later, Microsoft and Apple began to offer similar voice dictation products for personal computers. Bought out in 2000 by the Belgian company Lernout & Hauspie (L&H), however, Dragon Systems was dragged into the bankruptcy of its new owners and its assets acquired the following year by the emerging technology giant ScanSoft, later known as Nuance.

The dream of typing documents, opening and closing files, and issuing commands on a personal computer through voice alone, a dream pursued by IBM, Dragon Systems, and later by Apple and Microsoft, was never realized for a number of practical reasons. Chief among these was PC users' clear preference to control their computers by touch rather than speech. Typing, clicking, and double-clicking had become second nature and nearly effortless for most computer users, whereas speaking required more effort and could be impractical in many situations, such as in a noisy room or when sharing an office with other people, where the added issue of privacy arose when working on personal or sensitive documents.

After many years of research and development, dictation software had reached levels of performance that made it useful and effective—provided users trained their systems to their voices and corrected the systems' relatively few transcription mistakes by hand, or by voice in later versions. Few users, however, ever went through the training process, which required reading several paragraphs out loud until their systems adapted to their voices and reached satisfactory levels of performance. Fewer still adapted themselves to the software's idiosyncrasies to become proficient in its use. Thus voice dictation systems remained largely unused by the population at large, and even among users they were treated mostly as curiosities, to be cast aside a few days after purchase.

Another problem encountered by the speech dictation industry was that, as competition heated up, prices tumbled. The first commercial prototypes of voice dictation software by Dragon Systems were quite expensive. But, as soon as IBM and later Microsoft entered the market and their software reached comparable performance levels, a price war ensued, driving down the price of voice dictation systems to its virtual minimum. The war ended with Microsoft incorporating speech dictation software as part of the Windows operating systems in its desktops. In effect, general and basic dictation software became a free commodity available to anyone who owned a PC.

On the other hand, however, several niche markets developed. Certain professionals, accustomed to recording their findings or correspondence on tape for later transcription, adopted voice dictation software as an everyday tool in their work. Lawyers and medical doctors in particular welcomed customized versions of the software. Radiologists, for their part, found the dictation software helped them scale back their labor expenses by reducing their need for transcriber typists.

And the software proved valuable for the transcribers themselves, who were able to transcribe far more in far less time. Dictaphone's medical transcription service, grossing hundreds of millions of dollars of revenue in the mid-1990s before voice dictation systems were widely available but having to employ armies of human transcribers for what was called "carbon-based transcription," found it could transcribe more with fewer workers when they converted to "silicon-based transcription." Voice dictation systems could make a first recognition pass on recorded tapes, which could now be processed in batches, and produce first-draft transcripts; human transcribers had only to correct the systems' transcription errors to produce final-draft transcripts. Several transcription companies still use this semi-manual process to decrease their turnaround time and increase their profit margin.

Even though voice dictation software hasn't made typing on keyboards obsolete, at least not as I write these words, there's hope that it may do so yet. As the ever smaller computerized devices we proudly pull from our pockets—the smartphones—are becoming more and more our main, and often our only, means of communication with the rest of the world,[6] their keyboards or touch screens are becoming ever smaller, too—but not our fingers. Indeed, typing even a moderately long message on the miniature keyboard of a BlackBerry or touch screen of an iPhone is a challenge for anyone not equipped with Lilliputian fingers. Thus, perhaps, when and if the tiny keyboards and touch screens of pocket-size smart devices become the norm, voice dictation may yet become the only reliable and effective way to enter information of any length or complexity.

The Wildfire Effect

As you've seen, fostered by the various DARPA projects and competitions, the goal of the speech recognition research community in the early 1990s was to attain higher and higher recognition accuracy in more and more sophisticated tasks on the way to building machines with near-human speech and language capabilities. There was a widespread though unstated belief that, to build real-world machine-human dialog systems, you had to endow them with the ability to automatically recognize and understand spontaneous, unconstrained natural speech with ever higher accuracy and ever larger vocabularies. Contrary to this common belief, AT&T's voice recognition call processing system clearly showed that, by restricting the recognition task to as few as five keywords, you could build a machine that would bring tangible benefits to a company and its customers alike. Although speech researchers had little interest in pursuing such a simple, practical approach, entrepreneurs quickly saw its commercial possibilities. One such entrepreneur was Bill Warner, whose small, Boston-based company Wildfire would first draw the attention of the speech technology community to a revolutionary concept known as "voice user interface" (VUI).

Having explored the possibility of creating a computer video communication system with an interface "so cool that would spread like wildfire" in the late 1980s, Warner soon realized the time wasn't right for video communication and turned his energies to telephone communication instead, though he didn't give up on the idea of a "cool" interface. In 1991, Warner joined forces with Nick d'Arbeloff, former vice president of marketing at Avid Communications, Warner's short-lived video company, and young technology mavens Rich Miner and Tony Lovell to found Wildfire Communications.[7] The goal of the new company was to create a butler-like automated personal telephone assistant that, in the minds of its creators, would radically improve the experience of making and receiving telephone calls for nearly everyone.

Whenever you need to call someone, you have to look up the person's number, unless, of course, you know it already. But why do you *have* to know someone's number at all? Why can't you just say who you want to call? That was the idea behind Wildfire. You'd tell it who you wanted call, and Wildfire would dial that person's number for you. The only number you'd have to remember was Wildfire's. You could call Wildfire from any phone, and, as your personal assistant, it would be always ready to dial the number of anyone you wanted to call:

User: Wildfire.
Wildfire: Here I am.
User: Call.
Wildfire: Call whom?
User: Nick d'Arbeloff.
Wildfire: At which place?
User: At work.
Wildfire: Dialing <phone rings, Nick answers>[8]

Wildfire, like a good butler, wouldn't leave you alone during the call. It would always be there, discreetly eavesdropping. And if you said "Wildfire," it would come back and help you make another call or check your voicemail:

User: Wildfire.
Wildfire: What can I do for you?
User: Find.
Wildfire: Find what?
User: Messages.
Wildfire: I found four messages. The first is . . .

User: What's it say?
Wildfire: <plays the message>

And if somebody else called while you were on the phone, Wildfire would take that person's name and play it for you while announcing the incoming call, and your current caller would be briefly on hold and not hear it. You could then ask Wildfire to take a message or you could answer the incoming call by keeping your current one on hold. You wouldn't have to press keys or remember numbers. You could do all of this simply by asking Wildfire to.

Wildfire's speech recognizer didn't need to handle vocabularies of tens of thousands of words nor to understand syntactically complex utterances. And even though what you could say to Wildfire at each point of a conversation was very limited, it was also very intuitive. Rich Miner and Tony Lovell knew that building an automated telephone assistant to reliably understand everything you could say to it simply wasn't possible at that time, let alone practical. But if they could find a way to gracefully constrain what you said to Wildfire at each step of your interaction with it and to lead you, in an intuitive way, to say what Wildfire's recognizer could comfortably understand, the system could achieve a respectable level of performance. This was the beginning of the subtle art of prompt crafting. A good prompt could increase the performance of a speech recognizer without changing the speech recognizer itself. And it would do that by leading you to say what the recognizer wanted you to say in the way it wanted you to say it. A bad prompt would, of course, lead you to do just the opposite. For example, consider the difference between the following prompts:

Prompt 1:   Please confirm that your number is 555-1212

Prompt 2:   Is your number 555-1212? Please say yes or no.

To the first prompt, which doesn't ask you a direct question, you might respond in any number of ways:

Yes, that's right. My number is 555-1212.

Sure, that's correct.

You bet.

Indeed, for the first prompt, it would be hard to design a grammar that could cover all the things you might reasonably say. So the result would be a lot of misrecognitions for the many expressions not covered by the grammar. On the other hand, for the second prompt, a simple yes or no grammar, with a reasonable number of synonyms for yes and no, would most likely cover what you might say. Thus a grammar needed to serve a particular prompt, and if that prompt changed, most likely the grammar would need to change as well. Prompts and grammars were two faces of the same coin: a dialog turn interaction.

That well-crafted prompts and properly designed speech recognition grammars could recognize and understand the vast majority of user responses didn't simply diverge from what the speech researchers had seen as the ultimate goal of speech recognition technology—to recognize and understand unconstrained, natural, free-form speech. It also proved to be an effective strategy for building commercially successful speech recognizers. And so, while speech researchers still quested after the holy grail of what was known as "natural language" or "free-form dialog," pragmatic and business-oriented engineers built and deployed highly constrained recognition systems that gracefully and subtly directed users to say what the systems needed them to say—to engage in what was called "directed dialog."[9] The step-by-step crafting of voice interfaces, designing and testing prompts, and testing and optimizing the development of commercial spoken dialog systems came to be known as "voice user interface" (VUI) design.

Why Don't You Just Tell Me?

Although Wildfire was one of the first examples of voice user interface designs to use speech recognition technology, the art of VUI design started earlier than that. A few years before telephone applications of speech recognition technology became commercially viable, engineers had realized that the newer, touch-tone telephones had an input device that could be used as an effective means of communication between callers and automated systems, a twelve-key keypad, which supplanted the rotary dial of the older telephones.

Callers could use the twelve keys of the touch-tone keypad to make twelve different choices and communicate them to an automated system. When you press the keys to dial a telephone number, each key pressed sends a special dual-tone multi-frequency (DTMF) signal; together in series, these signals are easily and accurately recognized by the network switches to connect the caller to the specific telephone number you dialed.[10] Once you've made the call and the connection is established, you're free to send other touch-tone signals by again pressing keys on your keypad. How often have you called a toll-free number and gotten a recorded voice saying something like: "Press 1 for sales, press 2 for marketing, . . . or press 0 to speak with an operator"?

However, one of the problems with DTMF–based interactive voice response systems—or "DTMF IVRs," as they came to be called in the industry—is that the user's number of choices at each turn of an interaction is limited to twelve, the number of keys on the user's keypad. A service for which you have to choose among a larger number of options needs to be structured in successive layers of interaction, where you're presented with only a few options at each turn. Actually, even twelve options at each turn are too many. By the time you heard the twelfth choice, you almost certainly would have forgotten the first one. So, typically, IVR menus don't present more than five options at a turn, and the interaction often needs to proceed for several turns. If you were to draw a line diagram of all the options, suboptions, and so on from the start of your call to its end, it would look very much like a tree, where each branch represents a single key pressed at a precise turn in the interaction. IVR designers call this tree the "call flow" of a system.

Before speech recognition became part of our lives, voice user interface designers typically designed interactive voice response systems by sketching out their call flows. Unfortunately, even using only a few keys and offering only a few options at each turn, there are plenty of opportunities for bad designs, and some were so bad they gave rise to the epithet "IVR Hell." We've all experienced, at a some point, an IVR system so badly designed it drove us crazy, where customer representatives were unreachable, hidden behind layers of "Press 1s" and "press 2s," where cryptic prompts offered us too many options, and where we got lost in maze-like, circular interactions. Indeed, when used for number responses, those twelve keys on the telephone keypad have made far more of us unhappy than happy. But their use also set the stage for the next leap in technology, the speech recognition interactive voice response system.

Recognizing speech rather than key presses was the natural evolution of IVR applications. Speaking has several advantages over pressing keys. You can effortlessly speak many more choices and you're not limited to a maximum of twelve things.[11] Prompts don't have to associate options with numbers, and you can speak your choices directly, without having to think about their assigned numbers. As regards this last point, there were, and still there are, some naive, badly designed applications that mix voice and number responses, to produce prompts like

"Press or say 1 for billing, press or say 2 for technical support, press or say 3 for . . ."

That said, good VUI designers immediately realized there was no need to assign numbers to options:

"Please say 'billing,' 'technical support,' or . . ."

The new philosophy became "Why don't you just tell me?," as in the *Seinfeld* episode where Kramer pretends he is a touch-tone IVR system for movie locations, and George unknowingly interacts with him on the phone:

Kramer: Hello and welcome to Moviefone. If you know the name of the movie you'd like to see, press 1.

George: <pressing a key> . . . Come on!

Kramer: Using your touch-tone keypad, please enter the first three letters of the movie title now.

George: \<presses three keys\>

Kramer: \<puzzled\> . . . you selected . . . \<more puzzled\> "Agent Zero"? . . . If that's correct, press 1.

George: \<puzzled\> What?

Kramer: You selected "Brown-Eyed Girl" . . . if this is correct, press 1.

George: \<silent and more puzzled\>

Kramer: Why don't you just tell me the name of the movie you selected?

With speech recognition, prompts can become shorter, more intuitive, and the whole interaction can move along faster and more smoothly. Speaking is definitely more intuitive and natural than pressing keys. You don't have to take mental note of which number is associated with which option; you can just say the option. But there's more. Think of an application that, at a certain point, asks you to spell out part of the name of a city or an airport, or of a movie, as in the *Seinfeld* scenario. Say you're asked, "Please enter the first three letters of the city you want to fly to." If you want to fly to New York, you press 6 for N, 3 for E, and 9 for W. Unfortunately, the sequence 6-3-9 also corresponds to the first three letters of "Newark," "New Orleans," and even "Mexico City." So the system has to come back with yet another menu: "Press 1 for New York, press 2 for Newark, press 3 for New Orleans, press 4 for . . ."

Even in well-designed applications, spelling by telephone keypad is a slow and tedious operation. If you happen to have a telephone with the keypad right on the handset, or if you're calling from your cell phone, you have to remove it from your ear, press the right keys, and put it back on your ear to listen to the next prompt. And if it's dark, or you can't find your glasses, the operation becomes even more difficult. Wouldn't it be much easier, and faster, to just say it: "New York!" And what about times or dates?

Please enter the date of your trip: two digits for the month, two digits for the day, and the last two digits of the year, for example, for April 7, 2008, press 0 4 0 7 0 8.

Wouldn't it be easier to just say it?

Controlling Errors

To be honest, when compared with speech recognizers, touch-tone keys have one big advantage. They never make mistakes. If you press a 2 key, you can be 100 percent sure that the system on the other end will receive the number 2. A 2 pressed is a 2 sent is a 2 received. No question about it. No ambiguity, no statistical

variations. Instead, even with the tremendous advances in speech recognition technology, the smart use of well-crafted prompts to limit what you can say, and the
ever higher accuracy of speech recognizers, there's still a chance, however small, that
a speech recognition system will mistake one word for another: "Boston" can
become "Austin" sometimes, and if all you want is accurate flight information, that
can be really frustrating:

System: Please say the name of your departure city.
User: Boston.
System: Okay, Austin. Please say the name of your arrival city.
User: Er . . . no . . . it's not Austin, it's *Boston*.
System: Okay. Going from Austin to Boston. At what time?
User: No . . . I don't want to *go* to Boston, I am *leaving from* Boston!
System: Okay. There is a flight leaving Austin at 7:15 p.m. Would that be okay?
User: No, I am *not* leaving from Austin! I am going from *Boston* . . . B-O-S-T-O-N
. . . to San Francisco.
System: Is the 7:15 p.m. flight okay? Please say yes or no.
User: <hangs up>

To avoid such catastrophic dialog interactions, early VUI designers of speech recognition–based interactive voice response systems had to develop robust strategies
for error control. Here's what the above dialog might have sounded like if
the designer had taken into account that the speech recognizer actually make
mistakes:

System: Please say the name of your departure city

User: Boston

System: I think you said "Austin." Is that correct? Please say yes or no.

User: No.

System: Sorry, my mistake. Please say the departure city again.

User: Boston.

System: Got it! Boston. Please say your destination city.

User: San Francisco.

The strategy of asking for a yes or no confirmation, and in case of a no, of asking
again—called "reprompting" in the VUI jargon—which characterized all the early
dialog systems and most in use today, is called "two-step-correction." In reality, it
takes most systems at least two steps to recover from an error. Some recent systems,
however, have implemented what's called a "one-step correction," which is much
more efficient, at the expense of increased complexity in design:

System: Please say the name of your departure city

User: Boston

System: Was that Austin?

User: No, *Boston*!

System: Got it! Boston. Please say your destination city.

User: San Francisco

Error recovery can also make smart use of the past information. Early systems often fell into what was called the "infinite error loop" problem. Their simplified dialog logic didn't take into account the likelihood that a speech recognizer might make the same mistake over and over again. When you said no to a system's confirmation question, it made no use of that information:

User: Boston
System: I think you said "Austin." Is that correct? Please say yes or no.
User: No.
System: Sorry, my mistake. Please say the departure city again.
User: Boston.
System: I think you said "Austin." Is that correct? Please say yes or no.
User: . . . ?

Hearing you say no, smarter systems of the second generation would instead acknowledge that their previous answer had been wrong, and offer you a different one.[12]

Corona and Altech, Nuance and SpeechWorks

In January 2000, SpeechWorks was a company of 200 vibrant young people, with yearly revenue of $15 million and a sizable amount of capital in the bank, full of excitement at the prospect of a successful IPO at the peak of the Internet bubble. Headquartered in Boston, the historic cradle of speech research, next to the prestigious MIT, the rapidly growing company had offices in New York, San Francisco, Montreal, London, Paris, and Singapore. Every six months, all the employees from the remote offices would gather in Boston for "SpeechDays" to share their experiences, attend meetings, socialize, and have their leaders bring them up to date on developments in technology and business. Mike Phillips, one of the two founders, used to give a talk on how SpeechWorks came to be, for the benefit of the new hires, which started out like this:

On September 3rd, 1993, Mike [Phillips], Victor [Zue], Stephanie [Seneff, Victor's wife], Jim [Glass], and Dave [Goddeau] meet for a beer in Cambridge and decide it's a good time to start a speech company. On September 4th, Victor, Stephanie, Jim, and Dave go back to their MIT jobs, while Mike buys books on "how to start a company." In November 1993, Mike gets advice: "Find someone else to be CEO." In January 1994, Mike meets Bill O'Farrell at MIT's "how to start a company" course. Shortly after that, Bill visits MIT for demo and says, "Passes the cool test, let's do it!"

In 1994, Mike Phillips had already spent most of his career in speech technology, moving back and forth between research and commercial enterprises. In 1982, as a bright young programmer just out of college, he joined Scott Instruments. In 1983, he went back to research. In 1984, he joined the audio technology company SRS Labs, but six months later he again went back to research, first at Carnegie Mellon University and then at MIT, where he and Jim Glass built VOYAGER, one of the most impressive demonstration dialog systems in the speech community, in the laboratory of Victor Zue, who, as you'll recall, had years before pioneered the reading of spectrograms and had then created one of the strongest research teams in human-machine spoken communication and the GALAXY architecture. VOYAGER was able to carry on a dialog with a user and give information on restaurants in Cambridge in an almost colloquial fashion. Phillips was a constant presence at the DARPA evaluation meetings in the early 1990s. But, after a few years, he wanted to build systems "for real"; in February 1994, he and Bill O'Farrell founded Altech (Advanced Language Technologies), later renamed "SpeechWorks International," or "SpeechWorks" for short. SpeechWorks was one of two companies to play a pivotal role in the birth and rise of the speech industry.

The other was the West Coast Corona Corporation, later renamed "Nuance." Corona's founders, most notably Mike Cohen and Hy Murveit from the Stanford Research Institute, were researchers who, like SpeechWorks' Mike Phillips, had participated in the DARPA speech recognition evaluations, greatly contributed to the field, and felt that the time was ripe to start a speech company. Altech/Speech-Works started with technology developed at MIT; Corona/Nuance, with technology from SRI. Both shared the philosophy behind Wildfire and AT&T's voice recognition call processing system: they would build and sell speech systems that would be useful to companies and final users—systems with no pretensions to humanlike understanding.

With the shared backgrounds, experiences, and views of their founders and leading researchers, SpeechWorks and Nuance were like twins separated at birth. Once established, the two companies followed similar commercial paths. One of Nuance's first large-scale commercial dialog systems was designed for United Parcel Service (UPS) to provide its customers with package tracking information. A short time after that, SpeechWorks built a similar system for Federal Express (FedEx), UPS's largest competitor.

Package tracking is a relatively simple task for a dialog system: you read out the tracking number on your shipping receipt, the system recognizes it, finds out where your package is from the company database, and reads that information back to you. But, apart from the simplicity of their task, the UPS and FedEx dialog systems differed from the more sophisticated systems of the DARPA projects in one crucial respect. They were real-world systems deployed for real-world customers who were strongly motivated to use them under real-world conditions. That reality of purpose and the difficulties inherent in deploying dialog systems that had to work for the vast majority, if not all, of their real-world users placed demands on the systems and imposed constraints that required advanced technical solutions. They gave rise to the same types of questions that had arisen with AT&T's voice recognition call processing system, the five-option dialog application used by millions of telephone customers. For instance, what's the best way to get customers to say just what the system needs them to say—their tracking numbers—and to keep them from saying things the system won't be able to understand? Does everyone know what a tracking number is and where to find it, or does this need to be explained?[13] And even if customers do know where to find their tracking numbers, will they read them out as single digits, like "seven three four five one zero zero . . ." or as two- or-three digit numbers, like "seventy-three forty-five one hundred . . ."? Will they read out the leading zeros, if any, or simply ignore them? And what if a customer insists on speaking to a human agent? Or has a different request and got to package tracking by mistake? What if a customer has a strong accent? Or is calling from a noisy place? Or has lost the shipping receipt and thus also the tracking number? The list of "what ifs," even for this simple application, was almost endless. And only a VUI designer who had deep insight into the way people interact with dialog systems and who had carefully considered the possible consequences of every design choice could address all of them. The voice user interface design movement, which started with Wildfire, would, with the dialog systems of Nuance and SpeechWorks, spread throughout the industry.

The Art of Speech Design

With the evolution of the first large-scale commercial applications— package tracking, movie location finders, and flight status information for various airline companies—the profession of the voice user interface designer rapidly emerged to become an indispensable part of the speech technology industry. With imperfect speech recognizers that, despite the tremendous advances of recognition algorithms, kept making mistakes from time to time, building a commercially usable dialog system required a lot of experience and insight. Wording the prompts and designing the interface in the right way could make the difference between an application that worked and one that didn't, between an application that pleased users and one that drove them to swear and hang up in disgust. The secret to making a system that really worked could be summed up in a single word: design.

Everything we use today has been designed by someone. Almost every object, device, or tool has been, at a certain point in time, designed, redesigned, and improved, evolving from something less than fully usable to something we can enjoy using over and over again. Donald Norman, the usability guru behind some of Apple's sleek computer designs and the author of several books on usability and design of things, states that good design requires no instructions.[14] And he often illustrates this with a simple example, something we all know very well: a door. How many times have you encountered a door with a "Push" sign on one side and a "Pull" sign on the other?[15] Too many, I suspect, to even remember. But did you ever wonder why such a simple device as a door *needs* to tell you how to use it? It does for one simple reason, according to Don Norman: it's been badly designed. A well-designed door would have a large, visible handle on the "Pull" side and no handle at all on the "Push" side. The large handle would intuitively invite you to pull it, and the other side, for *lack* of a handle, would invite you to push it. If you consider the presence or absence of a handle on the side of a door to be the interface between you and the door, when that interface is well designed, you know what to do as soon as you see it; you don't need any instructions.

Like doors, vegetable peelers, and coffee machines, a well-designed interface for technologies would need no instructions. It would be intuitive and usable by everyone at the first sight. That was the idea behind the computer desktop interface icons invented by Xerox, and developed and marketed first by Apple and then Microsoft. Thus an icon depicting a folder, intuitively, meant something that contained documents. Dragging the folder icon to the trash can icon, intuitively, meant discarding the folder and all the documents it contained.

To see how the concept of a usable interface requiring no instructions applies to speech recognition, consider a voice-automated bank information system. You call your bank, and a robotic voice answers: "Welcome to Green Dollar Bank. Please say a command after the beep <beep>."

What would you say? Well, you know it's a computer and you have to say a command, but which one? Suddenly, you remember the bank sent you a little card listing all the commands. But you don't have it handy, and there's no time now to look for it. You start to panic, and, after a few seconds of silence, you mumble something like "How much money in my account? . . . my checking account." And the robotic voice replies: "Sorry, I did not understand what you said. Please say it again." "Checking account balance please." "Sorry, I did not understand what you said. Please say it again." This communication failure loop goes around a few more times until you either hang up or are put on hold to wait for "the next available agent."

The speech recognition machine did what it was designed to do. It couldn't do better than that since, as you know, it can't recognize everything you might say. So, if you say something that's not in its grammar, you're out of luck. That's why the bank sent you the card with all the commands its system can recognize. But if you need to read a card every time you want to talk to your bank, that's certainly not a very usable interface, is it? Here's where the art of speech design comes in. A well-designed interface requires no explanation; it's intuitive and easy to use. Consider what an improved version of your bank's information system might sound like:

Computer: Welcome to Green Dollar Bank. Do you need your account balance, fund transfer, or credit information?
You: Account balance.
Computer: Which account? Please say checking, savings, or credit line.
You: Checking.
Computer: You have five hundred and fourteen dollars in your checking account.

This improved version draws you into an intuitive exchange with the system: each prompt invites you to provide the correct answer. And if the system's voice is also pleasant, maybe you hang up with a smile on your face.

Inviting Computers to Dinner

After talking with the newly installed United Airlines flight information computer, one journalist wrote: "I found its voice so sexy that I wanted to invite it for dinner." United, American, and Continental were the first airlines to adopt speech recognizers to provide up-to-the-minute flight and gate information to tens of thousands of their customers every day. In a competitive market like flight travel, good customer care can make the difference between gaining—and keeping—customers and losing them to a competitor.

If you're like many of us, you've found yourself in a situation where you had to catch a flight or pick up a friend on one and you didn't want to get there too early and have to spend a lot of time waiting at the airport. Because the flight could be late or even canceled, before you left home, you called the airline to check on the status of your flight. If this had been back when flight information was handled by live agents, more than likely, you had to wait for the next available agent—sometimes for as long as twenty minutes because there weren't enough agents to handle all the calls—and, worse still, you had to listen to bad music all that time. So you finally hung up, jumped in the car, and rushed off to the airport because if you didn't and your flight was on schedule you'd have been late. And, more often than not, once you got there, you discovered that your flight had been delayed, maybe by several hours. At that point, you hated the airline not only for keeping you on the phone for twenty minutes listening to bad music, but also for making you wait much longer at the airport than you had to. What you experienced was bad customer care or, really, no customer care at all.

Flight information is just one of many examples where the cost of providing good customer care with human agents can be disproportionately high, compared to the economic benefit. In order to serve each of the thousands of customers that might call, especially during peak hours, as an airline, you need lots of agents. You need to recruit them, train them, pay them well, and continuously replace those who move on to different jobs. You also need to control the quality of their service and make sure that they're up to date on the newest database technology. Moreover, even though you'll lose your customers if you don't provide at least a reasonable level of customer care, you can't charge them anything for it, at least not directly. You need to find a way either to offset your increased labor costs with increased revenue or to reduce those costs. If you raise your fares, you'll also lose customers to competing airlines that offer cheaper flights. If you look for cheaper agents in countries where the cost of labor is definitely lower, you may have trouble finding, training, and supervising agents who are competent and who speak English decently. If you try to make do with ones who aren't that competent or who speak English with a heavy accent, your customers won't like that either. And, in the end, global labor arbitrage will more than likely make those agents nearly as expensive as in-house agents. So what do you do?

The solution to the customer care problem dilemma is automation, or self-service customer care. But what type of automation? The first attempts at automation used the telephone keypad as their input device, but as you've seen, that doesn't work very well in certain situations, especially when a caller has to select one of a large number of choices, such as all the airports in the country.

A few months after Nuance built the flight information system for American Airlines, SpeechWorks built a similar system for United. The prompts were recorded by Tom Glynn, a Boston musician and voice-over artist, whose warm voice so impressed the journalist at the start of this section. A call to the United flight information service might go like this:

Computer <Tom Glynn's voice>: Welcome to United Airlines flight information line. I can give you up-to-the-minute arrival and departure information for all United and United Express flights. And if you ever need assistance please say "Help" and I'll take things from there. Please say the United flight number or say "I don't know it" and we'll get the flight number in a different way.
Caller: I don't know it.

Computer: Would you like arrival or departure information?

Caller: Arrival.

Computer: Okay. I am going to ask you a few questions so we can find the right flight. Here's a hint. If you ever know the answer to a question I am asking, you can always interrupt me. And if you get stuck, just say "Start over." Here it goes . . . From which city is the flight departing?

Caller: Boston.

Computer: In which city does the flight arrive?

Caller: Chicago.

Computer: About what time of day is the flight scheduled to arrive?

Caller: Afternoon.

Computer: Let's make sure I've got it right. You are looking for a flight departing from Boston Logan which arrives in Chicago O'Hare today, January 19th, after 12 p.m. Is that right?

Caller: Yes.

Computer: Okay. I'll look up flights that have that itinerary . . . I found a few flights that just about match your itinerary. Three to be exact. Help me find the right flight. Here's the first one on my list. Option 1: flight 883 departing from Boston Logan to Chicago O'Hare is scheduled to arrive at 12:24 p.m. If this is the flight you want, say "This one." Otherwise, say "Next," or say "Help" for more information.

Caller: This one.

Computer: Please hold while I get the arrival information . . . United flight 883 will arrive in Chicago O'Hare at 12:34 p.m. today, Wednesday, January 19th, at gate E3 in terminal 2 . . .

SpeechWorks and Nuance played a catch-up game. In close but shifting succession, first one, then the other company would develop similar technology and deploy its applications for different customers in the same industries: delivery, transportation, banking, and stock trading. SpeechWorks and Nuance went head-to-head to establish market leadership. But even though their competition pushed both of them to become better and better, the technology and applications of one company did not substantially surpass those of the other.

Meanwhile, larger companies with a long history of speech recognition research, such as IBM and AT&T, played only a marginal role in this growing market, perhaps because they found it harder to move quickly, or because their higher costs wouldn't justify their entering into small deals, as Nuance and SpeechWorks could afford to do. But a more likely reason has to do with the strategy and structure of the two start-up rivals, which differed significantly from the strategy and structure of the long-established giants.

Products and Solutions

Since their founding, both Nuance and SpeechWorks were internally organized as two distinct but interrelated divisions: a product division and a solutions division. The goal of their product divisions was to develop and improve the core technology—to create more and more accurate, faster and faster speech recognition engines. Selling core technology can be a highly lucrative business. Once created by your research and development teams, often at considerable expense, this technology can be sold many times at little additional cost. This is particularly true for software products such as speech recognizers, which can be replicated as many times as you like at essentially their marketing and sales cost. Indeed, the sales model for software technology is to sell it as many times as the market and the competition will allow you to. Of course, you have to invest a portion of your sales revenue into research and development, as both Nuance and SpeechWorks did, to continuously improve your product and to keep ahead of your competition as best you can.

Mike Phillips, the founder and chief technology officer of SpeechWorks, used to motivate his speech recognition R&D teams by invoking what came to be known internally as "Mike Phillips's rule": the average error rate of the company's speech recognition engines must improve by 15 percent every six months. That amounted to halving the error rate every two years, pretty much in line with Moore's law of computer evolution.[16]

As a result of the two young companies' drive toward technological innovation, their speech recognizers evolved and improved in pretty much the same ways. But the question remained: how to sell them? Other companies before Nuance and SpeechWorks had built commercial speech recognizers for telephone applications. IBM had ViaVoice, which could be used to build dialog systems.[17] Bolt, Beranek and Newman had developed and marketed a commercial version of its research speech recognizer through BBN's subsidiary HARC, created in the early 1990s. AT&T's Watson, originally used on the company's telephone network in its voice recognition call processing system, was now a commercial product, as were the recognizers of Microsoft and a few European companies.[18] But sales of the larger corporations' speech recognizers, though they performed as well as, and sometimes better than, recognizers built by Nuance and SpeechWorks, had always been very limited. Why were these two small companies so much more successful than IBM, Bolt, Beranek and Newman, and AT&T in selling speech recognition engines?

One of the most likely reasons for the success of SpeechWorks and Nuance over the giants—apart from the start-ups' more focused and aggressive marketing and sales efforts—lay in their solution divisions, whose express objective was to create professional service or solution organizations to drive the sales of the companies' speech recognizers. These solution organizations would build speech applications using, and thus driving the sales of, the core technology products created and marketed by the sister organizations of their companies' product divisions.

Professional service organizations have a different business model from product organizations. Products are the same things built once and reproduced many times at little additional cost. Under favorable conditions, they recoup their substantial R&D costs through the sale of their reproductions to many different customers. In sharp contrast, professional services are different things built for different customers. The substantial development (mostly labor) costs of a particular service application often can't be recouped through its sale to other customers. The large corporations like IBM and AT&T that had developed their own speech recognizers had professional service—solution—organizations, too, but these were completely disconnected from the corporations' product organizations. As irrational as it may seem, the solution organizations of these giants were given no incentive to use the products developed by their sister product organizations, which often made little or no effort to convince them to do so. Shielded by layers of management from the real world, and receiving seemingly limitless corporate funds for R&D projects having little or no connection to paying customers, product organizations in large companies often feel they're immune to competition from small players, even aggressive ones, until it's too late. Thus, even as more and more speech recognition engines built by SpeechWorks and Nuance were sold and deployed, and even as the two small companies continuously promoted technological improvements to their products and created strategic partnerships that multiplied their ability to sell them, IBM, AT&T, and the other large corporations that had invested so much in research and development and had practically created speech recognition technology did little to commercially exploit it.

How May I Help You?

Limiting the possible responses of a caller to a small number of predictable words and phrases and combining directed dialog with menu options gave rise to a number of useful and commercially attractive applications. But there were some situations where either the number of options offered was too large to list them all or the options themselves weren't obvious. Take the task of automatically routing callers to the different departments of a large department store. To enumerate all the departments, the store's automatic information system would need an endless prompt:

Please tell me which department you would like to reach: Automotive, Appliances, Gardening, Entertainment Systems, Hi-Fi, Electronics, Fitness, Sporting Goods, Men's Clothing, Women's Clothing, Children's Clothing, Teens' Clothing, Men's Shoes, Women Shoes, Children Shoes, . . .

And, on top of that, callers wouldn't always know which department to choose. Say you wanted to buy a car radio, would you choose "Automotive," "Entertainment Systems," "Hi-fi," or "Electronics"? You wouldn't know. All you wanted was to buy a car radio, and, as soon as you said that, whoever answered the phone should be able to tell you the right department.

That simple expectation gave rise to a spoken dialog system developed by Al Gorin and other researchers at AT&T Laboratories in the mid-1990s that came to be universally known as "How May I Help You?"[19] The idea was to create an automatic association between anything a caller might say when responding to the question "How may I help you?" and a predefined number of categories, such as the departments of a store or the different services of a company, such as billing, sales, or technical support.

Every large (and many a smaller) company has a toll-free number that customers can call to connect to different services. Although human agents used to answer customers' calls and connect them to the right department or agent, with the advent of the dual-tone multi-frequency interactive voice response (DTMF IVR) technology, there was an exponential growth in demand for automated Press 1, press 2 systems to meet the exponential growth in the number of customer calls. But, for the reasons discussed before, when the options offered callers were either too many and or confusing, Press 1, press 2 systems didn't work very well, and a vast majority of callers either pressed a random number just to get out of the menu—typically 1, the first option—or pressed 0 to speak to a human operator. Choosing the wrong option, apart from irritating the callers themselves, created additional, "misrouting" costs for the call center whose wrongly chosen agents had to spend time *re*routing callers. A call center that received millions of calls every month could incur millions of dollars in misrouting costs each year.

By eliminating long and confusing Press 1, press 2 menus, routing calls based just on caller responses to a straightforward, open prompt, the How May I Help You? dialog system could enormously reduce misrouting costs. But for this to happen, the system needed to be highly accurate in identifying why callers were calling. To make it so, speech technologists turned to *statistical classification*, which uses supervised machine learning techniques to associate unknown patterns of speech to one of a number of predefined semantic categories. In the case of the new dialog system, the "unknown patterns of speech" were the strings of words in the caller responses or requests, and the "semantic categories" were the different distinct reasons why callers called.

Let's say you wanted to build a How May I Help You? call router for a telephone company's toll-free number. First, you'd need to identify the set of reasons why callers called the number, and assign each reason a symbol that represented a specific semantic category. When you did your research, you found out that callers called for each of the following reasons (followed by its category symbol in parentheses):

Pay a bill (PAY_BILL)

Ask a question about a bill (BILL_INQUIRY)

Locate a store (STORE_LOCATOR)

Subscribe to a service (SALES)

Add features to an existing service (UPDATE)

Get call rates (RATES)

Report a technical problem (TECH_SUPPORT)

Now you'd need to build your classifier module, which would assign the correct semantic category (reason) to each possible caller utterance spoken in response to the system's question "How may I help you?" So, for instance, if a caller said something like

I need to pay my bill,

Want to pay the bill,

Bill payment, or

I want to reconcile the outstanding balance of my bill,

your statistical classifier would need to assign the utterance to the PAY_BILL category. Or if the caller said something like

My telephone does not work,

The line is disconnected,

The telephone line is dead,[20] or

I can't make international calls,

the classifier would need to assign the utterance to the TECH_SUPPORT category, and so on.

So, after defining your set of semantic categories (reasons), you'd need to collect lots of examples of utterances assigned to each category. The more examples you collected, the more accurate your classifier would be. Collecting as many examples as you could for each one of the categories would be a costly, labor-intensive operation, but you'd want your examples to accurately reflect not only all the possible caller utterances, but also their true statistical distributions among your categories. To accomplish this, earlier systems typically took a Wizard of Oz approach, where one or more trained operators, the Wizards, would listen in on the toll-free line and route caller requests to the right destination by selecting the appropriate semantic category on an appropriately designed software dashboard. Callers thought their calls were being handled by a computer, but there was actually a human operator on the job. All caller utterances were immediately recorded and tagged with the category assigned by the Wizard. Recorded utterances were then transcribed into strings of words by a set of transcribers who listened to each one of them and wrote down exactly what was spoken. The set of transcribed utterances and the tags corresponding to their semantic categories—what speech scientists would call "a corpus of annotated utterances"—was then used to train the statistical classifier using a statistical learning algorithm.

About the time AT&T researcher Al Gorin published his first results on semantic classification of natural language utterances, other researchers were doing similar work at Bell and other research laboratories.[21] The main difference between the various research teams was in the specific learning algorithm each team used to build its statistical classifier. Although there are many ways to build a natural language statistical classifier, most are based on assigning numeric values to the strength of the association or relevance between the words spoken and each of the semantic categories. For instance, the words "pay" and "bill" together in the above examples are highly relevant to the PAY_BILL category, whereas the word "bill" by itself is equally relevant to the PAY_BILL and BILL_INQUIRY categories. *Functional words* such as "the," "am," "I," and "that" have no particular relevance to any of the categories.[22] Most of the statistical classifiers assign a relevance weight to each one of the words for each of the categories. So, for instance, the word "bill" would have a high relevance weight for both PAY_BILL and BILL_INQUIRY, and a very low relevance weight for the other categories. Functional words like "the," "am," "I," and "that" would have equally low relevance weights for all the categories. By combining the weights of each word recognized by the speech recognizer, you can compute a total relevance score for each one of the semantic categories and determine which is the most prominent, in other words, which most likely corresponds to the caller request. Classifier modules differ in how they compute the individual word relevance weights and combine them into a total relevance score for each category depending on their respective statistical learning algorithms.

So, once you'd assembled your large number of transcribed utterances and assigned them to their true semantic categories, you could use your classifier module, powered by your favorite statistical learning algorithm and working in conjunction with your speech recognizer, to assign a semantic category to any utterance spoken by callers. How May I Help You? systems perform a simple but effective understanding function by transforming utterances into corresponding semantic representations or meanings. Although they can be used anytime you're interested in interpreting speech with respect to a relatively limited number of possible meanings, they can't by themselves perform more complex understanding tasks, like the air travel information task of ATIS, for example.[23]

Automatic call routing systems based on spoken language understanding and semantic classification responded to a very precise business need. AT&T started to deploy natural language call routing in the early 2000s and created an organization called "Voice Tone" to build and host general speech interactive voice response systems. But the May I Help You? technology didn't really take off until SpeechWorks acquired the right to it from AT&T in 2000 and built SpeakFreely™. Nuance soon followed suit, with SayAnything™. Although both these first attempts to deploy natural language call routing were unsuccessful, the technology soon improved to the point that most large companies replaced the Press 1, press 2 systems on their main toll-free numbers with How May I Help You? systems.

9

The Business of Speech

Besides creating internal professional service organizations in their solution divisions to help drive the sales of the core technologies developed by their product divisions, SpeechWorks and Nuance made another smart move early on. Both companies realized that, to become a significant market presence, they needed the help of other companies to sell licenses to their core speech recognition engines and to build applications for them. At the same time, they realized that speech recognition engines, especially for telephone applications, needed to be tightly integrated into the infrastructure and the systems that would use them. The Press 1, press 2 or DTMF IVR systems had already been integrated as commercial platforms into telephone networks by AT&T and related companies. But, more significant, companies like Intervoice-Brite, Aspect, and Artisoft had developed commercial interactive voice response platforms that others could use to create and deploy the Press 1, press 2 systems. These companies and their platforms were the perfect vehicles for Nuance and SpeechWorks to promote sales of their speech recognition engines.

As noted in chapter 8, the old Press 1, press 2 interactive voice response systems were built on an interaction call-flow model, where all the possible paths and outcomes resulting from a caller's interaction with a system could be graphically represented in a treelike diagram. Let's take another, closer look at how those systems worked. Say you wanted to build a Press 1, press 2 information system for a bank. As soon as your system received a call, you'd have it play a prompt to greet the caller and offer a few options, as shown in figure 9.1.

At this point, the call could proceed in four possible ways: the caller could press 1, 2, or 3, or could choose to disregard the initial prompt and press some other key. This is represented by arrows coming out of the prompt box in figure 9.2, each labeled with the number of the key pressed and each leading to other prompts.

To deal with callers who chose not to press a 1, a 2, or a 3 key, but instead pressed another key, say a 0 or a # (pound sign) key—either of which your system would need to identify as "no match"—you'd have the system kindly remind them to press one of the allowed keys and send them back to the initial prompt. At that

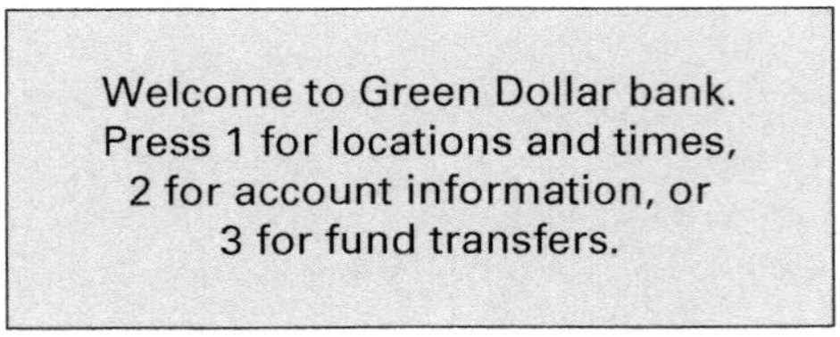

Welcome to Green Dollar bank.
Press 1 for locations and times,
2 for account information, or
3 for fund transfers.

Figure 9.1
Initial prompt of a call flow.

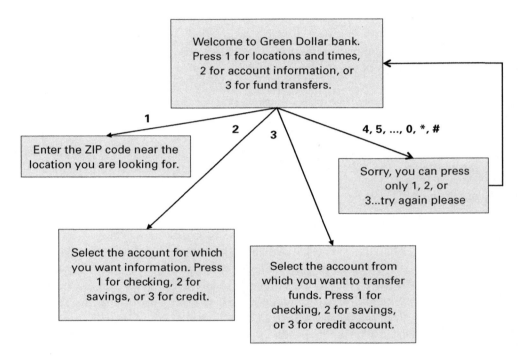

Figure 9.2
Touch-tone (DTMF) call flow showing all possible options after the initial prompt.

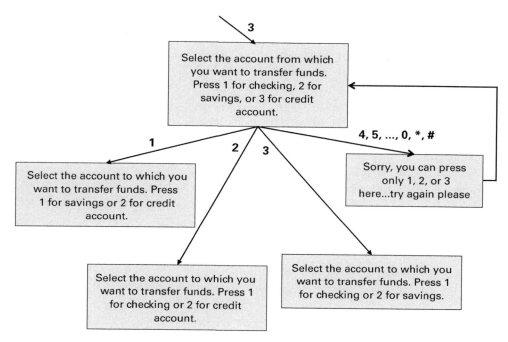

Figure 9.3
Continuation of call flow of figure 9.2.

point when, for instance, callers wanting to transfer money between accounts pressed a 3, your system would instruct them how to select the account from which they wanted to transfer money. After that, when they pressed the right key for the right account—checking, savings, or credit—your system would give them another prompt, and then another, and another, as shown in figure 9.3.

If you put together all the options for each prompt, you'd come up with a large call-flow chart that represented all the paths and outcomes of every possible choice a caller could make. But, typically, even the simplest applications required dozens of pages of call-flow charts like the ones in figures 9.2 and 9.3. And real-life designs needed to take into account that there were many more situations that might arise at each turn in the interaction between a caller and a system. As an effective designer, you might want your system to offer a special key—typically, 0—to let callers request a human operator and another key to let them hear that last prompt again or to give them additional information. If callers didn't press any keys after a reasonable amount of time—which your system would identify as "no input"—you'd want the system to remind them to press one of the allowed keys. And, finally, after callers had made a certain number of failed attempts, your call-flow design would need to provide for an exit outcome, like having your system say good-bye and hang up. Thus the number of possibilities at each node of the call flow—each turn of the interaction between caller and system—would increase with each set of options, and so would the complexity of the design.

As an IVR system designer, then, even with the simplest application, you'd end up creating very large call flows to represent all the possible options and make sure there were no unanticipated situations. Hypothetically, for a large-enough application, the call flow could become so unwieldy that no designer would ever be able to deal with it. Because of this, the touch-tone IVR industry created tools for both designing and testing call flows especially suited to handle complex applications. These tools were generally shipped with the interactive voice response platforms sold by companies like Intervoice-Brite and Aspect, and the professional call-flow designers who used them to design and develop large and complex touch-tone IVR applications became the first voice user interface designers.

Getting back to your simple bank information system, say you now wanted to transform it from a Press 1, press 2 to a voice recognition–based system. First, of course, you'd need to have your system, in its initial prompt, ask callers to speak certain words instead of pressing certain keys, as shown in figure 9.4.

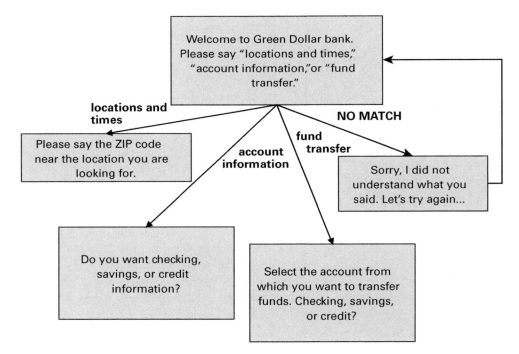

Figure 9.4
Simple speech call flow.

This is an overly simplified call flow even for a simple application such as your bank information system. In fact, in addition to the possibility of callers saying something other than what the prompt asked them to (no match), the design of your system would need to provide for the possibility of callers not saying anything for a certain amount of time (no input). Also, it would need to take into account the maximum number of consecutive instances of no match or no input you'd want your system to allow, say two or three, before it gave up and did something else, such as connecting a caller with a human operator. Moreover, you'd need to make sure that each no match or no input had a different prompt. But the point is that, at least in principle, to build a speech recognition–based interactive voice response system, you could rely on the same call-flow tools that were used to develop the Press 1, press 2 systems. That idea led both SpeechWorks and Nuance to come up with another: use the same IVR platforms that were used for touch-tone call flows by integrating the speech recognition engines into them. So that when IVR vendors sold one of their platforms, they'd also be selling the Nuance or SpeechWorks speech recognition engine embedded in it. IVR platforms thus became an effective way for SpeechWorks and Nuance to sell more speech recognizers.

From the developer's perspective, however, building speech recognition–based applications presented more challenges than Press 1, press 2 systems. The first challenge was to create grammars that would instruct the speech recognizer on which words and phrases would be allowed at each prompt. So, for instance, in response to the first prompt of your bank information system, its grammar would allow the following phrases:

locations and times

account information

transfer funds.

But that wouldn't be enough, as you well know. In fact, a large percentage of your callers wouldn't say exactly what the prompt asked them to. Some would add extra words, like

I want locations and times please.

Some would make slight variations to the required phrase:

transfer some of my funds

and others would say completely different things:

How much money do I have in my account?

Again as you well know, a speech recognition system can't recognize words or phrases not specified in its grammar. But when your system was a Press 1, press 2 one, it needed only to provide for the possibility of callers pressing keys other than the ones indicated by the prompt, a total of twelve overall, whereas now that your system is a speech recognition–based system, it needs to provide for an infinite number of things that callers can say and that aren't allowed by its recognizer's grammar—each of which your system's recognizer needs to identify as a "no match." If your caller says something like "I hate computers," your speech recognition system shouldn't misrecognize it as something that the system expected, like "location and times," or "account information," but needs to reject the input ; it should, in effect, bail out and avoid making hypotheses on what was said. As a result of that, your dialog system needs to do something like first apologize for not being able to understand and then reprompt your caller.

But, in going from a Press 1, press 2 to a speech recognition–based system, you'll encounter another, more important, difference. Touch-tone keys don't make mistakes. If your caller presses 1 on the telephone keypad, you can be 100 percent sure that your Press 1, press 2 system will interpret it as a 1. On the other hand, as we know well by now, speech recognition–based systems do make mistakes, however infrequently. If your caller says "locations and times," there's a small chance that your speech recognizer will misrecognize it as something else or will misidentify it as a no match. To avoid the potentially catastrophic consequences of speech recognition mistakes, VUI designers needed to apply special error control strategies at each step of the call flow, and that hugely complicated the already complex designs of their systems.

Error Control and Dialog Modules

Errors happen in speech recognition. You saw how the speech researchers struggled, year after year, to achieve higher and higher accuracy in their recognizers, but never quite reached 100 percent. Even in the best conditions, with the simplest and smallest of vocabularies—for instance, just "yes" and "no"—there's always a chance for the recognizer to mistake the wrong for the right answer. Even with a recognition accuracy of 99.9 percent, one in a thousand times a caller would say "no," and the recognizer would mistake it for a "yes." And that, in certain circumstances, could have catastrophic consequences:

Computer: So you want to transfer all your savings to the Adopt a Turkey for Thanksgiving Fund?
Caller: No.
Computer: Great! Your savings have been transferred . . .

Any interface that didn't account for the possibility of speech recognition errors would create huge interaction problems since even a single error could lead the dialog down the wrong path.

From their earliest systems on, voice user interface (VUI) designers considered the possibility of speech recognition errors and designed the interactions accordingly. The first thing to keep in mind is that speech recognizers don't just interpret what was said, but also assign a number to their interpretation—called the "confidence"— that represents the level of confidence the recognizer has in that interpretation.[1] Confidence can be a useful criterion for deciding whether to trust the response of the speech recognizer. So, for instance, after asking for the caller's departure city, a speech recognizer might interpret what the caller said as "Boston," and assign a confidence of 857—on a scale from 1 to 1,000, where 1,000 is certainty—to that interpretation. The higher the confidence number, of course, the more likely the recognizer's interpretation is correct. So, with an 857 out of 1,000 confidence level, the dialog system may decide to trust that the user actually said "Boston" and keep going. The lower the confidence number, the more likely it is that the recognizer's interpretation is wrong, and a very low confidence number means that the recognizer's interpretation is so unreliable it should be ignored. For instance, in the previous example, if the recognizer assigned a confidence lower than, for instance, 300, to "Boston," the dialog system should probably reject "Boston" and reprompt the caller (ask again for the caller's departure city).

Confidence is a powerful criterion that has been used to control speech recognizer errors. Typically, if the confidence is low, the system will ask for confirmation; if the confidence is very low, the system will reprompt, whereas if the confidence is high, the system will take the recognizer's interpretation as correct and go on to the next step of the interaction. The following is an example, with the corresponding recognition results, of a dialog where the flight information system performs error control for a particularly unlucky caller:

Computer: Please tell me the departure city.
Caller: Boston
(*Recognizer*:   "Austin" with low confidence)
Computer: I think you said "Austin." Is that correct? Please say yes or no.
Caller: No.
(*Recognizer*:   "No" with high confidence)
Computer: Sorry, my mistake. Please say the departure city again.
Caller: Boston.
(*Recognizer*:   "Boston" with high confidence)
Computer: Okay. Going to Boston! Please tell me the arrival city.
Caller: New York.
(*Recognizer*:   "Newark" with very low confidence)
Computer: I am not sure I understand. Can you please say it again?
Caller: New York.
(*Recognizer*:   New York with high confidence)

Computer: Got it. New York! Now, can you please tell me the approximate time of departure?
Caller: 5 p.m.
(*Recognizer*:   "9 p.m." with low confidence—second hypothesis "5 p.m.")
Computer: Is it 9 p.m.?
Caller: No.
(*Recognizer*:   "No" with high confidence)
Computer: So it's 5 p.m., then?
Caller: Yes.

Although such mistakes and corrections can be annoying if they happen frequently, error control is the only way, apart from improving the speech recognizer and tweaking its grammars, to effectively prevent more disastrous and unrecoverable mistakes during the interaction. The "I think you said" and "Got it!" error control strategy is a ubiquitous voice user interface practice in all speech recognition–based IVR systems, no matter which companies they're built for. It's become so associated in people's minds with the way "computers speak on the telephone" that even the popular TV comedy show *Saturday Night Live* dedicated a couple of skits to spoofing it. In one of them, Julie (which is also the name of the Amtrak system voice built by SpeechWorks) works as a voice talent for automated customer care systems and talks exactly like an IVR system:

Julie: Hi . . . I'm Julie.
Date: Doug told me you work in customer service.
Julie: That's right. I do the voice recording for companies like United Airlines, Blue Cross, and Amtrak . . .
Date: Wow . . . Amtrak . . . well, then, I have talked to you before . . .
Julie: I'm sorry . . . I didn't get that . . .
   . . .
Date: What do you think, Julie? . . . Latte or cappuccino . . . or something?
Julie: Did you say latte? Or cappuccino?
Date: I said both . . . Do you wanna latte or cappuccino?
Julie: My mistake . . . Cappuccino would be great.
   . . .
Julie: Before we go any further, let me get some information . . . Please say your age.
Date: I get that a lot . . . I know I look younger . . . but I'm actually twenty-nine.
Julie: I think you said "nineteen" . . . Did I get that right?
Date: No, twenty-nine.
Julie: I think you said "nine" . . . Did I get that right?

Date: No . . . *twenty*-nine!
Julie: Okay . . . Got it!

Because error control behavior followed pretty much the same pattern for any type of information a system tried to collect from a caller, the idea arose to embed it in a universal software construct—a "dialog module," as SpeechWorks called it, or a "dialog object," as Nuance did—to be used in many different applications, further evidence the companies were mirroring each other in technological innovation.[2] And, indeed, both companies built and sold specialized dialog modules (DMs) to collect the most frequent types of responses, to understand all possible variations of the responses, and to implement all needed error control behavior. Thus there were dialog modules to collect yes or no responses (these DMs are used in almost all speech recognition applications), U.S. currency responses, credit card number and expiration date responses, Social Security number responses, and date and time responses. There was even a customizable dialog module. These modules constituted the building blocks for many of the companies' commercial applications, whose creation was greatly simplified by putting together dialog modules with the right logic and configuration.

To the integration of their speech recognizers within existing IVR platforms, the provision of tools to design and test call flows for spoken dialog systems, and the invention of dialog modules, SpeechWorks and Nuance added another important element that promoted adoption of telephone speech recognition systems: formal definition of the development process from start to finish. Until then, spoken dialog systems, such as those developed during the DARPA Communicator project, were mostly the products of the inventiveness and talent of a very small team of skilled scientists and graduate students, usually led by a single researcher. When new members joined the team, it generally took them a while to become proficient in the use of the tools and software. Of course, building dialog systems as the products of a few scientists and researchers wasn't a sustainable practice for a commercial company, which needed to predict precisely how much time and money it would take to build each new system for its customers. As with all commercial products, defining a repeatable, predictable development process was essential to scale the business. But there was still another important factor that helped to stimulate the rapid growth of the speech recognition market.

The Rise of Speech Industry Standards

When Nuance and SpeechWorks couldn't grow fast enough to capture all the existing business by themselves and sought the help of partner companies, new companies sprang up to provide products and services in specialized areas such as tools for optimizing speech recognition performance, voice user interface (VUI) design, application development, and integration with third-party infrastructure. Software companies that had been providing platforms and infrastructure for call centers and touch-tone systems soon realized it was time to move from Press 1, press 2 to speech recognition–based systems and so began to integrate Nuance and SpeechWorks speech recognition engines into their platforms and tools. But, despite the rapid growth of the speech industry, potential business customers still considered its new technology to be highly risky. Chief among their objective reasons for doing so was the total absence of standards.

Although we often take standards for granted, we can be easily reminded of their importance. Think how frustrated you become when the charge runs out on your cell phone, your laptop, your digital camera, or your iPod, but you've left your charger at home and can't find anyone to lend you one of the same kind.[3] Now imagine an entire world of appliances and devices without standards. What if every electrical appliance had its own "proprietary" power plug or required a different voltage? What if every light bulb manufacturer used its own special type of attachment? What if your pocket MP3 player would only play audio files recorded using its proprietary standard? What if your computer could only read or print out files from computers of the same brand? Worse yet, what if your cell phone could only call and be called by cell phones of the same brand or with the same provider? It would be a nightmare all right, and certainly the adoption of new devices and appliances would be much slower than it is today. But such a nightmarish lack of standards isn't that far from the reality of past years: every new technology starts with no standards at all. Think of eight-track versus compact cassettes for audio recordings in the 1970s or of Betamax versus VHS for video recordings in the 1980s. In every case, mass adoption of a new technology took off only after manufacturers and vendors agreed on a single standard.

Although it may seem counterintuitive, competing companies often work together to create standards. Indeed, you'd think that doing so would make it easier for customers or clients to switch from a company to its competitors. Although that may be true, there are compelling reasons for standards that go beyond any tactical competitive advantage. For one, standards help grow the larger market. Most products and services don't exist in isolation but are used in conjunction and interact with other products and services provided by other companies. For instance, DVDs are used with DVD players, and DVD players are used with televisions and home theater systems. The more people buy DVD players, the more they buy DVDs, and the more they also buy large-screen TVs and home theater systems. The same is true for MP3 players. Companies that sell music tracks on the Web count on vendors to sell MP3 players. All MP3 player vendors stand to gain from having a single MP3 standard adopted by all music track sites: more and more people will buy their players. Similarly, if all cell phones can talk to one another, more people will buy and use them, and if you manufacture cell phones, you and your competitors will both end up selling many more of them than if your phones can only talk to other phones of the same brand. The larger the market, the larger its shares for everyone.

Mature industries understand the power of standards. Vendors often get together to decide on a standard that will help them grow the market faster. Competing standards may coexist for a time, but eventually, in most cases, one standard prevails and the others quickly disappear, even though the prevailing standard may not be either the best one or the one that provides the best value for the consumer since there are many different interests and forces at play.[4]

Given the momentum of the speech industry in the second half of the 1990s, IBM, AT&T, Motorola, and Lucent formed the VoiceXML Forum in March 1999 to formulate a standard for building and deploying spoken dialog applications. Exactly one year later, in March 2000, they published the VoiceXML 1.0 standard, which was gradually adopted by the few vendors of speech recognition engines at the time.[5] In 2001, a consortium led by Microsoft, and including Cisco, Comverse, Intel, Philips, and SpeechWorks, came up with a competing standard, called "SALT" (*Speech Application Language Tags*).[6] Although supported by the Microsoft speech recognition engine, SALT never achieved the market penetration of VoiceXML; it disappeared from the scene in 2006, when Microsoft decided to support VoiceXML. SALT was arguably a better standard, but market forces acted in such a way that Voice XML became the prevailing one.

Today almost all telephone speech recognition applications observe the VoiceXML standard, which is now managed by the main international organization for standards on the World Wide Web, the World Wide Web Consortium (W3C). But what have speech recognition technology and VoiceXML to do with the Web? Quite a lot it turns out since a spoken dialog system today is architecturally no different from a Web site, like that for Amazon.com or eBay. Moreover, speech recognition applications share some of the Internet protocols and standards that allow us to browse the Web. But to understand why this is so, we need first to review how the Web works.

The Voice Web

The traditional Web has become so pervasive in our lives it's invisible: we don't notice it, much less think about it; it's just there, all around us and everywhere. Indeed, the Web's become an extension of our minds: we count on it and we're almost lost without it. Do you remember what it was like *before* the Web, some twenty or more years ago? If you wanted to know what was playing at your local movie theaters, what flight was the best or cheapest one to get to where you needed to go, what the best brand of an appliance was and where to buy it at the best price—if you wanted to know any of these things, you had to spend a lot of time calling around or going from place to place. And if you wanted to find the name of the kid actor in *Kramer vs. Kramer* who won an Academy Award, well, you had to go to your public library and look it up or ask a movie buff if you could find one handy. Now think about all the other things you do and enjoy on the Web besides googling: e-mails, chats, blogs, and wikis; sharing pictures and home movies online; listening to the most recent songs on MySpace and buying them right away on iTunes. And what about reconnecting with your high school buddies on Facebook?

Well, it all started in 1989 with a young researcher, Tim Berners-Lee, working at the European Organization for Nuclear Research (CERN), in Geneva, Switzerland. Berners-Lee came up with three ideas, not to change the world, though they surely did, but rather to allow high-energy physicists to collaborate and share documents in real time no matter how far apart they happened to be. His genius was to take ideas that had been tried before—a common way to encode electronic documents, a protocol to transmit them over the Internet, and a program to display them on a computer—and put them together in a way that actually worked. The three ideas are known today as "HTML" (*HyperText Markup Language*), "HTTP" (*HyperText Transfer Protocol*), and the "Web browser," respectively.

Let's start with the Web browser. If you've browsed the Web at least once in your life—and chances are you've done so much more than once—you certainly know what a Web browser is. Depending on whether you're partial to Microsoft, Mozilla, Apple, or Google software, you may have chosen Internet Explorer, Firefox, Safari, or Chrome as your browser. But even though you use your browser to navigate the Web from morning till night, you still may not know exactly how things work when you do. Everything starts when you click a link or type a Web address in the address window of your Web browser and click the "go" icon. Either way, you'll be using what's called a "URL" (*Uniform Resource Locator*)—for instance, http://www.cs. indiana.edu/rhythmsp/ASA/highlights.html—to get to that Web address. A URL is actually a unique identifier of a file stored in a folder belonging to a specific computer located somewhere in the world, connected to the Internet and running a program called a "Web server." By clicking on a particular link or typing in a particular URL and clicking the "go" icon, you direct your browser to send a message into the Internet that will be routed by computers called "gateways" to that particular Web server. The message will ask the Web server to retrieve that particular document located in that particular folder. Your browser's message conforms to HTTP, a protocol language understood and spoken by Web servers. Besides the address of the Web server, the folder, and the name of the document, the HTTP message may also include other information, such as your encoded name or account number, or even your credit card number if you're actually making a purchase. As soon as the Web server, wherever it may be, receives the HTTP message, it "serves" the requested document back to your browser.

The document sent back is encoded in HTML, a language that describes how to format it and how to show still or moving images or play sounds. Web browsers understand HTML and know how to format each document with the right fonts, colors, and pagination, as well as how to display the images or play the sounds. The document displayed by the Web browser may include links, text fields, buttons, or icons you can click on, or type text in and click on, to send other messages to the same or a different Web server, and the whole process will start all over again.

Thus, overall, the concept of Web browsing is quite simple. By using your keyboard and mouse—your input devices—you direct your Web browser to request a document from a remote Web server through the HTTP protocol. The server then sends you back the document you requested, encoded in HTML, which your Web browser decodes to show and sometimes play you the document on your computer display and sound system—your output devices. Browsing the Web is like the turns of a dialog between you and a remote Web server. At each turn, you send a request to the remote Web server and receive a document as a response. Your Web browser is simply a mediator between your input and output devices, passing along the requests you send to the Web server and the responses the Web server sends back to allow you and the Web server to exchange information, as shown in figure 9.5.

Could the same mechanism be used and the same protocols and transport layers exploited for voice communication with computers? This question inspired the visionaries of the 1999 VoiceXML Forum to come up with a spoken communication analogue of the Web browser—the voice browser—and to create a standard that would change the way we build speech recognition applications. Though similar in many respects to a Web browser, a voice browser runs on a remote computer connected to the telephone network rather than on your home computer, and many people can interact with the same voice browser at the same time. They do so by dialing the telephone number associated with that particular voice browser and speaking on the phone or pressing touch-tone keys rather than typing on the keyboard or clicking the mouse of a PC. If the voice browser's speech recognizer works well, speaking to it or sending it signals by pressing touch-tone keys over the telephone is like clicking on a link or entering a Web address to your Web browser. As a result of that, the Web browser will then send an HTTP message to a remote Web server, which in turn will send back a document. But the document sent back by the voice browser will be encoded not in HTML, but in a different language—VoiceXML. And, whereas HTML coding instructs your Web browser to show you some text or images on your computer display or sometimes

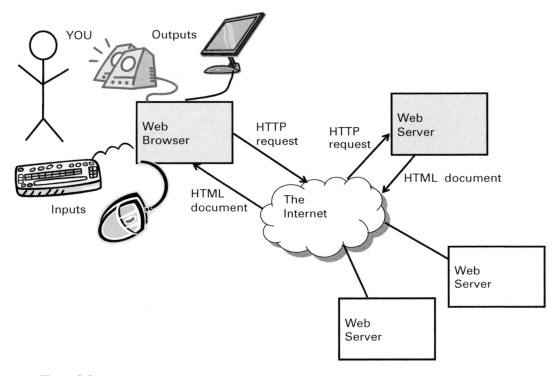

Figure 9.5
How the Web works.

to play you some sounds on your sound system, VoiceXML coding instructs the voice browser to play you audio files using its prompt player or to play you messages using its text-to-speech engine over the telephone, as shown in figure 9.6.

Now you can see the full analogy between a Web browser and a voice browser. The most obvious difference is that, because you interact with a voice browser by voice and touch-tone signals through the telephone network, rather than by keyboard and mouse on computer, you have no *visual* user interface with it.[7] Your voice and touch-tone signals provide inputs, with commands or statements, and a recorded or synthetic voice provides the outputs. But that difference in interface reflects a more fundamental one—in function.

Indeed, when the new voice technology was unveiled to the public in 2000, there was a lot of misunderstanding about its functionality. Many thought that voice browsers and VoiceXML would actually let them browse the Web with voice over the telephone, as Web browsers and HTML let them browse the Web with their

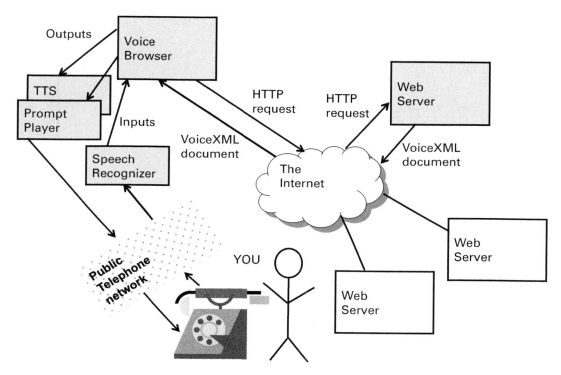

Figure 9.6
Web architecture of a modern spoken dialog system.

PCs. But, even though both HTML and VoiceXML are instruction or markup languages and both assume that a user is interacting with input and output devices, and even though both Web browsers and voice browsers are called "browsers," VoiceXML is *not* a way to browse the traditional Web with voice using a voice browser, but rather a way to build speech recognition applications leveraging the infrastructure of the traditional Web.

Inside VoiceXML

Among points in common between the visual and the voice Webs is what are called "forms," which can be found in many Web pages to collect information, such as your name, address, or account number. Figure 9.7 shows a typical form for a traditional visual Web browser, one you may have encountered many times.

HTML has specific formatting for how a Web browser should display a form: how many fields, the heading of each field, its size, position, and the type of input

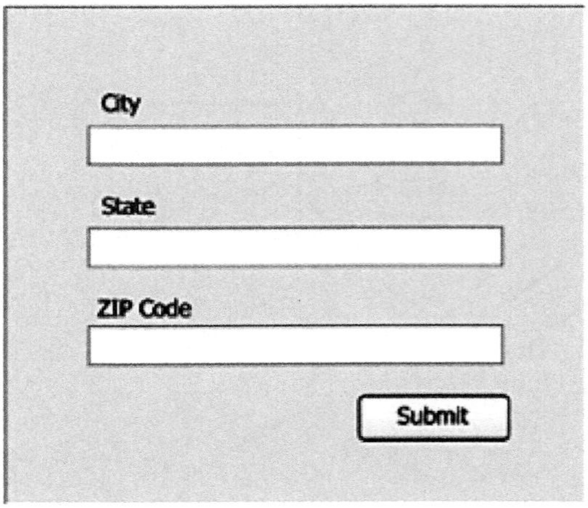

Figure 9.7
Web form.

each field will accept, such as free-form text or predefined options in a drop-down text box.[8] Typically, when interacting with a form, you fill in the requested information for each field, leaving some fields blank if that's allowed by the particular form. Once you click the "Submit" button, your Web browser sends an HTTP message to a particular Web server—the address of the server is specified in the HTML description of the form—along with the text you've typed in each field or the options you've selected. In response to this, the Web server will send you another HTML document, based on the information you sent, including text, pictures, sounds, or other forms to fill in. Sometimes the Web browser is instructed, by the HTML description of the form, to send the form only when certain requirements are met. For instance, you may not be allowed to submit the form if you leave one or more of the required fields blank, or if you fill in information that doesn't match what was expected, like writing letters instead of numbers in the ZIP code field. Today, the HTML descriptions of forms can even instruct your browser to verify the information you provide immediately before sending it to the server. For instance, HTML may instruct your browser to reject not only any letter in the ZIP code field, but also numbers that don't correspond to a valid ZIP code. In these cases, the browser won't send any information to the Web server until you fill in the correct and required information.

Now try to think about what a form would *sound* like in a nonvisual, voice-only interface. In an audio form, everything has to be spoken, the field labels as well as your input. Information that would be visually conveyed on a visual form needs to be spoken by voice prompts, and the inputs you'd normally type on your keyboard need to be collected by a speech recognizer. Thus the visual form in figure 9.7 might become the following audio form:

Computer: Say the name of the city.
You: Portland.
Computer: Say the state.
You: Maine.
Computer: . . . and the ZIP code
You: Hmm . . .
Computer: I'm not sure I got it right. Please say your ZIP code again
You: Zero four one zero six.
Computer: Thanks for filling in your location information.[9]

A voice browser can be instructed to speak the field headings and, for each one of them, to activate a speech recognition engine with a given grammar that corresponds to all the possible inputs. Moreover, as shown in this example, the voice browser can be instructed to reprompt for the same information again in case you hesitate or the speech recognizer doesn't understand what you said. VoiceXML allows developers of spoken dialog applications to define the audio form entirely, with all its prompts and grammars, and to apply a specific error management strategy in case something fails. And when the form is filled in as required, VoiceXML can instruct the voice browser to download a new document, including a new voice form, and continue the conversation:

Computer: Thanks for filling in your location information.
<the form is submitted to the server>
<a new VoiceXML form is sent to the voice browser>
Computer: Now, please tell me your telephone number.
You: Two zero seven . . .

And so on, until the end of the interaction. But, in fact, VoiceXML can do much more. The forum that defined the first VoiceXML specification thought that developers might want to use VoiceXML for more advanced applications than filling in forms one step at a time. Developers might want to let users take the initiative and fill in more than one field at a time:

Computer: Say the name of the city.
You: Portland, Maine.
Computer: . . . and the ZIP code.
Computer: Zero four one zero six.

In this limited instance of what researchers would call "mixed initiative," which we discussed in chapter 6, the user takes the initiative and changes the course of the dialog by giving more information than what was requested. VoiceXML allows a limited amount of mixed initiative. In particular, by using what's known as the "form interpretation algorithm" (FIA), a standard voice browser allows the user of a speech recognition application to fill the elements of a VoiceXML form in any order. The FIA algorithm works something like this:

• Cycle through all the fields in the form in the provided order;

• If a field has already been filled in, skip it; otherwise, ask the caller to supply the value;

• Continue until all the required fields have been filled in, and then request another form from the specified server.

Although far from mixed imitative in the normal sense, FIA provides a level of flexibility that may be useful in certain applications.

VoiceXML was simple enough to entice many developers unfamiliar with speech recognition technology to give it a try. Indeed, using Voice XML was almost like writing a Web page. And, by the early 2000s, many people knew how to write Web pages, many more than those who understood the complex intricacies of the speech recognition algorithms.

More Standards

Imagine you own a company that develops and sells speech recognizers and text-to-speech engines around the year 2000, when VoiceXML is first being adopted. Your competitors have started to integrate their recognizers and engines with voice browser platforms built by yet other companies. To maintain and perhaps improve your market position, you have to do the same. But unfortunately, each time another company markets a new VoiceXML platform, you have to do the integration work all over again. Even though all the platforms speak pretty much the same standard VoiceXML, each platform communicates with a speech recognizer, prompt player, and text-to-speech engine in its own particular way. So you have to adapt your speech recognizers and text-to-speech engines to each new VoiceXML platform, and that's a lot of work. You'd face exactly the same problem if your company sold VoiceXML platforms rather than speech recognizers or text-to-speech engines. You'd have to do the integration work all over again for each new system. On the other hand, if all available speech recognizers and text-to-speech engines spoke the same language so that all the VoiceXML platforms could communicate with them in the same way, the developers of both speech engines and voice browsers would have to do their integration work only once and could then plug in any engine or any platform at will.

To achieve interoperability—the ability of any platform to work with any speech engine and vice versa—the Internet Engineering Task Force (IETF) developed a standard called "MRCP" (Media Resource Control Protocol) in 2001. MRCP governs how speech recognizers and text-to-speech engines are instructed to perform elemental operations and to retrieve the results.[10] Thus, as long as the communication protocol is the same on both sides, any speech recognizer or text-to-speech engine can work with any VoiceXML platform and vice versa.

Although MRCP addressed the problem of integrating speech engines into voice browser platforms, VoiceXML itself left a lot of gaps to be filled. For instance, at the time VoiceXML started to be adopted, there was no standard governing speech recognition grammars. You could build a VoiceXML application and use it on different VoiceXML-compliant platforms, but when you wanted to use a different speech recognizer with that application, you had to reformat all the application's grammars. And there were other gaps as well. Simple grammars were unable to easily provide the same interpretation to all the variants that callers came up with in their responses to prompts. Thus, for a straightforward question like "Have you paid your last bill?," even though callers were expressly prompted to say "yes or no," they came up with a wide range of other responses like

"Mm-hmm," "Yup," "Sure," "Of course," "I did, I did," "Definitely," "You bet," "I paid your damn bill" or

"Uh-uh," "Nope," "No way," "Nay," "Negative" "I did not," "I didn't," "I didn't pay no stinkin' bill."

For the purposes of your VoiceXML application, the dialog system couldn't care less whether the caller said, "Mm-hmm," or "I paid your damn bill"—or simply said, "Yes." What counted was whether the response to the prompt was positive or negative, yes or no. Bare-bones grammars, like the regular grammars we discussed earlier, can describe all the possible answers but don't have a mechanism to represent the *meanings*, or what linguists call "semantics."

By embedding into the gramamrs a standard computer language called "ECMAScript," typically used by Web developers, for representing semantics the voice browser team of the World Wide Web Consortium produced the first standard on grammar formats, called "SRGS" (Speech Recognition Grammar Specification) in July 2000.[11] Though revised several times in subsequent years, SRGS is still not universally adopted as of this writing.

At the other end of the speech chain, the production of speech, the first standard on what a text-to-speech engine should say and how, called "SSML" (Speech Synthesis Markup Language), also appeared in the summer of 2000.[12] Like the other speech industry standards, SSML went through a series of revisions, which widened its scope, to include nonverbal forms of expression such as scoffing or giggling. And, finally, a standard governing interactions between voice browsers and telephone applications, called "CCXML" (Call Control eXtensible Markup Language), appeared in 2001.[13]

In a few short years, the speech industry witnessed the proliferation of standards around VoiceXML applications. These standards were instrumental in moving the industry from a largely closed circle of a few dominant companies to an extended ecosystem of many companies and organizations, each collaborating with and competing against one another to address one or more aspects of the technology.

From Clients to Servers

Let's get back for a moment to the visual Web, the Web as we know it. As you've seen, anytime you click on a link or enter a Web address, your Web browser requests a new document from the Web server, acting on your behalf as one of its many "clients"—all the browsers in the world currently requesting its service.

But where does the Web server keep all the documents that form a Web site? In the first years of the Web, each document—each Web page—was stored on a hard disk accessible by the Web server as a regular file containing lines and lines of HTML code. With the evolution of the Web, however, developers came to regard keeping static files for their Web pages as too restrictive. Soon enough, having dynamic information on Web pages became a compelling need. Current information such as the latest weather forecasts, traffic reports, stock quotes, or flight arrival and departure times proved more useful to clients than stale information updated only every now and then, as did personalized information such as the exact current balances in your bank accounts or current recommendations for books or music tracks you might like to buy based on your previous choices. Web developers felt that generating dynamic Web pages with updated information as soon as they were requested would open up a whole new universe of possibilities. And, because it made no difference to the client whether the requested document was a copy of a static file or created by the server a fraction of a second before, Web developers soon stopped writing Web pages as static HTML files and started writing computer programs that would generate HTML Web pages dynamically and include in them all sorts of dynamic information extracted from local or remote databases.[14] At the same time, programming languages such as Java Servlets and JSPs (JavaServer Pages) evolved to make it easier to generate dynamic HTML programs.[15]

As Web voice specialists, VoiceXML developers followed the same path. At first, they wrote spoken dialog applications as a set of static VoiceXML document files. After one file was executed, depending on the caller's response, the browser would request another VoiceXML file, and so on, with all VoiceXML files logically linked, pretty much like all the pages of a static Web site, to define the whole call flow. But soon, voice Web programmers, like their visual Web counterparts, started writing programs that would create dynamic documents as and when they were requested by a voice browser client.[16]

But the evolution of commercial spoken dialog systems had one more step to go. You've seen how the network of all possible dialog interactions can be graphically represented as a call flow, with nodes of the network representing actions—playing a prompt, activating the speech recognizer with a proper grammar, and so on—and arrows representing different conditions under which the dialog will move from node to node. In static VoiceXML dialog systems, at each node of the network, an individual VoiceXML document instructs the voice browser to play a specific prompt and activate the recognizer with a specific grammar. With dynamically generated VoiceXML, however, the program that manages the dialog on the Web server has a direct and clear representation of the call flow as a whole, rather than as individual VoiceXML files. The call flow drives the generation of VoiceXML files at each step of the dialog interaction. And, since one of the main strategies of software developers is to avoid doing the same work over and over again by reusing code, voice Web developers soon found it much more convenient to write, once and for all, a generic program that navigated a generic call flow of any complexity and to feed the specific call flow of each new application into this program. Some companies developed and marketed tools that enabled developers to create call-flow specifications, often in a direct, graphical manner, and an engine that would follow those specifications to generate VoiceXML files on the fly that could be used by any standard voice browser.

Although a call-flow description language would seem the perfect candidate for yet another standard, despite a number of attempts, no such standard has yet appeared, at least none as of this writing. And there's no industry-wide interest in creating one: a standard for an end product at the top of the speech industry food chain would fill no gap between levels of the chain. By contrast, a middle-of-the-chain standard like MRCP fills a gap between the VoiceXML browsers built by some companies and the speech recognition and text-to-speech engines built by others. Without it, vendors would have a hard time integrating different speech recognizers and text-to-speech engines into their platforms to offer their customers choice and flexibility. And companies that built speech recognition and text-to-speech engines would have a hard time selling their products to the many different platform vendors.

Large application developers have come up with their own proprietary call-flow description language, which they use internally. A standard call-flow description language would give them no market advantage but would instead encourage their customers to switch more easily to competing application developers who promised a lower price or better performance. On the other hand, a proprietary description language locks customers in by making it costly to switch to a different developer.

Companies that develop and sell tools to build applications have also come up with their own proprietary call-flow description language, having no interest in a standard for the same reason. Thus there may not be a standard until the call flow becomes an intermediate representation between two levels of the speech industry and no longer a top-of-the-food-chain end product. That could happen if the flow of interaction of a dialog machine ever becomes an ingredient of a higher-level reasoning machine. But that's not the case yet.

The Speech Industry Food Chain

In the beginning, the companies that made up the fledgling speech industry—for instance, AT&T at the time of the VRCP project and SpeechWorks and Nuance in their early years—did pretty much everything in-house. Often using the same people, they designed, developed, and deployed speech engines, tools, and applications all within their respective companies. But soon, as happens in most industries, the speech business evolved into an ecosystem of companies having mutual and competing interests, arrayed along a commercial food chain. The rise of industrial standards such as VoiceXML and MRCP served to catalyze this process.

At the bottom of the speech industry food chain is core technology, the enabler that makes everything above it work. The main driver of core technology companies is innovation, achieved through substantial investment of capital and personnel in research and development. Innovation in speech technology mainly aims at increasing the accuracy, speed, efficiency, and vocabulary size of speech recognizers, on the one hand, and the quality of speech synthesizers, on the other. The typical selling model of core technology software is what's known as "per session licensing," where a session is defined as a measurable unit of interaction with a piece of software. Thus, if you predict that ten of your customers will need to use the same speech recognition engine at the same time, you'd need to buy the license to use ten sessions at the same time. For telephone applications, the software sessions are referred to as "ports," and the number of ports you'd have to buy the license for corresponds to the maximum number of calls the speech recognition engine will need to handle at the same time.[17]

But core technology alone cannot fuel an industry and a market. It has to be properly integrated into the infrastructure and supported by the tools that allow people to use it. Speech core technology vendors typically sell their speech engines as integrated parts of VoiceXML platforms. Speech recognition alone and, to a certain extent, text-to-speech can't be easily used if they aren't integrated into a voice browser—at least for telephone network applications.

Thus the platform companies occupy the second level of the speech industry food chain, right above the core technology companies. They assemble platforms into which are integrated different pieces of core speech technology from various vendors. Whereas core technology companies strive for higher accuracy, larger vocabularies, greater speed, and more languages, platform companies strive for a greater number both of ports per computer unit and of different applications from different customers running on the same server—what today is known as "multitenancy." Their bread-and-butter issues are scalability, maintenance, reliability, and control. The customers of the platform builders fall into two groups: companies that deploy spoken dialog systems for their own in-house use and companies that deploy and maintain such systems for others.

Let's take a closer look at hosting companies. If you want to have a home page on the Web, you can buy a few gigabytes of space from one of these companies—and there are many of them—and, for a reasonable monthly fee, you can make sure that your Web page will be there until the end of civilization, the end of Internet, or the end of that company—whichever comes first. It's the job of hosting companies to store all the information, pages, and files, including the programs that generate dynamic Web pages, needed to maintain your home page, or any Web site, on the hard disks of computers located somewhere in air-conditioned rooms, with teams of computer technicians standing by to make sure that they don't crash, or if they do, that they're rebooted as soon as possible. They also make sure both that the hard disks never run out of space and that all information is periodically backed up on and off site, so if one of the hard disks dies, as happens sometimes, nothing's lost, and the information can be restored almost immediately, or if a tornado or flood destroys the primary facilities, operations can continue on the clone computers at the secondary site somewhere else. The air-conditioned, rack-filled, 24/7 monitored assemblies of computers of these hosting sites constitute the repository of the whole Web.

Hosting traditional Web sites requires both a substantial capital outlay to buy the Web servers and set up the necessary computer facilities and substantial recurring outlays for personnel, power, and high-capacity Internet pipes. Hosting companies that do their jobs well have thousands of customers paying monthly fees based on how much space they need on the hard disks, how many bits—how much information—they need to access through the Internet pipes every day, and how many ports they need for a particular software package. Hosting VoiceXML platforms works in much the same way. Racks of computers run voice browser platforms for speech recognition and speech synthesis engines to serve customers of companies that pay for every minute of every call received.

Founded in 1999 by Mike McCue and Angus Davis and located in Mountain View, California, Tellme Networks is one of the first start-up companies to envision the potential of hosting telephone applications. Before starting Tellme, McCue was vice president of technology at Netscape Communications Corporation, the pioneer computer services company best known for its Web browser Netscape Navigator. In 2000, McCue's new company launched one of the first telephone Internet portals: a platform able to deliver stock, weather, entertainments, and sports Web information to anyone who called its 1-800-TELL-ME service. The Tellme platform evolved to conform to the new VoiceXML standard, and the company moved toward large-scale hosting of general third-party applications. To help VoiceXML penetrate the large community of Web developers, it launched Tellme Studio, a free development environment that anyone could use over the Web to create a working sample application. If you were curious about speech recognition and the new VoiceXML technology, you could easily get a free account, take a short online tutorial, and build your own speech application—even you'd never heard about hidden Markov models or dynamic programming algorithms before—by using simple online tools without the need to buy expensive software or hardware. You could then test your application by calling it and having others do so as well over a toll-free number. Tellme Studio helped create a community of VoiceXML developers who built the most disparate applications, from video games to sports Internet portals that would keep you updated on the scores of your favorite baseball team. Tellme was eventually acquired by Microsoft in March 2007.

Thus, going up the speech industry food chain, core technology vendors cater to platform builders, platform builders cater to hosting companies, and hosting companies cater to speech technology adopters who don't want to bother with computer racks in air-conditioned rooms and Internet and telephone network connectivity issues. But who builds the speech applications themselves? Well, there are companies that design, develop, test, and even manage applications on a daily basis. These are the professional service or solution companies, which, using the software provided by the core technology vendors and integrated by the platform builders, deliver applications meeting the requirements of the final customers. Although they may develop their own tools, they often buy them from yet other companies that specialize in developing, testing, and monitoring software. And sometimes, tool companies sell to platform builders who integrate the tools directly into their platforms. Figure 9.8 shows a simple diagram of the speech industry food chain for telephone applications, with arrows pointing from vendors to buyers.

But the speech business ecosystem is more complex than that. There are companies that perform two or more roles at once. Thus both Nuance and SpeechWorks were at one and the same time core technology developers, application builders, and tool vendors; Nuance was also at a certain point a platform vendor. Some platform builders build tools and applications as well. Some hosting companies, such as Tellme, build their own platforms and tools. Some companies, such as Microsoft after acquiring Tellme, provide core technology, tools, and platforms; others provide these and hosting, too. Some tool companies prepackage prototype applications that

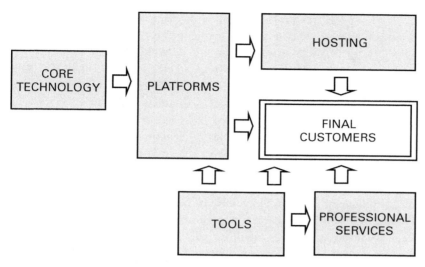

Figure 9.8
Speech industry food chain for telephone applications.

can be customized by professional service companies or by their final customers. And finally, some companies, like Google, a newcomer to the speech industry, build both technology and applications but sell something apparently much more profitable—advertising.

Expansion through Consolidation

The market for speech technology is potentially quite large. Take telephone applications alone. In 2006, U.S. companies spent more than $12 billion on telephonic customer care using human agents. Even though much of this service could be automated through speech technology, only a small part has been during the past few years. To increase their market penetration overall, speech technology companies have tried to expand and differentiate their speech technology in different dimensions.

To grow across several dimensions at once—speech recognition versus text-to-speech, network versus embedded engines, and different languages for the foreign market—companies needed to be quite large and to maintain a large product development team. Acquiring other companies or merging with them was a quick and often cheaper way to accomplish the same thing. The targeted acquisition of companies could rapidly expand the offerings of a company, with the additional benefit of eliminating potential competitors. And this is exactly what happened in the speech market.

Thus, in 1998, the speech technology company Voice Control Systems (VCS), which had previously merged with Scott Instruments in 1994, acquired Boston-based PureSpeech. In 1999, VCS was itself acquired by Philips, the well-known Dutch consumer electronics company, which had a telephone speech processing branch in Aachen, Germany. And, in January 2003, Philips's entire speech processing division was acquired by the scanner hardware and software company ScanSoft, which had entered the speech industry only two years before by buying up most of the bankrupt Belgian speech technology company Lernout & Hauspie (L&H). In August 2003, ScanSoft acquired one of the two largest speech companies in the United States, SpeechWorks, which itself had acquired Eloquent Technologies, a small text-to-speech company in Ithaca, New York, and SpeakEZ, a speaker verification technology spin-off from Rutgers University in New Jersey. But there was more to come. In 2003–2004, ScanSoft went on to acquire a large number of small, but important speech technology players, such as the Canadian speech application company Locus, the text-to-speech developer Rhetorical, the embedded speech recognition vendor Advanced Recognition Technologies (ART), and the directory assistance speech recognition company Phonetic Systems. What was left? Nuance, SpeechWorks' old-time rival, was still an independent company, but not for long. In September 2005, it merged with ScanSoft, although it retained its old name.

To expand its technological footprint, consolidate the market, and eliminate potential competitors, the new Nuance acquired still other speech technology companies—often at the rate of one every few weeks. And, as if that wasn't enough, in the spring of 2009, it acquired a large number of speech technology patents from IBM and the rights to its speech recognition engine as well.[18] With the result that, by 2010, Nuance controlled more than 80 percent of the speech technology market.[19]

What about the original speech technology giants, IBM, AT&T, and Microsoft? IBM commands a small share of the core technology market with its ViaVoice speech recognition engine. AT&T got out of the core technology market and went into the application development and hosting business through its subsidiary VoiceTone. Microsoft created a powerful dictation engine, which is today integrated in all Windows operating systems, and has placed its telephone application Speech Server on the market. Unfortunately, Microsoft couldn't compete with agile and energetic small companies like SpeechWorks and Nuance. While ScanSoft and then Nuance was getting more and more of the market, Microsoft's share, like that of the other giants, continued to shrink. That is, it did until March 2007, when Microsoft acquired the VoiceXML hosting company Tellme Networks for an industry record sale of $800 million. This acquisition puts Microsoft back in the speech technology game and may somehow offset Nuance's attempt to monopolize the speech industry.

Although it's hard to predict what the speech industry will look like in a few years, one thing is clear. Because speech recognition continues to attract research talents, industrial competition continues as well, and will do so for the foreseeable future. Even as Nuance acquires a larger and larger share of the market, other players are entering the fray, players with a completely different agenda. One such player is Google, which created a solid speech technology group by hiring key people from the largest organizations involved in speech research, like AT&T, IBM, Microsoft, and Nuance. Although it did so to develop its own technology, to automate telephone applications such as directory assistance, Google soon realized that speech recognition could help increase the traffic for its search engine, and thus also its advertising revenue. With that in mind, Google implemented one of the first *voice search* applications by allowing owners of smartphones, such as the iPhones and Android, to speak their search terms instead of having to type them on a cramped keyboard. That application, together with those of other companies like Vlingo and Microsoft, created a new wave of applications targeted at controlling smartphones with voice. But before exploring these, we need to briefly review what other new possibilities speech technologists are considering.

10

The Future Is Not What It Used to Be

The future is not what it used to be when first we dreamed of talking machines. Or is it? We dreamed of HAL 9000, a computer that could understand, reason, and speak in a soothing, humanlike voice—yet also murder without hesitation. We dreamed of androids, robots that could converse with us just as we did with one another. We dreamed of dictating memos, letters, and even books like this one to computers that could perfectly transcribe every word without our having to touch a keyboard. For hundreds of years, we dreamed of talking machines that could understand speech, and we worked toward that dream for more than fifty. And, truth be told, those dreams are still not realities.

Instead, we built simple machines that could recognize words, just a few at first and one at a time with pauses between them, and then more and more words—without pauses. In following the dream of artificial intelligence, we realized that the brute force of pattern matching worked better than we thought it might. We developed theories for understanding speech and extracting its meaning and theories to manage machines that could not only understand what we said, but also ask questions and perform actions. We developed practical talking machines from laboratory prototypes and created standards, infrastructure, and protocols to bring these machines to the marketplace, where they could help automate tasks and services under real-world conditions. And, though we're still far from realizing our dreams of talking machines in the ways we dreamed them, we accomplished a lot.

And think of all the other advanced technologies we have today. Before we had them, did we dream about them in the ways they actually turned out? Or did they take completely unexpected forms, unimagined in our dreams? What about the Web, DVDs, cell-phones, WiFi, digital cameras, MP3 players? Did we dream about them at all—or anything like them? If my grandfather were alive today, would he even recognize today's technologies from his dreams as a young man in the early 1900s?

Yes, you say, we have computers that talk to us on the phone, but only to ask us stock questions and give us stock responses, speaking in snippets of recorded

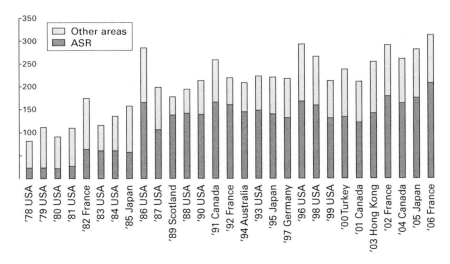

Figure 10.1
Bar graph of papers presented at ICASSP conferences (1987–2006), comparing the numbers of papers on speech recognition (ASR) to those on all other areas of research; courtesy of Sadaoki Furui of the Tokyo Institute of Technology.

voice. And yes, you say, we have dictation software on our personal computers, voice dialing on our cell phones, and voice activation features in our cars for climate control, navigation, and entertainment, but many of us have used these only once or twice out of curiosity, only to ignore them from then on. After years and years of research by thousands of people in dozens of laboratories and organizations, we seem to have just scratched the surface of our dreams. Is that all we can do? No, it's not. Although you may think of these speech technology devices as little more than gimmicks, they have, in fact, helped us reach a point where we may actually start to realize our dreams of talking machines, but in ways we never expected.

You've only to glance at figure 10.1 to see the ever growing proportion of papers on speech recognition at the annual sessions of the International Conference on Acoustics Speech and Signal Processing (ICASSP).

Indeed, that proportion has more than doubled, from some 30 percent in 1978 to nearly 67 percent in 2006, even as the number of papers on speech technology overall has quadrupled. The number of topics has also expanded enormously, to include speech-to-speech translation, speech mining, spoken dialog, emotion detection, speaker verification, speaker diarization, and spoken language understanding, among others.[1] A great deal of effort is being spent in many areas not only to improve speech recognition but also to find new and better applications of it, as you'll see later in this chapter.

If you can set aside expectations fed by years of imaginings, whether those of writers, moviemakers, journalists, or your own, you'll see that computer intelligence is steadily evolving in extremely useful ways, however different these may be from *Star Wars* or *2001: A Space Odyssey*. In chapter 3, we discussed the rise and apparent decline of artificial intelligence. Far from failing, however, AI has moved away from the goal of emulating and even replacing human intelligence into solid and mathematically sound machine learning aimed at building artifacts that actually help us accomplish our jobs, with no pretense of reaching our level of intelligence.

In a 1950 TV interview, replayed in the 1992 PBS documentary *The Machine That Changed the World,* Jerome Wiesner, an MIT professor of electrical engineering and scientific advisor to the White House, when asked whether machines could think, replied: "It's a very hard question to answer, if you had asked me the same questions a few years ago I would have said it is very far fetched. Today I just have to admit I don't really know. I suspect if you come back in four or five years, I'll say . . . sure, they really think." Speaking in the following decade in the same documentary, Oliver Selfridge, from Lincoln Laboratories, who came to be known as "the father of machine perception," said:

I am convinced that machines can and will think. I don't mean that machines will behave like men. I don't think for a very long time we are going to have a difficult problem distinguishing a man from a robot. And I don't think my daughter will ever marry a computer. But I believe that computers will be doing the same things that men do when we say they are thinking. I am convinced that machines can and will think in our lifetime.

And in a 1960s Paramount News feature dubbed "Electronic 'Brain' Translates Russian to English," also replayed in the documentary, a scientist in a room full of card-punching machines and spinning tapes stated without the slightest shade of doubt in his voice:

Scientist: We should be able to [translate]. . . about one to two million words an hour, and this would be quite an adequate speed to cope with the whole output of the Soviet Union in just a few hours' computer time a week. If our experiments go well, then perhaps [we should achieve that speed] within five years from now.
Interviewer: And finally . . . does this mean the end of human translators?
Scientist: I'd say, yes, for translators of scientific and technical material. But as regards translators of poetry and novels, no, I don't think we'll ever replace the translator of that type of material.[2]

Even though we're far from realizing the dream of the machine translation scientists of the 1960s, and our most advanced translation engines still make often laughable mistakes, machine translation has come a great distance since the early Cold War years, when it was considered primarily a weapon against Soviet espionage. Today there are powerful translation machines, many available for free on the Web, to help you when human translators are scarce, difficult to find, or too costly. And though they can't replace human translators, they can let you get at least the gist of a document in a completely unknown language. And there are also talking phrase books, like VoxTech's Phraselator, a pocket device built originally for soldiers serving abroad but now available to civilians for $50, to help you navigate foreign lands.

Language understanding is another area where you can see how computer intelligence is evolving in ways we didn't expect. Despite years of research, many attempts, and millions spent, the dream of AI scientists to create programs that would understand written, and even spoken, language without limitations and in a complete and unrestricted manner was never realized; nor did the highly ambitious Cyc project to compile all human knowledge and create a computer with humanlike common sense succeed in attaining even a fraction of human capabilities. Both efforts ran up against the unimagined complexity of human language and understanding, whose intricacies and levels of abstraction are still beyond our grasp. Instead, language understanding by machines has evolved toward what's called "information extraction," a new paradigm that has produced tools to help us extract knowledge from large sets of documents without actually having to read them. With this limited yet still very useful form of language understanding, programs can mine large collections of documents, such as those on the Web, for information like dates, names, locations, and the relationships between them. To that end, IBM launched a high-profile project in 2010 to build a supercomputer called "DeepQA" (*Deep Question Answering*) able to search through the millions of Web pages stored in its memory and successfully compete with the best contestants on the TV quiz show *Jeopardy!* Indeed DeepQA, also known as Watson, competed against Brad Rutter and Ken Jennings, all-time *Jeopardy!* record holders, and won by consistently outperforming them in three consecutive games on February 14–16 2011.

So the future of machinespeak, though not what we once imagined it might be, is nevertheless bright. Most likely you won't see, in your lifetime, a HAL 9000 or a C-3PO. But you will see other things that you couldn't even have imagined a few years ago, such as computers that help you solve problems over the telephone.

Solving Problems

Thank you for calling technical support. Please tell me the reason for your call.
I'm calling because my Internet connection never really worked since it was installed a few weeks ago. It goes on and off, and it's always very slow.
I understand you have a problem with your Internet connection, and it hasn't worked correctly since you installed it on May 25th. Is that right?

Yes.

Okay. I can help you with that. I'm going to send a ping signal to your modem and see if it responds back. Oh . . . I see. I can see your modem, but I can't see your computer online. Is your computer on?

Yes.

This dialog between a service customer and an automated technical support system is a great advance over the old "Please say 'arrival,' 'departure,' or 'gate information'" directed-dialog flight information systems of the mid-1990s. If you trace the evolution of interactive spoken dialog systems, you can clearly identify three generations. The first, informational generation corresponds to the early systems such as those for locating packages or missing baggage, finding current market or stock prices or the arrival and departure times of planes, systems built by companies like Nuance and SpeechWorks in the mid-1990s. They're called "informational" because the only thing they can do is exchange information. You give them one piece of information, like the tracking number of a package, and they give you back another, like where the package is.

Take the lost-baggage service the airlines once provided using live agents. When you had been sitting for what seemed like forever in a cramped economy seat, with little to eat and no sleep, and had landed two hours late, only to find your suitcase wasn't on the baggage carousel or anywhere else you could see, and when the small airport you'd finally reached was about to close, and there was no representative from your airline around, you were likely to be more than just surprised and disappointed. So you called an 800 number and, after long minutes of horrible music, finally reached a live agent, but all the agent could do was assure you that your suitcase would reach you eventually. Now you were really angry. Thus the reason airlines automated this service went beyond the reduced cost of computers as compared to human agents. After enduring continuous verbal abuse from frustrated passengers, many if not most agents would leave call centers for other jobs. High turnover cost the airlines a lot. Computers, of course, could stand verbal abuse very well. This is a perfect informational application.[3]

As the systems' ability to handle more complex dialogs increased, a second, *transactional* generation appeared, which could not only exchange information, but actually do things as well. The most popular applications were for securities and banking transactions, where you could buy or sell shares, check your balances, and make transfers from one account to another just by using your voice over the telephone.

A third, more sophisticated, *problem-solving* generation of spoken dialog systems appeared in the early 2000s, as a response to an all too common problem. How many times has your computer printer jammed or had configuration and communication problems just when you needed to print out a really important document?

You tried to find your printer manual, but it had disappeared in the general clutter of your work area. You went online for troubleshooting help but were overwhelmed by Web sites that weren't exactly user friendly. Wouldn't it be great, Zor Gorelov thought, if you could call a number and explain your problem to a computer, which would then give you step-by-step instructions on how to solve it? With that idea in mind, Gorelov together with Ruth Brown and Victor Goltsman, founded a company called "TellEureka," later renamed "SpeechCycle," in New York City in August 2001. His company produced the first commercially viable problem-solving dialog system to help consumers fix their home computer printers. But when the volume of calls for consumer printers didn't justify the investment necessary to build complex and sophisticated spoken dialog systems, SpeechCycle moved on to other, more promising telephone applications, called "automated agents," for digital service providers such as cable operators.[4]

Rich Phone Applications

Cable services have been growing in the United States for decades. Starting with the old analog television, they went on to digital and high definition TV, moving toward more interactive applications such as "on demand" and "pay per view" that allowed subscribers to order movies and sport events and watch them whenever they wanted. Next they provided Internet access and finally digital telephone access, known as "Voice over Internet Protocol," or simply "Voice over IP" (VoIP), for a "triple play" of all three main communication channels brought to your home through one or more cable boxes over a single cable. Cable operators, also known as "MSOs" (*Multiple System Operators*), rapidly grew their companies by creating infrastructure parallel to the telephone networks, infrastructure that reached even the more remote parts of the country. Small MSOs created local monopolies and were then acquired by larger MSOs, like Comcast, Time Warner, Cox Communications, and Charter. Though, for a long time, cable operators faced no real competition because of the local exclusivity of their service, that ended in the early 2000s, when satellite and telecommunications operators entered the market as television and Internet providers. Whereas, for Internet connectivity, satellite operators couldn't offer the same level of service as cable operators because of the difficulty of establishing and maintaining upload links through their satellites, telecommunication operators definitely could; with advances such as DSL (*Digital Subscriber Line*) and fiber-optic technologies such as Verizon's FiOS and AT&T's U-verse, they gained an ever larger share of the market. And of course the quality of service telecommunications operators could provide, and in particular the quality of customer service and technical support, at lower overall cost could convince even the most loyal cable subscribers to switch to them.

As competition from satellite and telecommunications operators mounted, cable operators faced another problem. The cost of customer care by human agents was becoming unsustainable, forcing more and more call centers to move offshore, with consequent reduction of the quality of technical support. Cable services—TV, Internet, and digital telephone—rely both on complex devices installed at home such as digital cable boxes and high speed modems, which interact with other complex devices such as digital TVs, VCRs, DVD players, home network routers, and PCs, and on a huge and complex network infrastructure. When something goes wrong and service is interrupted for some reason, cable customers are at a loss as to what they should do. There's an immediate need for competent and efficient technical support, which most often can't be met by poorly trained offshore personnel. But raising the quality of human agents would also raise the cable operators' overhead, further eroding their competitiveness. Automated agents, at a lower cost and at performance levels equal to or even better than human agents, were certainly an attractive prospect, one made even more attractive by SpeechCycle's business model, revolutionary for the speech industry.

Whereas deploying speech recognition devices from other companies required an upfront capital investment, SpeechCycle introduced the idea of "pay for performance." Rather than buy systems, customers would pay only for each call handled by its automated agents hosted by SpeechCycle, at a cost well below that of an equivalent call handled by a human agent.

But the most compelling feature of troubleshooting automated agents, called "rich phone applications"—and the key to their success—was their ability to extract information from customer databases, such as the type of modem and service level, and to run online diagnostics, often while talking to customers, which brought the performance of automated agents to levels comparable to, if not better than, those of human agents.

No Data like . . . Even More Data

At the time of the DARPA speech recognition projects, as you'll recall, herculean efforts were put forth to collect the vast amount of data needed to bring the DARPA systems to respectable levels of performance. Speakers were recruited and trained according to special collection protocols, special tools were developed, and special teams assembled to oversee the well-organized, articulated, and managed collection process. But with the deployment of large commercial systems, data started to flow in like water and in quantities far greater than researchers of the previous decade could ever have expected—indeed, several orders of magnitude greater. Thus an automated customer care system deployed for a single large cable operator received millions of calls per month. The differences between data collected by deployed systems and data collected by DARPA and other researchers in the 1980s and 1990s went beyond scale, however. For one thing, the deployed systems data was highly specific to the systems in question. It was mostly yeses and nos or specific answers to specific directed-dialog questions, with very few of the free-form, natural language responses so often encountered in the DARPA evaluations of the 1990s. It was therefore far more suited for improving those same systems than for general research in speech recognition and understanding. For another and more important thing, the data was real, that is, produced by real-world callers under real-world conditions, not by recruited speakers asked questions they really didn't care about.

Faced with data gushing like water from a fire hose, you need to make sure you can handle the millions and millions of utterances accumulating on your hard drives in an effective way. In particular, to use the data to improve your language models and evaluate your various voice user interface designs, you need to eliminate manual interventions in the handling of the data to the maximum extent possible. To that end, SpeechCycle automated the whole process of data handling, from collecting and transcribing speech data to generating grammars and language models.[5] And though data is still king, together with continuing the work on reinforcement learning we discussed in chapter 6, such fully automated data handling constitutes one of the first significant steps toward creating a system able to learn from its mistakes. We're still far from completely autonomous systems, but we're definitely moving in that direction.

Learning to Discriminate

The drive to improve the performance of speech recognizers did not, of course, stop with the invention of hidden Markov models and more effective use of greater amounts of data; using the HMM approach, researchers have gone on to achieve steady, incremental increases in speech recognition accuracy for quite some time. But still, there was one problem with the HMM theory that remained unsolved: the statistical learning of the hidden Markov model parameters was based on the intuitive, but mathematically unsupported assumption that, by probabilistically modeling the training data as best as you could, you'd attain the highest possible accuracy. Leonard Baum, in the early 1970s, had found a way to build extremely accurate statistical models of the training data with his training algorithm. But, from a real-world perspective, what was needed, instead, were models that, once deployed in a speech recognition system, would make the fewest errors possible. And representing the training data no matter how accurately was no guarantee that a speech recognizer would make the fewest possible mistakes.

Indeed, building models that did guarantee minimum recognition error proved to be extremely difficult mathematically. In the absence of a precise mathematical solution, speech researchers developed an approximation technique called "discriminative training" by which they could adjust their models to achieve targeted reductions in the error rate. To do this, however, they needed a third set of utterances, called "development data," besides training and test utterances, to use in iterated cycles of testing, evaluation, and adjustment aimed at reducing speech recognition error. Thus they would build models from training data, test and evaluate them on the development data, adjust the models to reduce the number of errors, test and evaluate the models again on the development data, adjust them again, and so on until they could achieve no further significant improvements. Then, in one last step, they tested the models on the original untouched test data for a final evaluation of their performance. Of course, the process turned out to be not that simple. For instance, if they started with a decent speech recognizer, they got very few mistakes on the development data, so they had very little to adjust. But researchers found ways to cope with this problem as well.[6]

Years after the invention of HMM–based speech recognizers, discriminative training, as a major, mathematically sound refinement of hidden Markov model theory, has brought solid and reproducible results. But what about efforts to go beyond HMMs altogether? Despite promising work aimed at merging statistical and linguistic knowledge and at generalizing the concept of hidden Markov models to develop still more powerful models, we've not seen any alternative that outperforms the HMM approach, at least not as of this writing.

Emotions

Most of us find it hard to hide our emotions. It shows when we're upset, negative about something, don't believe what others are saying, when we're afraid, deeply moved, or not moved at all. Our emotions visibly change the way we behave, and in particular the way we speak, which is often a telltale sign of how we feel. Can a machine detect that, and by listening to someone talk, have insight into the emotional state of that person? The answer is yes, at least to a certain extent.

Starting from the premise that certain clearly observable elements of speech change as the emotional state of the speaker changes, the recognition of emotions from speech has been a field of study in the more general computer speech discipline since the late 1990s. For instance, if you're upset, you may speak louder, faster, and the pitch patterns of your voice may differ from when you're calm and relaxed. As humans, all of us can detect that. Thus you can tell if someone's upset even if you don't know that person, even if you just heard the person's voice on the telephone or in a recording. And, of course, when someone says certain words rather than others, it can also be a clear indication of that person's emotional state. Can a machine detect emotions from the use of "certain words" or on a purely acoustic basis, by measuring the loudness, pitch, and the speed of someone's speech? Can it do so using other measures of someone's speech? Speech researchers set out to answer these questions.

The first problem they encountered as they looked at ways a machine might detect emotions from speech was defining the set of basic emotional states most of us could unquestionably identify. We've a certain intuitive idea of what being upset, afraid, or calm means. But, as in pretty much any attempt to classify things in rigid categories, the boundary cases are harder to classify, sometimes much harder. Because there was no formal, agreed-upon classification of basic human emotional states, with some psychologists listing fifty or more, emotional speech researchers decided to focus on only a small number, often as few as two or three, typically, anger, anxiety, and indifference, and to look at them in only two dimensions: *valence*, whether the emotion was positive, like confidence and interest, or negative, like sadness and anger; and *activation*, how strongly the emotion was felt, like sadness versus despair.

The second problem the researchers encountered was how to find enough speech samples that significantly represented each of the emotional states under study. Creating a corpus of speech samples for basic speech recognition experiments is relatively straightforward. You ask someone to read something, or you put someone in a situation where the person has to speak the words or phrases you need for your study. But how do you get someone to feel anger, annoyance, boredom, or surprise? You don't, unless that person happens to be a professional actor. And, indeed, the first studies on detecting emotions from speech drew on a corpus of emotional speech recordings made by professional actors asked to read neutral material, like dates and numbers, while acting different feelings like happiness, anxiety, and boredom, a corpus compiled by the Linguistic Data Consortium.

But, of course, it would be much more interesting if you could test automatic recognition of emotions with a corpus of speech samples from people who weren't acting but were really happy, anxious, or bored, say. You could use that corpus to train speech recognizers to detect anger or frustration in callers when they interacted with an automated call center machine or uncertainty in students when they interacted with automated tutoring systems, and you could then have your systems do something about it. Or you could use the corpus to train a recognizer to detect excitement in participants and thus identify important moments in a meeting.

While at SpeechWorks in the early 2000s, I collaborated with Shri Narayanan, from the University of Southern California (USC), and his student Chul Min Lee on machine detection of emotions from speech samples recorded when callers interacted with an automated lost baggage information system.[7] Many callers were clearly angry, and we could be quite confident that they weren't acting. We collected several hundreds of utterances from the deployed system and labeled the emotion clearly displayed by the caller in each utterance as either negative or nonnegative based on our perception. Then we statistically trained a speech recognizer to detect whether the emotion displayed by a caller in an utterance was negative or nonnegative from measurements such as the variation of pitch, loudness, and speed of speech. The results were encouraging. With the proper tuning and the proper learning algorithm, our recognizer was able to detect whether a speaker was displaying a negative emotion with an accuracy of about 80 percent. Narayanan and his team of USC graduate students continued to work on automatic detection of emotions for several years, obtaining more and more interesting results, and also raising the interest of the media. He appeared on CNN's *Paula Zahn Now* in a 2005 interview on advances in voice technology, and his research on emotion detection was featured in the *New Yorker* in 2008.[8]

Studies on detecting emotional states certainly generate a lot of interest. Take, for example, a 2006 study investigating how well various groups of people could detect lying. In it, the forensic psychologist Michael Aamodt and his colleague Heather Custer concluded that teachers were the best at detecting deception, with an accuracy of 70 percent, followed by social workers, criminals, secret service agents, and psychologists. Law enforcement personnel did worse, with police officers detecting liars 55 percent of the time, detectives 50 percent, and parole officers only 40 percent of the time.[9] Julia Hirschberg and her team at Columbia University wanted to find out whether a machine could be trained to detect when people were lying just from their speech. In her 2007 study, she found that by training on more than 150 speech features, including speaking rate, loudness, spectral characteristics, emotional words, and pleasantness of language, a machine could indeed detect liars, with an accuracy of slightly higher than 60 percent.[10] That's better than most law enforcement professionals. Julia Hirschberg's work continued with the automatic identification of charismatic speech and also of autistic behavior from speech alone.[11]

Distillations and Translations

In 2005, DARPA launched an ambitious new project called "GALE" (*Global Autonomous Language Exploitation*), under the leadership of Joe Olive, a former researcher in speech synthesis and director at Bell Laboratories. Reflecting DARPA's shift toward projects related to homeland security, GALE's mission was

to develop and apply computer software technologies to absorb, translate, analyze, and interpret huge volumes of speech and text in multiple languages, eliminating the need for linguists and analysts, and automatically providing relevant, concise, actionable information to military command and personnel in a timely fashion. Automatic processing "engines" will convert and distill the data, delivering pertinent, consolidated information in easy-to-understand forms to military personnel and monolingual English-speaking analysts in response to direct or implicit requests.[12]

There are vast amounts of text and recorded speech all around us: not only in text and audio files on the Web, but also in audio recordings of all types, from TV and radio to questionably legal recordings of telephone conversations. Faced with the ever-present threat of terrorist attacks, it's imperative that we be able to mine all these written and spoken documents for information vital to our national security. But Arabic, Farsi, or Korean interpreters aren't always available. GALE was intended to foster technologies that would allow English-only speakers to extract information from non-English audio sources. So that a military commander, combat soldier, or decision maker could make a query in English, such as "Where was Abdul Qadir last seen?," and the specialized search engine would search all documents that might lead to an answer, not only those in English, but also those in Arabic, Farsi, and any other language of interest, and present the answer back in spoken English. The process of extracting information from documents, whether written or spoken, is called "distillation." A key ingredient of distillation, of course, is automatic translation, without which only documents that matched the specific wording of the query would be searchable. But translation, especially from speech, is a very difficult job for a computer.

In simplest terms, a *speech-to-speech* translation system would link a speech recognizer to a text machine translation system to a text-to-speech synthesizer, as shown in figure 10.2.

As always, however, things were more complicated than putting together three existing technologies. Besides the intrinsic complexities of speech recognition, translation, and text-to-speech, there were other problems. The English text generated by the source language speech recognizer lacked both capitalization and punctuation, which made correct translation quite hard. Without capitalization, words that could be either proper or common nouns, such as "Brown" or "brown," "Cook" or "cook," and "Wood" or "wood," might be incorrectly translated. And without punctuation, determining the beginning and end of phrases and sentences was very difficult. So capitalization and punctuation had to be reconstructed automatically using contextual information. Researchers were able to do this quite effectively

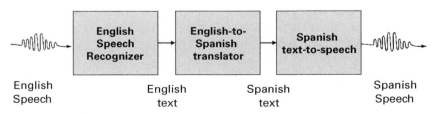

Figure 10.2
Speech-to-speech translation system.

using statistical methods to determine which sequences of words were likely to begin or end a phrase or sentence.

But one of the major issues with translation in general, and speech-to-speech translation in particular, is the absence of a clear criterion for evaluation. How do you determine which of the many ways to translate a sentence, all conveying essentially the same meaning, is best?[13] And how do you determine which among different translation systems is the best? Consider the differences between evaluating a speech recognizer and evaluating an automatic translation system. To determine the accuracy of a speech recognizer, you need a correct transcription of the actual words that were spoken in each one of a set of test utterances. Even though there are words or phrases that can be transcribed in different ways, such as "work out" or "workout," and "hang up" or "hang-up," most transcribers, taking their cues from contexts, would transcribe the same utterance in the same way. Moreover, as you've seen in previous chapters, the process of transcribing a large corpus of utterances for test and training purpose can be done quite effectively and economically by nonspecialists. Using special tools, laboratories and speech recognition companies can generate transcribed speech corpora with millions and millions of utterances. This is not the case with translation. Different human translators would most likely provide different translations of the same utterance, all of them preserving the same meaning. Moreover, translators for certain languages are expensive and hard to find. The most notable attempt to evaluate automatic translation systems, called "BLEU" (*BiLingual Evaluation Understudy*), was invented by IBM and is used by most researchers interested in machine translation today.[14] BLEU computes the accuracy of a system by comparing how many chunks of consecutive words in the system's translations match those in a set of reference translations made by human translators. Nevertheless, the problem of effectively and reliably evaluating machine translation systems remains.

Voice Search

Without a doubt, searching is one of the things we do a lot, whether for things at home, for telephone numbers, for that restaurant we heard about, for old friends, or for memories. Indeed, we spend much of our time searching. And that's certainly true on our computers. Take note of what you do from the moment you boot up. First, you search for your e-mail client on your desktop, then you search for the day's e-mails, then for the one your boss sent you a couple of days ago in the pile of e-mails you left unanswered. Then you go back to your documents and search for the one you were working on, open it, search for the point where you left off yesterday, and start writing again. A little while later, you suddenly think of a movie someone told you about, but you can't remember its title or who played in it. You go to the Web, open up your favorite search engine page, type in a few keywords, and find the movie Web site with everything you wanted to know. Then you search for the closest theater showing the movie and also for a restaurant not too far away to go to after the show. Thus many, if not most, of the things we do on a computer amount to some sort of search.

With the advent of smartphones, like the BlackBerry, iPhone, and Android, any computer search is at your fingertips at any time, in any place. But typing may not be all that practical. For one thing, smartphone keyboards are tiny, and your fingers aren't. For another, you may have only one hand free for your smartphone while carrying something else with your other. Or your eyes may be busy, as when you're walking along a busy sidewalk. Or maybe you left your glasses at home, and you can't see a thing. If you could avoid typing, say by speaking the terms of your search, your life might be quite a bit easier.

The mass adoption of smartphones with ubiquitous high-speed Internet connection and tiny keyboards and the increasing importance of Web search in our everyday lives gave rise to the idea of voice search: speaking rather than typing your search into your favorite search engine. Yahoo, Google, and other search engine sites today have their own voice search you can use on your smartphone. Say you want to find a Mexican restaurant in the Hell's Kitchen neighborhood of New York City. You pull out your iPhone, tap the Google search icon, and say: "Mexican restaurants in Hell's Kitchen." In a second or two, the display will show you a list of appropriate restaurant Web sites. Or say you're sitting on your couch watching a movie about Robert Kearns, who invented the intermittent windshield wiper only to have his invention stolen by Ford and Chrysler, and you want to know more about that. You reach for your smartphone, tap the search icon, say "Robert Kearns," . . . and the *Wikipedia* page is right there for you to read. But how many words would a search engine's recognizer need to know to be really useful for any search you cared to make? Probably millions. Could a speech recognizer with millions of words fit into the limited memory of your smartphone and still be fast enough to do the job? Probably not. Perhaps someday, but certainly not today. So how does voice search work?

The idea of *distributed speech recognition* (DSR) came into play when the first data links on mobile devices started to become available. As you may recall, a speech recognizer can be said to have two components: the first collects speech and compresses it into sets of feature vectors, and the second, working with millions of hidden Markov model states, computes the most likely sequence of words. The recognizer's two components need not be located in the same place. If the Internet connection between them is fast enough, the speech collecting and compressing device can be in one place and the "find-the-best-sequence-of-words" device in another, far away. And today's data connections are fast enough, indeed. That's how voice search is realized today.

Because the search engine's speech recognizer can use the data it receives to continuously improve its performance, the more people use voice search, the better it becomes. And because the same person uses the same phone most of the time, the speech recognizer can be personalized for individual voice search users, by learning their acoustic characteristics and the statistics on their choice of words. It's interesting to note that we seem to have come full circle here. Speech recognition technology started with speaker-dependent systems, systems completely attuned to the voice of single users. Researchers and developers then struggled for years to find ways to achieve speaker independence and avoid having to train systems for each individual user in real-world applications. Now, with smartphones, which are personal devices, we're going back to tuning speech recognizers to individual users. Moreover, another speech technology, known as "speaker verification" or "speech biometrics," has come into play to secure the personal information we all keep in our smartphones, such as passwords and account numbers. Speaker verification detects whether an utterance belongs to an authorized speaker who has gone through an enrollment process or to an impostor. In the years to come, we'll almost certainly see more and more of both adaptation and verification technologies in speech recognition applications for smartphones.

Put That There!

Except for when we talk with one another on the telephone, we humans don't communicate with speech alone. We communicate with our eyes and facial expressions, gestures, and touch, we gaze at one another or look away, we make marks on paper or type on computer keyboards, and we do many other things besides speaking and understanding speech. Steve Springer, a leading voice user interactive system designer at SpeechWorks (and later ScanSoft and Nuance) once asked, why, if you want to buy something, say a pastry in a pastry shop, you can point to it and simply say, "I want that one," why couldn't a computer let you do the same kind of thing?

An increasingly large community of scientists is creating machines that can do just that, using what they call "multimodal interaction." The idea dates back to one of the first and best-known examples of a multimodal interactive device, built by Chris Schmandt and his colleagues at MIT in 1978. They equipped their interactive "Media Room" with speakers, a giant display, light beams, touch-sensitive pads, and, of course, a speech recognizer. In "Put That There," one of several early public demonstrations, Chris Schmandt sat in front of a giant screen showing colored geometric figures. Pointing with a light beam to a particular figure, say a green triangle, and then to a particular location, say to the right of a yellow square, Schmandt would give the command "Put that there," and the interactive room would execute his command by moving the figure to the correct position.[15]

Clearly, adding an interactive display makes spoken interaction simpler and more natural in any number of situations. Say, as a visitor to New York City, you wanted to find somewhere to grab a bite to eat. With an interactive map you could talk to, you could circle the area where you happened to be on the map and say something like "Find a good Chinese restaurant around here," and the system would promptly oblige. This was actually done by Michael Johnston and other researchers at AT&T Laboratories on a touch-tablet demonstration computer called "MATCH" (*Multimodal Access To City Help*; figure 10.3).

Let's go back to our flight information directed-dialog example for a moment. As you'll recall, when the system's speech recognizer is unsure what you've said, the system tells you what it *thought* it heard and asks you to confirm. When you say no, the system apologizes for its mistake and tries to correct it:

Computer: Please tell me the city from which you want to leave.
User: Boston
Computer: I think you said "Austin." Is that correct?
User: No.
Computer: My mistake. Was it Houston?
User: No! BOSTON!!!
Computer: Got it. Boston.

Sometimes the system has to go through a whole list of possible candidates before arriving at the correct one, and you can get quite frustrated. But if you had a display you could interact with, the system could show you a list of likely words, and you could click on or touch the correct choice right away, without having to go through an awkward conversation. This is a lot like what you do when you search for something on the Web. You get a long list of ranked sites, and you scroll through them to find the best choice. But what if you had to *speak* each site out loud to see whether it was the right one? It would take forever!

Making Friends

In the classic 1982 sci-fi movie *Blade Runner,* J. F. Sebastian, a small man affected by the rare Methuselah syndrome, which makes him look much older than he actually is, lives alone in a run-down and deserted part of the city. When the sexy replicant Pris asks him whether he gets lonely, he answers: "Not really, I make friends." In fact, Sebastian genetically engineers his friends.

But "making friends" isn't that far from what we can dream of accomplishing today by combining speech recognition with other cognitive technologies. Yorick

Figure 10.3
Multimodal interface on a smartphone using speech and gestures. Courtesy of AT&T Labs and Michael Johnston.

Wilks, a professor at the University of Sheffield with an endless list of accomplishments, awards, and appointments in the fields of artificial intelligence, information processing, and language understanding, often talks about one of the special projects he's coordinated. Funded by the European Committee and with fourteen industrial and academic partners across Europe, the Companions project brings together several advanced technologies, including speech recognition and understanding, to create a virtual companion, an artificial entity that carries on regular conversations with the same person, in much the same way a human companion might.[16] Of course, the aim of this project is not to replace real human companionship, but to create machines that continuously learn about their human companions, track what they do, and that, eventually, are able to help them with tasks such as cooking, shopping, or making reservations and even to suggest things to do, as well as simply chat whenever their human companions feel like it. In its first embodiment, the companion looks something like a toy rabbit. Sitting on your kitchen table and connected to the Internet through WiFi, it's always ready to chat.

Here's one conversation between a user, Markku, and his virtual companion:

Companion: Hi, Markku! How are you doing today?
Markku: I'm fine, thank you.
Companion: How about taking a look at your eating habits?
Markku: Sure, why not.
Companion: Would you say yesterday was an average day?
Markku: Yes, I guess so.
Companion: What time did you wake up?
Markku: At seven o'clock.
Companion: Do you usually wake up around seven in the morning?
Markku: No, usually around eight in the morning.
Companion: What did you eat and drink between getting up and going to work?
Markku: Some coffee and juice.
Companion: Did you eat something between getting up and going to work?
Markku: Yes, I had toast.
Companion: Did you have milk or sugar in your coffee?
Markku: Yes, both milk and sugar.[17]

Not a bad start, but obviously there's still a lot of work to be done before you'll see a well-mannered android like C-3PO sitting across from you at your kitchen table, ready to talk intelligently about almost anything.

What We Must Do

One obvious question arises regarding any developing technology, and in particular the speech understanding technology we've dealt with in this book. What must we do to make it as close to "perfect" as we can? For "perfect" to have any meaning, however, it needs to be defined by a valid and appropriate criterion. If, by "perfect" for talking machines, we mean "humanlike," several choices for that criterion come to mind: we can say that talking machines' use of speech is definitely humanlike when people prefer to talk to machines rather than to humans, or at least when they don't insist on talking to humans *instead* of machines. Or when, in blind tests of those machines, human judges can't tell whether they're conversing with humans or machines. Thus we might also say that talking machines are "perfect" when their speed, accuracy, transaction success rate, and pleasantness of interaction aren't just comparable to but *indistinguishable* from those of humans.

A veteran in speech recognition technology, David Thomson worked first at AT&T's Bell Laboratories from 1984 to 2002, then at several start-up and commercial firms in the speech industry, before returning to AT&T in 2010. Thomson has been a pioneer and leading advocate of VoiceXML and is now part of the Advanced Dialog Forum, a not-for-profit organization with members from leading speech technology companies. At a speech technology trade show held in New York in 2010, he spoke of seven steps we must take if we're to create "human-equivalent" dialog systems:[18]

Raise the systems' speech recognition accuracy to human levels.   We've not yet reached human performance levels in any speech recognition task. Getting as close as possible to human accuracy will greatly facilitate using speech as an input modality for dialog systems. But, of course, speech recognition accuracy is only one essential factor. Others, like the ability to understand what was said and the logic of the dialog, need to be raised to human levels as well.

Optimize the analysis and selection of system architectures.   Architectural choices strongly influence the capabilities and the limitations of any speech recognition and understanding machine we might build. Since the first large systems of ARPA's Speech Understanding Research project in the 1970s, there's been much discussion on what the best structure for a dialog system should be. How should its modules collaborate? Should speech recognition be fully integrated into the language parsing structure, as in Harpy, or should it collaborate with all the other modules in a massive parallel architecture, as in Hearsay's blackboard or MIT's Galaxy? Should an algorithm coordinate the generation of hypotheses coming from each module and select the winning one? Or should the speech recognition resources be assigned to a remote server dynamically driven by markup documents, as in the VoiceXML Web model? Or perhaps even distributed between client and server, as in current smartphone voice search applications? One thing is clear: advances in computer architectures such as cloud computing will give rise to new models, structures, and algorithms for dialog systems not possible before.

Automate the building of systems by exploiting their ability to learn. Today's systems are heavily handcrafted. From their voice user interfaces to their grammars and tuning, dialog systems require the labor and expertise of software architects, programmers, and speech scientists. But every system built by hand is bound to have limitations, whether in its performance or its scalability, unless it can improve that performance by learning from new knowledge and experience in an autonomous way.

Find the right dialog algorithm. Although the call flows or finite state machines used by most commercial dialog systems today are quite effective for modeling simple interactions, they are far from endowing the systems with humans' ability to react to unexpected turns in a conversation, to get the conversation back on track, and to deal with uncertainty. There's great hope that, by pursuing reinforcement learning for talking machines, speech technologists will come up with an algorithm that will enable dialog systems to converse like humans by learning what was good and what went wrong in their previous dialog experiences.

Expand and perfect systems' models of language and semantic interpretation. Even if dialog systems learn to recognize speech as accurately as humans can, they still need to interpret what was said. Our statistical models of language understanding, for all their mathematical elegance and power, fall far short of giving dialog systems the ability to comprehend any utterance they might encounter.

Make world knowledge a central part of their language understanding. As you'll recall from chapter 1, not all meanings expressed by a sentence make sense within our world knowledge—our highest level of abstraction, just above semantics, the first linguistic level. Thus when you hear someone ask, "Where can I buy china?," your world knowledge tells you right away the asker has tableware rather than the world's most populous country in mind. If intelligent dialog systems are to make humanlike language judgments of this kind, they must also have access to world knowledge. A logical source for them would be the Web, which has grown enormously since its inception to include much of our world knowledge. Whether we'll be able to harness all that knowledge, however, and build intelligent dialog systems that can rely on it remains an open question.

Make the systems domain adaptable. The speech recognition engines in most commercial dialog systems must be customized to specific applications by specifying the vocabularies and grammars or language models needed to deal with what their likely users might say. But creating general speech recognition engines to deal with the set of virtually all expressions in the language of choice and making the dialog systems domain adaptable would bring them that much closer to human performance levels. Today we can largely automate the transcription and correct semantic labeling of each of a large number of utterances recorded during the deployment of an application.[19] If we could find a way to fully automate these processes, we could build dialog systems that, through unsupervised adaptation and by learning and improving continuously, could adapt to any domain, as humans can.

When, if ever, will we take these steps to achieve "human equivalence" in our dialog systems? That very much depends on the economic forces that shape the direction of scientific and technological research. Is there enough interest in pursuing the dream of talking machines to foster creation of the new algorithms, architectures, and standards to make the needed breakthroughs? If so, you'll see ever greater progress in perfecting dialog systems and speech technology more generally. If not, progress will be more limited, with dialog systems serving as a useful, but marginal component of other interaction technologies.

Invisible Speech

We have come to the end of our journey. We have delved into the complexity of human speech, and we have walked through the first attempts to tame that complexity. We have seen the excitement of elegant artificial intelligence projects, the power of rigorous mathematical approaches, and the steady gains won by brute-force engineering. We have witnessed the rise of an industry that uses speech technology for resolving problems of cost and scale, and we have glimpsed what the future can bring.

We can see that every dream of replicating human capabilities has followed a similar course. Starting with enthusiastic optimism, it has finished with resigned acceptance of the reality that we humans are the most sophisticated, the most complex, the most irreplicable machines of all. But that doesn't mean we should abandon our dream—if only to learn more and more about ourselves.

Speech as an effective medium of communication with computers will reach "perfection" when the technology becomes invisible to us. Your keyboard and mouse are clear examples of invisible technologies. You don't even think about them when you enter data or command your computer to do something: you rely on what they do and pay no attention to how they work, which they always do. And because they're so invisible, they've become an extension of your communication capabilities. Speech technology is not there yet, but as long as researchers and scientists continue to share that dream, it will get there. Sooner or later.

Epilogue: Siri . . . What's the Meaning of Life?

42! The meaning of life is 42, as everyone who read "The Hitchhiker's Guide to the Galaxy" knows very well. And Siri knows that too.

In 2007 a group of entrepreneurs and scientists from SRI International founded a company called Siri with the goal of creating a voice-interactive intelligent assistant—also called Siri—that would be available to everyone's smartphone. Siri was designed to respond properly to a wide variety of expressions and requests like "What movies are playing at the theaters nearby?" "Reserve a table for two at the Red Cat," or "Set up an appointment with Jonathan for this Friday at 3 p.m." Seamless integration with popular Web applications for finding movies in theaters and reserving tables at restaurants and with the contact list and calendar on your smartphone made Siri more than a cool toy, rather a useful and seemingly intelligent virtual aide. It made its first debut as a free application on the Apple App Store early in 2010, and was downloaded by a substantial number of enthusiastic smartphone owners. However, that was just the beginning.

In April 2010, Apple acquired Siri for a rumored $200 million. It was not the first time that Apple ventured into speech recognition technology. The dream of a human-like talking virtual assistant had been Apple's vision for a long time. In 1987 Apple produced a commercial clip showing a talking avatar—called Knowledge Navigator—on a then futuristic computer tablet, with the look, the attitude, and the dry sense of humor of a butler assisting its master in all sorts of tasks, from answering the phone to finding answers to scientific questions posed in the most natural conversational manner. Later Apple built a dictation machine integrated into their MacIntosh computer that could also respond to commands, such as opening or closing files, or setting appointments on the calendar. However, Apple's speech recognition software did not produce much commercial traction and the company, in spite of its team of renowned speech research luminaries, did not mass market any mainstream products in that area for years. But this time it was a different story.

On October 4, 2011, one day before the death of Steve Jobs, Apple announced that the fifth generation iPhone would have a Siri personal assistant integrated in its operating system. And a few days later, on October 14th, the new iPhone 4S hit the stores. Siri immediately became a mass phenomenon. Thousands of Facebook and Twitter posts, blogs, and newspaper articles inundated the Web with discussions about Siri, speech recognition, and artificial intelligence. Its ease of use, its catchy personality, and its sense of humor gave rise to what many believe is the most positive reaction toward computers that understand speech expressed by the broadest and more diverse population of consumers in the whole history of this technology.

In principle, Siri works like many other speech recognition applications available on smartphones, such as Google's Voice Search or Microsoft's Bing. You speak to your smartphone, which collects and digitizes your speech, and sends it, via Internet, to a remote speech recognition server. After a fraction of a second, once the result is available, the speech recognition server sends the textual transcription of what you said back to your smartphone. But Siri does not do just that, it does something more. Siri tries to understand the meaning of what you said. For instance, Siri can understand that you wanted to make an appointment with someone called Jonathan. It also understands that you want that appointment to be set for next Friday at 3 p.m. It then looks into your contacts to see if there is someone named Jonathan and, if there is more than one Jonathan, Siri will ask you to specify which one. It then looks into your calendar to check if you have a slot available for 3 p.m., and if not, it asks you whether you want to cancel the appointment or change the time. And if you ask to find a movie, or to reserve a table at a restaurant, or whether it is going to be sunny tomorrow, Siri goes to the movie, restaurant, and weather applications on the Web and gives you an appropriate response. More than that, its designers gave Siri a quirky personality with a slight attitude and a sense of humor; it is always ready to surprise you with witty answers to questions on the meaning of life or on its own whereabouts and beliefs.

In principle, there is nothing dramatically different in Siri's technology from what we have seen in the previous decades. As you may remember, during the DARPA ATIS and the Communicator projects, many labs built very sophisticated machines that could understand what you said with a high degree of confidence and act upon that. At that time MIT, and other labs, built several applications that could help you find restaurants, movies, and what the weather in any city around the world is like. Many small and large companies built commercial telephone systems that understand what callers want and provide adequate customer care, and even provide assistance with complex technical problems. Siri, which is perceived to work quite well, takes advantage of the most modern technology that evolved incrementally from all the past attempts. It uses a commercial speech recognizer—rumored to be Nuance's, even though that was never confirmed. It is extremely well integrated within the iPhone's operating system, with its applications like the calendar or the contact list, and with many external Web applications. It is an excellent work of engineering. Better, but technologically not different than the technology that was developed before; it is a beautiful product but not a technological breakthrough. So why has Siri been so successful right the minute it hit the Apple stores? One of the reasons of this success, undoubtedly, is that Siri happens to be in the right place at the right time. It is available to the largest number of consumers as an integral part of one of the most coveted devices, and rides on the waves of the persuasive and pervasive marketing of one of the most loved computer manufactures of the decade.

As this book goes to press, we are seeing more and more applications of Siri, we are feeling it is getting better and better every day, we are seeing the first Siri competitors hit the application markets for other devices than the iPhone, while it is gaining popularity even among the most technologically averse consumers.

Is Siri the gentler version of HAL we have been awaiting for more than 60 years? Is Siri what the scientists of the field hoped for to recover from all the frustration and unpopularity that speech recognition small and big failures have raised in the popular culture? Is Siri a beginning or an end? Are we going to see more and more computers that understand speech used by nearly everyone, or is Siri just a fad that will vanish and be forgotten soon? The answers to all these questions lie ahead of us, probably only just a few years ahead, but this is definitely an exciting time for all who have contributed, with their talent, their perseverance, their belief, and their vision to the science and technology of the voice in the machine.

Notes

Introduction

1. D. Bohus and E. Horvitz, "Models for Multiparty Engagement in Open-World Dialog," in *Proceedings of SIGdial'09: The Tenth Annual Meeting of the Special Interest Group on Discourse and Dialogue*, 225–234. London, September 2009.

2. The prestigious Italian telecommunication research center CSELT was located in Turin. Created in 1964 as a research laboratory of the government-controlled STET holding company, CSELT served to guarantee the reliability and quality of the telephone switch equipment during a time of maximum expansion of the Italian telephone network. After Telecom Italia reorganized in 2001, CSELT was first renamed "Telecom Italia Lab" and then completely integrated into other organizations within the company.

3. *Minicomputer* was a term used in the 1970s and early 1980s to denote any of an intermediate class of computers, such as the DEC PDP 11 series, that were considerably smaller and less expensive than mainframes. Typically, minicomputers were the size of one or two filing cabinets and were used by small groups of people.

4. A teletype (TTY) was a primitive computer terminal resembling an electric typewriter. It had no display, but both the operator input and the computer output were typed out, line by line, on a roll of paper.

5. That the acronym HAL can be formed by replacing each letter of IBM with the one immediately before it in the alphabet gave rise to the belief that this wasn't by chance. From the movie *2010: Odyssey Two:* "Is it true, Dr. Chandra, that you chose the name HAL to be one step ahead of IBM?" "Utter nonsense! Half of us come from IBM and we've been trying to stamp out that story for years. I thought that by now every intelligent person knew that H-A-L is derived from *Heuristic ALgorithmic*."

6. See D. G. Stork, ed., *HAL's Legacy: 2001 Computer as Dream and Reality* (Cambridge, Mass.: MIT Press, 1996).

7. The popular song "Daisy Bell" was composed in 1892 by Harry Dacre (source: *Wikipedia*, "Daisy Bell"). The lyrics are better known than the song's title: "Daisy, Daisy, give me your answer do. / I'm half crazy, all for the love of you. / It won't be a stylish marriage, / I can't afford a carriage. / But you'll look sweet upon the seat / Of a bicycle built for two."

8. Created by the inventor Rotwang in the image of his dead lover, Futura is called a "Maschinenmensch" (machine-human) in the original German.

9. This quote, as reported by Larry Rabiner, comes from a luncheon meeting in 1967 when W. O. Baker (then vice president of research and later president of Bell Labs) spoke to new employees about the needs of the Bell System.

Chapter 1

1. Although, by "speaking" here, I refer mainly to the acts of producing and understanding speech, *speaking* in the larger sense involves a rich repertoire of nonverbal communicative acts, including gestures, facial expressions, postures, and nonverbal sounds.

2. S. Pinker, "Language Acquisition," in *An Invitation to Cognitive Science*, ed. L. R. Gleitman, M. Liberman, and D. N. Osherson (Cambridge, Mass.: MIT Press, 1996): 135–182.

3. R. Goulden, P. Nation, and J. Read, "How Large Can a Receptive Vocabulary Be?" *Applied Linguistics* 11 (November 1990): 341–363.

4. Pinker, "Language Acquisition," 139–145.

5. One famous example of a feral child is Genie, the thirteen-year-old girl who was found by the police in 1970 in the suburbs of Los Angeles after having been kept in isolation by her parents since birth. Despite her substantial vocabulary, Genie had very limited language skills and was never able to form grammatically correct sentences, even though she was judged to have no serious intellectual or motor impairment. See, for instance, M. Pines, "The Civilizing of Genie," *Psychology Today*, September 1981, 28–34.

6. The thesis that a child cannot learn language given only the limited amount of linguistic data to which it's exposed during the first years of life is known as the "poverty of the stimulus" argument; it directly supports Chomsky's hypothesis that language learning is an innate, albeit short-lived capability of the human being. The term *poverty of the stimulus* was introduced by Chomsky in his book *Rules and Representations*. (Oxford: Blackwell, 1980).

7. Indeed, there are species of chimpanzees that use sounds and gestures to communicate. But despite several attempts to teach chimps a more sophisticated language, and even after intense periods of teaching by human instructors, their ability to communicate didn't evolve beyond the repetition of a few signs for requesting food or play. Whether some animals may be able to acquire a language as sophisticated as the human language is still somewhat controversial; many believe that any observed animal language capability is a sort of instinctive reaction, far below the cognitive level of humans. For an interesting discussion on the superiority of human linguistic capabilities, see T. W. Deacon, *The Symbolic Species: The Co-Evolution of Language and the Brain* (New York: Norton, 1997).

8. For an accessible discussion about Chomsky's language organ hypothesis, see S. Pinker, *The Language Instinct: How the Mind Creates Language* (New York: Morrow, 1994), 297–331.

9. Creole languages originated during the sixteenth and seventeenth centuries in the American, African, and Pacific colonies among the descendants of mostly uneducated immigrants from around the world. First-generation immigrants communicated with an ungrammatical mix of words from their different languages called "pidgin." Their children, however, spoke creole languages, comparable in grammars and sophistication to those of their parents' original languages. Scholars of creole languages, like Derek Bickerton, found evidence of common

grammatical features among the creole languages themselves and the established older languages from which they evolved, evidence that supports Chomsky's language organ hypothesis. D. Bickerton, "Creole Languages," *Scientific American*, December 1983, 116–122.

10. Pinker, "Language Acquisition," 135–182

11. Linguists distinguish between *phonemes*, the idealized basic sounds that compose words, and *phones*, their acoustic realization. So, for instance, the first and only vowel sound of the word "caught" can be represented as the idealized sound or phoneme /oh/ but is realized as different phones by speakers in New York and Boston. Here, for the sake of simplicity, I use the term *phoneme* to refer to both idealized and realized speech sounds. See P. Ladefoged, *A Course in Phonetics* (Orlando, Fla.: Harcourt Brace, 1993), for a general introduction to phonetics.

12. L. J. Whaley, *Introduction to Typology: The Unity and Diversity of Language* (Thousand Oaks: Sage, 1997), 32.

13. U. Eco, *Semiotics and the Philosophy of Language* (Bloomington: Indiana University Press, 1986), 136.

14. By "knowledge" here, I mean a representation that's available to our brains but that we may not be consciously aware of. For instance, the acoustic knowledge about how to articulate each sound of the language we speak is somehow coded in our brains, but we may not be consciously aware of that. We can't even explain or describe how we humans articulate, but our brains definitely know how. This is different from our conscious knowledge of facts, like, for instance, our own names and our dates of birth or that Rome is the capital of Italy.

15. See T. Norretranders, *The User Illusion: Cutting Consciousness Down to Size*, trans. J. Sydenham (New York: Penguin, 1998), 23–44 and 83–87, for an interesting discussion about the power of information reduction by selection and its relationship to the concept of thermodynamic depth information measure. According to this concept, the informative content of a message is related to the amount of information discarded in the creation of a message itself. The more information is discarded, the higher the value of the message is. S. Lloyd and H. Pagels, "Complexity as Thermodynamic Depth," *Annals of Physics* 188, no. 1 (November 1988): 186–213.

16. This and other semantic formulas in the main text are simplified forms of what is known as a "semantic network," a graph that represents the semantic relationship among conceptual entities. For an introduction on semantic networks see J. Sowa, ed., *Principles of Semantic Networks: Explorations in the Representation of Knowledge* (San Francisco: Morgan Kauffman, 1991).

17. See D. B. Lenat and R. V. Guha, *Building Large Knowledge-Based Systems: Representation and Inference in the Cyc Project* (Reading, Mass.: Addison-Wesley, 1990).

18. N. Siegel, K. Goolsbey, R. Kahlert, and G. Matthews, "The Cyc® System: Notes on Architecture," Cycorp, Inc., November 2004, http://www.cyc.com/copy_of_technology/whitepapers_dir/Cyc_Architecture_and_API.pdf.

19. J. Friedman, "The Sole Contender for AI," *Harvard Science Review*, October 22, 2003, http://www.scribd.com/doc/1814/An-Article-about-the Cyc-Project.

20. For an introduction to semantic Web see J. Davies, *Semantic Web Technologies: Trends and Research in Ontology-based Systems* (Chichester, UK: Wiley: July 11, 2006).

21. *Pidgin* is a simplified language typically used by groups of people who don't have a language in common and is usually characterized by sequences of words, often in different languages, put together without and proper syntactic construct. See note 9 on Creole languages.

22. The observation that nearly all English speakers can understand Yoda English is thanks to an anonymous reviewer of this book.

23. There's plenty of evidence that languages tend to become more and more regular with the passage of time. For instance, in E. Lieberman et al., "Quantifying the Evolutionary Dynamics of Language," *Nature* 449 (October 2007): 665–667, the authors report that, during the past 1,200 years, irregular verbs in English became regular at a speed proportional to the square of their frequency in the language: "A verb that is 100 times less frequent regularizes 10 times as fast."

24. For my nonspecialist readers, I use here a simplified set of parts-of-speech elements, disregarding number (singular vs. plural) and verb tenses, and a simplified, single equivalent form of the three grammar rules traditionally used by linguists to describe plain sentences: *Sentence → Noun_Phrase Verb_Phrase; Verb_Phrase → Verb Noun_Phrase;* and *Noun_Phrase → Determiner Noun.*

25. "Colorless green ideas sleep furiously" is a famous example presented by Noam Chomsky in 1957 to show that a meaningless sentence can be readily recognized as grammatical by a native speaker. In *Syntactic Structures,* 2nd ed. (Berlin: Walter de Gruyter, 2002), 15, Chomsky contrasts it with "Furiously sleep ideas green colorless," which, though containing the same words as the original sentence, is both ungrammatical and nonsensical, and he observes that "any search for a semantically based definition of 'grammaticalness' will be futile."

26. As we saw earlier for the vocabulary rules, by using disjunctions, you can add any number of rules to the right-hand side of the grammar formalism, each using the same symbol that appears on the left-hand side and each representing one of its alternative expansions. For instance, you could write the three rules *NP → N; NP → ADJ N;* and *NP → ADJ NP* in a single, more compact form, as *NP→N, ADJ N, ADJ NP.*

27. This powerful formalism, which allows us to represent an infinite number of expressions by using recursion, is called a "context-free grammar." Context-free grammars are just one of the four types of grammars of the hierarchical categorization introduced by Chomsky in his "Three Models for the Description of Language," *IRE Transactions on Information Theory* 2 (1956): 113–124. The first type, *regular grammars,* on the lowest level of the hierarchy, allows recursion only at the beginning or end of the right-hand side of a rule. The second type, *context-free grammars,* allows recursion in any position within the right-hand side of the rule (also called "embedded recursion"). The third type, *context-sensitive grammars,* allows any number of symbols on the *left*-hand side of the rule. And, finally, the fourth type, *unrestricted grammars,* allows the rule to assume any form at all. There is also a relationship between the type of grammar and the type of memory structure required to implement a parsing algorithm with the corresponding grammar. Thus a regular grammar requires only a finite state machine, whereas a context-free grammar requires a memory stack.

28. This sample, as originally transcribed with no punctuation other than a final question mark, was judged to be the most ungrammatical spontaneous sentence among those recorded by the MADCOW committee in the early 1990s, during the DARPA ATIS project, which will

be discussed in chapter 5. Typically, transcribers of recorded spontaneous speech in the United States provide other punctuation marks besides question marks—commas, hyphens, dashes, ellipsis points, or periods—to reflect their (and ordinary listeners') sense of when a speaker pauses or hesitates, prolongs a sound, breaks or trails off, or seems to halt. Without these punctuation marks, transcribed spontaneous speech looks more incoherent than it would have sounded to someone listening in.

29. P. A. Barbosa, "On the Defense of Von Kempelen as the Predecessor of Experimental Phonetics and Speech Synthesis Research," in *History of Linguistics 2002: Selected Papers from the Ninth International Conference on the History of the Language Sciences*, 101. São Paulo-Campinas, August 27–30, 2002.

30. X-rays were first used in speech research in 1904 by J. F. Fischer and J. Moeller, who studied the shape of the larynx (upper trachea or windpipe) for obtaining different pitch levels. See J. Moeller and J. F. Fischer, "Observation on the Action of the *Cricothyroideus* and *Thyroarytenoideus internus*," *Annals of Otiology, Rhinology, and Laryngology* 13 (1904): 42–46. E. A. Meyer applied X-ray analysis to the study of vowels in 1910. See E. A. Meyer, "Untersuchungen über Lautbildung," in *Festshrift Wilhelm Viëtor* (Marburg: Elwert, 1910).

31. http://www.langsci.ucl.ac.uk/ipa/.

32. Zulu and a few other Southern African languages have peculiar sounds called "clicks," such as the interjections to express disapproval or to signal horses. Ladefoged, *A Course in Phonetics* (Harcourt and Brace: 1975), 135–137.

33. You can experience the continuous transition from one phoneme to the next with the help of a sound-editing program available on any home computer. Record an utterance, for instance, the word "away," as in our example. Then look at the waveform of your recording. Use the edit tool to select out the initial part, the one corresponding to /əw/. Listen to it. Now try to separate the /ə/ and the /w/. You'll find that, no matter where you put the separation boundary, you'll still hear a little bit of /w/ in the /ə/ and a little bit of /ə/ in the /w/. And, as a matter of fact, you'll hear a little bit of the third sound, /a/, in the /w/, too.

34. In speech science, *fundamental frequency* is the actual frequency of vibration of the vocal cords, whereas *pitch* is the subjective perception connected to the *change* in fundamental frequency. Fundamental frequency and pitch are formally distinct because the relationship between the two is a nonlinear one. Nevertheless, for the sake of simplicity in the course of this chapter, I use *pitch* as a synonym for *fundamental frequency*.

35. To be precise, "to determine lexical stress *variations* in a particular word." As in the word "present," stressing one syllable in a word induces vowel reduction in its unstressed syllables. So as soon as you stress one vowel sound in a word versus another, all the vowel sounds change. Unstressed English vowel sounds often reduce to /ə/, the "schwa" or "neutral vowel" sound. For instance, the nouns "present" and "sofa" are phonetically rendered /'pre-zᵊnt/ and /'sō-fə/, respectively. The same is true for the verb forms of other English words such as "addict," "address," "combat," and "conflict." This explanation was kindly provided by James Mesbur at SpeechCycle, Inc.

36. Pinker, *The Language Instinct*, 209.

37. This approach to the generation of synthetic speech is known as "articulatory synthesis," and will be described in chapter 7.

38. H. Moravec, *Robot: Mere Machine to Transcendent Mind* (New York: Oxford University Press, 1999), 56–57.

Chapter 2

1. T. Sandage, *The Turk: The Life and Times of the Famous Eighteenth-Century Chess-Playing Machine* (New York: Walker, 2002).

2. A. Doyon, L. Liaigre, and B. Gille, *Jacques Vaucanson: Mécanicien de génie* (Paris: Presses universitaires de France, 1966).

3. Bell Telephone Laboratories was created in 1925 with the consolidation of Western Electric Research Laboratories and some of the engineering departments of AT&T. Its headquarters were in Manhattan until the 1940s, later moving to a number of other locations in suburban New Jersey before settling in Murray Hill.

4. Recordings of the original Voder can be found at http://www.youtube.com/watch?v=mSdFu1xdoZk and http://www.cs.indiana.edu/rhythmsp/ASA/highlights.html.

5. L. J. Raphael, G. J. Borden, and K. S. Harris, *Speech Science Primer: Physiology, Acoustics, and Perception of Speech* (Philadelphia: Lippincott Williams & Wilkins, 2007), 24.

6. V. Bush, "As We May Think," *Atlantic Monthly*, July 1945, http://www.theatlantic.com/magazine/archive/1945/07/as-we-may-think/3881/.

7. On the controversial connection between the invention of the carrier multiplexing technique by Major Squier of the U.S. Signal Corps and its initial deployment by AT&T during World War I, as well as its subsequent commercial exploitation, see M. Schwartz, "Origins of Carrier Multiplexing: Major George Squier and AT&T," in *Proceedings of the 2004 IEEE Conference on the History of Electronics*, Bletchley Park, UK, June 2004, http://www.ieeeghn.org/wiki/images/7/77/Schwartz.pdf.

8. To limit the frequencies of a signal, electrical engineers use electronic devices called "filters." Low-pass filters limit the highest frequencies of a signal, high-pass filters limit its lowest frequencies, and band-pass filters limit both its highest and its lowest frequencies. The proper design of filters is an electrical engineering discipline.

9. I. B. Crandall, "The Composition of Speech," *Physical Review,* 2nd ser., 10 (1917): 75.

10. Ibid. More often spelled "soffit," a *soffet* is the underside of a building member, typically an eave or staircase support.

11. Although the bandwidth of the standard telephone signal is assumed to be roughly 4 kHz, in fact, the higher frequencies of telephone signals attenuate above 3.4 kHz and are completely filtered out above 4 kHz. Similarly, the lower frequencies attenuate below 400 Hz and are completely filtered out by 0 Hz. So the net bandwidth of the standard telephone signal is effectively 3 kHz, from 400 to 3,400 Hz.

12. H. W. Dudley, "System for the Artificial Production of Vocal or Other Sounds," U.S Patent 2,121,142, filed April 7, 1937, and issued June 21, 1938, p. 2.

13. James L. Flanagan, Electrical Engineer, an oral history conducted in 1997 by Frederik L. Nebeker, IEEE History Center, New Brunswick, New Jersey.

14. K. H. Davis, R. Biddulph, and S. Balashek, "Automatic Recognition of Spoken Digits," *Journal of the Acoustical Society of America* 24, no. 6 (November 1952): 637–642.

15. Quote, which appears on source pp. 637–638, reprinted with permission from Davis, Biddulph, and Balashek, "Automatic Recognition of Spoken Digits." © 1952, Acoustic Society of America.

16. J. L. Flanagan, S. E. Levinson, L. R. Rabiner, and A. E. Rosenberg, "Techniques for Expanding the Capabilities of Practical Speech Recognizers," in *Trends in Speech Recognition*, ed. W. E. Lea (Englewood Cliffs, N.J.: Prentice Hall, 1980), 426.

17. Quote, which appears on source p. 639, reprinted with permission from Davis, Biddulph, and Balashek, "Automatic Recognition of Spoken Digits," © 1952, Acoustic Society of America.

18. Many of today's speech recognition systems greatly improve their performance through *speaker adaptation*—by adapting themselves to a small sample of their users' speech; for instance, certain dictation systems require users to speak a number of "training" sentences provided by the system. In modern voice Web search, as in Google mobile search on smartphones, such as the iPhone, Blackberry, or Android, adaptation is performed automatically when the remote server receives new voice sounds from the same device, assuming that the same user is using an identified phone. Adaptation procedures adapt the system to the acoustic parameters of users, their speaking style, such as the frequency of words used and their specific pronunciation of words.

19. Twice the highest frequency of a signal is thus called the "Nyquist frequency."

20. C. E. Shannon, "A Mathematical Theory of Communication," *Bell System Technical Journal* 27 (July 1948): 379–423, and (October 1948): 623–656.

21. Unfortunately, because we can't measure signals or anything else with infinite precision, the numbers of our measurements and thus the digital representation of a signal aren't as exact as we would like them to be. The imprecision of sample values gives rise to a distortion of the original signal known as "quantization noise." Fortunately, with careful management of numeric approximation for each sample, quantization noise can be made insignificant for all practical purposes.

22. Jim Flanagan, personal communication, February 2005.

23. In practice, the most successful features extracted from the speech signal, which result in speech recognition of the greatest accuracy, are based on a nonlinear scale of frequency known as the "mel scale" (derived from "melody") and proposed first in S. S. Stevens, J. Volkman, and E. Newman, "A Scale for the Measurement of the Psychological Magnitude of Pitch," *Journal of the Acoustical Society of America* 8, no. 3 (1937):185–190. This scale characterizes the approximately logarithmic perception of pitch by the human ear, which perceives only a linear increment in pitch when the actual frequency of a sound doubles.

24. A feature vector can be considered as a point in a multidimensional space, where each element of the vector is a dimension, and thus the geometrical distance among them, for instance, can be used as a measure of how different the corresponding speech frames are. The geometrical distance between points in a multidimensional space corresponding to feature vectors is a reasonable and intuitive choice to compute a *dissimilarity* score between frames of different utterances. On the other hand, that's not always the best choice as far as accuracy in speech recognition is concerned. Several researchers have explored different types of distance measure in conjunction with different types of features, including weighted distances—where each feature is weighted in a different way according to its importance in the

discrimination of sounds—and more complex distance measures motivated by perceptual studies of human hearing.

25. RAND Corporation, located in Santa Monica, California, is a nonprofit organization established by the Douglas Aircraft Company in 1948 for fostering research focused on the welfare and security of the United States.

26. Bellman tells how he came to choose the term *dynamic programming* in his *Eye of the Hurricane: An Autobiography* (Singapore: World Scientific, 1984), 159:

The 1950s were not good years for mathematical research. We had a very interesting gentleman in Washington named Wilson. He was Secretary of Defense, and he actually had a pathological fear and hatred of the word "research." . . . His face would suffuse, he would turn red, and he would get violent if people used the term "research" in his presence. You can imagine how he felt, then, about the term "mathematical." The RAND Corporation was employed by the Air Force, and the Air Force had Wilson as its boss, essentially. Hence, I felt I had to do something to shield Wilson and the Air Force from the fact that I was really doing mathematics inside the RAND Corporation. What title, what name, could I choose? In the first place I was interested in planning, in decision making, in thinking. But "planning" is not a good word for various reasons. I decided therefore to use the word "programming." I wanted to get across the idea that this was dynamic, this was multistage, this was time-varying—I thought, let's kill two birds with one stone. Let's take a word that has an absolutely precise meaning, namely "dynamic," in the classical physical sense. It also has a very interesting property as an adjective, and that is it's impossible to use the word "dynamic" in a pejorative sense. . . . Thus, I thought "dynamic programming" was a good name. It was something not even a Congressman could object to. So I used it as an umbrella for my activities.

27. T. K. Vintsyuk, "Speech Discrimination by Dynamic Programming" (in Russian), *Kibernetika* 4, no. 1 (1968): 81–88; English translation in *Cybernetics* 4, no. 1 (1968): 52–57.

28. H. Sakoe and S. Chiba, "A Similarity Evaluation of Speech Patterns by Dynamic Programming" (in Japanese), presented at the 1970 National Meeting of the Institute of Electronic Communication Engineers of Japan, 136. July 1970.

29. See F. Itakura, "Minimum Prediction Residual Applied to Speech Recognition," *IEEE Transactions on. Acoustics, Speech, Signal Processing* 23, no. 1 (February 1975): 67–72.

30. H. Sakoe and S. Chiba, "Dynamic Programming Algorithm Optimization for Spoken Word Recognition," *IEEE Transactions on. Acoustics, Speech, Signal Processing* 26, no. 1 (February 1978): 43–49.

31. As this book goes to press, some speech recognizers embedded in small devices, like low-end mobile phones, still use dynamic time warping with whole-word template matching for simple command and control of the device functions or limited name dialing. These simple applications require the user to speak an example of each word into the speech recognizer before using them.

32. One of the popular approaches for building speaker-independent template-matching speech recognizers was to collect multiple templates for a large number of speakers, representative of the whole population of possible users of the system, and to perform matching with all of them. The DTW algorithm would find one among all templates from the entire collection that would best match the voice of the current user. Because increasing the number of templates increased the computational requirement, and thus slowed down the process of

speech recognition considerably, researchers investigated a technique called "template cluster-ing," whereby the whole multispeaker collection of templates for each word in the vocabulary would be merged into a single representative archetype, or a limited number of them. See, for instance, L. R. Rabiner, S. E. Levinson, A. E. Rosenberg, and J. G. Wilpon, "Speaker-Independent Recognition of Isolated Words Using Clustering Techniques," *IEEE Transactions on. Acoustics, Speech, and Signal Processing* 27, no. 4 (August 1979): 336–349.

33. According to *Wikipedia,* "Kludge": "A *kludge* (or *kluge*) is a workaround, a quick-and-dirty solution, a clumsy or inelegant, yet effective, solution to a problem, typically using parts that are cobbled together. This term is diversely used in fields such as computer science, aerospace engineering, Internet slang, and evolutionary neuroscience." See http://en.wikipedia.org/wiki/Kludge.

Chapter 3

1. C. Shannon, "A Chess-Playing Machine," *Scientific American,* February 1950, 48–51. *Symbols* are objects, names, or images that represent, by association, something else. *Symbolic*—as opposed to *numeric*—*processing* in computer science refers to the ability to process knowledge and draw conclusions from it.

2. "SHRDLU" is derived from the nonsensical phrase "ETAOIN SHRDLU," made up of the twelve most commonly used letters in English in descending frequency.

3. T. Winograd, "Procedures as a Representation for Data in a Computer Program for Under-standing Natural Language," *MIT AI Technical Report* 235 (February 1971).

4. For a more complete conversation with SHRDLU and for other information, including the program's source code, see Terry Winograd's Web page: http://hci.stanford.edu/~winograd/shrdlu/.

5. B. G. Buchanan and E. H. Shortliffe, eds., *Rule-Based Expert Systems: The MYCIN Experiments of the Stanford Heuristic Programming Project* (Reading, Mass.: Addison-Wesley, 1984).

6. MYCIN was never put into practice. The problem wasn't its performance: it actually outperformed members of the Stanford Medical School in tests. And though ethical questions were raised about using MYCIN on real patients, that wasn't the problem either. Apparently, the problem with MYCIN was that it required users to enter all the necessary information by hand and that, even when they had, there was no network infrastructure to connect users to mainframes—PCs and the Internet hadn't been invented yet. An interaction with MYCIN took more than 30 minutes, an unacceptably long time for a clinician. *Wikipedia,* "Mycin," http://en.wikipedia.org/wiki/Mycin.

7. According to Malcolm Gladwell, writing in his bestseller *Blink,* experts can draw extremely accurate conclusions in a very short time—using what Gladwell refers to as "rapid cognition." For instance, art experts can "intuit" that a piece of art is a forgery, or police officers, that a person in the street is a criminal, "in the blink of an eye," and their intuitions are often more accurate than decisions arrived at rationally after pondering the facts and evidence for a long time. If this is true, it would raise interesting questions about experts' conscious explanation of rules in a field. M. Gladwell, *Blink: The Power of Thinking without Thinking* (Little, Brown, 2005).

8. There's evidence that the perceptual difference between an unvoiced (voiceless) plosive, such as /p/, and a voiced one, such as /b/, is determined by the duration of the pause (closure). L. Lisker, "Closure Duration and the Intervocalic Voice-Voiceless Distinction in English," *Language* 33, no. 1 (January–March 1957): 42–49.

9. The theory of *fuzzy sets*, developed in 1965 by the mathematician Lofti A. Zadeh, permits a nonbinary assignment of truths to membership functions. Thus, according to Zadeh, you could assign a person measuring 5'7" a fuzzy membership of 0.6 in the set of tall people and a person measuring 6'2" a fuzzy membership of 0.9 in the same set. This would allow you not to reject any hypothesis on the basis of a true-false decision, but to maintain it using different values of fuzziness. Zadeh developed also a theory of fuzzy *logic,* popularly used in the field of automated controls, around the concept of membership function. See L. A. Zadeh, "Fuzzy Sets," *Information and Control* 8, no. 3 (1965): 338–353.

10. J. R. Pierce, "Whither Speech Recognition?," *Journal of the Acoustical Society of America* 46, no. 4B (October 1969): 1049–1051. Quote, which appears on source p. 1049, reprinted with permission from J. R. Pierce, "Whither Speech Recognition?," © 1969, Acoustic Society of America.

11. Jim Flanagan, personal communication, February 2005. The discipline of talker or speaker identification attempts to build speech recognition machines that can identify a speaker among a limited set of potential speakers based on one or more utterances.

12. U.S. Department of Defense Directive Number 5105.15, February 7, 1958.

13. The agency's name has changed three times since its inception in 1958. President Richard Nixon first changed it to DARPA in 1972; President Bill Clinton then changed it back to ARPA in 1993; and President George W. Bush changed it a third time, again to DARPA, in 1996. It's still called "DARPA," as of this writing. See http://inventors.about.com/library/inventors/blARPA-DARPA.htm. ARPA (or DARPA) has been one of the main funding resources for the development of many technologies that changed U.S. history, such as the Internet, for instance, which evolved from the ARPANET, the first large- scale computer network installed in 1969 at University of California, Los Angeles (UCLA), with the goal of sharing expensive computing resources among ARPA's own research contractors. Today DARPA is still one of the main sources of government funding for advanced industrial and academic research in the United States, strategically targeted toward achieving defense and homeland security objectives.

14. Allen Newell, as quoted in Committee on Innovations in Computing and Communications: Lessons from History and the National Research Council, *Funding a Revolution: Government Support for Computing Research* (Washington, D.C.: National Academy Press, 1999), 204. This and other information on the ARPA SUR project, unless otherwise noted, is from *Funding a Revolution.*

15. D. H. Klatt, "Review of the ARPA Speech Understanding Project, " in the *Journal of the Acoustical Society of America* 62, no. 6 (December 1977): 1345–1366.

16. Computers were so expensive in the 1970s that the cost of understanding one utterance was estimated to be about $5.00. Lowerre, B. and Reddy, R., "The Harpy Speech Understanding System, in Trends in Speech Recognition," edited by Wayne Lea, Speech Science Publications, 1986, 341. As for their speed, by way of comparison, a top-of-the-line computer of the 1970s like the PDP-KA 10 used by Carnegie Mellon in the SUR project ran at 0.4 MIPS, whereas a top-of-the-line microprocessor of 2010 like the Intel Core i7 Extreme Edition

i980EE used in home computers runs at 147,600 MIPS—almost 60,000 times as fast. And the world's most powerful computer processor of 2010 is almost four times as fast as that. *Wikipedia*, "Instructions per second," http://en.wikipedia.org /wiki/Instructions_per_second.

17. According to SUR reports, the SDC system showed inferior performance due to the loss of one computer. Computers being as expensive as they were, a project could often not afford to replace them.

18. In a two-year project funded by IPTO, researchers visited the SUR sites to learn what "had been accomplished and what the issues were, what the failures were, and what the positives were." They produced an extensive 1979 report and a 1980 book edited by W. A. Lea entitled *Trends in Speech Recognition*.

19. In reality, most advanced isolated-word DTW alignment techniques allowed for some flexibility in matching the end points of the templates and the unknown utterance in order to compensate for possible errors of the end-point detector.

20. Even with a digit vocabulary, you can exclude some of the sequences. For instance, if the sequences of digits to be searched are telephone numbers, only sequences of seven and ten digits are permissible. So you can exclude sequences of two to six digits, eight or nine digits, and more than ten digits. And because, at least in the United States, neither the area codes nor the seven-digit telephone numbers can start with zero, you can also exclude all sequences like 056 987 3456 or 234 076 3456 from the best-path search. That said, excluding all these sequences from the whole set of potential digit sequences saves very little computation.

21. Only grammars without *embedded recursion*—where an infinite number of phrases are embedded within, rather than at the beginning or end of, a sentence—can be represented as finite state machines. Constructions like "The cat (which ate the mouse (which broke the vase (which . . . (which . . . (which . . .))))) sat on my sofa," are examples of embedded recursion. Grammars without embedded recursion are a subset of *context-free* grammars in Chomsky's hierarchical classification of grammars.

22. The same set of sentences represented by the finite state machine in figure 3.5 can also be represented by the rules of the following context-free grammar:

S → VP1|VP2

VP1 → ("PUT"|"MOVE") NP1

VP2 → "REMOVE" | ("TAKE" "AWAY") NP2

NP1 → OBJ PSTN

NP2 → OBJ

OBJ → "THE" CLR SHP

CLR → "RED"|"GREEN"|"YELLOW"

SHP → "CUBE"|"SPHERE"|"PYRAMID"

PSTN → ("ON" "TOP")|("TO" "THE" RL) "OF" OBJ

RL → "RIGHT"|"LEFT"

There is a one-to-one correspondence between a finite state machine representation of a grammar and its representation using context-free rules.

23. Transitions with no symbols, commonly represented as unlabeled arrows, are called "null transitions" and involve a change of state without taking any action.

24. A *finite state transducer* (FST) is an extension of a finite state machine where every state transition has an output symbol in addition to the input symbol. The integration of phonetic, lexical, and syntactic knowledge, as described here for the Harpy system, can be algebraically expressed as a *composition* of finite state transducers, each representing a specific level of knowledge. See M. Mohri, F. C. N. Pereira, and M. Riley, "The design principles of a weighted finite-state transducer library," *Theoretical Computer Science*, 231, 17–32. Most modern commercial speech recognizers are based on finite state transducer theory.

25. Harpy didn't use templates of phonemes, which would be of the order of 40 for English, but 98 smaller constituent elements of portions of phonemes. For instance, a plosive phoneme like /t/ was broken down into constituent elements like "pause" and "burst." That gave Harpy's designers more flexibility to represent transitions between consecutive words and to cope with the problem of coarticulation.

26. Collecting and preparing templates by hand is a laborious job. You have to record utterances from each participant speaker, then analyze them and cut them into the individual phoneme-like templates using a sound editor program. Any way to speed up the process would have the advantage of allowing more speakers to use the system at a reduced cost.

27. One of the most popular inventions to come out of Reddy and Lowerre's work with Harpy is known as "beam search algorithm," and it's still used today in modern speech recognizers. Rather than searching through all the points of the alignment grid, the dynamic programming algorithm considers only decision points for which the cumulated score is within a predefined delta (deviation) from the best score for that input frame. The search thus proceeds on a "beam" that follows the locally best path. Of course, if the locally best path deviates from the global best path by an amount larger than the beam size, the best path disappears from the search and is never recovered. This event can be made quite unlikely, however, by choosing a conservative beam size. And, most often, a large number of suboptimal paths still go through the correct words, thus producing correct recognition results despite the suboptimality of the search.

Chapter 4

1. Fred Jelinek confirmed he did indeed make this remark, famous among speech technology scientists, during his talk "Applying Information Theoretic Methods: Evaluation of Grammar Quality" at the Workshop on Evaluation of NLP Systems, Wayne, Pennsylvania, December 1988.

2. Jelinek, who sadly passed away in September 2010, was the first recipient of the Antonio Zampolli Prize, awarded by European Language Resource Association (ELRA) to speech and language scientists for "Outstanding Contributions to the Advancement of Language Resources and Language Technology Evaluation within Human Language Technologies." Professor Antonio Zampolli, from the University of Pisa, was ELRA's first president. Jelinek told his story in the course of his acceptance speech, which he entitled "Some of My Best Friends Are Linguists."

3. This is expressed by the fundamental equation of statistical speech recognition:

$$\hat{W} = \arg\max_{W} P(A \mid W) P(W)$$

which states that the most probable sequence of words,

$\hat{W}$

is the one that maximizes the product of two factors. The first factor,

$P(A \mid W)$

is the probability of the acoustic observation conditional on a sequence of words,

W.

The second factor,

$P(W)$,

is the probability of that sequence of words.

4. This is a restatement of the so-called Anna Karenina principle, derived from the opening sentence of Leo Tolstoy's *Anna Karenina*: "Happy families are all alike; every unhappy family is unhappy in its own way." Jared Diamond associates the principle with an endeavor where the failure of any one factor leads inevitably to the failure of the whole endeavor—where there's only one way to succeed, but many possible ways to fail. J. Diamond, *Guns, Germs, and Steel: The Fates of Human Societies* (New York: Norton, 1997), 139.

5. C. Shannon, "A Mathematical Theory of Communication," (July 1948): 379–423, (October 1948): 623–656.

6. With the greater computational memory and power provided by today's computers, modern speech recognizers today often use sets of four and even five consecutive words (quadrigrams and pentagrams), which can significantly improve on the recognition accuracy provided by classic trigrams.

7. The *chain rule* in probability theory allows you to compute the probability of joint events, like that of a sequence of words, as the product of their conditional probabilities. For instance, you can exactly compute the probability of a sequence of words

$w_1, w_2, ..., w_T$,

expressed as

$P(w_1, w_2, ..., w_T)$,

as the product of the conditional probabilities of each word, given the preceding ones, that is,

$P(w_1, w_2, ..., w_3) = P(w_T \mid w_{T-1}, w_{T-2}, ..., w_1) \cdot P(w_{T-1} \mid w_{T-2}, w_{T-3}, ...w_1) \cdot ... \cdot P(w_1)$.

Because, in *n*-gram theory, you disregard the effect of the preceding words except the most adjacent $(n - 1)$ words, you can approximate this product by taking the product of *n*-gram probabilities, that is, for $n = 3$:

$P(w_1, w_2, ..., w_T) \cong P(w_T \mid w_{T-1}, w_{T-2}) \cdot P(w_{T-1} \mid w_{T-2}, w_{T-3}) \cdot ... \cdot P(w_1)$.

8. In a "dictation" machine, the word "period" is actually pronounced at the end of a sentence, thus its trigram probabilities have to be computed as those of a regular word.

9. The estimation of unseen events is based on the probability of other facts that may be related to the event itself. For instance, the probability of an unseen trigram can be estimated from the corresponding bigram and unigram of the current word.

10. The algorithm to find the most likely sequence of hidden states of the hidden Markov model that generated a given observation is called a "Viterbi algorithm," after its inventor,

Andrew Viterbi, an Italian American electrical engineer, businessman, and university professor. See A. J. Viterbi, "Error Bounds for Convolutional Codes and an Asymptotically Optimum Decoding Algorithm," *IEEE Transactions on Information Theory* 13, no. 2 (April 1967): 260–269.

11. See L. E. Baum, T. Petrie, G. Soules, and N. Weiss, "A Maximization Technique Occurring in the Statistical Analysis of Probabilistic Functions of Markov Chains," *Annals of Mathematical Statistics* 41, no. 1 (February 1970): 164–171.

12. See L. R. Welch, "Hidden Markov Models and the Baum-Welch Algorithm," *IEEE Information Theory Society Newsletter* 53, no. 4 (December 2003): 1, 10–13.

13. When you estimate the probability of an event, you need to base your estimate on a statistically significant number of observations of that event. For instance, you can't accurately claim that the probability of rain in New York is 50 percent if you just look at two randomly chosen days and one of them happens to be rainy. Statistical significance of data is measured by different formulas (called "tests") that are able to quantify the amount of error involved in the estimation of probabilities, averages, and the like, most often expressed as "with an error of plus or minus [such and such] percent."

14. Speech recognition researchers use the forward-backward and closely related iterative algorithms to automatically segment any large *corpus*—test or training set—of utterances into phonemes, as you'll see in the discussion of corpus-based text-to-speech systems in chapter 7.

15. Even if you know the words that were spoken in each one of the recorded utterances, you can't assume that you know exactly the sequence of phonemes. Some words may be subject to phonetic variations because of the speaker's pronunciation habits, like /tomahto/ and /tomeito/, the coarticulation between consecutive phonemes, or other effects. In any case, modeling the string of words of each training utterance as a finite state machine with all the possible variations will still allow you to train hidden Markov models without the need for an exact phonetic transcription and segmentation.

16. Statistically modeling the relationships between two or more different languages is at the basis of what's called "statistical machine translation" or "statistical MT." Statistical MT systems, which require extensive parallel sets of documents in the target languages, far outperform traditional rule-based MT systems. Indeed, most automatic translation systems today are based on statistical principles.

17. See T. K. Moon, "The Expectation-Maximization Algorithm," *IEEE Signal Processing Magazine*. 13, no. 6 (November 1996): 47–60.

18. Iterative maximization doesn't guarantee that you'll find the absolute maximum—or absolute best—value you're seeking but only a relative maximum that depends on your specific initial choice of parameters. Think of it as trying to find the absolute top of a mountain, its highest peak, by starting from an arbitrary point on the mountain's slope and proceeding upward step by step until any little move you can make won't take you any higher. That procedure will stop with the first peak it finds, even if it's not the highest one.

19. Even though feature vectors are neither symbols nor finite, the first HMM–based speech recognition systems represented each frame of speech by associating each feature vector with a symbol drawn from a finite set of representative vectors called a "codebook." The idea of a codebook came from a popular speech coding technique in the 1980s called "vector quantization." See J. Makoul, S. Roukos, and H. Gish, "Vector Quantization in Speech Coding,"

Proceedings of the IEEE 73, no. 11 (November 1985): 1551–1588. When computers became more powerful, most of the speech recognition labs modeled the distribution of the feature vectors directly in a multidimensional space without going to the symbolic level, using what are called "continuous density HMMs," which proved to yield higher performance than the "discrete HMMs" they replaced, and thus are still in use today.

20. Having characterized a phenomenon as belonging to a particular probability density with a particular functional shape, mathematicians can then compute the specific function parameters that would best characterize the probability of the phenomenon, given the shape of the function. One shape of particular interest is called a "Gaussian probability density," the classic bell shape, which mathematicians find attractive in that, in the case of a one-dimensional event—for instance, the height of people in a given population—it can be defined by two parameters only: the mean value—in other words, where the center of the bell shape is located—and the variance, which controls the width of the bell shape. Gaussian probability densities can also be used in a multidimensional space, where they're characterized by a mean vector, which corresponds to the center of the bell shape in a multidimensional space, and a covariance matrix, which determines the width of the bell shape across any pairs of dimensions. To model the probability density of feature vectors, which can be more complex than a simple multidimensional bell curve, with several peaks and valleys, speech scientists used what's known as a "mixture distribution model," mixing together, for each state of a hidden Markov model, a number of multidimensional Gaussian distributions, each characterized by its own mean vector and covariance matrix, and each providing a different contribution to the mix by the particular setting of a weighting factor. So, once they defined the number of mixture density functions for each state of a hidden Markov model, the training problem became that of estimating, for each density function in the mixture, its mean vector, its covariance matrix, and its weighting factor. See J.-L. Gauvain and C.-H. Lee, "Bayesian Learning for Hidden Markov Model with Gaussian Mixture State Observation Densities," *Speech Communication* 11, nos. 2–3 (June 1992): 205–213.

21. Perhaps the most crucial missing detail that prevented other researchers from readily reproducing the IBM results was the solution to the "scaling problem." Since the absolute values of the probabilities associated with acoustic events in the intermediate steps of the forward-backward algorithm were very small, and since the algorithm proceeded by multiplications of probabilities, these values became smaller and smaller, and all attempts by other researchers to implement the HMM training process with mathematical precision using a computer failed. The solution consisted in scaling the probability to a common multiplier at each frame of the training utterances and using the set of multipliers to rescale the probabilities back at the end of the calculation, a simple and quite effective technique without which implementation of HMM training was practically impossible.

22. L. R. Rabiner, "A Tutorial on Hidden Markov Models and Selected Applications in Speech Recognition," *Proceedings of the IEEE* 77, no. 2 (February 1989): 257–286.

Chapter 5

1. The annual ICASSP is a major conference sponsored by the Signal Processing Society, one of the largest branches of the Institute of Electrical and Electronic Engineering (IEEE). As described by its Web site at www.ieee.org/index.html, IEEE is the "the world's leading professional organization for the advancement of technology," counting more than 350,000

members from all branches of technology, including circuits, broadcasting, aerospace systems, communications, computers, devices, medical engineering, information theory, and pattern recognition. For many years the most important venue for speech technology research, ICASSP brings together at its annual gatherings some 2,000 scientists in all engineering disciplines related to speech, including speech coding and compression, speech synthesis, and speech recognition. Among the other conferences specialized on speech research, Interspeech, known as "Eurospeech" in the 1980s, was the annual conference of the European Speech Communication Association (ESCA) and was held every two years in Europe, in alternation with another U.S. conference, known as the "International Conference on Speech and Language Processing" (ICSLP). In September 1999, ESCA changed its name to "International Speech Communication Association" (ISCA) and joined the Eurospeech conference with ICSLP to form an annual conference called "Interspeech." Each year, Interspeech attracts some 1,500 scientists and technologists from all over the world. Although ICASSP and Interspeech are the largest conferences where the latest advances in speech recognition and spoken communication with machines are discussed, small workshops such as the IEEE Workshop on Automatic Speech Recognition and Understanding (ASRU) and the IEEE Workshop on Spoken Language Technologies (SLT) also serve as important venues.

2. During the mid- to late 1980s, the technology known as "artificial neural networks" (ANNs), which had proved to be useful in other areas of pattern recognition and machine intelligence, acquired significant relevance in speech recognition research. *Artificial neural networks* are massively parallel networks of simple computational elements, called "artificial neurons," which are interconnected in a multilayer structure, where the neurons of one layer receive the outputs of the previous layer and generate the inputs to the next. Although ANNs were previously known in computer science as "multilayer perceptrons," it was only after David Rumelhart, Geoffrey Hinton, and Yann LeCun, working in parallel from 1984 to 1986, invented and developed the back-propagation algorithm that they assumed an important place in pattern recognition. The back-propagation algorithm allowed researchers to learn the weights of the connections among neurons from training data in order to approximate any arbitrarily complex function. Artificial neural networks have been very successful in recognizing images and characters and in tasks where pattern classification doesn't require sophisticated representation of time varying phenomena. Although much work was devoted to adapt ANNs to the speech recognition problem, the results did not prove to be superior to the statistical methods. Artificial neural networks are used today in some commercial speech recognizers to model the probability density of feature vectors, where the time sequencing is still modeled by hidden Markov models. See, for instance, R. P. Lippmann, "Review of Neural Networks for Speech Recognition," *Neural Computation* 1, no. 1 (Spring 1989): 1–38.

3. The term *corpus* (plural *corpora*) in this context refers to a collection of utterances with various degrees of annotation used for experimental and comparative purposes in speech research. When the speech community approached the problem of spoken access to relational databases (such as flight databases in the ATIS project described later in this chapter), the term *database*, which had also referred to a collection of utterances, became ambiguous and fell out of use in that sense.

4. G. R. Doddington, "Whither Speech Recognition?" in *Trends in Speech Recognition*, ed. Wayne A Lea Editor (Englewood Cliffs, N.J.: Prentice Hall: 1980), 561.

5. See R. G. Leonard and G. R. Doddington, "A Database for Speaker-Independent Digit Recognition," *Proceedings of the IEEE International Conference on Acoustic, Speech, and Signal Processing* 9 (March 1984): 328–331.

6. There are five or six basic dialects in the United States as defined by linguists. The twenty-one dialectal regions represented in TI-DIGITS reflected marked acoustic or phonetic variations over these basic dialects.

7. The erroneous substitution of "nine" for "five" is the most common error in digit recognition for the English language. "Nine" and "five" have the same vowels, and the sounds /f/ and /v/ can be confused with /n/ in presence of noise, or bandwidth limited telephone speech. This is why in the NATO international alphabet, or international radiotelephony spelling alphabet, "nine" is pronounced as "niner," to help distinguish it from "five."

8. The principle often used as a tiebreaker in science is called "Occam's razor," attributed to the fourteenth-century English philosopher William of Occam. Most often rendered "Entities must not be multiplied beyond necessity," it refers to the scientific practice of always choosing, everything else being equal, the simplest explanation of an observed phenomenon among competing explanations.

9. Larry Rabiner, personal communication, January 2005. Segmental characterization of the digits, also called the "head-body-tail technique," was invented at Bell Telephone Laboratories. Using this technique to optimize the number of units and their characterization of the possible coarticulation phenomena at the boundary of each sequence of two adjacent words, Bell Labs researchers broke down each digit into three parts—"head," "body," and "tail"—corresponding to the initial, central, and final part of the utterance. Assuming that the body of each digit is insensitive to coarticulation phenomena, there are only 11 (the ten digits plus OH) body units. Then, considering also the possibility of silence either before or after each digit, there are $12 \times 12 = 144$ possible sequences of tail-head units characterizing the juncture between the final part of the preceding digit (or silence) and the initial part of the following digit (or silence). Thus, with $144 + 11 = 155$ units, the researchers could create robust recognition elements optimized for digit strings. Of course, using hidden Markov model training, they didn't have to exactly specify the head-body-tail segmentation for each digit, but could let the training algorithm discover the optimal segmentation. See C.-H. Lee, E. Giachin, L. R. Rabiner, R. Pieraccini, and A. E. Rosenberg, "Improved Acoustic Modeling for Large-Vocabulary Speech Recognition," *Computer Speech and Language* 4 (1992): 103–127.

TIMIT, a corpus of read speech originally intended to provide data for acoustic-phonetic research and phonetic speech recognition, was jointly designed and developed by MIT, Stanford Research Institute, and Texas Instruments. As opposed to the TI-DIGIT corpus, which represents all digits in all possible numeric contexts, the TIMIT corpus represents all phonemes in all possible phonetic contexts. Each of its 630 speakers reads ten phonetically rich sentences. See the LDC Catalog at http://www.ldc.upenn.edu/Catalog/CatalogEntry .jsp?catalogId=LDC93S1. See also V. Zue, S. Seneff, and J. Glass, "Speech Database Development at MIT: TIMIT and Beyond," Speech Communication 9 (1990): 351–356.

Wall Street Journal(WSJ), the first large-vocabulary, general-purpose corpus of speech, was jointly developed by AT&T, Bolt, Beranek and Newman, Carnegie Mellon University, Dragon Systems, IBM, Lincoln Laboratories, MIT, the National Institute of Standards and Technology, Stanford Research Institute, and Texas Instruments. It consists of 400 hours of speakers reading passages from the *Wall Street Journal* and amounts to 47 million words.

10. Writing all the sentences in capital letters was one of several conventions established for the representation and documentation of the Resource Management corpus.

11. See K.-F. Lee, *Automatic Speech Recognition: The Development of the SPHINX Recognition System*, Springer International Series in Engineering and Computer Science (Boston: Kluwer, 1989). See also http://cmusphinx.sourceforge.net/.

12. P. J. Price, "Evaluation of Spoken Language Systems: The ATIS Domain," *Proceedings of a Workshop Held at Hidden Valley, Pennsylvania, June 24–27,* 1990, ACL Anthology, http://www.aclweb.org/anthology/H/H90/.

13. The most common "relational" types of databases used today can be queried in SQL.

14. Today speech recognition is also called "speech-to-text," "STT," or "S2T."

15. Feeding the language understanding system with the best string of words out of a speech recognizer is a highly practical, albeit crude, approach. Although the full integration of semantic knowledge into the chain of models (acoustic, phonetic, and syntactic) would be computationally expensive, as an approximation of that, modern speech recognizers can make use of a more complex structure where several competing word hypotheses are present. Such a structure, in the most complex situations, can be represented by a network of word hypotheses called a "lattice."

16. L. Hirschman, "Multi-Site Data Collection for a Spoken Language Corpus: MADCOW," *Proceedings of the International Conference on Speech and Language Processing*, 903–906. Banff, Alberta, October 1992.

17. By today's standards, 25,000 utterances is a relatively small number for a corpus in speech recognition and understanding research. Tests and experiments are typically carried out using hundreds of thousands, if not millions, of utterances. In the early 1990s, however, it was a more than respectable number for the speech research community.

18. "Wizard of Oz," named, of course, after the famous movie, alludes to the tiny old man who turns out to operate the big scary Wizard machine, which hums and puffs and speaks in an intimidating deep voice. In a similar fashion, the operator—the "Wizard"—of a WoZ data collector sits concealed from view while the subjects believe they are interacting with a machine. Some call this collection paradigm "PNAMBC" (*Pay No Attention to the Man Behind the Curtain*). On the other hand, openly using humans to perform tasks that would otherwise be assigned to computers is a sort of inverse artificial intelligence, or "artificial artificial intelligence," an expression often used to refer to the "Mechanical Turk," and infrastructure created by Amazon.com to enlist for pay large numbers of people on the Web to perform simple tasks that can't be easily automated, such as recognizing or classifying patterns (also known as *crowdsourcing*).

19. You can always and indefinitely complicate any simple sentence by recursively substituting the corresponding dictionary definition for each word. You can take, for instance, the sentence "The dog ate the sausage" and, using the online version of Webster's, look up the words "dog," "ate" (or "eat"), and "sausage." When you substitute their definitions for the words themselves, the simple initial sentence becomes something like "The highly variable domestic mammal took in through the mouth, as food, the highly seasoned minced meat usually stuffed in the casing of prepared animal intestine." You can do this again by substituting definitions for some of the words in this longer sentence. And you can continue this process indefinitely, obtaining longer and longer, and more and more complicated sentences. The more you try to explain, the less obvious the meaning is.

20. "There is no data like more data" was what an IBM researcher stated during a DARPA meeting in 1985 when the participants were discussing how much data was considered to be enough.

21. Indeed, some of the ATIS collection sites defined formal English grammar, which was used to rephrase every user utterance. The formal English rephrasing of utterances was then automatically translated into SQL for database access.

22. See R. Pieraccini, E. Levin, and C.-H. Lee, "Stochastic Representation of Conceptual Structure in the ATIS Task," in *Proceedings of the Fourth Joint DARPA Speech and Natural Language Workshop*, 121–124. Pacific Grove, Calif., February 1991.

23. See R. Pieraccini and E. Levin, "A Learning Approach to Natural Language Understanding," in *Speech Recognition and Coding: New Advances and Trends*, ed. Antonio J. Rubio Ayuso and Juan M. Lopez Soler, NATO ASI Series/Computer and Systems Sciences (Berlin: Springer, 1995), 139–156.

24. D. S. Pallett, J. G. Fiscus, W. M. Fisher, J. S. Garofolo, B. A. Lund, A. Martin, and M. A. Przybocki, "1994 Benchmark Tests for the ARPA Spoken Language Program," in *Proceedings of the 1995 ARPA Human Language Technology Workshop* (San Francisco: Morgan Kaufmann, 1995), 5–36.

Chapter 6

1. Although the ATIS task was restricted to a relatively small number of U.S. airports, sentences like "I need to fly to San Francisco" caused problems for the scoring program, which had to compare quite large result tables. In particular, in the ATIS corpus, there were sentences like "I need flight information" that were known to crash the evaluation program because it couldn't handle the large size of the result table. That very simple sentence would cause, in a compliant ATIS system, the display of the whole flight database: tens of thousands of records.

2. This quotation and the VOYAGER dialog example are taken from V. Zue, J. Glass, D. Goodine, H. Leung, M. Phillips, J. Polifroni, and S. Seneff, "The VOYAGER Speech Understanding System: A Progress Report," in *Speech and Natural Language: Proceedings of a Workshop Held at Cape Cod, Massachusetts, October 15–18, 1989* (San Mateo, Calif.: Morgan Kaufmann, 1989) ACL Anthology, http://www.aclweb.org/anthology/H/H89/.

3. See D. Goddeau, E. Brill, J. R. Glass, C. Pao, M. Phillips, J. Polifroni, S. Seneff, and V. W. Zue, "Galaxy: A Human-Language Interface to On-Line Travel Information," *Proceedings of the Third International Conference on Spoken Language Processing (ICSLP 94)*, 707–710. Yokohama, September 1994.

4. In linguistics, sentences like "Do you have anything cheaper?" are known as "elliptical sentences," whose missing parts are to be inferred from context or convention. For instance, the sentence "Do you have anything cheaper?" most likely means "Do you have anything cheaper than what you've just shown me?," but, of course, in a well-defined context, its meaning would be clear even without the added clause. Sentences that refer to information contained in previous sentences are called "anaphoric sentences." For instance, "I want to go there tomorrow" is an anaphoric sentence because "there" refers to what was said in a previous sentence, like "I need to fly to San Francisco."

5. Marvin Minsky introduced the term *frames*, meaning data structures for representing arbitrary knowledge in a hierarchical way, in 1974. See M. Minsky, "A Framework for Representing Knowledge," MIT–AI Laboratory Memo 306, June 1974, reprinted in *The Psychology of Computer Vision*, ed. P. Winston, (New York: McGraw-Hill, 1975).

6. Be careful not to confuse the term *frame* meaning a data structure used to represent knowledge with the term *frame* meaning an elemental interval of speech, typically 10 milliseconds, used to construct the feature vector representation of an utterance.

7. HUB programs were written in a special scripting language designed and implemented by the MIT speech research group. The program shown here is an English rendition of a possible HUB program.

8. Allen Sears, speaking at the first DARPA Communicator coordination meeting, held at MIT in 1996, which I attended.

9. In 1996, AT&T was divided into three different companies in what was called its "trivestiture," playing off the famous AT&T divestiture of 1984. The trivestiture gave rise to Lucent, a telephone equipment manufacturing company, and AT&T, the telephone operating company. Bell Telephone Laboratories remained with Lucent, which merged with the French company Alcatel on December 2006. Right after the trivestiture, AT&T created Shannon Laboratory, which included some of the former Bell Labs scientists and was headquartered in Florham Park, New Jersey.

10. Byron Reeves and Clifford Nass, from Stanford University, give another reason for a positive bias in automated surveys in their bestseller book *The Media Equation: How People Treat Computers, Television, and New Media Like Real People and Places* (Stanford, Calif.: CSLI, 1996), 65–72. Asked to rate a computer's performance, their experimental subjects tended to give better ratings when they responded on the same computer than when they did so on a different computer. This phenomenon, Reeves and Nass claim, is equivalent to asking someone to give an evaluation of a person to that same person as opposed to a different person. People tend to give better evaluations of the persons they're evaluating to their faces and worse ones behind their backs. Apparently, they do the same with computers.

11. Often people surveyed a few hours after an interaction with a computer have only a vague recollection of their experience. Thus some users who interacted with a commercial telephone computer system by pressing numbers on the keypad, when surveyed hours later, clearly stated they had "talked" to a computer, even though the computer had done the talking and they had just pressed keys. Personal conversation with VUI team at SpeechWorks, June 2002.

12. Companies that regularly perform customer surveys acknowledge that very few users, often no more than 20 percent, will agree to take part in a survey when reached a few hours after interacting with a telephone computer system. Personal conversation with service providers, December 2005.

13. See M. A. Walker, D. J. Litman, C. A. Kamm, and A. Abella, "PARADISE: A Framework for Evaluating Spoken Dialogue Agents," in *Proceedings of the 35th Annual Meeting of the Association for Computational Linguistics and Eighth Conference of the European Chapter of the Association for Computational Linguistics*, 271–280. Madrid, July 1997.

14. See R. Likert, "A Technique for the Measurement of Attitudes." *Archives of Psychology*, no. 140 (1932): 1–55.

15. See R. S. Sutton and A. G. Barto, *Reinforcement Learning: An Introduction* (Cambridge, Mass.: MIT Press, 1998).

16. Imagine you're playing a special slot machine with *two* arms—a "two-armed bandit"—rather than a typical one with a single arm. One of the machine's arms is known to give a higher return than the other, but you don't know which. You've a lot of coins, and you want to maximize the amount of money you'll win in the long run. What's your best strategy? At first, you try each of the arms randomly, on a fifty-fifty basis. As soon as you start winning a few jackpots, however, you start to favor the arm that's given you the higher return to that point. But since you haven't played all that many games, you can't be sure that's actually the winning arm. So, while favoring the arm that's given you more money, you keep trying the other arm, until you're *sure* which arm's the winning one. Which is to say, while you're *exploiting* what you've observed, you keep *exploring* because you don't have sufficient evidence to be sure.

17. E. Levin, R. Pieraccini, and W. Eckert, "A Stochastic Model of Human-Machine Interaction for Learning Dialog Strategies," *IEEE Transactions on Speech and Audio Processing* 8, no. 1 (January 2000): 11–23.

18. Whereas a Markov decision process (MDP) assumes that the machine accurately knows the current state of the environment at any point in time, a partially observable Markov decision process (POMDP) assumes that the machine has only a vague knowledge of that state, represented by a probability distribution. POMDPs reflect the fact that certain elements of a dialog, such as the meaning of what the user said, aren't determined with certainty, but with the likelihood represented by the speech recognition and language understanding accuracy. For an accessible description of POMDPs in dialog technology, see S. Young, "Cognitive User Interfaces," *IEEE Signal Processing Magazine* 27, no. 3 (May 2010): 128–140.

Chapter 7

1. See H. Dudley, R. R. Riesz, and S. S. A Watkins, "A Synthetic Speaker," *Journal of the Franklin Institute* 227, no. 6 (June 1939): 739–764.

2. See C. G. Kratzenstein, "Sur la formation et la naissance des voyelles," *Journal de Physique* 21 (1782): 358–380.

3. Hermann Ludwig Ferdinand von Helmholtz (1821–1894) was a German physician and physicist who made several significant contributions to several areas of science, including physiology (and the physiology of speech in particular), psychology, and physics. On Wheatstone's and Willis's contributions to speech science, see, respectively, B. Bowers, *Sir Charles Wheatstone FRS, 1802–1875*, 2nd ed., ed. M. Wilson (London: Institution of Electrical Engineers, 2001), 34–35; and M. R. Schroeder, *Computer Speech: Recognition, Compression, Synthesis* (Reprint, Berlin: Springer, 2004), 27.

4. J. Groundwater, *Alexander Graham Bell: The Spirit of Invention* (Calgary: Altitude, 2005), 30.

5. See F. S. Cooper, A. M. Liberman, and J. M. Borst, "The Interconversion of Audible and Visible Patterns as a Basis for Research in the Perception of Speech," *Proceedings of the National Academy of Science* 37 (1951): 318–325.

6. The time patterns of PAT's six parameters—the three formant frequencies and type, amplitude, and frequency of the excitation signal—were painted on a sliding piece of glass; through an optical mechanism, these controlled the synthesizer and generated an acoustic signal that could be perceived as an utterance. Although for the sake of simplicity we discussd only the first two formants, the third formant is also used for a more accurate characterization of speech sounds. W. Lawrence, "The Synthesis of Speech from Signals Which Have a Low Information Rate," in *Communication Theory*, ed. W. Jackson (London: Butterworth, 1953): 460–469.

7. G. Fant and J. Mártony, "Instrumentation for Parametric Synthesis (OVE II), Synthesis Strategy and Quantization of Synthesis Parameters," *Speech Transmission Laboratory: Quarterly Progress and Status Reports (STL-QPSR)*, no. 2 (1962): 18–24.

8. J. N. Holmes, "Research on Speech Synthesis Carried Out During a Visit to the Royal Institute of Technology, Stockholm, from November 1960 to March 1961," Joint Speech Research Unit Report JU 11.4 (1961), British Post Office, Eastcote, UK.

9. J. Allen, M. S. Hunnicutt, and D. Klatt, *From Text to Speech: The MITalk System* (Cambridge: Cambridge University Press, 1987).

10. G. Rosen, "Dynamic Analog Speech Synthesizer," Technical Report 353, February 10, 1960, Massachusetts Institute of Technology, Research Laboratory of Electronics, Cambridge, Mass.

11. Speech synthesis scientists have spent a considerable amount of time developing algorithms that allow individual snippets of sounds to be concatenated in a seamless manner.

12. L. Truss, *Eats, Shoots & Leaves: The Zero Tolerance Approach to Punctuation* (New York: Gotham Books, 2004), 2.

13. A. Black and P. Taylor, "Festival Speech Synthesis System: System Documentation (1.1.1)," Human Communication Research Centre Technical Report HCRC/TR-83, University of Edinburgh, 1997.

14. Mike Phillips, personal communication, September 2002.

Chapter 8

1. Jay Wilpon, personal communication, March 2009.

2. F. P. Brooks, *The Mythical Man Month: Essays on Software Engineering*, 2nd ed. (Reading, Mass.: Addison-Wesley, 1995).

3. B. W. Arthur, *The Nature of Technology: What It Is and How It Evolves* (New York: Free Press, 2009), see esp. 167–189

4. Larry Rabiner, personal communication, January 2005.

5. During a session on the history of speech recognition at the 2006 Interspeech Conference in Pittsburgh, Janet Baker told how, needing speakers to train their recognizer, Dragon had advertised for anyone fluent in Klingon (spoken by the humanoid Klingons of the popular sci-fi television and movie series *Star Trek*). Much to everyone's surprise, a long line of Klingon speakers showed up in front of Dragon's Newton, Massachusetts, office the next day, having waited there since the early hours of the morning.

6. I'm referring here to the fact that more and more households, at least in the United States, are abandoning landline phones for cell phones and smartphones, indeed, 25 percent of them

had already done so by 2009, according to a survey by the Center for Disease Control. See S. J. Blumberg and J. V. Luke, "Wireless Substitution: Early Release of Estimates from the National Health Interview Survey, July–December 2009," CDC study, released May 12, 2010.

7. Rich Miner would go on to cofound Android, Inc., with Andy Rubin, acquired by Google in August 2005, less than two years after its start-up. Android would form the basis of the Android operating system powering several types of smartphones.

8. This and the following Wildfire examples are taken from "Wildfire Communications: 'What Can I Do for You?'—Speech Recognition Interface Simplifies and Expedites Telephone Use." Release 1.0, October 1994.

9. The term *natural language* is overused, and often misused, by the commercial speech recognition community. In theory, everything we say is "natural language," whether it be the simple yes or no response to a properly crafted yes or no prompt or the long and articulated answer to an open prompt, such as "How may help you?" In practice, however, "natural language" came to indicate only the free-form response to an open prompt.

10. Dual-tone multi-frequency (DTMF) signals, generated by pressing keys on a telephone keypad, are mainly used to control telephone switches in call dialing. Each key, when pressed, sends a signal generated by merging two tones with the frequency on its row and column. The characteristic sounds we hear when we dial our touch-tone phones are easily recognized by network switches or other devices at the other end of the line.

11. Of course, a touch-tone interactive voice response system can also associate pairs or triplets of key presses to increase the number of choices, but that would result in an extremely complex interface.

12. Jonathan Bloom, an experienced and widely recognized VUI designer, standup comedian, and writer, illustrates the difference between science fiction prediction and reality with his reinterpretation of a famous dialog between HAL, the *2001:A Space Odyssey* computer, and Dave Bowman, the astronaut. In one of the most dramatic scenes of the movie, HAL has found out that Dave suspects it of "terminating" his fellow astronauts and wants to deactivate it. So while Dave's outside on a space walk, HAL tries to prevent him from getting back into the spaceship.

Dave: Hello, HAL do you read me, HAL?

HAL: Affirmative, Dave, I read you.

Dave: Open the pod bay doors, HAL.

HAL: I'm sorry Dave, I'm afraid I can't do that.

Dave: What's the problem?

HAL: I think you know what the problem is just as well as I do.

Dave: What are you talking about, HAL?

HAL: This mission is too important for me to allow you to jeopardize it.

Dave: I don't know what you're talking about, HAL.

HAL: I know you and Frank were planning to disconnect me, and I'm afraid that's something I cannot allow to happen.

Dave: Where the hell did you get that idea, HAL?

HAL: Dave, although you took thorough precautions in the pod against my hearing you, I could see your lips move.

If HAL had indeed been built with the actual IVR speech technology of the year 2001, and by a not-so-experienced designer, the dialog as Bloom tells it might have instead gone like this:

Dave: Hello, HAL do you read me, HAL?

HAL: Welcome to HAL. Please listen carefully, as our options have changed. You can say, "Open the pod bay doors," "Play chess" . . .

Dave: Open the pod bay doors, HAL.

HAL: Sorry, I didn't understand. You can say, "Open the pod bay doors" or press 1, "Play chess" or press 2, "Learn the alphorn" or press 3 . . .

Dave: <presses 1>

HAL: Around what time would you like the pod bay doors to open? You can say "Today," "Tomorrow," . . .

Dave: Now! Damn you!

HAL: Main menu. Please listen carefully, as our options have changed. You can say, "Open the pod bay doors," or press 1, "Play chess" or press 2 . . .

Dave: <emphatically presses 1 multiple times>

HAL: I'm really, really sorry. Even though your call is really, really important to us, this mission is even more important, and I can't allow you to jeopardize it.

Dave: I don't know what you're talking about, HAL.

HAL: I know you and Frank were planning to press 0 for an agent, and I'm afraid that's something I cannot allow to happen.

Jonathan Bloom, personal communication, March 2010.

13. Indeed, experienced VUI designers can tell countless stories about applications that failed because they asked for information that users didn't know how to find. For instance, "Please say your account number," "Account number? Which account number?" "I am sorry, I did not get that. Please say your account number." A problem like that can be fixed by slightly changing the prompt: "Please say your account number, which is written on the top right corner of your membership card." For an introduction to the principles of Voice User Interface design and its application on commercial dialog systems, see B. Kotelly, *The Art and Business of Speech Recognition: Creating the Noble Voice* (Addison-Wesley Professional, 2003) or M. H. Cohen, J. P. Giangola, J. Balogh, *Voice User Interface Design* (Addison-Wesley Professional, 2004).

14. See, for instance, D. Norman, *The Design of Everyday Things* (New York: Basic Books, 2002).

15. I heard this example of bad and good design in doors during an invited talk by Donald Norman at Bell Laboratories in the mid-1990s.

16. Intel's cofounder Gordon Moore noticed that the power of computers, measured by different related quantities such as the number of transistors in their integrated circuits, their speed, or their memory capacity, doubled roughly every two years, even as their cost halved in the same time. Moore published his observation, which came to be known as Moore's law, in a 1965 article. See G. A. Moore, "Cramming More Components onto Integrated Circuits," *Electronics Magazine,* April 19, 1965, 114–117. The exponential growth in computer power continues at this writing and is expected to do so for the next decade or even longer.

17. IBM called its whole family of speech recognition products "ViaVoice": ViaVoice dictation, ViaVoice speech recognition server, for telephony applications, and later ViaVoice embedded for automobile applications.

18. The name "Watson" for the AT&T speech recognizer comes from Thomas A. Watson, who was Alexander Graham Bell's assistant and the first person ever called by Bell himself

during the first telephone experiments. According to Bell's laboratory notebook, the first words he said one the telephone were "Mr. Watson, come here. I want to see you."

19. See A. L. Gorin, G. Riccardi, and J. H. Wright, "How May I Help You?" *Speech Communication* 23, no. 1–2 (October 1997): 113–127.

20. Presumably, the caller in these three instances, and in some of the other examples, was using a different telephone line to call for technical support.

21. See, for instance, J. Chu-Carrol and B. Carpenter, "Vector-Based Natural Language Call Routing," *Computational Linguistics* 25, no. 3 (September 1999): 361–388. Remember that, as of 1996, because of AT&T's trivestiture, Bell Laboratories and AT&T Laboratories were headquartered in different locations, the first in Murray Hill and the second in Florham Park, both in New Jersey.

22. These and other functional words which can be filtered out of an utterance without affecting its semantic categorization are also called "stop words."

23. Semantic classification could, in principle, be applied to more complex understanding tasks if used in conjunction with other techniques. Before development of the How May I Help You? technology, Roland Kuhn and Renato De Mori at McGill University in Montreal applied a semantic classifier to the ATIS task to assign each utterance to one of a list of possible high-level meanings, such as "request for flight," "request for fare," "request for itinerary," and so on. Using different techniques, they then filled in the missing information: departure and arrival airports, exact departure and arrival dates and times, and so on. See R. Kuhn and R. De Mori, "The Application of Semantic Classification Trees to Natural Language Understanding," *IEEE Transactions on Pattern Analysis and Machine Intelligence* 17, no. 5 (May 1995): 449–460.

Chapter 9

1. A straightforward way to compute the confidence of a given recognition is to use a normalized form of the maximum likelihood obtained during hidden Markov model alignment. Although the maximum likelihood represents the "resemblance" of the recognized utterance to the best path through the network of HMMs, however, it's not related to the probability of the recognition being correct. More sophisticated forms of confidence scoring have been developed to approximate that probability. See, for instance, H. Jiang, "Confidence Measures for Speech Recognition: a Survey," *Speech Communication*, no. 45 (2005): 455–470.

2. On dialog modules, see E. Barnard, A. Halberstadt, C. Kotelly, and M. Phillips, "A Consistent Approach to Designing Spoken Dialog Systems," *Proceedings of the 1999 IEEE Workshop on Automatic Speech Recognition and Understanding (ASRU99)*, 353–362. Keystone, Colorado, December 1999.

3. After many years of frustration for ever larger numbers of cell phone users, the major handset manufacturers announced in 2009 they had agreed on a standard for a universal cell phone charger.

4. If you were around in the 1980s, you certainly remember the videotape wars. At first, in the early 1980s, there were several types of videotapes, such as Betamax from Sony, Video 2000 from Philips, Laserdisc from MCA, and VHS from JVC, that were incompatible with any but their respective VCR systems. If you bought a Sony VCR at that time, you could

only view and record Betamax videotapes on it. If your neighbor wanted to share a copy of the season finale of M*A*S*H that you missed, and the neighbor happened to have a JVC, while you had a Sony, well, you were just out of luck. Eventually, VHS prevailed. Although Betamax was arguably superior, VHS was the one that survived the wars. Soon, no one was able to play Betamax or Video 2000 tapes anymore, and they became collector's items.

5. VoiceXML 3.0 is the most current working draft released by the World Wide Web Consortium (W3C) as of this writing; see http://www.w3.org/TR/2010/WD-voicexml30-20100831/. VoiceXML 2.0, released in March 2004, is the most recent recommendation used for commercial purposes; see http://www.w3.org/TR/2004/REC-voicexml20-20040316/.

6. See K. Wang, "SALT: An XML Application for Web Based Multimodal Dialog Management," in *Proceedings of the Second Workshop on NLP and XML* (NLPXML-2002), 1–8. Taipei, September 1, 2002.

7. Spoken dialog systems can still resort to touch-tone commands in certain situations. For example, after a certain number of failed attempts to recognize a caller's voice, the system can request a touch-tone interaction (for instance, "Press 1 for yes and 2 for no"), or it can offer callers the option of entering sensitive information like their credit card numbers by touch-tone, especially when they're in public places; and the system can always have the "0" key available for immediate human operator requests.

8. To show the basic simplicity of the HTML language, here's the HTML code representing the form shown in figure 9.7:

```
<form method="post" action="getCityStateZIP.cgi">
    City <br>
    <input name="city"><p>
    State <br>
    <input name="state"><p>
    ZIP Code <br>
    <input name="zipcode"><p>
    <input type="submit" value="Submit">
</form>
```

The action tag specifies the name of the program on the server that will handle the information, such as the state, city, and ZIP code, to be encoded in the HTTP message from the browser to the server once the "Submit" button is clicked.

9. Here's the code from a basic and extremely simplified VoiceXML program to implement the main-text dialog on a standard voice browser:

```
<form>
    <field name="city">
        <prompt count="1">Say the name of the city</prompt>
        <prompt count="2">I am not sure I got it right.
        Please say the name of the city again.</prompt>
        <grammar src="cities.grm"/>
    </field>
```

```
<field name="state">
      <prompt count="1">Say the state</prompt>
      <prompt count="2">I am not sure I got it right.
      Please say the name of the state again.</prompt>
      <grammar src="states.grm"/>
</field>
<field name="zip">
      <prompt count="1">...and the ZIP code</prompt>
      <prompt count="2">I am not sure I got it right.
      Please say your ZIP code again</prompt>
      <grammar src="ZIP.grm"/>
</field>
<submit next=http://localhost/handler/>
</form>
```

This code directs the voice browser to play each prompt with its text-to-speech engine and to activate its speech recognizer with the specified grammar at each turn. It directs the browser to play a second prompt at each turn when speech recognition fails on the first attempt. After information from all fields is collected, the recognition results are submitted to the URL indicated by the "Submit" element at the end of the form.

10. Cisco, Nuance, and SpeechWorks collaborated on the first draft of the MRCP standard. See http://tools.ietf.org/html/rfc4463.

11. ECMAScript is a scripting language standardized by Ecma International, founded in 1960 as the "European Computer Manufacturers Association," but renamed in 1994 as "Ecma International: European Association for Standardizing Information and Communication Systems" to more closely reflect its mission. ECMAScript includes several "dialect" languages such as JavaScript, Jscript, and ActionScript. On SRGS, see http://www.w3.org/TR/speech-grammar/.

12. On SSML, see http://www.w3.org/TR/speech-synthesis/.

13. On CCXML, see http://www.w3.org/TR/ccxml/.

14. For an entertaining book about initial trends in creating dynamic Web pages, see *Database-Backed Web Sites: The Thinking Person's Guide to Web Publishing* (Emeryville, Calif.: Ziff-Davis Press, 1997) by computer scientist and photographer Philip Greenspun. The full text and images of the book, first published as a Web book under the title *How to Be a Web Whore Just like Me,* can be found at http://philip.greenspun.com/wtr/dead-trees/.

15. See, for instance, B. W. Perry, *Java Servlet & JSP Cookbook* (Sebastopol, Calif.: O'Reilly Media: 2004).

16. Although VoiceXML language allows developers to use ECMAScript code to place dynamic information within static files, doing so imposes certain limitations on the dynamic information and gives rise to a variety of technical problems. Thus the developers of most high-end voice Web applications choose simply to create dynamic VoiceXML pages on the server instead.

17. Call centers typically use three parameters to determine the number of ports required: average daily volume of calls, percentage of daily calls allocated during the busiest hour of the day, and average duration of a call. Using the appropriate formula, they can get a good estimate of the number of concurrent calls, and thus the number of ports required, with just these parameters. But, of course, to face exceptional and unpredicted spikes in traffic, they need to increase that number by a safety factor.

18. Unfortunately, the speech industry fell into the deplorable practice of "patent trolling"— acquiring patents for the sole purpose of suing smaller companies for infringement. The trollers would then force these companies either to pay large settlements, to exit the market, or to be acquired for a price well below their real valuation.

19. In August 2011, Nuance announced the acquisition of the Italian Loquendo, which among the smaller speech technology companies was the one with the larger speech recognition market share.

Chapter 10

1. *Speech mining* extracts information such as names, dates, and places from a speech stream or recording. *Speaker verification* determines whether the speaker of a number of utterances is who he or she claims to be, based on previous recordings or "voice prints" of the speaker. *Speaker diarization* segments the voices of different speakers in a multispeaker recording, as of an interview, meeting, or telephone conversation, and assigns to each one of them a unique speaker identity label within the recording. For instance, speaker diarization can separate the voice of the interviewer from that of the interviewee in a recorded radio or TV interview.

2. Jerome Wiesner, Oliver Selfridge, and scientist interviewed in Paramount News feature, as quoted in "The Thinking Machine," episode 4 of the documentary *The Machine That Changed the World,* jointly produced by WGBH Boston and BBC for release in the United States in January 1992.

3. Even though this may be a perfect application for solving a business's human agent problem, it's far from perfect for customers angry over the loss of their baggage, who now have to talk to a computer instead of a human agent.

4. See K. Acomb, J. Bloom, K. Dayanidhi, P. Hunter, P. Krogh, E. Levin, and R. Pieraccini, "Technical Support Dialog Systems, Issues, Problems, and Solutions," in *HLT 2007 Workshop: Bridging the Gap: Academic and Industrial Research in Dialog Technology,* 25–31. Rochester, New York, April. 26.

5. D. Suendermann, K. Evanini, J. Liscombe, P. Hunter., K. Dayanidhi, and R. Pieraccini, "From Rule-Based to Statistical Grammars: Continuous Improvement of Large-Scale Spoken Dialog Systems," in *Proceedings of the 2009 IEEE Conference on Acoustics, Speech and Signal Processing (ICASSP 2009),* 4713–4716. Taipei, April 19–24.

6. See K. Vertanen, "An Overview of Discriminative Training for Speech Recognition," technical report based on "Computer Speech, Text, and Internet Technology," master of philosophy thesis, University of Cambridge, 2004.

7. See C. M. Lee, S. Narayanan, and R. Pieraccini, "Classifying Emotions in Human-Machine Spoken Dialogs," in *Proceedings of ICME 2002, the IEEE International Conference on Multimedia and Expo,* 737–740. Lausanne, August.

8. *Paula Zahn Now,* CNN, July 27, 2005; J. Seabrook, "Hello HAL," *New Yorker,* June 23, 2008, 38–43.

9. M. G. Aamodt and H. Custer, "Who Can Best Catch a Liar?" *Forensic Examiner,* Spring 2006.

10. F. Enos, E. Shriberg, M. Graciarena, J. Hirschberg, and A. Stolcke, "Detecting Deception Using Critical Segments," in *Proceedings of Interspeech 2007,* 2281–2284. Antwerp, August 2007. An interesting result from this study is that words associated with positive emotions and pleasantness of conversation correlate better with deception, whereas filled pauses in speech correlate better with someone telling the truth.

11. See F. Biadsy, A. Rosenberg, R. Carlson, J. Hirschberg, and E. Strangert, "A Cross-Cultural Comparison of American, Palestinian, and Swedish Perception of Charismatic Speech," in *Speech Prosody 2008,* 579–582. Campinas, Brazil. Julia Hirschberg, personal communication, August 2008.

12. See http://www.darpa.mil/IPTO/programs/gale/gale.asp.

13. I'm not talking here about literary translation, which requires a deep understanding of the text and discriminating judgment in choosing which content to translate. The writer Umberto Eco, in *Experiences in Translation,* trans. Alastair McEwen (Toronto: University of Toronto Press, 2001), talks about the impossibility of being able to fully translate the many contents carried by a literary work. Besides the literal translation of sentences, there are the more subtle meanings that need to be preserved, and the translator needs to negotiate which of these meaning to keep in the target language. The choice to preserve some of the meanings will inevitably lead to the loss of others.

14. Papineni, K., Roukos, S., Ward, T., Zhu, W.-J., "BLEU: a Method for Automatic Evaluation of Machine Translation," in *Proceedings of the 40th Annual Meeting of the Association for Computational Linguistics (ACL),* 311–318. Philadelphia, July 2002.

15. C. Schmandt and E. Hulteen, "The Intelligent Voice Interactive Interface," in *Proceedings of the ACM Conference on Human Factors in Computer Systems,* 363–366. Gaithersburg, Maryland, 1982.

16. D. Benyon and O. Mival, "Introducing the Companions Project: Intelligent, Persistent, Personalised Interfaces to the Internet," in *Proceedings of the 21st British HCI Group Annual Conference on People and Computers: HCI . . . but Not As We Know It* 2: 193–194. University of Lancaster, September 3–7, 2007.

17. See *Companions Project Newsletter* (University of Sheffield), no. 1 (January 2008).

18. Panel on "Towards Anthropomorphic Systems," at SpeechTek 2010, August 4, 2010.

19. See Suendermann et al., "From Rule-Based to Statistical Grammars."; D. Suendermann, J. Liscombe, and R. Pieraccini, "How to Drink from a Fire Hose: One Person Can Annoscribe One Million Utterances in One Month," in *Proceedings of SIGDIAL 2010:The Eleventh Annual Meeting on the Special Interest Group on Discourse and Dialogue,* 257–260. Tokyo, September 24–25.

Index

Printed in Great Britain
by Amazon

79820283R00201